JOHN PARIS
CHRISTMAS
FROM:
MARLYN . DAVID

COWS,

COWBOYS,

CATTLEMEN, &

CHARACTERS

with best wishes

Leonard Friesen

A History of the Calgary Stockyards, 1903 - 1989

By: Leonard Friesen

ISBN 0-9699641-0-2

Canadian Cataloguing in Publication Data

Friesen, Leonard, 1926-
Cows, cowboys, cattleman, & characters

1. Livestock—Alberta—Marketing—History.
2. Stockyards—Alberta—Calgary—History.
3. Animal industry—Alberta—Biography. I. Title
HD9433.C23C34 1995   380.1'416'0097123   C95-910821-1

Cover photo by
Harry and Viv Hewitt

Cover designed by
Jon Paine

Published by Friesen Cattle Company
Box 3511
Airdrie, Alberta, Canada
T4B 2B7

Printed and bound in Canada by Friesens Corporation
Ste. 120 - 3016 - 19th Street NE
Calgary, Alberta
T2E 6Y9

ACKNOWLEDGEMENTS

In my "*Cattle Call*" column in *Alberta Beef,* February 1993 issue, I mentioned that I was thinking about writing a history of the Calgary Stockyards. Even though my telephone number was inadvertently misprinted in the column, I still received a number of phone calls encouraging me to write this book. I also received a number of letters—all expressing the same thing: go ahead and write the book. I visited with dozens of people at auction markets, bull sales, and 4-H shows as well as other places where cattle people gather; and they were all very positive that I should write this book. Unfortunately, I cannot begin to enumerate all of the ones who talked to me about this endeavour.

The people who phoned me were: George Anderson, Hussar; Wes Alm, Claresholm; Duan Friesen, our grandson; Sam Fulton, Carstairs; Albert Galarneau, Hanna; Henry Hansma, Dalemead; Ken Karsten, Claresholm; Bill Lumley, Didsbury; Alan Rand, Innisfail; Borge Rasmussen, Spruce View; Mike Rogers, Delbourne, Ted Shipley, Glenwood; Ken Sietz, Strathmore; Ed Silbernagle, Water Valley; and Wilson Trotter, Brooks.

The people who wrote to me were: Leona Akitt, Vulcan; Carl Anderson, Brooks; Gordon Boyd, Hanna; Don Chalmers, Balzac; Grant and Denzil Cameron, Cayley; John R. Craig, Eckville; Phil Doan, Castor; Dwayne Friesen (not related), Airdrie; Orrin Hart, Claresholm; Mel Johnston, Brooks; Hugh and Marion Kennedy, Turner Valley; Gene, Mary and Zack Johnston, Iddesleigh; Ron McCullough, Edmonton; Hank and Joyce Pallister, Stettler; Bax Slemp, Castor; Jock Stevens, Morinville; Joyce and Martin Tyress, Elnora; Albert Widmer, Olds; and Herb Widmer, Olds.

When I was gathering details, I phoned and visited certain individuals to seek dates or incidents. I talked to some of these people only once or twice. With others, I had a good bull session or two, at which times we recalled the good old days at the Stockyards. I want to thank you people for your input. I promise I will not blame any of you if some of the information is a little off base. It was strictly up to me to ensure everything in this book was as accurate as possible.

The people that I phoned or visited were: Henry Bridgewater, Jim Bridgewater, Paddy Brown, Pat Collins, A. J. E. Child, Dr. Bob Church, Jo-Ann Crook, Don Edge, Bill Furgeson, Bruce Flewelling, Murray Flewelling, Jim Friesen (nephew), Lee Friesen (son), Neil Friesen (nephew), White Garries, Bob Green, Ken Hurlburt, Will Irvine, Roy Gilkes, Ronnie Ostrim, Harvey Jamison, Harry McWilson, Vern Miller, Mel Morrison, Gordon and Dorothy Rauch, Jim and Isabel McPherson, Buck Rothwell, Cathy Schimpf, Hank Schimpf, Ray Starke, Eric Tribble, Shelley Trodden, Lorne Wells, Larry Harding, Hank Pallister, Donalda Hotomanie, Jo Hutchinson, Redvers Perry, Bill Bateman and Dr. Brian Edge.

Some of the material for this book was obtained from the Stockmen's Memorial Foundation in Cochrane. The Glenbow Museum in Calgary had a good source of information, especially about the early years of the Calgary Stockyards. Information was also obtained from the Land Titles Office, The Calgary Public Library and the City of Calgary Archives.

The pictures in this book are by the courtesy of: Henry Bridgewater, Bill Furgeson, A. J. E. Child, Vi Burwash, Tom Copithorne, Dale Christiansen, Don Edge, Lester Gurnett, Norman Edge, Lee Gunderson, Bruce Flewelling, Larry Petherbridge, Lorne Wells, *The Calgary Livestock Market Journal, The Market Examiner* (both of which are now out of print), *Alberta Beef, The Calgary Herald,* and the Glenbow Archives.

Dorothy Edge has definitely gone the second mile. She did a super job of taking some of the kinks out. She has spent a lot of hours on her computer making sure everything was as correct as possible. She also had a lot of good suggestions, many of which I incorporated into this book.

Last, but not least, I want to thank my wife, Edna, for her patience and for putting up with me while I was writing the manuscript. You have heard of golf widows; well, I guess you could call Edna a writer's widow. During the years our children were growing up, I spent a lot of time at Burns and the Stockyards—for this reason I want to dedicate this book to my wife, Edna, our six children: Lee, Ward, Melody, Dee, Graham, and Trent (deceased), their respective spouses and our grandchildren.

A big thank you to all the people who helped make this book possible.

CONTENTS

CHAPTER I

THE EARLY YEARS
(FROM THE BEGINNING TO 1903-1910)

For thousands of years, Western Canada was a vast empty land where a few tribes of Indians lived and moved around in a nomadic fashion. Their existence depended almost entirely on the buffalo that roamed this large domain in huge numbers. The seasons came and went with virtually no change from year to year.

However, this primitive lifestyle did change with the introduction of horses about three hundred years ago. The horses were brought over from Spain by the Spanish Conquistadors in the 16th century. It took over a hundred years for the horse population to work its way north into what is Western Canada today.

Approximately a hundred years after the horse's appearance, firearms were introduced to the Indians. These firearms came from the early fur-traders and explorers. The combination of firearms and horses made it relatively easy for the Indians to secure an adequate meat supply in a short period of time.

This enhancement also gave them a lot of time to play games, enjoy the great wonders of nature, and steal horses—a favourite pastime, which was quite a legitimate thing to do in their culture. This in turn led to many a pitched battle between the various tribes.

Young men had to distinguish themselves in battle in order to become full-fledged warriors, and this was the goal of every young Indian boy.

In many ways, the Indians had a pretty good life. They were their own masters. This bliss, if you could call it that, was rudely shattered by the fast westward migration of the so-called white man. Somebody once said that when the explorers arrived in North America they found a native society that had no central government, no income taxes, and the women did most of the work. Then, along came the white man to improve the system. In the last few years, we have gone back to some of that same system since about half of our workforce outside the home, now, are women. (I dare say that women do about 85 percent of the work in the home.)

When the early pioneers saw this ocean of grass, they sensed that here was a land on which thousands of cattle would thrive. In the 16th century, the Spaniards introduced cattle to Mexico, which, in those days, included Texas. Many cattle escaped and literally became wild. They roamed by the thousands in Texas and were called Texas Longhorns. Nobody paid much attention to them except to shoot an occasional one for its hide and a bit of stringy beef.

However, after the Civil War in the USA, some hard-up but ambitious entrepreneurs found a market for these cattle further north. The hides were a big factor, although the meat was also needed for the hungry, hardworking people in the large northeastern, eastern and mid-west cities where the population was increasing rapidly through immigration, mostly from Europe. The trick was how to get the cattle up there. There were no railroads in the South. In fact, there were hardly any railroads anywhere.

History has a way of converging a lot of different events at the same time. Within a 30-year period, from 1860 to 1890, so many things happened that it is hard to comprehend it all: First, there was the Civil War won by the North, setting the slaves free. Also, huge immigration was taking place. Next, there was the settling of the West by ranchers and homesteaders. This in turn caused big confrontations between the settlers and the Indians.

In the end, the Indians were placed on reservations. The treaties gave them bare existence. The almost complete demise of the buffalo led to two important results: First, it deprived the Indians of their food source. Second, it left the land vacant for the establishment of large herds of the white man's buffalo (cattle).

Railroad construction also began during this era. Most railroads, as they still do today, went from east to west, not from north to south. When the railroad arrived in Kansas, the Texans saw their opportunity and trailed millions of cattle to the railheads in Kansas. At the same time, many large herds were trailed to Colorado, Wyoming, Montana and finally into Alberta to establish ranches on all this grass recently acquired at the expense of the natives.

The natives' cattle (bison/buffalo). Fortunately, they won't become extinct because of some people with foresight. This one made a brief stopover at the Calgary Stockyards in 1976 on its way to Don and Dorothy Edge's ranch at Cochrane, Alberta.

Here is a recap of what took place in that short period (not necessarily in this order):

- Civil War in the USA
- Freeing of the slaves

- Cattle moving from the South to the North

- Indian wars in the USA; peace treaties in Canada—both had the same end result

- Indians placed on reservations

- Nearly all the buffalo were killed by the white men: sometimes, only for sport and their tongues

- Settling of the West: first, by ranchers; then, by homesteaders

- Legends of the West were born: cowboys, rodeos, etc.

- Introduction of windmills and barbwire

- Building of the railroads

- Major stockyards were built at railroad terminals: Chicago, Kansas City, St. Louis, Omaha, and Sioux City

In Canada, we were slightly behind the United States in these developments. In many ways we paralleled them, but usually in a slower, more conservative fashion. Many of Alberta's present day ranches were started in the late 1870s up to about 1900—at which point the homesteaders started arriving in large numbers. The railroad arrived in Calgary in 1883. (This was two years after my dad was born in Manitoba, south of Winnipeg.)

In Manitoba there was an Irishman by the name of Pat Burns who came from Ontario as a young man. He filed on a homestead in the Minnedosa country. It did not take long for him to get bored and restless on the farm, so he began to buy and sell cattle. He also butchered cattle for whatever meat trade he could muster.

In 1890 Pat arrived in Calgary where he saw a lot of opportunity to establish a meat trade. During this same year, he built a small slaughterhouse and meat-packing plant as well as some yards to house livestock. His first contracts were with the railroad builders. The railroad construction between Calgary and Edmonton required a lot of men and a lot of meat. Pat Burns supplied that meat. He also supplied meat to several other railroad construction gangs in Saskatchewan.

In the late 1890s, several of Pat's top hands (Bill Henry from High River was one of them) trailed and barged cattle to the Yukon

10

to feed the hungry gold miners. During the next ten years, he acquired several ranches, some from early ranchers and others he more or less started from scratch. At one point, he owned at least eight big ranches.

After the railroads were built, cattle were shipped from Calgary, Lethbridge, and Medicine Hat to Eastern Canada and some US destinations. A few years later, they were shipped from some of the branch lines as well, such as Cayley, Innisfail and other country points.

With all this cattle activity, it stood to reason that Calgary should have a major stock yards market operation managed by an autonomous body. Such a terminal marketing facility would need to handle cattle, swine, sheep, horses and mules. So, Pat Burns and some other interested parties decided to build a major stockyards facility similar to some already built in many US cities. Several meetings were held by these men of vision and action to discuss the venture. Most of the ground work was done by a person named John Hall, a lawyer in Calgary.

Accordingly, the preliminary City By-Law, dated April 6, 1903, authorized Mayor Thos. Underwood and Clerk Chas. McMillan to execute an agreement with John S. Hall respecting his request for the City to convey certain lands for the purpose of establishing a stock yards market.

This extensive Agreement, dated April 14, 1903, allowed the City to allocate some parcels of land (19 and 80/100th acres, excepting road allowance) in the NE/4 of Section 11, Township 24, Range 1 W5M (adjacent to holdings owned by Patrick Burns and the Calgary and Edmonton Railway Company) to John S. Hall, or proposed company, for $990 cash to commence the City's stock yards market operation to last for 25 years; and, nowhere else within the limits of the City would there be another market place allowed to operate during such period. Active construction was to commence within three months of the date of the Agreement, and $6,000 worth of improvements were to be built the first year. As well as fences, pens, sheds, and barns, the conditions also included that offices and business buildings as well as a boarding house were to be constructed. Once all conditions were met, final transfer of land title would take place. A default would revert the property back to City ownership at same price. The land, valued at $50 per acre, was not yet in the City limits. This detail was taken care of at the next session of the North West Assembly.

It was also stipulated in the initial Agreement that the City of Calgary would have access to the Company's books to verify all sales and collections; and the City would impose market fees, in respect to animals brought to the market for sale, barter, storage, or exchange, to be paid to the City, which were not to exceed the following amounts:

"For every calf, swine or sheep . . . . 1¼ cents
For every head of horned or hornless cattle . . . 5 cents
For every horse, mare, gelding or mule. . . . . . .10 cents"

By the Memorandum of Association (by-laws) of The Alberta Stock Yards Company Limited, dated May 23, 1903, the capital of the company was fixed at $200,000 and divided into 2,000 shares of $100 each.

On June 1, 1903, The Alberta Stock Yards Company Limited was incorporated in the Northwest Territories capital in Regina (called Pile o' Bones in the real old days). This incorporation took place two years before Alberta became a province in 1905. The name *"Alberta"* was already being used for the district and people were pressing for independence from the NWT government. The name *"Alberta"* appeared on all the Company's official documents, but the stockyards setup they built in Calgary was usually referred to as the Calgary Stockyards. (Later, The Alberta Stock Yards Co. built and owned the Lethbridge Stockyards.)

On June 5, 1903, the first officers elected were: R. J. Hutchings, president; C. W. Peterson, vice president; and John S. Hall, secretary-treasurer. The rest of the board members were: R. B. Bennett, James Lougheed, Pat Burns, Dan Riley, William Pearce, Jack Hall, and Fred Black.

By the time the Company was operational, in March of 1904, shares were issued to the following men—all from Montreal: B. McKellan, Jas. A. Cuttle, C.M. Kinghorn, R. H. Carlin, C. E. Gault, James McDonnell, A. E. Cooke and J. E. Wilder. H. C. Telfer, also from Montreal, was a shareholder right from the very beginning. I doubt very much if any of these Montreal gentlemen knew one end of a cow from the other, but the West was opening up and they wanted part of the action. (Over the years, I have also invested in some ventures about which I knew very little.)

12

With all conditions being satisfactorily met, the official "Transfer of Title," became effective September 14, 1905, and the blocks of land were transferred from the City to the Company. This document is signed by Mayor J. Emerson and Clerk H. E. Gillis. By 1906 the lands together with all buildings and improvements were valued at $8,000. The "Certificate of Title" bearing the name "The Alberta Stock Yards Company Limited" is dated, May 22, 1906.

The Canadian Pacific Railway Company, whose holdings were about 13.44 acres with some yards for livestock, was also very interested in the promotion of the stock yards market in Calgary right from the start. It is recorded that by 1911 Pat Burns was the biggest shareholder in the Company. On August 22, 1911, he sold his shares to the CPR. There was land swapping involved as well. I am not sure about those details, but, what I do know is that Pat Burns received $59,587.50 for his preferred and common shares. This really was not very much money when you consider that the original investment to start the Company was $200,000. Pat Burns' initial investment was approximately $50,000, plus some land.

Over the many years, key personnel at the Stockyards were: Donald A. Cameron-manager & treasurer (1906); Thomas Bellew (1907-10); J. A. McLaughlin (1911); Leonard Gates (1912-13), who later became livestock manager for Burns; D. C. Coleman-president, J. Halstead-vice president, Edward Evans-manager, and J. W. Hugill-secretary (1914); Edward Evans-manager (1915-1918); E. Ward Jones-manager & secretary (1919-29); Walter M. Ripley-manager, Tom Connelly-secretary (1929-1938); Tom Connelly-manager, Charlie Kennedy-assistant manager (1938-1941); Charlie Kennedy-general manager (1942-76); and Eric Tribble-general manager (1976-81).

In 1881 there was a grand total of 127,309 horses, cattle, hogs and sheep in the Northwest Territories. By 1910 there were 1,668,259 head of livestock in Alberta alone. I cannot find any record as to how many cattle were handled or sold by the Alberta Stock Yards Co. in its first few years of operation. There were no commission firms to start with. The Company conducted its own business. What usually transpired was that a rancher would ship in several carloads of range cattle. Pat Burns and a few smaller butchers would then buy a certain number of them. Of course, there were often more cattle to sell than the local trade could absorb, so the surplus cattle were then fed, watered, and shipped to either Eastern Canada or to the

13

USA. Some went by rail to Montreal; then they went by ship to Great Britain. There were many days when no cattle were sold at all; they were all shipped to other destinations.

By this time, the Burns establishment owned a number of ranches. Quite often they had enough cattle of their own to supply their slaughter requirements. They also bought cattle from some of their neighbours' ranches. Any cattle shipped in from the neighbouring ranches were unloaded at Burns' unloading chute, not at the Alberta Stock Yards unloading chutes.

(Incidentally, one of Burns' brands was NL (/L), which stood for "never lock," referring to ranch house doors or gates. The hospitality mat was always out.)

Branding at Burns' chute, 1920. Barney Walsh and Leonard Gates, branding. (Note brand on the chute gate.)

Over the years, I occasionally heard stories about Pat Burns that cast some doubt on his character. One story was that he had a "long rope" and that is why he was so successful in becoming a very wealthy man. I say "hogwash"! Pat Burns was a shrewd operator, but he was not a cattle rustler. Most of that kind of talk came from small minds who were jealous of Pat's success. The false tales were passed on from father to son to grandson, each embellishing them a little bit to

14

make a better topic of conversation. For starters, I do not think Pat Burns knew how to rope. Secondly, he certainly would not instruct any of his men to steal cattle.

During the Depression, many of Burns' rancher friends fell on hard times. On whom did they call to bail them out? Pat Burns, of course. He was about the only person around with a bit of money. He helped at least three major ranchers that I am aware of. I will not reveal their names because they were good people who still have descendants running those same ranches today. Pat could have foreclosed on at least a few of them. He chose not to do so. When things improved a bit, these people paid him back and retained ownership of their ranches. Maybe some people will be surprised that I would write about this in this book; but, for years, it has bothered me whenever I heard some snide remarks about Pat Burns. I know he was human, but I also know he helped a lot more people than he ever hurt. "May He Rest In Peace"—an old Jewish saying.

CHAPTER II

GOOD, LEAN AND BETTER YEARS
(1910 - 1949)

By 1910 the Alberta Stock Yards Co. had decided to sell cattle more or less on a daily basis. This is when commission firms were established. I have searched everywhere to find out who those very first firms were, but information on this is rather sketchy. I do know that D. P. McDaniel hung up his shingle about that time as a livestock commission merchant and forwarding agent. He had two cattle salesmen working for him by the names of W. J. Hunter and C. J. Hardin. Another outfit was a Farmers' Co-op. Some of the other early commission men were A. H. Mayland, D. S. "Dunc" McIntosh, Tom Cadzo, and Ot Hammill. After several years, one of D. P. McDaniel's salesmen, C. J. "Cliff" Hardin, went on his own. He was one tough hombre. If he ran into trouble, he settled it with his fists.

These early commission men had little shacks on the docks where the rail cars were unloaded. In those days, cattle were usually shipped to the Calgary Stockyards; and, when they arrived, there was a real battle as to which firm would handle the cattle. Like I just mentioned, this often resulted in a few black eyes. Hardin wasn't the only one who could handle his dukes.

In 1911 there were 2,098 carloads of livestock (the bulk of which were cattle) unloaded at the Calgary Stockyards. That same year there were 1,730 carloads of livestock shipped out. This tells us that for 368 carloads, Calgary was the final destination. There were also a lot of cattle trailed into Calgary with horses. When those numbers are added to the ones shipped in by rail, it amounts to a lot of stock. The charge for unloading and loading was 5 cents per head for cattle and 2 cents per head for horses and sheep. (I do not know why it was so cheap for horses.) By 1915 the charge for unloading and loading a car was 75 cents.

A view of the commission firms' offices at the Calgary Stockyards, 1919, on the unloading dock before the Livestock Exchange Building was built.

(Looking southwest) Cattle waiting for "Private Treaty" sale, 1919.

(Looking northwest) Stockyards and Burns' plant, 1919.

Around 1912, when the CPR became the majority shareholder in the Alberta Stock Yards Co., they decided to expand the capacity of the Yards. J. E. Dennis was in charge of those operations. (I have no record of the transactions, but, within the next few years (after 1912), the CPR acquired all of the shares and became the sole owner and proprietor of The Alberta Stock Yards Company Limited.)

From 1912 to 1919, a number of facilities and buildings were constructed. They built some railroad loading chutes on the west side, a chute where a wagon or possibly a very early version of a truck could unload a few head, a hog and sheep scalehouse, and a Livestock Exchange Building. A modest hotel with a restaurant had been built in 1907. It was called the Alberta Stock Yards Hotel.

During the 1920s they built a number of pens with roofs over them. In fact, on the west side of Portland Street nearly every pen had a roof over it. They also built a dipping vat.

From 1929 to 1962 very few improvements were made to the existing facilities. Some exceptions were: more truck chutes; two rather makeshift sale rings; and a building with a squeeze chute for testing cattle for TB and brucellosis—the latter of which is generally referred to as "Bang's disease."

The old Alberta Stock Yards Hotel met its demise sometime in the mid-20s. Kemo Inamasu, the proprietor, moved his restaurant from that hotel into the basement at the back of the old Livestock Exchange Building, where it remained until that building was demolished in 1962. Mickey Dirrane told me a lot of tales about the old hotel. Some stories were pretty raunchy. Often the people who stayed there had sold some cattle on the market, so they had a little loose change in their jeans. Throughout history wherever there are men and money, the ladies of the night soon make their appearance. This was no exception. It was not officially declared a red-light hotel; however, it often harboured girls from the red-light district of East Calgary. They were classified as casual visitors. Of course, not all of the men who stayed there availed themselves of these ladies. There were also many land, cattle and horse deals consummated within the confines of that old hotel.

Back to the commission men: In 1915 George Denoon, who came from Guelph, Ontario, and Vern Parslow, who was born and raised in Calgary, teamed up and formed a commission firm called Parslow & Denoon. That firm was in business for 66 years, which is the longest any commission firm operated at the Calgary Stockyards.

Harvey Adams and Roy Furgeson arrived at the Yards in 1919 to start the firm of Adams, Wood & Weiller. Harvey came from the "Show Me" state of Missouri. When he came to Canada, he landed at Tofield, Alberta, where he stayed until he moved to Calgary. AWW was in business at the Yards for 62 years, which is the second longest any commission firm operated at the Calgary Stockyards.

Stan Denoon and Pete Adams were partners in the Calgary Public Livestock Market Ltd., which was a new company we formed in 1981. So, all together, a Denoon had a presence on the Calgary market for 71 years and an Adams for 67 years. From 1986 to 1989, with the exception of Cecil Barber (former Paul & MacDonald man), none of the initial commission men were involved with the Calgary Public Livestock Market Ltd.

There were also a number of other commission firms that operated at the Yards from 1910 to 1981. Some changed hands several times. A few simply went out of business. I have not been able to secure the exact dates or time spans that these firms operated, but, as near as I can ascertain, there were 17 commission firms that operated at the Calgary Stockyards.

The people who operated commission firms at the Calgary Stockyards from 1910 to 1981 were: <u>D. P. McDaniel</u>, <u>Cliff Hardin,</u> and

A. H. Mayland, who eventually sold out to Punch Barhan and Bud Sewall. These two men did not operate the firm for very long. The Depression caught up with them. United Grain Growers (UGG) did not last too long either. It was producer-owned. D. S. McIntosh Co. was around for a lot of years. There was one Jewish commission man who operated at the Yards during the 1920s and early 1930s. His name was Benny Katchen. He was the father of Myer and Sammy Katchen, who later built a packing plant just south of the Yards. Another early commission firm was Gavin Jack. His trademark was a big cigar. He was a feisty individual who could hold his own in the rough and tumble game of the early cattle business. Central Livestock was owned by Ot Hammill, who, after many years, sold out to the Alberta Livestock Co-op in 1942. The ALC was producer-owned with George Winkelaar at the helm. There was Tom Cadzo, who sold out to W. W. Starke and Pat Trainor in 1944. In a few years, Starke bought Trainor out. In 1951 Starke sold out to Jim Paul and Danny MacDonald, and they renamed the firm Paul & MacDonald. In 1958 Jim Paul sold his interest to Cecil Barber and Doug Keer. After Danny MacDonald passed away in the mid-1970s, Cecil bought Danny's share. Several years later, when Doug passed away, Cecil became the sole owner of the firm. He never changed the name; it remained Paul & MacDonald. In 1971 the J. C. Wheatcroft Co. Ltd. opened up a commission firm. This was after ALC had moved out to the Agri-Mart. Producers' Livestock was owned by Alex Beveridge and Irish Johnston. They folded sometime in the mid-60s.

W. J. Elliott, 1922
(with UGG)

Gavin Jack, 1922
Jack Gavin Commission Co.

21

Dunc McIntosh, 1922
(McIntosh & Co.)

Eddie McIntosh, 1922
(McIntosh & Co.)

Harvey Adams, 1922
(Adams, Wood & Weiller)

Roy Furgeson, 1922
(Adams, Wood & Weiller)

George Denoon, 1922
(Parslow & Denoon)

Vern Parslow, 1922
(Parslow & Denoon)

Benny Katchen, 1922
(Katchen Commission Co.)

C. E. Bain, 1922
(Dominion Livestock Branch)

23

Bud Sewall, 1922
(Mayland Commission Co.)

Punch Barhan, 1922
(Mayland Commission Co.)

From 1903 until the Second World War (1939), many cattle and horses were trailed to the Stockyards from the surrounding areas of Calgary. Most of the cattle trailed in originated from the city limits to a perimeter of about 15 miles out; this included places like Langdon, Delacour, Balzac, Midnapore, Cochrane, Shepard, sometimes Airdrie, Millarville, Priddis, Conrich and so on. Many of these places are very close to the city limits these days, but in those days, they were a fair distance away. From places like Crossfield, Carstairs, Okotoks, and Strathmore the cattle were nearly always shipped in by rail. Quite a few were shipped in by rail from Cochrane and Airdrie as well. The rule of thumb was that, if it took more than one day to trail them to the Stockyards in Calgary, then it was best that they be shipped by rail. To give you an example—say, the ranch was six to twelve miles west of Cochrane, it made more sense to trail the cattle as far as the Stockyards in Cochrane, then load them onto rail cars and ship them out from there. If, however, the ranch was located in Springbank, or between Cochrane and Calgary, then they often were trailed directly to the Calgary Stockyards.

I heard a lot of stories about cattle being trailed into the Calgary Stockyards from the north and crossing the Bow River at Centre Street, or, in the real old days, swimming the river. In the latter years, they crossed over the Centre Street Bridge or sometimes the Langevin Bridge. From the south they often moved the cattle along the west side of the Bow River. A lot of the cattle from the south belonged to the Burns outfit, since they owned most of the land along the river.

(Looking east down Ogden Road)
Cattle being trailed to the Stockyards, 1924.

There were a fair number of wrecks on any given drive. Sometimes, an Old Tin Lizzie (Model T Ford) was involved. Sometimes, teams of horses would spook and bolt. Another real problem was caused by little backyard gardens. Many a potato patch and other vegetables got trampled by rambunctious steers. More than one cowboy got jerked off his horse when a backyard clothesline caught him under the chin. I personally know several people who had this happen to them. Sympathy was strangely lacking for the cowboy by the people who owned the garden and the clothesline.

In those days, the City Police fully cooperated with the people moving cattle. Any young person who reads this will find it hard to believe that cattle could be chased down the streets of Calgary. If your grandfather and grandmother are still alive, ask them about it.

(Looking east) Herd of cattle leaving Stockyards, 1924.

Frank Hutchinson from Cochrane used to write a column in some of the local papers called *"Wit and Wisdom."* One time he wrote about a cattle drive they made from his ranch at Lochend to the Calgary Stockyards. His sister-in-law, Jo Hutchinson, gave me the story to reprint. Here it is:

"The year 1935 found us on the trail down Nose Creek with a bunch of steers bound for the Calgary Stockyards. We knew of at least two drives that failed to reach the Yards that fall. One was from Beiseker. Very, very early on the final day

we made our drive into the sleeping town. As we approached the end of Nose Creek our troubles began. There were barking dogs that lived at the many little squatters' shacks that fringed the outskirts of Calgary, especially along Nose Creek. These squatters were very clean people. Their clotheslines were long, always full and waving merrily in the morning breeze. Chickens? There were a few in the right places at the wrong time; we were making some headway, but the steers were very tense. Then ahead of us down by the creek was a family milk cow on a picket. This looked like a break to ease our bunch along. But, just before they reached her, the lady of the shack in a long flowing skirt made a wild dash to get her picketed dairy cow. This was it—the herd broke and stampeded for safety! After a wild ride that took a good hour or two, we got them turned and were almost back to the dairy cow when help arrived in the form of Mickey Dirrane from the Stockyards. Mick was the rider who handled cattle in the Yards—there were no foot cowboys in those days. Mick was leading a long, lean, gentle cow. Her calf was in the Stockyards waiting for breakfast. Mick turned her loose among the steers. She took the lead into town with our bunch following her through the shack town to the bridge over the Bow. Just east of McLellan Coal Yard the steers overtook the cow and here they balked. Finally Old Bossy took the lead over the bridge and held it right to the Yards. As far as I know, this was the last successful drive from the north side. I believe they made it in from the south for a couple more years. It was a long ride home that afternoon. It was after dark when we reached home. It was also the last long ride with Dad as he had a heart attack that night, and after that he rode only short gentle rides on the ranch.

"The official last cattle drive into Calgary was just before Stampede Week in 1946. Clem Gardiner of Pirmez Creek drove the rodeo and bucking stock in for the Stampede. This was a drawing card for the Calgary Stampede. It was run live on the radio with much advertising ahead of time. The photographers and press were all out. Also, the Police kept the traffic off the route. People came from far away places to watch. Clem Gardiner with Noel, Joan and Audrey,

27

Lennie Mickle, Geoff and Winston Parker, Frank Gattey, Dave Wheatcroft and Vincent Robinson were the riders. Old Jim "what-is-his-name" drove the chuckwagon on the lead."

There was also another aspect to trailing cattle in the early years and that was moving cattle from the Stockyards to outlying farms and ranches. Of course, there were a lot more cattle trailed to the Yards than there were from the Yards. Nevertheless, without trucks available, or nearby railway service, many cattle were trailed to the country.

Henry Loose, who was born in 1910 and lived on Symons Valley Road west of Airdrie, told me that they often trailed cattle home from the Yards. That would be approximately 20 miles. His dad had George Denoon Sr. buy the cattle for him. The cowboys from the Yards would chase the cattle across the Langevin Bridge. At that point, the Looses would take over. Once they crossed 16th Avenue North, they were in open country all the way home. There were a lot of other people in the surrounding areas of Calgary who did the same thing.

From 1903 till the late 1920s, the Stockyards used loose hay and not bales, like they did later on. This loose hay was purchased from various farmers around Calgary's perimeter. It was hauled with horses, sometimes with sleighs, but nearly always with wagons. Southern Alberta is poor country for sleighs. High winds blow the snow into drifts, and Chinook winds make snow disappear like magic. I have experienced a temperature change of 67 degrees Fahrenheit within a 24-hour period.

C. Redvers Perry, who lives in the Balzac district, is quite an historian. He has written a column in some of the local rural newspapers for a number of years. He is also very involved with the Nose Creek Historical Society. Every year they publish a booklet in which the history is given about the various aspects of pioneer life north of the Bow River. In 1985 Redvers wrote the Fourteenth Local Historical Recognition booklet entitled *The Hay Trail from 1875 to 1930s.* He does not mention anything about hay being delivered directly to the Calgary Stockyards, but I have talked to some other old-timers who said that some of that loose hay did end up at the Yards.

The following is an excerpt from Redvers' booklet:

"Haying was usually done in July and August. Usually, two years' growth was quite acceptable. The current year's green growth made it most attractive in quality and pleasant odour. The term used by old-timers was to "hit the hay trail," which meant off to town with a load of hay. Trails, which we are paying tribute to today with a plaque in memory of those respected old-timers, were the paths of travel taken to the hay's destination. Trails wandered in seemingly endless miles on lines of least resistance. They avoided wet marshes, steep hills, rough rocky terrain, tipsy valleys and were careful to select a nice gravel base with not too many steep creek banks when fording a creek or river. Snowdrifts in the winter or icy terrain, which may occur after a Chinook or warm spell, also had consideration. So, as one can see from all these conditions, it is no wonder that our hay trails on maps, or that can still be seen on open prairie areas, take on an aimless here, there and everywhere pattern. The goal was the HAYMARKET—weigh, sell, unload, eat a meal at one of the hospitable cafes and get home before dark or storm.

"The Haymarket in Calgary for those who did not have private deals previously arranged, was just opposite the Langevin Bridge on 4th Street East, just north of the Cecil Hotel along the riverbank. I well recall the horses and wagons lined up there in the 1920s and the City weighscales. Vivid hay trails over the prairies were still used, in part, up until 1930; but, with road development and tractor power and larger trucks in operation, the hay trail died from existence along with the pioneer hay haulers. Some of us nearing the "three score years and ten" bracket still had lots to do with upland prairie hay but on the level of hauling it home to feed our own livestock. The same prairie wandering trails saw many a settler's wagon drawing oats to town for the horses that kept the City going, from the business executive's driving horse, to the grocer's and butcher's delivery rigs; the local ambulance, fire brigade, and the "end of the trail" undertaker's hearse, to one's last resting place in the Union Cemetery, Calgary's south side, are not forgotten. So, from beginning to end, the HAY TRAIL was

Calgary's first "energy pipeline" and also served for a well-worn path for the settlers and their families to go to town and shop for weekly provisions.

"As one wanders over the few pasture lands yet untouched in our district, the faint two-rut trails remind one of the great hope and confidence those hardy pioneers, who were yet young and ambitious, had in the western prairies. I often think: "OH! IF THOSE TRAILS COULD TALK—WHAT SECRETS THEY HOLD." Like our respected old-timers—they fade away, but never to be forgotten."

The Bank of Montreal had a branch at the Stockyards for approximately seventy-four years. It would be interesting to know how many dollars' worth of livestock money passed through that bank. At least 85 percent of all the business transacted at the Yards was funnelled through it. I hope the bank's Board of Directors in the East appreciated the "little milk cow" they had at the Calgary Stockyards.

Prices so high — lone bandit "hits" Stockyard branch of Bank of Montreal

Headline news—bank robbery incident, Calgary Stockyards, May 14, 1978. The "culprit" got an undisclosed amount of cash at gunpoint and was never apprehended.

Another outfit that made its appearance at the Calgary Stockyards in 1915 was the Hartford Insurance Co. They still do business at the Calgary Stockyards Ltd.-Strathmore. That gives them a tenure of eighty years. They have paid out a lot of claims, but, like most insurance companies, they must have made money or they would not have stuck around for eighty years. In 1915 Hartford's rate was 10 cents a carload. At least that is what the records state. I personally wonder if it wasn't 10 cents per head.

As we all know, from the late 1870s until 1900 or thereabouts, the newcomers to the West were ranchers. In many cases, they were rich eastern or British gentry who employed managers to run their spreads. One example of this was the Cochrane Ranche, which was under lease by Senator Matthew Cochrane from Montreal. I am sure the Senator never pulled a steer out of a snowbank or checked on his cattle in a snowstorm in Alberta. Another example was the Matador Ranch, which had operations in Texas, North Dakota, and southern Saskatchewan. This outfit was owned by a gentleman from Dundee, Scotland. Their head office was in Denver, Colorado.

After 1900 the homesteaders started to move in. At first, it was a trickle, which, by 1908, had developed into a flood. When I was a boy, I heard countless stories about homesteading as told to me by my dad. He was a homesteader, who came from Manitoba in 1906. He homesteaded 28 miles northeast of Swift Current, Saskatchewan, on the south side of the South Saskatchewan River, directly across from the Matador Ranch. Many homesteaders in that area came from Ontario and from the northern part of the USA.

My dad, C.W. Friesen, filed for his homestead the same year Saskatchewan became a province, in 1905. He and my mother, whose name was Katherine, did not take possession until 1906. At Morris, Manitoba, Dad loaded his "settler's car" with two horses, one cow, and I think one ox, a few chickens, a walking plow, some small harrows, a few bags of grain for seed, some household items, and a little feed for his livestock. Dad slept with a few blankets on some straw in one corner of the rail car. Meanwhile, my mother, and my oldest brother, a babe in arms, rode in style on the passenger train. They unloaded at Herbert, twenty-eight miles southeast from where their homestead was located. This scenario was repeated by thousands of other settlers between 1903 and 1915.

Here is where the Stockyards in Calgary come into the picture. Hundreds of these settlers' cars were unloaded at the Stockyards. Eventually, the CPR built a special platform where people had room to store their goods for a few days while they got their bearings.

Often, they would go over to 9th Avenue to buy a few supplies. The Stockyards also provided pens for their travel-weary stock for a few days. Finally, they would make their way to their new homes, albeit sod shacks. Many of these young homesteaders became very successful farmers. Most of them acquired some cattle and hogs. Of course, they all had horses, since farming was done with horses as well as oxen. Many of them remembered landing in Calgary at the Stockyards where they had sometimes witnessed a number of carloads of ranch cattle being unloaded. When it came time to sell stock, where else would you go but to the Calgary Stockyards?

Heard Around Calgary Yards

WEDNESDAY

H. J. Flack had a car of cattle shipped down to the U.G.G. from Raley.

Kline & Son shipped a car of hogs down from Penhold, handled by the Mayland Commission.

W. S. Paris shipped a car of cattle in from Sentinel, billed to the U.G.G.

H. C. Beckner shipped a car of hogs to the market from Carstairs, selling through the U.G.G.

C. E. Dovey, the local feeder, started turning off his bunch of finished hogs this week-end, selling through Parslow & Denoon.

The Mayland Commission shipped a car of cattle out from A. Linton, at Islay.

The Harden Commission shipped a couple of cars of cattle out to L. Mercier, at Chilliwack.

Willows shipped a car of hogs down to G. I. & F., Winnipeg.

Adams, Wood & Weiller shipped four cars of cattle over to Bogan, at Portland.

The Harden Commission shipped a car of calves down to L. C. Low; at Cardston.

THURSDAY

Wm. Elliott shipped a car of hogs in from Irricana, consigned to the Mayland Commission.

J. S. Earle shipped a co-operative load to the market from Acme, handled by the U.G.G.

B. Hashman shipped a car of hogs in from Acme, which was handled by L. B. Katchen and shipped through to Rosenbaum at the coast.

Storey & Gibbons shipped a car of hogs to the market from Beiseker, billed to Parslow & Denoon.

J. T. Evans shipped a car of cattle up from Bassano, selling through the Harden Commission.

E. Fonder had a car of hogs in from Trochu to the U.G.G., and they also handled a car of cattle for W. Williams from the same district.

Wilson shipped a car of hogs down from Huxley, to be sold through Gavin Jack.

There was a car of stock in the yards which G. Scott was shipping from Killam to Salmon Arm.

A. Music shipped a car of hogs down from Coronation, to be sold through the U.G.G.

W. E. Tees had a shipment of stock through from Tees to R. A. Wallace,

down, to be sold through Parslow & Denoon.

H. A. Thomas shipped a car of cattle and hogs to the market from Bassano, selling through the U.G.G.

The Pincher Creek Co-operative members at Brocket shipped a car of hogs up, handled by the U.G.G.

Ramage & Walls shipped a car of hogs up to the Swift company from Claresholm.

Blackie U.G.G. members shipped a car of hogs up, to be sold through their live stock branch.

McKenzie shipped a car of hogs down from Halkirk to the Swift Co.

Puffer had five cars of hogs down from Ponoka, two billed to the Canadian Packing and three to the Harris Ab., Toronto.

Dovey turned off a bunch of 60 hogs today, selling through Parslow & Denoon.

The U.G.G. shipped five cars of hogs down to H. P. Kennedy, Ltd., at Toronto.

Paulin & Frazier shipped four cars of cattle out; one to G. S. Eckers, at Watt, Sask.; one each to R. G. Smith and R. Grant, at Teeswater, Ont., and the other load to A. W. Massie, at Carstairs.

Parslow & Denoon shipped eight cars of cattle down to the Canadian Packing, at Montreal.

FRIDAY

Railway shipments, 1922.

It is of interest to note that a large percentage of the cattle and hogs received at the Yards came from medium to small operations. This is still the case at the auction markets today.

Many of the children, grandchildren and great-grandchildren of those early pioneers are still in the livestock business. Some of them are the owners of huge feedlots. Very few of their cattle are marketed through a ring these days, although some are sold on the computer. These large feedlots do support the Calgary Stockyards Ltd. at Strathmore (and other markets) by purchasing a lot of their feeder cattle from them. Many of the large ranches sell on the computer, like the Douglas Lake Ranch in British Columbia.

In spite of all the technical advances in the last twenty-five years, plus all the changes in the ways we conduct our cattle business, two things do not change: one is price, which is governed by supply and demand, and the other is principle. So, like I always say, methods may change, but the principles of honesty and integrity are the same today as they were hundreds of years ago. In the cattle business, we owe much to our pioneer forefathers (and mothers too). They left us a good legacy that I hope doesn't die in the foreseeable future.

Sorry for digressing into a bit of philosophy, but, while writing this book, I got quite nostalgic thinking of all the people I have met over the years. They all deserve to be in some kind of Hall of Fame.

I might mention those homesteaders who were smart, or lucky, or maybe both, to file on land close to Calgary. They became multimillionaires, or should I say their children and grandchildren did. Much of that land is covered with houses today.

The history of the Stockyards can be broken down into ten eras, as follows:

ERA 1, 1903 to 1910 - The Early Days: When the Stockyards were first built, the ranchers showed good support right from the start. The Alberta Stock Yards Hotel made its appearance.

ERA 2, 1910 to 1919 - Progress and Development: The establishment of commission firms took place. It was during this timeframe that the two longest operating commission firms set up shop: Parslow and Denoon in 1915 and Adams, Wood and Weiller in 1919. The formation of the Calgary Livestock Exchange with its federal trading rules came into being. More facilities were built—including the Livestock Exchange Building. They poured concrete in many pens and alleys. This period also included World War I. Many cattle passed through the Stockyards on their way to Britain to feed the soldiers and others.

ERA 3, 1920 to 1929 - The Roaring Twenties: Things were in high gear. Everyone made money. Burns was going full tilt and expanding right across Canada. Several other plants and abattoirs joined forces and became Canada Packers. Swift Canadian and Union Pack were cutting a wide swath. It was during this era that the hog population rapidly increased. There were a number of large sheep ranches south and east of Calgary. The Stockyards also had a number of horse dealers using the premises; in fact, they had a special horse sale ring located approximately 300 yards north of the old Livestock Exchange Building where they held horse auction sales for a twenty-five-year period. All this activity created a lot of business for the Alberta Stock Yards Co. and the commission men. The Calgary Stampede, founded in 1912, was by now well established as an annual event.

Norman Edge, Bar 14 Ranches, Cochrane, Alberta (south of Bow River), never worked at the Calgary Stockyards, but he was a great supporter. This picture of Norman, riding a horse called "Cougar," was taken at the Calgary Stampede, 1928.

ERA 4, 1929 to 1939 - CRASH: As the old saying goes, all good things must come to an end. These years are usually referred to as the Great Depression, and indeed it was. I can remember those years as a child. I was born in 1926. Many people were in dire straits.

The bottom dropped out of everything, including commodities. Wheat went down to 20 cents a bushel, hogs were only a few dollars each, and old canner cows went down to 2 cents a pound. I remember my dad and my brothers shipping some cattle to Winnipeg in 1936. They got 5 cents a pound for two-year-old steers. They were quite happy. That was more than they had received for the last few years. Meanwhile, at the Calgary Stockyards things got pretty tough. Receipts declined. They had to lower their selling rate. People were laid off, and it was very grim. Many unemployed hobos (a term given to young men bumming a ride on a freight train) availed themselves of sleeping in a haystack at the Yards. Many people could not afford to drive their cars. In the cities, they rode the old street cars, while, in the country, many converted their cars into Bennett buggies, which were then pulled by horses. R. B. Bennett was the Prime Minister of Canada from 1930 to 1935. Many people blamed him for the bad state of affairs, but the fact was that the whole world was experiencing a major depression. It was kind of ironic that this was the same R. B. Bennett who was one of the early directors of The Alberta Stock Yards Company Limited.

REPRESENTATIVE SALES AT CALGARY YARDS

THURSDAY, DEC. 21

BUTCHER CATTLE

Steers

Number of Animals—Price per Cwt.

7 @ $4.50   1 @ $4.35   2 @ $4.25
19 @ 4.00   11 @ 3.85   2 @ 3.75
6 @ 3.60   3 @ 3.35   2 @ 3.00
1 @ 2.50

Heifers

1 @ 2.85   12 @ 2.75   5 @ 2.65
2 @ 2.50   1 @ 2.35   1 @ 2.25
2 @ 1.50

Cows

12 @ 3.00   1 @ 2.85   11 @ 2.75
80 @ 2.65   10 @ 2.50   15 @ 2.40
1 @ 2.35   18 @ 2.25   12 @ 2.00
1 @ 1.25   2 @ 1.00   3 @ .75

Bulls

1 @ 21.00

Calves

7 @ 3.00   21 @ 2.10   3 @ 1.50

STOCKERS AND FEEDERS

Steers

25 @ 3.35   30 @ 3.25   35 @ 3.15
1 @ 3.10   77 @ 3.00   13 @ 2.85
1 @ 2.75   5 @ 2.50   10 @ 2.25
2 @ 1.75   1 @ 1.50

Heifers

12 @ 2.50   17 @ 2.35   3 @ 2.25
21 @ 2.00   10 @ 1.85

Cows

7 @ 2.00   1 @ 1.75   27 @ 1.50
1 @ 1.40   13 @ 1.25   5 @ 1.00
12 @ .75

Mixed Cattle

2 @ 2.25

FRIDAY, DEC. 22

Steers

3 @ $3.75   3 @ $3.25   5 @ $3.00
12 @ 2.80   21 @ 2.75   2 @ 2.50
1 @ 1.75   4 @ 1.50   2 @ 1.25

Heifers

13 @ 2.40   4 @ 2.25   2 @ 1.75
2 @ 1.50

Cows

2 @ 2.50   5 @ 2.25   3 @ 1.75
26 @ 1.50   1 @ 1.35   1 @ 1.25
5 cows and 2 calves   150.00

Bulls

1 @ 1.25

Calves

1 @ 3.25   6 @ 2.75   6 @ 2.50

SATURDAY, DEC. 23

Steers

Number of Animals—Price Per Cwt.

15 @ $4.85   4 @ $2.75   2 @ $2.25
1 @ 2.00   3 @ 1.50   2 @ 1.25
1 @ 1.00

Cows

3 @ 1.50   1 @ 1.00   3 @ .75

Stags

1 @ 1.25

Bulls

1 @ 1.75   1 @ 1.50   2 @ 1.25

TUESDAY, DEC. 26

Steers

4 @ 3.00

Heifers

21 @ 2.50

Cows

3 cows and 3 calves $110.00

WEDNESDAY, DEC. 27

Heifers

12 @ 2.75

Cows

6 @ 2.10   1 @ 2.00   22 @ 1.65
8 @ 1.60   5 @ 1.00

Calves

9 @ 3.00   2 @ 2.00

HOGS

WEDNESDAY, DEC. 27

Select Bacon

5 @ $10.01

Thick Smooth

42 @ 9.35   11 @ 9.10

Lights

19 @ 8.75

Heavies

1 220 8.10

Sows

2 265 7.10

THURSDAY, DEC. 21

Select Bacon

28 @ 10.06½   4 @ 9.90

Thick Smooth

1087 @ 9.15   172 @ 9.00   19 @ 8.90
196 @ 8.65   33 @ 8.50   20 @ 8.40

Feeders

15 @ 8.50   51 @ 8.25

Heavies

14 @ 8.15   3 @ 8.00   2 @ 7.15

Livestock prices at the Calgary Yards.

ERA 5, 1940 to 1946 - The Second World War started in August of 1939: Once again, this had a very profound effect on the Stockyards. Within six months, the employment situation did a complete turnaround. The so-called hobos were suddenly first-class soldiers. Not only the unemployed joined the armed forces; thousands of young men and a fewer number of women either joined or were conscripted into the military. Suddenly the Alberta Stock Yards found itself short of help. Charlie Kennedy was the young man in charge of the operations at the Yards. Charlie rolled up his sleeves. One of his moves was to employ a large number of Indians to keep the Yards operating. They set up their own tipi village on the Stockyards property. There were not as many of them as there were at the signing of Treaty No. 7 at Blackfoot Crossing in 1877, but almost as many as there are at the Indian Village every summer at the Calgary Stampede grounds. Along with the Indian folk, he hired many of the people who were not medically fit to be in the armed forces. Needless to say, this crop of mixed rookie employees often caused Charlie to wring his hands in frustration; but, in the end, they always got the job done. Suddenly, the livestock receipts increased and the price also moved up. Once again, the good times had arrived back at the Stockyards.

ERA 6, 1947 to 1953 - The postwar years proved quite interesting: Many of the boys who returned from the War came back to work either for the Stockyards, the commission firms, the packer buyers, or one of the other sectors of the Stockyards family. Many of them had seen action overseas. They were ready to contribute to society both in business and socially. This era also saw the embargo on shipping cattle to the USA lifted in 1947. Then, early in 1952, hoof-and-mouth disease broke out in Saskatchewan. It was also in this period that the selling of cattle at the Stockyards switched from so-called private treaty to the auction method. Calgary was the first major cattle market in Canada to sell by auction. During these years, cattleliners made their appearance.

ERA 7, 1954 to 1970 - Many changes took place during these years: The price of cattle was not real high; however, because of the grain glut, many farmers started to feed more cattle. Up to this time, there were only a handful of small feedlots, although some people had been feeding cattle for the last thirty or forty years, say 1915 to 1955. A few of the feedlots that come to mind are Burns Ranches, Alex Gillespie, Peter Massie, and the DeWitts on Nose Creek. From 1955 to 1975 there were a lot of little feedlots around Calgary. During the grain glut, not only farmers started feeding cattle: this was also the time when many of today's large custom and private feedlots started their operations. Other developments were the country auction markets. In 1962 a new Exchange Building was constructed. In 1966 two new sale rings were built, back to back, to replace the two old rings.

Calgary Stockyards, 1968.

Old Livestock Exchange Building, built in 1921.

The old Exchange Building comes tumbling down. Bill Furgeson caught this action shot. (Wearmouth Demolition)

Partial view of new Livestock Exchange Building
(Alberta Stock Yards Building) built in 1962.

ERA 8, 1971 to 1981 - This was the most erratic cattle market the industry ever experienced: For the Alberta Stock Yards Co., the order buyers, and the commission men, these were wonderful years. The receipts were really good. One year, I think it was 1976, 320,000 cattle were sold through the Yards. In 1973 President Nixon put a freeze on the price of beef. This proved a disaster for our cattle prices in Canada. I remember that, during one week at Burns, the dressed price dropped ten dollars a hundredweight. By 1975 there was a huge sell-off of cows. This paved the way for what happened to the cattle market a few years later. By 1977 the prices began to rise. This lasted to the end of 1980. During those four years, small fortunes were made feeding cattle. I know, because we (Friesen Cattle Co.) were in on it. It was also during the 1970s that Eugene Whelan (our Federal Minister of Agriculture at the time), and people like him, desperately tried to foist a cattle marketing board on us. To this day, I am glad that we, as cattlemen, resisted this plan. We never got a marketing board!

ERA 9, 1981 to 1986 - The Alberta Stock Yards Co. and the commission men ceased to exist: Amid new prevailing marketing strategies, the commission men et al. formed a new company called the Calgary Public Livestock Market Ltd. I mentioned how much money was made feeding cattle in the late 1970s; well, we gave it all back in the early 1980s, even though many of us so-called free enterprisers received some government subsidy for a few years. The first few years of this new company's operation were good, but then the receipts trailed off.

ERA 10, 1986 to 1989 - Computer selling: Once again, a new regime took over at the Stockyards. This time it was Will Irvine and Don Danard; initially, Cec Barber was included, as he was the president of the Calgary Public Livestock Market at the time. During this era, the computer method of selling cattle became a reality.

When dealing with selling and shipments of livestock, two separate categories were used: those shipped in and "sold locally," and those unloaded, fed and watered, loaded back up again, and shipped out "thru-billed" to another destination.

During the first three years of the Depression, 1930, 1931 and 1932, the receipts were a disaster. More than once Harvey Adams (who was not a quitter) had to be persuaded by his partner Roy Furgeson to keep the doors open as better times were coming; and, indeed, better days did come. Vern Parslow always specialized in hogs, so when the Depression hit, P&D were a little better hedged than those firms that depended almost solely on cattle. As you can see by the figures that follow, there were more hogs sold than cattle in those first three years.

The grand total of cattle handled (sold locally and thru-billed) by the Yards during the first three years of the Depression (1930-32) was 153,511 head for an average of 51,170 per year. That is 57,518 fewer per year than were handled in each of the next seven years (1933-39).

The grand total of hogs handled was 286,126 head for an average of 95,375 per year. That is 40,010 fewer per year than were handled in each of the next seven years (1933-39).

The grand total of sheep handled was 72,334 head for an average of 24,111 per year. That is 52,665 fewer per year than was handled in each of the next seven years (1933-39).

The grand total of horses handled was 4,440 head for an average of 1,480 per year. That is 3,680 fewer per year than were handled in each of the next seven years (1933-39).

It is easy to see why those were tough, difficult days. They handled 153,873 fewer animals per year than they did in each of the next seven years (1933-39).

From 1933 on it was still a battle to keep the wolf from the door until the War started in 1939. This sounds like war brings prosperity; well, it usually does, unless it is fought within the borders of your own country. I am opposed to war, but sometimes we have no choice. If democracies had not stood up for what is right in the last three hundred years, I cannot imagine the mess we would be in today. Don't get me wrong, we are still in a mess, but, at least, we still retain most of our personal freedoms, even though at a high price to the tax man. Sir Winston Churchill once said: "Democracy is a very poor form of government, but it is the best we have discovered so far." How does war bring prosperity? Jobs are created. This means full employment. The more money in circulation, the more prosperity— unless inflation takes over at an unbridled pace. During World War II, Britain needed our agricultural products, especially things like bacon, cheese, butter, and meat.

Pen full of sheep at the Yards, 1920.

41

Just to give you an idea of the amount of livestock that passed through the Yards, I have researched and found the total numbers of cattle, hogs, sheep, and horses that arrived at the Yards during three consecutive, seven-year periods.

Here is the tally of livestock handled by the Yards for the commission firms from 1933 to the end of 1953, a twenty-one year period:

1933 to 1939 - The Depression Period: During these seven years, they sold 540,853 head of cattle for an average of 77,265 head per year. There were 219,960 thru-billed cattle for an average of 31,423 head per year, making a grand total of 760,813 or 108,688 head per year.

They sold 817,104 hogs for an average of 116,729 per year. There were 130,588 thru-billed hogs for an average of 18,655 per year, making a grand total of 947,692 or 135,385 head per year.

They sold 109,636 sheep for an average of 15,662 per year. There were 427,798 thru-billed sheep for an average of 61,114 head per year, making a grand total of 537,434 or 76,776 head per year. To me, these thru-billed numbers for sheep are quite amazing; but, they are factual, I got these figures from some old Stockyards' records stored at the Glenbow Museum.

They sold 2,708 head of horses for an average of 387 head per year. There were 33,413 thru-billed horses for an average of 4,773 head per year, making a grand total of 36,121 or 5,160 head per year. Many of those thru-billed horses were headed for Quebec where they would be "skid" horses pulling logs out of the bush for the rest of their lives.

To recap the 1933 to 1939 period, the Yards handled 2,282,060 head of cattle, hogs, sheep, and horses for an average of 326,009 head per year.

1940 to 1946 - The Wartime Period: During these seven years, they sold 906,332 head of cattle for an average of 129,476 head per year. There were 285,748 thru-billed cattle for an average of 40,821 head per year, making a grand total of 1,192,080 or 170,297 head per year.

They sold 962,558 hogs for an average of 137,508 head per year. There were 283,620 thru-billed hogs for an average of 40,517 head per year, making a grand total of 1,246,178 or 178,025 head per year—almost the same numbers as the cattle.

They sold 162,627 sheep for an average of 23,232 head per year. There were 354,585 head of thru-billed sheep for an average of 50,655 sheep per year (approximately, 1,000 head per week), making a grand total of 517,212 or 73,887 head per year.

They sold 2,182 head of horses for an average of 312 head per year (less than one a day). There were 30,112 thru-billed horses for an average of 4,302 head per year, making a grand total of 32,294 or 4,613 head per year.

To recap the 1940 to 1946 period, the Yards handled 2,987,764 head of cattle, hogs, sheep, and horses, for an average of 426,823 head per year.

1947 to 1953 - The Postwar Period: During these seven years, they sold 1,350,764 head of cattle for an average of 192,966 head per year. There were 332,369 thru-billed cattle for an average of 47,481 per year, making a grand total of 1,683,133 or 240,447 head per year.

They sold 594,378 hogs for an average of 84,911 per year. There were 344,837 thru-billed hogs for an average of 49,262 head per year, making a grand total of 939,215 or 134,174 head per year.

They sold 111,154 sheep for an average of 15,879 per year. There were 247,887 thru-billed sheep for an average of 35,412 head per year, making a grand total of 359,041 or 51,292 head per year.

They sold 2,567 horses for an average of 367 head per year. There were 15,680 thru-billed horses for an average of 2,240 head per year, making a grand total of 18,247 or 2,607 head per year.

To recap the 1947 to 1953 period, the Yards handled 2,999,636 head of cattle, hogs, sheep, and horses for an average of 428,519 head per year.

It is interesting to note that the total number of livestock handled during the seven wartime years and the seven postwar years were almost identical. I rechecked my figures. They are correct. Actually, the cattle receipts showed a substantial increase, but the hogs, sheep and horses all decreased in numbers.

From 1954 to 1976 the cattle receipts levelled out at approximately 250,000 head per year with several peak years of over 300,000 head (367,000 head in 1957).

Meanwhile, the sheep and lamb business succumbed to New Zealand imports in the 1960s, and the hogs to direct sales and finally to a marketing board in the 1970s.

As for horses, they just kind of petered out once every phase of our farming and ranching operations became mechanized, although there are still some meat horses handled through the Stockyards at Strathmore. Bruce Flewelling is the kingpin of this industry.

It has been estimated that the Stockyards in Calgary handled between forty-five and fifty million head of livestock in its 86-year history.

Cattleliner loading up at the huge Calgary Stockyards, 1957.

CHAPTER III

THE MATURE YEARS
(1950 - 1980)

When I arrived at the Stockyards on January 25, 1950, it looked like an institution that would survive forever. Actually, I started to work for Burns Foods, as it was called in those days. Since the Stockyards' inception in 1903, Burns and the Stockyards were interlinked. They joined each other from the railroad tracks on the east side to Portland Street on the west side. Burns always had been and continued to be a big supporter of the Stockyards. Burns bought a large percentage of their daily kill at the Yards. This included cattle, sheep and hogs. In those days, they tossed a coin to see who had first chance to bid on the cattle that were for sale by the various commission firms.

One of my first jobs was to go to the Stockyards, along with several other men, to gather the cattle the Burns buyers had bought that day. Some of my other duties were to help sort cattle that came in directly to Burns from the country in railroad cars. I also had the pleasure of watering those cattle. In winter this was no small task because the waterers froze up on a regular basis.

After about six months, my boss, Mickey Dirrane, let me buy a few cattle "off trucks" that farmers delivered to the Burns plant.

What a thrill! I was now a cattle buyer, not big-time, but it was a start. After several years, Mickey asked me to become a lamb and hog buyer at the Stockyards. I must admit I was not very happy to leave my off-truck buying, but when you work for a big outfit and you are a rookie, you do as you are told if you want to keep on collecting a paycheque. This new role was quite an experience. The sheep and hog scalehouse was located on the west side of Portland Street. I went over there every day to "match" on the hogs and sheep that were for sale. If I got lucky, we would own quite a few on a given day. On other days, I either lost the coin match or did not have enough money to buy the stock.

At that time, there were five commission firms operating at the Yards: Alberta Livestock Co-op (ALC); Parslow & Denoon (P&D); Adams, Wood and Weiller (AWW); Paul & MacDonald (P&M); and Producers' Livestock. Each firm had a salesman at the hog house, which was often referred to as "The Den of Iniquity."

Ook McRae was the salesman for the ALC. Ook was a straight-shooter. I really liked buying lambs from him. We could usually make a deal.

Maule McEwen was the salesman for P&D. I got along pretty well with him although, on a given day, he could be tougher than whalebone—often on the day I needed to buy lambs or hogs the most.

Cliff Green was the salesman on deck for AWW. He was the toughest of the lot. I can still see Cliff, or "Gandhi" as Maule called him, looking over his glasses at me without blinking and asking me and every other buyer an outrageous price for a pen of lambs. Sometimes those lambs or feeder hogs would be there for weeks before he finally sold them.

Bill McRae, Ook's brother, was the salesman for P&M. Bill's main occupation was telling stories. Selling livestock was his secondary pursuit. Bill was easy to buy from, but he did not receive a whole lot of hogs or sheep to sell.

Walter Dancocks was the salesman for Producers' Livestock. Walter considered himself a "fancy Dan." He was always dressed to the "T." He looked quite out of place in the hog alley. Walter tried to be tough, but he soon wilted under pressure.

The boys (when I say "boys," it refers to any man at the Yards from sixteen to ninety years of age) had card games at the scalehouse every single day—sometimes for small stakes; other times for big stakes. I never participated in those games. There were several others who did not play, either. Some people came there to play cards even though they weren't selling any livestock.

The sheep and lamb sales were very legitimate; however, the hog selling left much to be desired. It was pretty well rigged. By that, I mean the packers would collude on the price. For many years, the price set at the Yards would set the price the packers paid for their direct receipts at the plants. They would never admit to price fixing, but it was very evident to everyone around when all the major packers would come out with identical bids.

The commission men would often secure orders for hogs from plants outside the province of Alberta. When this happened, the apple cart upset. Katchen Bros. paid no attention to this game played by "the big three" (Canada Packers, Burns, and Union Packing, which was owned by Swift Canadian). So between Katchen Bros. and the outside orders, the hog market had a semblance of competition. Every once in a while, the big three would get into a disagreement and things went wide-open. I remember one such time, and, on that day, I bought about 1,000 hogs. That was quite a lot of hogs in those days.

Burns was the most aggressive lamb buyer on the market. I bought lambs for them nearly every day. When the market closed, I would call the old Scotsman at Burns, Pete Murry, who would then come over with his sheepdogs and chase the lambs across Portland Street to the Burns plant. To this day, I still know how the back of a lamb has to feel in order for it to catch the top grade. It was not uncommon to feel the backs of at least half the lambs in a pen of 10 to 100 lambs.

In 1951 the province had only two major markets, Calgary and Edmonton. Lethbridge was just getting started. Approximately 75 percent of the cattle were still being shipped in by rail. This included cattle shipped directly to packers. Cattle shipped out of the province went 100 percent rail. From 1951 to 1955, the increase in cattle trucked to the Yards was dramatic. By 1957 I dare say that 90 percent arrived by truck. I remember the first cattleliner I ever saw. It came up from the US in 1951. It was only about 26 feet long, but it sure looked big to me. Shortly thereafter, the McElroys from Lethbridge and George Eamor, originally from Vulcan, each got a few liners from the USA. Within the next two years, there were quite a few cattleliners. In spite of this, the bulk of the cattle were hauled by "body-jobs" (truck body and box with racks on same chassis). As for shipping long distance, the railroads continued to handle most of that business well into the 1970s.

Ever since the commission men first made their appearance, starting from 1910 until 1952, the cattle offered for sale were all "matched" for in fair competition. Here is how it was done: A farmer or rancher would ship his cattle to the market. After the cattle arrived, either the owner or the trucker would tell the Alberta Stock Yards person receiving the cattle which commission firm he wanted to sell his cattle for him. The cattle would then be "yarded" in a pen in the alley that was assigned to that particular commission firm. Usually the cattle were delivered in the late afternoon or evening. The next morning each commission firm would take a group of registered buyers to its alley to show them the cattle for sale that day. The number of interested buyers would vary from day to day. Usually there were six or seven men (they were all men). Each buyer would then toss a coin to see who got the first turn to bid on the cattle. They would match all the way down till every man had a bidding position. Each producer's cattle were bid on separately. Each commission firm would have anywhere from 5 to 40 pens of cattle for sale from different owners.

If the market was strong on a given day, quite often the first man that the cattle were offered to would buy them at the money the commission man had priced them at. On most days, they all got a chance to bid on the cattle; if that happened the highest bidder bought the cattle. If there were two identical bids, the cattle went to the man who was ahead in the match line-up. If the market was under pressure, the commission firm often "passed" the cattle (no sale). The firm would offer them again the next day. This could go on for a week, although it seldom did. Usually, after two or three days, it was obvious that the market was down, so they sold the cattle at the lower price. After the cattle had been sold, the alley boys would chase them to the weighscale where they would be weighed and then put in the new owner's pen.

On a hot summer day, people like Buck Rothwell, Jimmy Marsh, Len Rowland and a few others would have a little cache of beer stored under the old bridge next to the Stockyards. While they were waiting for their turn to weigh their cattle, they would hop over the fence to quench their thirst. Somehow, there were very few mix-ups. The boys did a good job.

Incidentally, all this cattle trading could only begin when the old Union Jack was raised at 9 a.m., and ended when the flag was lowered at 4 or 5 p.m. Anyone breaking those and other trading rules could be fined or even suspended from the privileges of trading cattle on the market. Usually after a fine and a lecture, the guilty party was reinstated. This flag raising and lowering was discontinued after the auction method of selling cattle was implemented.

In the summer of 1951, George Winkelaar, commission man, and Tom Farrell, Burns' ranch manager, came up with the idea of selling cattle by auction; to start with, only the Burns Ranch cattle were auctioned. They sold them on the west side. Since there were no sale rings, they auctioned them off in the pens.

By the summer of 1951, all the commission firms began to sell their cattle by auction. They built two rings, each in a different location. At first, these selling facilities were very primitive. They consisted of a small auctioneer's stand with a pen between it and the buyers, who sat behind some hastily installed windows. These windows would frost up in winter so the buyers could not see the cattle. The only way to correct this problem was to remove the windows. Now, everybody would shiver—cattle, buyers and any spectators who happened to be there. The temporary heaters they installed had very little effect. The two buildings were just shells with no insulation. In the next few years, they made improvements and insulated them to where it was at least halfway warm on cold winter days. One ring was located close to the road, just south of the gatehouse. ALC and P&D used this ring for selling their cattle. The other ring was located about five or six hundred yards to the east, directly south of the Burns scalehouse. AWW and P&M sold their cattle in that ring. Every packer would have a buyer in each ring. I nearly always bought cattle in the east ring from AWW and P&M.

The feeder cattle were bought by the commission firms and the licensed order buyers. It was not until the mid-'70s that any amount of outside buying took place. (By that, I mean other order buyers or producers or even the feeders themselves.) Calgary was often criticized for having a so-called closed market. Actually, people were allowed to buy cattle for themselves, but not many people knew this

49

or took the privilege of doing it. Order buying for other people was another matter: Unless you had an approved license from the Federal Government, administered by The Alberta Stock Yards Company Limited, you were not allowed to operate on the market.

The commission firms did not want too many order buyers. The reason for that was because it took away some of their orders. The primary function of the commission firms was to sell cattle for producers; however, order buying either "fat" or "feeder" cattle gave the commission firms an extra income. You can almost count on one hand the number of order buyers that operated at the Yards after the end of World War II. They were: C. W. Johnstone; Ted Nicholls; J. C. Wheatcroft; Bridgewater Livestock; Friesen Cattle Co.; and Sonny and Scott Gray, partners.

The Calgary market had a lot of stability. Sure, the market would fluctuate, but not like it did at some of the smaller auction markets. When auction markets started to spring up all over the country, things changed fast. This resulted in a lot of new order buyers in the Province all vying for a share of the business. Many farmers and small feeders started to buy their own feeder cattle. Because of this increased number of buyers, the prices would often vary a lot from week to week. At Calgary the price was more stable. Some weeks the markets down the road would be several dollars higher than Calgary. This would cause some producers to switch to that particular market. Lo and behold, the next week they would be a few dollars lower than Calgary. I have some firsthand experience in this matter. On several occasions, I heard there were some cheap cattle to be bought at a certain market. So, like everyone else who had heard that same story, I went to buy some of those cheap cattle. You already guessed it, that week the cattle were sky high because every man and his dog were there. This went on for about a decade from the mid-'60s to the mid-'70s. Since then, things have really evened out. These days the markets are all pretty even because of better market information, better transportation, and the order buyers have matured. In fact, there are fewer people buying cattle for themselves than there were ten years ago. This is as it should be—let the professionals do it. In the long run it is cheaper. I have observed that, on the big feeder-cattle markets in the United States, 90 percent of the cattle are bought by order buyers.

For the first twenty years that I bought cattle at the ring, they were weighed after you bought them. This meant you had to be good at guessing weights. It was ultra-important to buy the right weight cattle for each order. This applied to both "feeder" and "fat" cattle. For instance, if a farmer or feeder wanted you to buy some 500-pound calves, he did not want to end up with 600-pound calves because you had misjudged their weights. The same thing applied to "slaughter" cattle. If the packer wanted 1,150-pound steers, your goose was cooked if they happened to weigh 1,300 pounds. I should not boast, but I very seldom missed the weight of cattle by more than twenty or thirty pounds a head. Often, I was right on. This applied to most of the regular packer and order buyers. This method of operation was one of the main reasons there were very few outside buyers on the market. They just did not want to take a chance on buying cattle that weighed more or less than what they wanted them to. It could also be embarrassing. After we changed to weighing the cattle before they were sold, there was a huge increase in the number of people who bought cattle on the market. Today, all markets weigh the cattle before the sale. In fact, even for me it has become a "crutch." I am too lazy to guess the weight, so I usually wait till it flashes on before I bid. Actually, I liked the old system. It kept you sharp. There were three factors to consider when buying cattle: weight, quality, and price. Today, you have to know only quality and price.

Ever since the first trail herds arrived in Alberta from the USA, the import and export of cattle between the two countries has been an ongoing thing. Sometimes, there are long periods when there is very little activity in the export or import of cattle. Over the last hundred years, I am sure a lot more cattle have been exported from Canada to the USA than were imported from the USA. From 1895 to 1929, fairly large numbers of three- and four-year-old steers were shipped to Chicago and St. Paul from Canadian ranches. During the Depression there were very few cattle shipped either way. When World War II came along in 1939, the Canadian government stopped what few cattle were being exported by placing an embargo on cattle exports. In 1947 they lifted this embargo. The result was about a 30 percent increase in the price of cattle in Canada. A few people, who had an idea this might happen, made a small fortune on cattle that they had bought or tied up before this happened. Early in 1952 hoof-and-mouth disease broke out in Saskatchewan. So, once again the

USA closed the border to Canadian cattle. It reopened in less than a year. There was no drastic price increase this time around.

The reason I mention all this Canada-USA cattle activity is that it directly affected the commission men and order buyers who operated at the Calgary Stockyards. The Calgary market was the host to dozens of US buyers who came to buy cattle in Canada during the '50s, '60s, '70s and '80s. Both slaughter and feeder cattle were purchased by these buyers. There often were American buyers on the Calgary market representing their respective US firms, although most of the cattle that were going to the US were bought without the American buyer being present. Sometimes, these American orders caused resentment. The Canadian packing plants had to pay more money for their cattle because of the extra competition. Even some of the Canadian feeder cattle buyers felt they were facing unfair competition when a chap like Bill Torme, an American cattle buyer from Spokane, blew into town and started to "windrow" cattle. For the past dozen years or so, most of the cattle that have gone to the US are slaughter cattle shipped directly from the big feedlots. Many of them are contracted in advance. The US has always been a big bologna bull market for our Canadian bulls. This continues to be the case to the present time. The majority of the bulls that came to the market ended up in the US.

There were five, what I call "bull kings" on the Calgary market over a 40-year period. By that, I mean the firm that bought the bulk of the bulls to ship to the US. In the '50s, it was Shorty Ross. He worked for ALC. In the '60s, it was the J. C. Wheatcroft Co. In the very late '60s to the mid-70s, it was Bridgewater Livestock, and then it was Friesen Cattle Co., which had acquired the order-buying division of Bridgewater Livestock. From the mid-70s to the early '80s, it was P&D with Stan Denoon at the helm. After that, it was George and Terry Prescott. They are still at it to this day. During those four decades, there were a few others who also bought some bulls—Larry Farrell, John Pahara, AWW, and, occasionally, a local packer. I am not exactly sure why we played musical chairs in the bull-buying department. I do know why I quit doing it. Bulls are difficult to handle, hard to move and they tear up a lot of fences. One day, I finally said: "We have lots of business. We can live without the bull trade." We had been shipping one or two potloads to the US every week; so, with that, we ceased buying them. That's when Stan Denoon took up the slack and started shipping lots of bulls to the US. Most of our bulls had gone to the state of Washington. I think Stan shipped most of his to Idaho.

Livestock holds a fascination for people. It is a worldwide fact of life. Where there are people there will be livestock. A lot of women like horses. A recent survey done by the American Veterinary Association found that in the USA, 70 percent of all pleasure horses are owned by young women between the ages of twelve and twenty-eight. (A lot of men like horses as well.) Many urban professional and business people own acreages, farms, or ranches where they love to spend their weekends. They get a little of that "stuff" on their boots and often do menial tasks that they would never think of doing in the city. Sometimes, it may be for a tax shelter, but, I suspect, more often than not, it is because of their desire to own and enjoy their own livestock. Usually the livestock are cows and horses with a few dogs on the side—although these days some are getting into buffalo.

During the forty years I was at Burns and the Calgary Stockyards, thousands of people visited the premises. Some were on conducted tours; others came in small groups. Many times whole classrooms of school children, chaperoned by their teachers, came to enjoy looking at the livestock, usually cattle. There also were a lot of foreign visitors from overseas. There were seldom any from the US, except the ones who were buying cattle. Others came from the various provinces in Canada. Alberta is cow country—so, they came to look for themselves; however, most of the groups were local. Many individuals who lived in the City dropped in to see what was going on as well as look at livestock.

Whenever a group was there, whether it was big or small, the auctioneer would stop the sale and announce who the visitors were and where they were from. Then he would welcome them to the Calgary Stockyards. Everyone would clap and the sale would continue. Depending upon how many good-looking ladies there were among the visitors, the prices and action would sometimes increase. People like Davey Dvorkin and a few others could put on quite a show. It was a standing joke at the Yards that, if a producer wanted to receive top dollar for his cattle, it would be wise for him to enlist a few of his good-looking neighbour ladies and have them seat themselves directly behind certain buyers. Their very presence would automatically raise the price a few cents a pound. As far as I can remember, very few ever sat behind me. If they did, it did not really affect my performance. Another favourite trick some of the auctioneers liked to pull was to knock cattle down to some visitor, usually a woman who was gesturing with her hands as she talked to the person sitting next to her. This always brought a laugh from the crowd because the person to whom the cattle had supposedly been sold to was not sure if the auctioneer was serious or not. They often turned as red as a beet and stammered out something to the effect, "I wasn't bidding!" The auctioneer would say, "I saw you bid, you raised your hand." Then, after a few more moments, the victim realized it was all a joke at their expense. I do not remember a single one of them ever getting angry. Like Davey Dvorkin used to say: "Who has more fun than people?—more people!"

Like all businesses we received our share of complaints—many of them unfounded. This applied at Burns as well as at the Calgary Stockyards. I will relate a few that come to mind. Nearly all of these complaints came from either purebred breeders or dairy farmers. Do not get me wrong, there are many excellent purebred people as well as good dairy operators. But, for some reason, whenever they sold one of their "cull" cows or bulls, they expected more money than the animals brought.

There was one Angus breeder who often brought one or two crippled or otherwise cull cows to Burns. He always had to have the head buyer look at them and price them. He just did not like dealing with "underlings," even if that buyer had bought thousands of cattle—some of them big strings. After I became the head buyer for Burns, I had to do this, even though I had three or four other buyers who were quite capable of pricing his cows. It was something like going into a large department store to buy a toaster and demanding that the manager be called to sell it to you.

The biggest hassle I ever had over one animal was the day a dairy farmer sent in a cow to be "rail graded." She was what we called an "old crock"—real thin, big bag, etc. It was doubtful she would pass the health of animals inspection. That is why she was sold subject to inspection before we paid for her. Well, she passed inspection—so we paid for her hanging carcass weight at the going price for that day. When this dairyman got his cheque, he went ballistic. He drove to Calgary, rushed over to Burns and proceeded to give me a tongue lashing like I could not believe. (To this day, I am still astounded that I kept my cool. I was about twice his size.) His complaint was that he had been paid for the wrong cow. Of course, this was virtually impossible because all subject cattle had an ear tag attached to their ear with a number on it. After the cow was killed that tag was pinned to the carcass. Now, we know a tag could fall off; however, on this particular day, there were no other cows slaughtered that this old crock could have gotten mixed up with. We checked everything out with a fine-tooth comb, and there was no mix-up. His Daisy was worth more money than he had received and that was that! I guess he was so used to getting subsidy money for his milk, he wanted someone else to subsidize his old cull cow as well. I held my ground because I knew he had been paid for the right cow. He went to his grave thinking we had paid him for the wrong cow.

Another class of animal that caused us a lot of problems were the so-called virgin bulls. In the beef industry a virgin bull is basically just that. He is a young grain-fed bull that will catch a steer grade 97 percent of the time, provided he is not extremely coarse and heavy. The ideal weight is between 1,100 and 1,300 pounds at approximately 14 to 16 months old. The problem we had was that some purebred breeders would deliver a handful of bulls on a rail-grade basis. The bulls often were two to two-and-a-half-year-olds weighing anywhere from 1,400 to 1,900 pounds. Some of them graded as bulls. A few caught steer grades, but the carcass weight was way too heavy for what the meat trade wanted, so we had to mark them down to a price where we could sell the meat. Well, those purebred breeders just could not understand why their bulls did not bring more money. No matter how well you explained the problem to them, they usually left thinking they had been ripped off.

The commission men had their share of troubles as well. They spent many hours on the phone each year explaining why certain cattle had not brought more money. I am not down on the little guy, but, nine out of ten times, the complaint came from people who had only sold a few animals. The problem was that they just did not understand how markets work and they often overestimated how good the quality of their cattle actually was. There were very few complaints from the owners who sold big bunches of cattle. They knew the quality of their cattle, be it good or bad. They also understood that markets do fluctuate.

55

One day a producer brought in some real junky yearlings. I mean, they were a sad sight. He was very agitated when they began to sell the stock. Suddenly, he called the sale off and took the balance home. As far as I know, he never came to the market again. This was an exception and not the rule. A year later, I heard he had gone right out of the cattle business.

On more than one occasion, one of the commission firms would come and ask me if they could redeem a certain animal that I had bought because the owner wanted it back. I always returned it unless it had already been shipped out with a load of cattle. Very seldom was the animal worth more than I had paid for it, so it was really no hardship for me to give it back.

I do not want you folks to get the impression that all producers were difficult to deal with, for this definitely was not the case. Ninety-nine percent of them were great people to do business with, but, like in all other segments of business and society, there were always a few difficult ones. Also, remember, I am talking of a time span of the forty years that I was at the Yards. Two incidents a year would amount to only 80 situations that tested one's patience—not bad for a handshake-type of business.

The Stockyards was an interesting and exciting place—at least, it was for me. It was inhabited by a bunch of real characters. There were usually anywhere from 150 to 200 people working around the Yards on a daily basis, representing the various firms. Later, in this book, I list many of them, complete with a brief profile on each.

The people at the Yards came from a mix of urban and rural backgrounds. I knew a lot of top-notch cattle buyers who had never lived on a farm or ranch. They learned their trade at a packing plant or at the Stockyards. I always felt good about the fact that I had a rural background. Whenever I talked to farmers or ranchers, I knew where they were coming from. I know what it's like to feed cattle when it's 30 below, drag a cow out of a bog, pull a calf, or rope an animal and treat it. Many other workers at the Yards also had this same background.

Over the years, the Yards was a haven for rodeo cowboys, ex-rodeo cowboys and would-be cowboys. Many of the commission firms would hire some of them for short periods in between rodeos, especially in the fall.

Here are the names of a few that come to mind (probably, there were some others that participated in rodeo as well): Dave Abrahams, bronc rider; Larry Adams, bronc rider; Harold Bissel, calf roper; Eddie Bowlen, calf roper; Paddy Brown, bronc rider; Duane Bruce, bronc rider; Robin Burwash, bareback rider; Archie Bushfield, bronc rider; Kent Butterfield, calf roper; Jim Cammarent, bareback rider; Dale Christiansen, bareback rider; Frank Cockx, bullfighter; Mason Cockx, bareback rider and steer wrestler; Bill Collins, calf roper (Rodeo Hall of Fame); Warren Cooper, rodeo announcer (Rodeo Hall of Fame); Tom Copithorne, steer wrestler; Tom Crow, bronc rider; Don Edge, steer decorator/wrestler; Rudy Evenson, calf roper; Ken Fisher, steer wrestler; Bruce Flewelling, pick-up man and cow milker; Art Galarneau, calf roper (Rodeo Hall of Fame); Clarence Gingrich, pick-up man (Rodeo Hall of Fame); Gene Gunderson, bareback rider; Lester Gurnett, bronc rider; Bob Hartell, bullrider and bareback rider; Dick Havens, bareback rider; Gerry King, bareback rider; Roddy MacDonald, steer wrestler; Bryan Mandeville, steer wrestler; Vern Miller, bareback rider; Rocky Ostrim, steer wrestler; Ronnie Ostrim, steer wrestler; Larry Petherbridge, bullrider; Terry Prescott, steer wrestler; Lee Price, bronc rider; Sykes Robinson, bronc rider (Rodeo Hall of Fame); Bob Robinson, bronc rider; Mark Roy, steer wrestler; Cody Seitz, calf roper; Merle Sorenson, bullrider; Gary Sparshu, bullrider and steer wrestler; Russel Swain, chuckwagons; Cliff Vandergrift, calf roper, wild horse race and wild cow milking (Rodeo Hall of Fame); Harry Vold, auctioneer, rodeo stock contractor (Rodeo Hall of Fame); Lorne Wells, calf roper; and Marty Wood, bronc rider (Rodeo Hall of Fame).

There were also quite a few ex-boxers around the Yards. Some of them ranked fairly high. These are the names of a few of them: Art Adams, Jim Beal, Bob Bertram, Russ Boyer, Stan Denoon, Rusty Edwards, Gerry Going, Bob Keddie (karate), John Pahara and Augie Sauer.

There was also a lot of interest in horse racing; some owned horses, some were jockeys and others just gambled on the races. The list to follow will not be quite complete. I do not know who played the horses occasionally, but I do know who the regular ones were: Joe Casey; Norman Dalstro; Don Danard; Bill Duggan; Dave Dvorkin; Dr. Brian Edge, veterinarian at racetrack; Dr. Jack Evans; Vic Hammill; Dr. Morris Hanson, veterinarian; Don Hockley;

Albert, George, Harry and Jim Inamasu; Mark Jenkins; George Johnson, Al Lennox; Al MacDonald; Danny MacDonald; Billy, Charlie and Bob Marsh; Jim Marsh Sr.; Jim Marsh Jr.; Gary and George McLean; Ron McRae; Vern McRae; George O'Bray; Sam Raskin; Dutch Ryder; Billy Taylor; Ted Umphrey; and Ray Witney.

These days nearly everyone is into golf. In the old days, it was not as common; however, for some reason, there were a lot of golfers at the Yards, even years ago. I am not going to list them, but there were a number of good golfers around the Yards who played once or twice a week. I even won a trophy one year. It was a kind of hollow victory since it was played under some sort of handicap system. The low net score that year belonged to Claude Shackell. When Claude was younger, he was a member of the Wellington Cup Golf Team.

One of the problems at the Stockyards was alcohol; in a general sense, I saw a lot of good men go down the tube. There were binge drinkers, secret drinkers, party drinkers, occasional drinkers, and some plain old drunks. It is not a pretty sight to see people slide downhill because of drink. Very often the people with the problems were some of the best men around. When they were sober, you could not fault them. I talked to many of them about their problem in a concerned way and not by preaching to them about the evils of alcohol. They knew I was a teetotaller, so I was extra careful not to give them the impression that I was better than they were. They were friends of mine and it hurt me to see them go downwards due to liquor. Two of them committed suicide, and a number died premature deaths because of booze. There were also many who quit drinking altogether and stayed sober for the rest of their lives.

I will never forget the old Livestock Exchange Building with its creaky old wooden floors that were well oiled. There was no intercom system, people just hollered at the top of their voice if they were looking for someone in another office or hallway. I am not sure about every office location, but I do remember that the Bank of Montreal, Parslow & Denoon and J. C. Wheatcroft were located downstairs. W. W. Starke (later P&M), Adams, Wood and Weiller and the Alberta Livestock Co-op as well as Producers' Livestock were on the main floor. The Alberta Stock Yards Company Limited and the Canadian Pacific Railway Company offices, plus a few "snake" rooms (lunch rooms) were upstairs. There were also other offices in the building whose locations slip my mind, such as CP Telegraph, Hartford Insurance and others.

One of the favourite pranks the boys pulled was to drop a big brown paperbag filled with ice-cold water onto someone's head as he stepped out the doorway on the main floor of the Exchange Building. The prankster was impossible to catch, since he had a lot of time to make his getaway before the victim could run up the stairs to see who did it. It was a lucky thing that no one ever had a heart attack when that cold water hit him on a hot day! Another thing that was common around there was the guys putting their arms around some of the girls or even patting their bottoms. Nowadays, they would be charged with sexual harassment. An odd guy got a slap on the "chops" by some of the early liberated ladies. On the other hand, there was a lot of hanky-panky with the cooperation of both sexes. Human nature hasn't changed much since Adam and Eve or Samson and Delilah.

One day there was a sow that had to be delivered to either the MacLean Auction Mart or a packing plant, I am not sure which. What I do know is how it was delivered: Buck Rothwell asked Art Adams if he could use his car to make a small delivery. Art never turned anyone down, so he tossed the car keys over to Buck. The car happened to be a brand new Nash. The item to be delivered was that sow. (Of course, Art did not know that.) Buck and Len Rowland loaded the sow into the backseat. She was a fairly large sow, so they opened the window in the back door just enough so the sow could stick her head outside to enjoy the scenery. They then circled around to Ogden Road on the north side of the old Exchange Building. Here, they stopped the car long enough to make sure Art and a few other people saw the old sow wisely looking at them from the rear door window of the new Nash. It looked so comical that anyone who saw it had to burst out laughing, including Art. Before anyone could approach the car, they sped off to the sow's final destination. Hog manure has an extremely strong smell and, no matter how much they scrubbed the car, the odour remained quite distinct. I think Art spent a small fortune on deodorants, but he never lost his cool—it was all in a day's activities. Buck worked for Art and things continued as usual.

There was a similar incident involving Art. He and his wife sometimes took a little trip down South in the wintertime to enjoy the sun. One year, the day before they left, the boys put a fish under the front seat. We all know the result of a caper like that. On about the third day of their trip, they started to notice a peculiar smell. They thought maybe it was a sour gas well or some dead stock close to the roadside, but it wasn't. The odour persisted. They checked their luggage; everything was okay there. Finally, about the fifth day, they could no longer tolerate the stink, so they searched the car completely; and, there it was, a rotten fish stuffed into a corner under the front seat. Personally, I do not think this was a very good prank. Why spoil people's vacations? I don't think Art ever found out who did it, although I am sure he had a pretty good idea.

Another favourite trick the boys pulled around the Yards was to walk up behind somebody when they were in conversation with someone and grab a good hold onto the top of their pants, then give a mighty tug downwards. The result: the pants lay on the ground leaving the person standing there in his underwear. Since the guy's feet were still in his pant legs, it worked like hobbles, which prevented him from running after the culprit even if he wanted to. Larry Farrell used to love pulling that prank on Danny MacDonald. Danny had a slim waist with narrow hips so his pants dropped down very easily. To my knowledge, this stunt was never pulled on any of the women. There was a little chivalry around the Yards, even though it got pretty raunchy sometimes.

There was a time when the Stockyards gang had a difficult time securing a place to hold a social affair such as a Christmas or retirement party. Calgary was much smaller in those days so your reputation caught up to you fast. Word got around that the "cowboys" from the "stockyards" could cause quite a stir—disorderly conduct, wrecking a little furniture and things like that. This was grossly exaggerated. The boys got a little rowdy at times, but not nearly as bad as their reputation was made out to be. During the last twenty years of the Stockyards' existence in Calgary, the boys' reputation improved a whole bunch. There were also more facilities available in the City then, and their business was, in fact, solicited by some of the newer hotels and caterers.

In 1962 the CPR built a new Exchange Building right across the street from the old building. The boys became a little more sedate for a while. It was something like putting on a new suit. Eventually, though, everyone got used to it and things continued more or less like they had in the old building. There was a bootwash by the back door, but, somehow a lot of the "stockyards" got tracked into the building. To a stranger it had quite a strong aroma. I hardly noticed it. One day we hired a new clerk for the office. However, when she arrived and sniffed the odour, she suddenly changed her mind. In fact, we had several women looking for work who left in a hurry. Maybe it was the smell, or maybe it was Danny MacDonald's voice and words drifting upstairs in the heat of a craps game.

In 1966 the Alberta Stock Yards Co. built a new sale ring at the same location where the old east ring had been. This time they had two rings in the same building, back-to-back. This made it a lot easier, since we were all in one area. If the need arose, one man could work both rings, which I did once in a while if we happened to be short a buyer. Larry Palata used to stand at the top, buying cattle in both rings. He bought a lot of big, heavy cattle that went to Ontario. He made a lot of people nervous, but to my knowledge nobody at the Yards was hurt by his activities. There were a few questionable country deals settled in court.

Like most societies and businesses, the Stockyards had a pecking order. It was not always visible and certainly often not fair. But, it did exist. I am not going to say who was at the top of the pecking order, although it is not hard to figure out. It was not real extreme, and maybe it was more a state of mind of the individuals than a reality. Like I have already mentioned in this book, we were all one big happy family having a quarrel now and then that usually ended in an amicable truce.

The people in this book consist of commission men, commission firms' office staff and a few commission buyers, plus a fairly large group of people who sorted and moved cattle. (The latter were sometimes called alley rats, a term I did not like and did not use.) There were also order buyers (sometimes referred to as brokers) and packer buyers, as well as Alberta Stock Yards personnel including management, secretaries, clerks, foremen and yardmen. (It was the yardmen's job to receive cattle for sale. They had to feed, water, unload and load livestock into railroad cars, as well as repairing the Yards to keep them functional.) There were a lot of small feedlot operators who came to the Yards to buy feeder cattle for themselves. There were the bank manager and his staff, the Hartford Insurance Company and staff, the restaurant owners and their crew, plus a bunch of local truckers. We had at least four different government agencies operating at the Yards; two were federal and two were provincial. The federal government had a grading service and market reporting staff. It also had a Health of Animals Division headed up by a veterinarian. The provincial government looked after brand inspection. In later years, the provincial government had health and animals personnel at the Yards as well.

Besides all the people mentioned above, there were always a lot of cattle producers (farmers and ranchers) at the Yards. Some were big operators while others sold only a few head once or twice a year.

The Calgary Livestock Exchange governed the trading practices at the Stockyards. There was a membership involved, allowing a member to vote at the annual general meeting, at which time a board of directors was elected. The people holding seats on the Exchange voted on who would be admitted as a new member (pretty much like a private golf club operates). A membership only cost $150. This was not an obstacle; being "approved" was much more difficult. The membership basically consisted of the owners of commission firms and a few of their top people and order buyers, as well as the manager of the Alberta Stock Yards Co. and his assistant. Over the years, a few other people were accepted. Some that come to mind are: Bob Campbell, manager of Burns Ranches; Larry and Mike Farrell; and Bob and Barrie Smolkin. I do not remember a single government person ever being a member. I think you get the picture. The people who made up the Exchange were the power brokers. Let me hasten to add that all those other people were just as important when it came to keeping the Yards operating; and, over the years, quite a few of them became members also. The Board had the power to suspend its members or fine them for any infraction of the rules. Nearly every principal of the various firms served as the president at one time or another in the forty years that I was there. I had the privilege of serving several terms. I was the second last president to hold that office. Pete Adams was the last. He was elected president in March 1981, and on October 1, 1981, we disbanded the Exchange after which time we formed a new company called The Calgary Public Livestock Market Ltd.

It was not a good idea for anyone to get high on themselves. Nobody at the Yards liked a "stuffed shirt." People who put on "airs" or thought they were really important were soon brought down to earth. They were ignored or ridiculed—either of which soon deflated their ego. In spite of the pecking order I mentioned, everyone talked to everyone else, which was something I always appreciated about being involved at the Stockyards. We were an experienced bunch of cattlemen doing our best, and that's what democracy and free enterprise is all about.

For at least twenty years of the Stockyards' existence, we had Friday feeder sales at the Yards. In the fall, these sales often lasted till three or four o'clock in the morning. Everyone thought the price would go down when it got late. The truth was, this very seldom happened; in fact, it often got higher. In the early days, the cups the boys were drinking from after 10 p.m. contained something other than coffee or water. Although I hardly ever saw anyone really sloshed at a sale, a few got a little tipsy once in a while. If this was evident, the auctioneers would conveniently miss their bids. By 1980 we started to organize community sales. This really took a lot of pressure off the Friday sales. Some of the sales that come to mind are: Elbow Slope, Millarville, Airdrie, and Madden. They still hold them at Strathmore.

I read somewhere recently that the receipts at the Yards were way down and stayed down as early as 1968. This is not true. From 1967 to 1977, the receipts hardly declined; in fact, one year we came close to setting a record with 320,000 cattle sold. There was only one year that we sold more, and that was in 1957, with 367,000 head.

Red Wheatcroft, our outfit (Friesen Cattle Co.), and the commission firms shipped thousands of cattle to Eastern Canada and to the USA. Most of these cattle were shipped on double-deck railroad cars. Red owned a whole fleet of them. We had a few also. The cattle going to the States went by cattleliners. It was quite an ordeal to load all those rail cars. I must say, the Stockyards crew did a good job of loading them. It took two or three "spots" to get them all loaded. There were 16 railroad loading chutes. Rail cars were ordered from the CPR or the CNR a day in advance. On the day that the stock was to be loaded and shipped, the train arrived with the empty cars. The train engineer would push all 16 rail cars into position at each chute. This was referred to as spotting cars. The chutes were spaced so that each chute matched the door in the rail car. If there were 48 cars to be loaded on a given day, it meant that the engineer had to make three spots to load all 48 cars. Eric Tribble told me that one night they loaded 100 railroad cars of livestock—that would be about seven spots.

Besides cattle, there were hogs and sheep that had to be loaded into rail cars. Whenever the Stockyards crew was loading pigs, you could hear the squeals half a mile away. The pigs always expressed their displeasure about being crowded into a railroad boxcar. Five minutes after the door was closed, all the noise subsided and pretty soon they were on their way over the mountains to the Coast.

Then there were the sheep. That's a different story again. A sheep or lamb makes very little noise, even under stress, except for maybe an odd little bleat. Sheep could not be chased like cattle or hogs—they have to be led. So, how do you lead them? At the Burns yards we used to catch one of them by the front leg and gently pull it up the loading chute into the railroad car. It's hard to believe, but the other sheep followed the one that was being pulled. By this time, you were at the far end of the car. Once all the sheep were in, you had to make your way back to the door, unless you wanted to make a trip to Vancouver with a load of sheep. Most of the hogs and sheep were shipped in double-deck cars, so you had to perform the same act for the bottom deck. (The top deck was always loaded first.)

At the Stockyards, they used a slightly different method for loading sheep. They had what they called the "Judas goat." This goat would gleefully run up the chute with all the sheep following him. When they were all loaded, the goat would nonchalantly stroll down the ramp where the next group of sheep would be waiting. On a few occasions, after the last car was loaded, the boys forgot to let the goat down the chute before closing the door. I have a sneaking suspicion they sometimes forgot about him intentionally. When this happened, the Judas goat got a free ride to the Coast or to wherever the sheep were being shipped. At the other end, the men would unload the sheep. When they saw the goat, they would put him back into the car with a little feed and water and bootleg him back to Calgary. I guess you could call that travelling first class. One goat to a whole car. You could almost see the self-satisfied smirk on the Judas goat's face as he walked down the ramp. This was in sharp contrast to the real Judas, who, after he had betrayed Jesus, felt such remorse that he cast the thirty pieces of silver he had received onto the ground. Then he went and hanged himself.

64

The brand inspectors were another fact of life around the Yards. They were employed by the provincial government. Their job was to make sure that the brands on delivered cattle matched with the brands recorded on the trucker's manifest. If an animal did not carry the present owner's brand, he had to produce a bill of sale, or if a brand appeared to be less than 30 days old, it often had to be verified. Hard-to-read brands usually had to be "clipped." Extra long hair in bad weather made this inspection difficult because their hand-held clippers clogged up with wet hair; they always carried old toothbrushes to clean the clippers' teeth.

Most of the brand inspectors had a farm or ranch background. One reason for this was that they had to know how to rope. (Things did get a little western at times!) They were kept very busy during peak cattle receipts. About eight of them, including the head brand inspector, who also did some of the paperwork, were on duty every day inspecting cattle for the various packers and commission firms in their separate alleys.

On most days, at least several cattle had to be roped and clipped to expose a brand. This procedure really bugged Henry Bridgewater. He just detested it when cattle came into the sale ring, often clipped in three or four locations. I have to admit I did not like it very much either, especially in wintertime. Sometimes I know it was necessary; however, at times it was done by an over-zealous inspector.

When I first came to the Yards, Dave Wheatcroft was still using a horse for a lot of his work. After Dave's retirement, the inspecting was done on foot. I am not sure why it is, but these days I see a lot fewer cattle being clipped than there were in the old days. Maybe today's brand inspectors have better vision. There was one old boy by the name of Dalfas Roy who did not clip many. He could read a brand that I could not even see, and I have 20-20 vision. Dalfas was often "three sheets to the wind," but, I must say, it did not affect his performance.

Some of the cattle dealers, who delivered cattle to Calgary for resale, were often quite unhappy about the brand system. At times, cattle cheques were held back weeks, or even months, before the brand problem got cleared up. The brand boys caught quite a few strays through inspection, but hardly any rustlers that I am aware of. If they did catch one, the judge usually let him off with a slap on the wrist.

Unloading, loading, moving and sorting cattle was a big job. The only tool the men needed was either a cane, a buggy whip, or an electric stock prod. The prod was only used for putting cattle through the testing and branding chutes. Most of the truckers used them as well. Personally, I never did and still do not like electric cattle prods. If used lightly or sparingly, they do help to move some stubborn bulls or cows through the chute. Using them indiscriminately just riles the cattle up and makes them hard to handle. Buggy whips were nice and light to carry and you could not inflict much damage with them, but I did not like them for sorting cattle in the alley. If you tried to stop a critter coming at you by snapping the whip in front of it, it often ignored you and ran right on by. Sometimes, if you were not careful, the little lash at the end of the whip would hit them in the eye, causing the eye to water and this could partially blind the animal. For this reason, I seldom used a whip. The best thing to use was a sturdy wooden cane. The cane also had to be used with care. Some people used a cane far too roughly; they would beat the animal unmercifully, especially if the they lost their temper. More than once I told people not to beat the cattle with their canes. The packing plants often had to trim bruises off beef carcasses; so, besides being cruel to the cattle, it also caused financial losses. Fortunately, most of the men used common sense and did not abuse the cattle. A cane properly used was the right tool with which to handle cattle. With a cane you could poke the cattle to make them move or a light tap on the nose usually stopped an animal when sorting in an alley. A cane also gave you protection if an animal actually charged you. In a situation like that you had to use a cane like a club. It was strictly self-defence. It did not happen very often; but, when it did occur, it often saved a person from getting injured. I know of several occasions when I might have become history or at least been seriously injured if I had not had a cane. The "stockman's cane" became a symbol of the Stockyards.

The weather had a huge impact on working conditions around the Stockyards—in the late fall and winter, snow and ice; in the spring knee-deep muck; and in the summer and early fall, slop if it had rained, or dust, if it hadn't.

Icy alleys, which occurred every winter, were a hazard to man and beast. Cattle, hogs, and sheep do not like ice. They try to avoid stepping on it. So, whenever the alleys became icy, it was hard to move the stock. Sometimes a critter would slip and spread itself. This means that a cow's legs would slip in opposite directions causing the pelvic bones to separate. The animal was then unable to walk, so it had to be put down. Often, this happened to hogs as well. I suppose the saying "ornery as a pig on ice" comes from a situation like this. There were miles of alleys. It was almost impossible to scatter enough rock salt to relieve the slippery conditions, so it was applied only in the alleys that were frequently used.

Spring always resulted in a lot of muck when the winter's accumulation of snow, ice, and manure melted to make a soupy mess, about a foot deep. It was a great day when the Stockyards' crew got around to cleaning those pens and alleys. It was a pleasure to once again walk on clean cement.

If there was a long drought in the summer or early fall, the Yards became very dusty, due to the cattle stirring up the dust whenever they were moved. It would sting your nostrils and make your eyes water. Dry shavings were spread in the sale rings every morning; then they had to be sprinkled with water to keep the dust down. This treatment could not be done in the pens and alleys; there, you had to live with the problem. On the other hand, there was often a lot of rain. This created conditions similar to what we had in the spring, only the waste was not quite as deep.

Wet snow in the early fall made a real mess. Often when we had a big run of cattle, the Yard conditions were at their worst. I cannot count the number of times that I, or anybody else, who was sorting or moving cattle got covered from head to foot with that liquid fertilizer. When those conditions prevailed, we wore rubber boots and rainwear, but not always. Whether we had some protective clothing or not, our faces were exposed, so at the end of the day we looked like coal miners coming out of a mine. The only difference was, miners were black. We stockmen were kind of a dark-brownish color. But, as the boys used to say: "It's only grass and water—it will wash off."

Regardless of weather, the show had to go on. We enjoyed taking care of the cattle, rain or shine. I actually kind of liked working in the rain. I knew that, out in the country, the grass was growing and the winter feed supply was assured. This meant a healthy cattle industry and that was good for future business at the Yards. Also, when it rained, the farmers and ranchers who patronized the Yards were always friendly and in good spirits, and usually had some time to linger over a coffee and shoot the breeze with us in the Stockyards Cafe.

In 1977 the Calgary Stockyards hosted the World Livestock Auctioneer Championship, sponsored by the Livestock Merchandising Institute out of Kansas City. I was the president of the Calgary Livestock Exchange, so they told me how they wanted the contest set up. It was up to me to make all the arrangements—such as providing a variety of cattle to sell and selecting judges. It was a very successful affair. The commission firms and the Stockyards workers gave their cooperation 100 percent. Everybody pitched in and did their best.

Bobby Russell from Canton, Missouri, was the Champion, and Johnnie Charlton from Brooks, Alberta, was the Reserve Champion. I think our American guests were quite impressed by how well we Canadians handled the event. After the contest was over, the Board of Directors from the Livestock Merchandising Institute, headquartered in Kansas City, asked me to become a trustee. I stayed on as trustee until the organization disbanded a few years ago.

Bruce Flewelling, center, Stampede Park, 1979.

Shortly after that competition, Ted Pritchett, Keith MacKinnon, and I decided we should have a Canadian contest. So, at the Round-up Show in 1979, we had our first Canadian Auctioneers Market Championship contest. This annual competition was held until 1985 when they switched it to the International Livestock Auctioneer Championship contest. This allowed American auctioneers to enter. (Something like the Canadian Football League is doing these days.)

I am sure that most of you know what "futures" are. In case you don't, they are future contracts of commodities such as cattle, hogs, pork bellies, grains, coffee, sugar, orange juice, etc. You can either buy or sell contracts for future buy or delivery. All cattlemen know about cattle futures. Many use them in their daily operation of a feedlot. They can be a real tool to hedge against future losses; however, there are times when large losses can be incurred. This often happens when a "Texas Hedge" is used. Texas Hedge simply means you already own a bunch of live cattle in your feedlot, which will be ready for market in two to three months, but instead of selling them on the futures market for a small future profit, you elect to buy more future contracts. If the price moves up in the next several months you hit a home run; however, if the price moves down, as it often does, you lose a bundle. I know, it has happened to me—both ways. Often the future months are so low you have no chance to lay your feedlot cattle off. This is pretty dicey business and not designed for the fainthearted. Of course, there are very few fainthearted cattlemen.

The Chicago Mercantile Exchange is the only place where cattle futures (both feeders and fats) are traded these days. (A contract consists of 40,000 pounds of live cattle.) These futures are very controversial in the cattle community. Many producers think they are manipulated by the large packers and other speculators. You do not have to own any cattle to buy or sell them, and anybody who wants to gamble can participate. (It was reported that Hillary Clinton made $100,000 on cattle futures one year. Not bad for a lady who does not know a cow from a billy goat.)

Where does the Calgary Stockyards fit into this picture? For a number of years the Winnipeg Stock Exchange traded in Canadian Cattle Futures. In the mid-70s, the Calgary Stockyards' premises were designated as a receiving point for live cattle to be delivered.

If the producer chose to do so, when his contract expired, the cattle had to measure up to the "specs" that the Winnipeg Exchange had established. These included quality, grade, and weight. A panel of three cattle buyers were appointed to evaluate those cattle. I was one of the three panel members. I will not name the other two—they were good cattlemen and friends of mine, but when it came to judging those contract cattle I did not agree with their assessment. In my opinion, they were far too tough on the producer who delivered the cattle. The result was "a hung jury," except it did not work that way. On a panel of three, the decision of two against one wins. As a result, there were no more contract cattle delivered to Calgary. The Canadian cattle futures were very thin traders. (In other words, not many people availed themselves of this service.) It was hard to buy or sell any amount of contracts. Sometimes, you had to wait several days before you could either buy or sell a contract, let alone multiple contracts. In Chicago, you can buy or sell a contract in a matter of minutes.

The Winnipeg Exchange finally decided to cease trading cattle futures. The two main reasons were: lack of trading activity and the problem of cattle evaluations at both Calgary and Winnipeg. I was sorry to see this happen. Once more we were the "little boy on the block." We were too conservative and cautious to develop our own cattle futures program in Canada. It is fortunate that we have "Big Brother" to the south to fall back on.

The Calgary Livestock Exchange always played a big role in the National Livestock Markets' Association. In APPENDIX A, I list the American markets that were in existence in 1914. I am not exactly sure how many markets Canada had at that point in time; however, when I became a member of the Calgary Livestock Exchange in 1967, the Canadian markets (also listed in APPENDIX A) represented in the Association were: Montreal, Toronto, Winnipeg, Regina, Saskatoon, Prince Albert, Edmonton, and Calgary. These markets were usually referred to as "terminal" markets (meaning a major junction within a transportation system).

The Association held annual meetings, which were always well attended. There was always a wide range of issues to be discussed that affected all of the cattle people in Canada. It was not just the marketing of cattle that concerned us—there were health of animals problems, American and Canadian imports and exports, offshore beef quotas, staving off the implementation of a beef marketing board, (which was one of Agriculture Minister Eugene Whalen's pet projects,) interprovincial trade, and a host of other things that we as cattlemen had to deal with. Of course, the Association was not alone in dealing with cattle issues affecting us. The Canadian Cattlemens' Association, The Western Stockgrowers' Association, and, in later years, the Alberta Cattle Feeders' Association each took a stance similar to ours on the things that affected the cattle industry.

We definitely were a bunch of "right-wingers." Each of the Canadian markets would send two delegates to the annual meetings, which usually alternated between the East and the West. From these delegates, a board of directors was elected. A president and a vice president were then elected from the directorship. I had the privilege of being president for two terms. I was first elected at Toronto in 1977 and at Banff in 1978.

The following is an extraction of that Banff meeting as reported in the May 20, 1978 issue of *The Calgary Livestock Market Journal:*

> *"Leonard Friesen, President of the Calgary Livestock Exchange, Calgary, was re-elected as President of the National Livestock Markets' Association. The election took place at the Annual Meetings of the National Livestock Markets' Association which were held at Banff Springs Hotel, Banff, Alberta, April 19-22.*
>
> *"Doug McDonell, Toronto, General Manager, Ontario Stockyards, was re-elected as Vice President. Members elected on the National Bodies Board of Directors included: Roy Gilkes, Calgary; Mackie McCallum, Edmonton; Allen Stewart, Prince Albert; Garry Craig, Saskatoon, Don Allewell, Regina; Ed Oldershaw, Winnipeg; Murray Morrison, Toronto; Terry Maher, Montreal; Mr. Dick Triscott, Edmonton Stockyard Manager; and Mr. Art Larson, Winnipeg Stockyard Manager.*
>
> *"The three-day convention was well attended by approximately 120 members, delegates, and their wives. All business meetings were to a standing room only capacity, which showed the keen interest within the Livestock Marketing Industry in Canada. Other speakers included Mr. Harvey Cochrane and Dr. J. E. McGowan of the Canada Livestock Department with discussions relating to present day livestock marketing legislation.*

"*The National Livestock Markets' Association is the association representing all the terminal markets in Canada and represents Calgary, Edmonton, Prince Albert, Saskatoon, Regina, Winnipeg, Toronto and Montreal. The members are proud of their role in the livestock industry and spent considerable time at the convention discussing how more markets could be included in the Association so that a wider cross-section of the industry could be represented. Several markets have expressed interest in becoming classed as a terminal market, and the future of competitive livestock marketing in Canada is very bright.*

The Association is founded on a ten-point operation code which is as follows:

1. *To provide the functions and the facilities to meet the marketing demands of livestock producers in a changing livestock industry.*

2. *To maintain the purpose and philosophy of the free-enterprise system of marketing.*

3. *To promote and encourage the producers to expose their livestock through competitive selling by the use of the Central Markets.*

4. *To continually explore and develop new demands and outlets for producers' livestock, both at the domestic and export levels.*

5. *To guarantee the producer immediate full payment at accurate weights for all livestock sold through the Central Markets.*

6. *To provide accurate weights on government-inspected and approved scales by Federally approved and Bonded weighman operating independently of buyer and seller.*

7. *To provide current and accurate livestock market information on a daily basis.*

8. *To ensure that trading practices and all business are conducted in an ethical manner conducive to good business practices.*

9. *To ensure that all business be conducted in accordance with the Federal Livestock and Livestock Products Act and the regulations thereunder.*

10. *To provide a round-the-clock service for the handling and care of livestock.*

"James L. Smith, Chief of Procurement, Packers and Stockyards Administration, United States Department of Agriculture, Washington, addressed the convention and gave an excellent outline of payment policies in effect in the United States. The member markets of the National Livestock Markets' Association have the best financial protection that is available to producers at the present time but are looking to avenues where this can be improved.

"A highlight of the convention was a panel discussion entitled, "The Central Market - Right or Wrong." Panel members were Mr. C. A. Gracey, Manager, Canadian Cattlemen's Association; Mr. D. McDonell, General Manager, Ontario Stock Yards, Toronto; Mr. Mac McKinnon, General Manager, Lakeside Packers, Brooks, Alberta and Mr. Ellis Reimer, Feedlot Operator, Linden, Alberta.

"Mr. Reimer praised the market for opening up more sales areas by picking up Eastern and American orders. This stimulated the market in total and any patron of the market could take immediate advantage of these opportunities."

In the next year, Kitchener and Brandon also became members in the National Livestock Markets' Association. Sometimes truth is stranger than fiction. None of us realized at Banff that our days as an Association were numbered. In two years, a major reorganization took place. The Auction Markets of Canada and the National Livestock Markets' Association amalgamated to become the "Livestock Markets' Association of Canada." All the markets in Canada, large and small, were united and they still are to this day.

A report covering that organizational meeting, which was held in Edmonton in April of 1980, is as follows:

"Auction Market and Terminal operators from all over

Canada met recently at the Macdonald Hotel in Edmonton to form a new association, "Livestock Markets' Association of Canada." The new body is structured in such a way that every province will have equal representation of two voting members. These will be selected from each provincial or territorial association.

"Ralph Vold, Ponoka, Alberta, was elected president; Emerson Gill, Grand Bend, Ontario—Vice President; John Milne, Fort Macleod, Alberta—Secretary-Manager. Other directors are as follows: British Columbia: Bruce Whyte, Kamloops; Soren Jensen, Abbotsford. Alberta: Eric Tribble, Calgary; Leonard Friesen, Calgary. Saskatchewan: Gary Craig, Saskatoon; Stuart McDonald, Regina. Manitoba: Art Larson, Winnipeg; Don Rogers, Gladstone. Ontario: Emerson Gill, Grand Bend; Lex Rutherford, Toronto.

"As of now these are the provinces fully organized. Quebec and the Atlantic provinces will name their representatives as soon as they complete organizing their own associations.

The objects of the Association are:

(a)   To foster and advance a spirit of cooperation among persons, firms and corporations engaged in the marketing of livestock.

(b)   To promote, foster and advance the auction method of competitive marketing in the livestock industry.

(c)   To otherwise promote, foster and advance open and fair competition in the marketing of livestock.

(d)   To establish improved standards in customs and trade practices in the marketing of livestock and to achieve greater uniformity in customs and trade practices in the marketing of livestock.

(e)   To safeguard and improve the operations of persons engaged in the marketing of livestock in the best interests of producers, brokers, dealers, buyers, and sellers of livestock.

(f)   To aid in improving measures to assure financial protection for producers, brokers, dealers, buyers and sellers of livestock.

(g)   To prepare and distribute educational, statistical and economic information pertaining to the livestock industry and livestock marketing.

(h)   To formulate and recommend plans and measures to protect and promote the welfare of the livestock industry.

(i)   To advocate the enactment of appropriate laws, whether statute or regulation, affecting the marketing of livestock and the livestock industry, and to make representation therefore to any federal, provincial, municipal or other regulatory authority.

"The new association will represent approximately 60 percent of all cattle marketed in Canada.

"The meeting was adjourned in an atmosphere of accomplishment. The next Annual Meeting will be held in Toronto on April 24 and 25, 1981."

The daily physical operation at the Calgary Stockyards, encompassing 22 acres of pens, was not easy. The pens were constructed of big wooden planks and posts. It was only natural that time would take its toll. Wood becomes brittle; it also rots. Consequently, there had to be repairs made nearly every day—gates fell off, planks broke, water troughs leaked, etc. Bulls also caused a lot of damage. They would get into fights when you assembled them, which was daily. The results were crashed gates, shattered pens, upset troughs—you name it. In the last ten years of the Stockyards' existence, several sturdy bull pens were built. These special fortified pens could withstand a lot of bull-battering.

Cleaning pens was also a never-ending chore. In the old days they would load the manure onto the railroad cars and then haul it to Airdrie. There they dumped it into a boggy area between the railroad tracks and Nose Creek. Airdrie was only a small hamlet in those days but, even so, I am surprised that the residents put up with that kind of activity. In later years, the Stockyards' crew found some farmers east of Calgary who were more than happy to have this type of fertilizer spread on their farmland. I am sure that the enrichment of that soil still benefits those farmers to this day.

The feed and hay supplies were another big item at the Stockyards. Over the years, thousands of railroad cars of cattle and hogs were unloaded at Calgary for feeding and watering before continuing on their journey to their final destination. I must say, the hog feeding left a lot to be desired. They always had some barley chop on hand, but the feeding facilities were not good. Often, the chop was dumped into the pen along the fence. A lot of it got trampled into the dirt and manure before the pigs could eat it. The cattle had a better deal—they had feed racks. They were fed small square bales, which had to be loaded up, and then tossed onto a narrow plank catwalk above the feed racks. The strings or wires were then cut and the hay was dropped into the racks.

The owner of the livestock or his agent would put in a hay order at the Alberta Stock Yards office stating how many bales each pen was to receive. For instance if a load of cattle consisted of, say, 30 head, the feed order would probably request eight bales to be fed. I am sure these cattle often received only six or seven bales. Multiply that by 40 pens and you have a short fall of anywhere from 40 to 80 bales. Before you jump to the conclusion that the Company was dishonest, let me assure you they were honest. It was an occasional employee of the Yards who was lazy and dishonest. When it's 20 below and you are alone feeding cattle and feeling sorry for yourself, why not feed them a little less, no one will ever know. After all, you are not really stealing from your employer, you are stealing from the outfit that owns the cattle—probably a rich packer. This was the reasoning of a handful of employees. Most of those haymen were hardworking, conscientious, honest people, but, unfortunately, we will always have a few of the others with us.

Your logical question is, why would they not notice this overage of hay supply in the office? There were several reasons: First, all of the hay was bought by the ton, but it was sold to the cattle owners by the bale. Each ton can vary as to how many bales it contains. The

Company had to mark the hay up some to cover the overhead of handling it, and they also wanted to make a small profit. Second was the theft factor. On the east side of Portland Street, they kept a supply of hay on the plank walks above the feed racks. This hay was intended for cattle that did not get sold or, sometimes, for cattle being assembled for shipment. In most cases, the owners of these cattle would feed their cattle themselves. Even basically honest people thought nothing of feeding a few bales to their cattle, then conveniently forgetting to report it to the office. (This is something like people eating fruit at a Safeway store before they have paid for it.) I can honestly say we never indulged in this practice, nor did 97 percent of the other operators, but I know for a fact it happened. Third, there was spoilage. A lot of this hay was stored outside, so there was always a little waste at the bottom, plus some broken bales. In the final picture, the Company came out even or maybe sometimes made a little profit, but I know they did not get rich on hay sales.

The Alberta Stock Yards Co. also owned and operated the Lethbridge market. At that market, hay was supplied by a man named A. E. Kerslake. Every now and then, Calgary needed extra hay, so Kerslake would truck it north to Calgary. For many years, the Boothbys from Cochrane supplied most of the hay that the Calgary Stockyards used. It was "prairie wool," which is the best hay in the world, bar none. It is high in protein and other nutrients. Cattle never bloat on it. My friend Don Edge and several other people in the Cochrane district still put up some prairie wool. In the '70s and '80s, the McBains from Cremona, (George and his sons, Doug and John,) supplied all the hay the Yards needed. This was "tame hay," not as good as prairie wool, but good hay nonetheless.

The Stock Yards Co. also bought straw for bedding railroad cars. It took four to six bales to bed a car. With all those "thru-billed" cattle and hogs, plus cattle bought and shipped from the market, a lot of straw was required.

One of the great mysteries is that more fires were not started in all that straw and hay. There were a few, but only one fairly big one. A hayshed with at least 50 tons of hay went up in smoke. There were also several smaller fires that got doused. Access to that hay and straw was easy. Anyone could climb the fence and make themselves at home, and many did. Quite often, transients, bums, and hard-luck people (today we call them street people) found a good place to spend the night. Once in a while, a young couple bedded down for an hour or two. It was much more comfortable than the backseat of a car and a lot cheaper and more private than a motel room. Of course, they were playing with fire, but it was not the kind that burns up haystacks. Eric Tribble told me one day that they had discovered some person or persons who had tunnelled right into the center of a huge strawstack. They had hollowed out a fair-sized room and even furnished it to some degree. (Sure beats high rent.) Like I said earlier, it is absolutely amazing that there were not more fires started in the tinder-dry feed.

Calgary Stockyards, 1923. Aftermath of haystack fire.

The roads to and around the Yards became a troublesome factor in later years. In the late '60s and early '70s, when they were constructing the Deerfoot and Blackfoot Trails, things became pretty hectic around the Yards. Sometimes the cattle trucks faced long delays in the areas where road construction was taking place. Even without road blockages, there often were long lineups stretching for half a mile or more over the Alyth Bridge. They also lined up to the north well past the Shamrock Hotel. This usually happened in the fall of the year. A lot of credit goes to the patience of the truckers who had to endure this inconvenience.

Another bottleneck was Portland Street. It ran right through the middle of the Stockyards splitting the acreage into 8 acres on the east side and 14 acres on the west side. There were two big gates made of planks that had to be swung out across the street to meet in the middle in order to close the road off from traffic whenever cattle had to be moved from one side to the other. This would happen many times each day. Oftentimes, irate motorists would have to sit there in a line-up waiting for the gates to be swung open before they could proceed. (It always amazed me that the Alberta Stock Yards Co. was not able to negotiate a deal with the City of Calgary to close down that road to public transportation. It would have caused no real hardship to anyone, since motorized traffic could easily access Burns, 9th Avenue, or downtown Calgary by driving down Ogden Road, then turning north on 11th Street.) Every once in a while, when the gates were not across the road, a vehicle would roar through there at a high rate of speed. It is amazing that no one ever got killed on that road, because to get from the Livestock Exchange Building to the truck chutes and gatehouse as well as to the sale rings, this road had to be crossed. Many a motorist got a tongue lashing by a patron who was crossing the road. Of course, they seldom heard this verbal abuse because they were long gone.

One of the miracles, in my opinion, is that there was never a major wreck in our city caused by an escaped critter from the Yards. It is my guess that there were approximately 20 such incidents in the forty years that I was at Burns and the Calgary Stockyards—in other words, one every other year. I recall several of them.

One episode was when a wild-eyed steer got away from the Burns unloading chutes. The boys took after him with a roper standing in the back of a pickup. He roped the steer, quickly jumped out of the truck, and dallied the rope around a medium-sized fruit or ornamental tree. When the steer hit the slack, the tree got jerked out of the ground—away went steer, rope and tree. The boys finally managed to catch the steer and hold onto him after he had terrorized the neighbourhood for half an hour. No one was hurt except for Burns' bank account—they had to pay damages.

Another time, a wild cow got away from the testing chute. She was completely goofy. She ran at full-throttle for about two miles, dodging in and out of traffic on the Blackfoot Trail. To this day, I cannot believe that not a single vehicle was damaged. This time the police and a City animal control officer ended her short-lived freedom with a tranquillizer dart.

Another day, Harley Earl, from High River, unloaded a few head of steers at the Stockyards. He was not backed up to the chute straight on, so there was quite an opening on one side. One of the steers decided to go back into the truck, and when he saw that opening, he stuck his head into it. There was just enough room for his lanky body to pass through, so he dropped to the ground and away he went.

It just so happened that Harley had a few horses with saddles on them in that same truck. He quickly unloaded one and took after the steer. By this time, the steer had run underneath the Alyth Overpass. This led him to the Kerr Packing plant. Harley shook out a loop and caught him on the pavement in the yard of the plant. His horse was not shod. The steer only weighed a few hundred pounds less than the horse, so quite a tug-of-war ensued. The steer would gain a few feet, then the horse would pull it a little way. After about ten minutes of seesawing back and forth, Harley finally got the steer to a pen where they closed the gate on him. Again, no real damage done, except a tired horse and a somewhat frustrated Harley.

About two years before the Stockyards closed shop, a cow got loose. She ended up on the railroad switching tracks where the trains shunted back and forth. This time the police acted a little too hastily in my opinion. They shot her. I think the boys could have chased her back into the enclosure. Anyway, 600 pounds of meat was wasted.

When I was a partner in Rivercrest Ranches at Okotoks, we had a reckless Newfoundlander working for us by the name of Joe. One day, Joe was coming to Burns with 12 steers on a body-job. He only had one gear and that was ahead as fast as the old truck would go. When he exited the Blackfoot Trail to circle onto Portland Street, he was going about 25 miles an hour too fast. What happened was, the bolts that held the truck box on the chassis sheared off. The box with twelve 1,150-pound steers in it sailed right onto the CIBC Bank parking lot where the box tipped over and spilled all the steers to roam the streets of Calgary at will. A roundup ensued. After a few hours, every critter was gathered. The damage was some bruised beef carcasses, but, believe it or not, no broken legs. There were no humans hurt in this episode either.

I mentioned the wooden gates that closed off Portland Street. They had to be closed every time cattle were moved across to the west side. Whenever Canada Packers bought cattle at the sale, which was nearly every day, their men would gather those cattle and move them across that road to the west side; however, there were no gates across Ogden Road. In order to move those cattle into the Canada Packers yards, they had to cross over this road too. It took anywhere from five to seven men to get the job done. Two or three people would stand on each side of where the cattle had to cross. Another man was behind the cattle chasing them. Even in those days, Ogden Road was a very busy thoroughfare. It is almost impossible to believe, but only a few head ever escaped from this route; but, one day a snaky wild cow broke the rules and dashed for freedom. She ran to 9th Avenue in East Calgary. From there she proceeded to travel downtown. When she got to about 6th Street East, she veered off to the right and ran onto the ice on the Bow River. We had been experiencing really cold weather, so the river was frozen over except a few open spots where the current was fast. She came to a stop on the ice, just east of the Centre Street Bridge. About six Canada Packers' employees, including my nephew, Jim Friesen, were in hot pursuit. By this time, the City Police also had joined the fray. Soon, 15 or 20 policemen and Canada Packers employees were standing on the bank of the frozen river pondering their next move. The police decided to use a shotgun. (Don't ask me why—a rifle would have made more sense.) The policeman using the shotgun was not a very good shot. He let a blast go, missed the cow, but managed to spray birdshot on a would-be photographer, who was perched in a tree trying to get some pictures of the action. Fortunately, he was far enough away so that the pellets only stung him, but he vacated the tree in a mighty big hurry. (I am sure he had to attend to some laundry when he got home.) As for the cow, she took off at the crack of the shotgun. Strange as it may seem, I have forgotten exactly how they finally captured her. I am not sure if she was dead or alive.

Another time, when a cow escaped, she went visiting in an East Calgary residential area. It so happened that a young mother had put her baby outside to take a nap in its carriage. The carriage was parked on the old-fashioned veranda, so the baby could enjoy some fresh air. This particular cow decided to mount the steps onto the veranda, which surrounded the house. When she got up the stairs she raced back and forth like a maniac, dodging the carriage each time she passed it. Finally, she decided to jump over the railing to look for wide-open spaces. The baby slept through the whole episode. Not a hair was harmed on its head. I am sure there was a guardian angel watching the baby that day. This incident was related to me by Pat Collins.

Here's another incident that I found kind of humorous. One evening, it was not quite dark yet when a stray coyote made his appearance in the stockyard pens on the west side of Portland Street. The nightman on duty called the police. (Don't ask me why—unless maybe he thought Mr. Coyote was after some fresh lamb.) When the City Constable arrived, he jumped from his car and went coyote hunting. He had his pistol drawn and was sneaking down the alleys in a crouched position. It looked like he was approaching the shootout at the OK Corral. You already guessed it: The coyote was long gone. He had slipped through the fence, ran past Canada Packers and up the hill to look for a grouse for supper instead of lamb. After about fifteen minutes, the police officer sheepishly got into his car and drove off. It's much easier to catch two-legged thieves than a wily coyote.

Calgary Livestock Exchange - Board of Directors, 1964. (L-R) Bud Parslow, Vern McRae, George Winkelaar, Art Adams, Larry Farrell, Charlie Kennedy, George Hopkins, Cecil Barber, Sonny Gray, and Henry Bridgewater.

AWW crew, 1963. (L-R) Peter Adams, Morris Gunderson, Mel Morrison, Doris Cushnuk, Buck Rothwell, Pat Willis, Roy Furgeson, Art Adams, Ray Brown, Larry Stiff, Henry White, Archie Lamont, Jim Adams, and Al Jordan. Picture on wall is the founder of AWW, Harvey Adams.

Calgary Livestock Exchange Board of Directors for 1978

The 62nd annual meeting of the Calgary Livestock Exchange was held March 3, 1978. Leonard Friesen was elected as president for the second term. Roy Gilkes vice president. Secretary Treasurer Gordon Rauch.

LEONARD FRIESEN
President

ROY GILKES
Vice President

ERIC N. TRIBBLE
Director

CEC BARBER
Director

STAN DENOON
Director

MEL MORRISON
Director

GEORGE DENOON
Director

PETER ADAMS
Director

WILL IRVINE
Director

Calgary Livestock Exchange - Board of Directors, 1978.

Parslow & Denoon, Livestock Commission Agents, 1962. (L-R) Bud Parslow, Jim Suitor, Peter Holt, George Jamison (peeking), Stan Denoon, Shorty Watson, Ken Denoon, Hughie Kane, Vern Parslow, David Denoon, Fred Blazenko, Vern McRae, Bill Revelly, Ronnie Byers, and Maule McEwen.

J. C. Wheatcroft crew. (L-R) Bill Perlich, Mary Craig, Roy Gilkes, Dave Milton, Lynn Watson, Murray Flewelling, and Mason Cockx.

Alberta Livestock Co-operative Limited, 1963. (L-R) Lloyd Lumhiem, Ook McRae, Mike Spence, Chris Jacobson, Bob Blyth, John Allan, Dave Hedley, George Hopkins, Shorty Ross, Bill Duggan, Don Ritchie, Jim Hogg, and Jim Blain.

Small portion of the Alberta Stock Yards Co. crew, 1965. (L-R) Bill O'Gryzlo, Phil Pust, Harvey McEwen, Ken Gingrich, Don Olsen, Ray Eagleson, Frank Carr, John McCaffery, Hank Schimpf, and Jack Beacham.

Banquet time. (L-R) Frank Cockx, Hughie Kane, Stan Denoon, Art Adams, Vern Parslow, and White Garries.

Story time. (L-R) Roy Furgeson, unknown, Danny MacDonald, unknown, Art Adams, Doc Armour, and Earl Galvin. (Two backs, unknown.)

PETER ADAMS

JIM ADAMS

RON WARD

MEL MORRISON

R.W. (BILL)FURGESON

DORIS CUSHNUK

Adams, Wood and Weiller's logo and crew.

BUD PARSLOW
RES. 249-6908

STAN DENOON
RES. 242-2717

63 YEARS OF PERSONALIZED SERVICE ON THE CALGARY PUBLIC LIVESTOCK MARKET

With continual and rapid
changes taking place, minute to
minute in the beef trade ...
Price can only be related by offering
your stock to all demands.

BRING EM TO THE MARKET!
MAKE ALL BUYING POWERS WORK FOR YOU

AT THE CALGARY PUBLIC LIVESTOCK MARKET

MAUL McEWEN
SALESMAN
RES. 271-9106

HUGHIE KANE
BUYER
RES. 281-5424

GEORGE DENOON
BUYER
RES. 253-0800

CHAPTER IV

THE FINAL RUN
(1981-1989)

In the fall of 1979, Eric Tribble, his son Gary, my son Lee and I flew to Wyoming to look at a ranch that was for sale. We flew in a private plane. Gary was the pilot, and a good one. As it turned out, we did not buy the ranch, but it was on this jaunt that Eric and I got into serious discussion about the future of the Calgary Stockyards. The old system of operation had worked well for the past seventy-some years; however, circumstances had drastically altered things in the last ten years.

We both agreed that change was inevitable, so we came up with a very radical idea. Why not all join together and form a company? We knew it would take a lot of work and persuasion to have everyone agree to this innovative concept; and, when our idea was first broached to the various principals of the commission firms, it was met with mixed reaction. We must remember that these people had been each other's competitors for the last three generations.

In the old days, when only the Calgary and Edmonton markets were involved, the commission-man method worked well. The system amounted to competition between the various firms all seeking customers and doing the best job they could. If they didn't perform, the producer would sell through another firm.

During the late 1970s, it had become evident to the commission firms that their competition for cattle was not with each other at the local market, but rather from all the auction markets surrounding us.

Back in 1963, the CPR had transferred all of their real-estate operations in Canada over to Marathon Realty Co. Ltd., a public company. This changeover included handling the dealings with the Alberta Stock Yards Co.

In our discussions, Eric Tribble, who was the General Manager of the Alberta Stock Yards, told me that Marathon Realty, the parent company, would like to get out of the livestock handling business. The CPR had been heading that direction for quite a while. They hauled very little livestock by the late 1970s, and, in the early 1980s, they ceased hauling livestock altogether.

With Eric as the chief spokesman, we started negotiating a deal with Marathon that we thought was fair to them and to ourselves. We came up with a plan to lease the Stockyards for a five-year period at a price of $8,000 per month, or $96,000 per year. We then called a meeting with the future shareholders disclosing our plans to form a new company. Eric and I explained the terms and conditions of our proposed lease agreement with Marathon. After much discussion, they all agreed we should pursue the deal. Time changes things and concepts; this reorganization would be no exception. In subsequent meetings with Marathon, we made a few minor changes; but, basically, it was a done deal.

At that point we incorporated a new company called the Calgary Public Livestock Market Ltd. The shareholders were Cecil Barber; Stan Denoon; J. C. Wheatcroft; and Pete Adams—all commission men; Eric Tribble, retired General Manager of the Alberta Stock Yards; Sonny Gray; and me, Leonard Friesen—order buyers. I was elected President, Cec Barber was elected Vice-president, and Eric Tribble, was elected Secretary-Treasurer in charge of Operations. Roy Gilkes was our sales manager. Will Irvine, Ronnie Ward, Don Ritchie and Bill Perlich were our country reps. Our auctioneers were Bruce Flewelling and Lester Gurnett. After the incorporation date of our new company, October 1, 1981, Marathon dissolved The Alberta Stock Yards Company Limited. At this time, we also disbanded the Calgary Livestock Exchange, then reshuffled the offices in the Exchange Building and were ready for business.

Calgary Public Livestock Market Ltd., October 1981. Back row, (L-R): Mel Morrison, Charlie Kennedy, Eric Tribble, Leonard Friesen, Cecil Barber, Pete Adams, Brian Maitland, person unknown, and Harold Hanna. Front row, (L-R): Stan Denoon, Roy Gilkes, Larry Adams, Keith Svienson, and person unknown.

We all had a good feeling about our new venture. After all, Calgary was "Cowtown"—and we had just preserved the tradition of a Stockyards in Calgary! As it turned out, however, it was only for eight more years. (A similar type of amalgamation and reorganization took place in Edmonton and Saskatoon shortly thereafter.)

During the last six or seven years, I have heard by word-of-mouth that the Yards were in utter disarray by 1986 when I left to go to the USA. The receipts did decline sharply from 1983 to 1986, but this was due to certain extraordinary circumstances.

Through the years, many changes had evolved: first came the cattleliners, then the outlying auction markets and, last, but not least, the big custom feedlots.

Fancy Charolais waiting for sale.

Over the years, the Calgary market had more or less set the price for "fat" cattle. We also handled a lot of "feeder" cattle through the Calgary market. I can still hear George Winkelaar's gravelly voice on the radio at noon hour telling the country folks what the price of cattle and hogs was for that day. Adams, Wood and Weiller also had a morning broadcast, featuring Wilf Carter as the singer.

The large custom feedlots had expanded rapidly and this caused many of the smaller farmer-feeders to shut down their operations. Some of them started to feed their cattle at these big custom feedlots. Consequently, their cattle by-passed the Calgary market because they were all sold on the private bid system. This even included our own cattle that we (Friesen Cattle Co.) custom-fed. There was no way that the big feedlots were going to load up all those cattle and put them through a sale ring when they could sell them right at home. So, slowly but surely, the slaughter receipts declined at the Yards.

By 1986, there were virtually no fat cattle sold through the ring. At that point, Will Irvine, who had departed, but returned to become a shareholder in the Company, got the franchise for selling cattle by computer, an electronic marketing method. This solved the problem of all the fat cattle bypassing the Calgary market and saved the day for the Company. Most of the fat cattle these days are sold on the tape at Strathmore, or by bids, or by direct, or forward contracts.

In a period of about five years, four packing plants located near the Yards had closed. They were Burns Foods, Canada Packers, Kerr Packing, and Dvorkin's. Union Packing had closed years earlier. XL Beef, a public company, is still operating.

Another factor in the decline of receipts was the fierce competition for feeder cattle by surrounding auction markets. These other markets convinced many producers that they could do as good a job as the Calgary Stockyards could and with much easier access. This was partly true, although not altogether correct. The access to the Stockyards from the north, east, and south was very good. From the west it was more difficult. In spite of this, it seemed to me that our company's most loyal customers came from the west. (Many of these same people still support the Calgary Stockyards Ltd., at Strathmore.)

It was in the fall of 1989 that Marathon gave notice for the Calgary Public Livestock Market and its current Stockyards' crew to vacate the premises. They would not renew the lease. The excuse was that they had sold the property. I suspect the real reason was that they wanted out of the Stockyards business. To them tradition meant nothing. So what, if the Stockyards that had operated in Calgary for the past eighty-six years became history. If I sound a little bitter, maybe it's because I am. It was the end of an era; it all seemed so ruthless.

I'm sure glad that Marathon or some other Eastern entity does not own Stampede Park. They might shut that down as well—no more Stampede! My intention is not to denigrate Eastern Canadians. There are a lot of fine people in the East. I know many of them who are in the cattle business in Ontario and Quebec, and we speak the same language. What does bug me, though, is any big faceless corporation, be it in the East or West. They have no sense of history. They only care about the bottom line.

I want to make it very clear that if it hadn't been for Cec Barber and me, plus a few other people, the Calgary Stockyards would have closed in 1984. The reason I go into such great lengths about the era of the mid-'80s is because those were difficult days. The pressure was on. Hard economic times usually bring about change. In an attempt to optimize business, we (our new company) started a number of district calf and yearling sales in the fall as well as special bred-cow-sales. Sometimes this was not too successful; the bred cow market was lousy. We also cut overhead wherever we could.

The outcome of the commission firms' amalgamation in 1981 resulted in our Company reporting the following returns: 1981, fair profits; 1982, good profits; 1983, good profits; 1984, sharp decline, barely broke even; 1985, small loss; 1986, same story.

Annual Elbow Slopes calf sale, October 1982. Picture taken in Livestock Exchange Building, Board Room. Standing, (L-R) Leonard Friesen, Raymond Nicholl, Stubby Foster, Wayne Sibbald, David Edge, Ernie Geiger, John Sibbald, Floyd Pointen, Vern Pointen, Bob Fullerton, Jim Copithorne, Hugh Wearmouth, Charlie Fullerton, Bill Bateman, David Flundra, Dave Glaister, Mike Hawes, Lindsay Eklund, Tom Bateman, Susan Hawes, Roy Gilkes. Seated, Brenda Geiger, Lucille Glaister, Pat Bateman, Beryl Sibbald, Kathryn Pointen. Kneeling, Liz Mitchell, Pat Fisher, Kathy Flundra.

I commend Will Irvine for introducing computer selling when he arrived back at the Yards in 1986. I know this saved the day; but, I want to emphasize that the Calgary market was not in disarray. We had maintained our integrity. Things were at a low ebb, but we had kept the embers alive for Will and Don Danard, a commission man from Edmonton, to take over the Company and eventually relocate to Strathmore.

Many of you know how computer selling works. For those of you who do not—this is how it is done: The producer, or cattle feeder, who has cattle to sell phones the market to list the cattle he has for sale. At that point, one of the field men drives out to the country to look at the cattle. This person then makes an assessment on breed, quality, weight, sex (steers or heifers). If they are slaughter cattle, he must also determine what grade they fall into. He relays this information to the person operating the computer. This is usually done anywhere from a day to a week before the computer sale is to take place. The main computer in the Stockyards office is linked to numerous other computers around the country. Potential buyers all know the exact hour when the sale will start. They look at the screen on their computer. On it will be displayed the description of the cattle for sale. It also states who looked at the cattle and made the assessment. The operator at the main terminal then starts the cattle at a price somewhat lower that what the cattle should actually bring. For instance, if a group of feeder steers is worth about 98 cents a pound, they may start them at 95 cents. Immediately someone will punch in a bid which always goes in quarters, so now the screen reads 95.25 cents. The price rises fairly rapidly as a number of other buyers start punching in as well. When the price has risen to, say, 97.50, the bidding starts to slow up. However, it may continue to go up to 98, 98.75, 99, or even $1.00. If there is no bid for 15 seconds the bidding is finished. The highest bidder owns the cattle, unless the owner of those cattle decides to pass (no sale) the cattle. One of the advantages of this method is that most of these cattle are hundreds of miles away from the market munching on feed or grass until the day they are shipped to the new owner. Often, they are sold to a buyer who lives close to where the cattle originate. One of the disadvantages is occasionally the cattle do not measure up to the buyer's expectations. This is just a very brief description of how the system works. There are many other details to this method such as weighing conditions, delivery date, the "slide" which means if the cattle weigh more or less than described, the price goes either up or down. No one knows who they are bidding against until the sale is finished.

These days, there is also video marketing, which is similar to computer selling except the cattle are described and shown on your television screen. I have bought quite a few cattle in the US on this system.

When I left the Yards March 1, 1986, to go to the USA, Cec Barber took over and owned the Company outright. (I continued to buy cattle at the Yards during the next three fall seasons.) Cec was the last of the original seven owners. Then Will joined forces with him. Eventually, Cec sold his shares to Don Danard. Will and Don became partners in 1988 and operated the Calgary market until they moved the operation to Strathmore January 1, 1990. There was a short period when the Nilsson Brothers from Clyde, Alberta, were involved with the market as well. I do not know exactly how many shares they owned, but Don Danard bought their shares a while before they moved to Strathmore.

(L-R) Don Danard and Will Irvine, 1995.

So, there you have it, folks, the demise of large "terminal markets" had been going on in the United States for years, and Canada was just a few years behind them.

On December 15, 1989, the Calgary Stockyards conducted their last cattle sale. It was attended by a "standing room only" crowd. At the end of the regular sale they featured five special cattle for sale. The first one was a Charolais cow consigned by Barber Land and Cattle Company. It was sold to Ken Hurlburt for $1,296.75. The second one was a cow consigned by Sears Ranches, Nanton, and it sold to Frank Gattey for $1,250. Frank immediately donated the cow back. The second time it sold to Dr. Bob Church for $1,500. The third consignment was a Highland cow and calf pair consigned by Sears Ranches. They were sold to Friesen Cattle Ltd. for $1,500. The final animal sold at the Calgary Stockyards was a seven-year-old Luing steer consigned by Dr. Bob Church. It was purchased by the Calgary Stockyards Ltd. for $3,700. This steer had never been in a corral until the day Dr. Church shipped him to Calgary. All the money generated from the above sales was donated to the Stockmen's Memorial Foundation. The cheque issued to them amounted to $9,246.75.

The Highland cow's head is presently being mounted by Boland Taxidermists Ltd. at Cochrane and will be displayed in the sale ring at Strathmore. (I sold this cow to the Calgary Stockyards in the spring of 1994.) The heifer calf is now a six-year-old cow which we still own (Friesen Cattle Co.). She has raised four excellent calves.

On the evening of December 15, 1989, we had a "Stockyards-closing" party at the Sandman Inn. Six hundred people attended. I am sure there would have been more, but that's all the facilities could handle. I had the privilege of being the master of ceremonies. For me, and many other people, it was a sad day when the Stockyards closed after eighty-six years of operation in Calgary. It was always a beehive of activity, and the Yards full of livestock was a beautiful sight to see.

I am really happy that Don Danard and Will Irvine are running a successful auction market at Strathmore. I wish them nothing but the best. They have built a very functional stockyards facility. They displayed wisdom when they changed the Company name to "Calgary Stockyards Ltd." in 1988. This was a very fitting tribute respecting the long historical presence of the Stockyards in Calgary. The Company's head office is still located in the Livestock Exchange Building on Portland Street in Calgary.

This is the last animal (Luing steer consigned by Dr. Bob Church) of the many millions of cattle that were sold through the Calgary Stockyards in its 86-year history.

CHAPTER V

BRIDGEWATER AND FRIESEN CLIENTELE

The number of ranchers, farmers and feedlot operators who sold cattle at the Calgary market far exceeded the number of corporations or individuals who purchased cattle. There were many small consignments along with the larger ones. On the buying side, there was a relatively smaller number of packing plants, feedlot operators, and other individuals who bought cattle. The seller/buyer ratio was probably about seven to one. In other words, if there were 350 consignors in one week, the number of buyers would be approximately 50.

All the commission firms had their pet customers. By that, I mean some producers were completely loyal to the commission firms with which they dealt. Other producers sold their cattle through several different firms. The important part was that they all supported the Calgary Stockyards.

I will give you a small example of this producer loyalty. The Ushers from Scollard, Alberta, sold their cattle through AWW at Calgary for seventy-five years; Sam Fulton, Carstairs, fifty years; and Alvin Scheer's father from Carstairs started shipping to AWW in 1919; Alvin sold his last cattle at Calgary in 1989. The Amerys from Madden dealt with P&D for seventy-five years. This list could go on, but I just wanted to give you an idea of how loyal many people were.

Alberta Stocker and Feeder Show and Sale, 1924. First prize carload two-year-old Aberdeen Angus steers bred and exhibited by Usher Bros., Scollard, Alberta.

Hiro Takeda and his father, Naka, at the Calgary Stockyards, 1967.

I know there were at least a hundred ranching and farming families who shipped cattle to the Yards for forty to seventy-five years, spanning three or four generations. One day, at the sale ring, there were four generations of Kings sitting at ringside: Ansley, Carman, John and John's son. The Kings' operation was located west of High River.

Bob Hope and George Burns are not the only two people who plied their careers into ripe old age. There were two gentlemen cattlemen, who did not come to the Stockyards very often, but they certainly were very active buying cattle in the country and at country auctions. One was Jack Harrison from Crossfield, Alberta, and the other one was R. C. Fraser, from High River, Alberta.

In the Dirty Thirties Jack would start to buy cattle at Cremona, then Madden. By the time he trailed them into Crossfield, he had quite a little herd gathered. At Crossfield, he loaded the cattle into railcars and shipped them to the Calgary Stockyards. Jack continued to buy cattle till he was almost 90 years old.

R. C. Fraser was a real gentleman. I loved to visit with him. He continued to buy cattle till he was 90 years old. Occasionally, he came to the Calgary Stockyards with his son, Ron. R. C.'s grandsons, Dave and Bob Fraser, are good calf and team ropers. Both R. C. and Ron have passed on. I recently had a nice visit with Ron's wife on the phone.

At one point, I had decided to list all the producers who patronized the Calgary Stockyards; however, after compiling a list of several hundred names, I realized I had only scratched the surface. There were just too many for this book, and, I know for a fact, I would have missed some, so I scrapped the idea.

We bought cattle for many companies. When I say "we" I mean Bridgewater Livestock; later, Friesen Cattle Co. We also bought cattle for approximately 20 different packing plants in both Canada and the USA, including Ontario. We sent some cattle to B.C. as well. Many of these people's names have slipped my memory.

From 1967 to approximately 1977, we shipped thousands of cattle to Jack Daines at Innisfail. In the late 1960s, we shipped cattle to Perlich Bros. in Lethbridge.

Some of you may wonder how we could ship cattle for resale when we had so many other customers. There are 52 weeks in a year, and, in those days, the Calgary Stockyards operated two sale rings, five days a week. That amounted to about 500 sales a year. In other words, there were enough cattle available for everyone.

I hope Jack Daines and Tony Perlich will forgive me when I state that our farmer and feeder customers came first. I am sure they knew that even in those days. When their auction markets first started, they needed cattle, so we supplied whatever we could. After a while they phased us out because they were starting to get good receipts on their own. It was a good arrangement. It helped us when we needed orders, and it helped them get started. Incidentally, our orders increased after we quit shipping to them. Our volume was actually bigger than before.

Calgary Stockyards, 1978. "Fall"—harvest time for the cattlemen.

We bought feeder cattle for many good customers. These people supported us by giving us their buy orders; therefore, I want to give them recognition in this book. Some were big orders year in and year out; others were medium to small. Here then is a partial list of those people—forgive me if I missed you:

Jake Aleman, Seven Persons; Bill Amery, Crossfield; Bauman Ranches, Claresholm; Archie Bushfield, Calgary; Bill Byma, Carseland; Lou Callahan, High River; Dave Carlson, Lethbridge (a few loads of heiferettes); Cattleland Feedyards (Pat Fisher), Strathmore; Augie Christianson, Drumheller; Richard Copithorne, Springbank; Albert DeWitt, Airdrie; Diamond-Five Cattle Feeders, Calgary; Murray Dodds, Olds; Dodds Bros., Rumsey; Hymie Dvorkin, Calgary; Morton Dvorkin, Calgary; David Dyrholm, Calgary; Mickey and Tom Earl, Cremona; Jack Evans & Sons, Balzac; Bill Fokkens, Spruce View; Corny and Bill Friesen (not related to me), Lethbridge; Pete and Bob Friesen (my brother and nephew, respectively), Chilliwack, B.C., (these cattle were fed in Alberta); Larry Green, Bow Island; Clayton Griffin, Cochrane; Art Griffith, Calgary; Wayne Harris, Shepard; Bruce Hastie, Trochu; Mike Haverland, Calgary; Hawk Bros., Parkland (only once); Gene Helfrich, Strathmore; Hans Hindbo, supervisor for Raven Feeders Association, Spruce View; Dennis and Barb Holmes, Cochrane; Ron and Kim Holmes, Cochrane; Wes Houchin, Bowden; Pat Hutchinson, Cochrane; Rob Jackson, Calgary; Bill Jansen, Red Deer; Joe Jeffray, Airdrie; George Jones, Crossfield; Frank July, Calgary; John Klassen, Vauxhall; Lakeside Feeders, Brooks; Bob Lausen, Carseland; Gerry Lavoy, Strathmore; John Lozeman, Claresholm; Albert Lutz, Olds; Bill Massey & Sons, Calgary, now Granum; Roy McArthur, Dog Pound; George McBain, Cremona; Mowat & Sons, Forest Lawn in those days, now Langdon; Archie Nauta & Sons, High River; Harvey Neufeld, Didsbury; Fred Ollerenshaw, Shepard, later Calgary; Parkland Colony, Stavely; Bob Poffenroth, Midnapore, now Nanton; Dave Poffenroth, Midnapore, now Mossliegh; Harry Ramsey, Markerville; Borge Rasmussen & Sons, Spruce View; Jim Reed, Medicine Hat; Rivercrest Ranches, Okotoks; Gordon Robertson, Hanna; Bill Saxby, Calgary; Herb Serfus, Turin; Jack Smylie, Madden; Don Snyder, Crossfield, now Ponoka; Rudy Stepper, Calgary; Thiessen Farms (Ed and Rick Thiessen), Carseland; Thorlakson Feedyards (Ben Thorlakson), Airdrie; Dean Ulseth, Coronation; Howard Waite, Calgary; Art Warner, Calgary; Don Wathen, Midnapore; Ian Watt, Cremona; Western Feedlots, Strathmore and High River; Keith Wheeler, Strathmore; George Whitlow, Cremona; Walt Wilson, Stavely; Ray Witney, Calgary; and Cam Wray, Crossfield.

Approximately 15 percent of these people have passed away. In a few cases, their sons and daughters are carrying on in the cattle business. Approximately 40 percent (including the 15 percent deceased) of these corporations and individuals are no longer in the cattle business. That leaves about 60 percent who are still going strong. Thanks folks, we enjoyed doing business with you.

CHAPTER VI

BURNS

P. Burns and Company Limited, as it used to be called, played a huge role not just at the Calgary Stockyards, but in the early days of Calgary and the surrounding area as well. For this reason, I am including a chapter about Burns and my involvement with them over a period of twenty-four years.

Much has been written about Pat Burns and his achievements by people like Grant McEwen and other authors. Just in case you have not read any of these accounts, I will endeavour to give you a small glimpse of Burns' activities from the early days until the Calgary plant closed in 1984.

Pat Burns came from good Irish stock. He was born and raised in Ontario. In 1878, when he was twenty-two years old, he headed west—Winnipeg to be exact. Pat and his brother John heard there was good homestead land at Minnedosa. After a week's trek, they arrived at their homesteads.

During the next eight years, Pat proved up on his homestead. He did custom plowing and hauled freight to and from Brandon and Winnipeg as well as other towns. He also traded a few cattle with his neighbours. Occasionally, he bought some cattle, slaughtered them, and sold the meat.

In 1886 Pat took on a contract to supply beef to the railroad building crews working between Regina, Saskatoon and Prince Albert. The beef was slaughtered at a small plant he built in Saskatoon on the banks of the South Saskatchewan River.

In 1890 Pat moved to Calgary where he built another small plant to supply beef to the railroad crews building the railbed between Calgary and Edmonton. In the next ten years, he expanded rapidly. He sold beef contracts to the Indians. He also barged and trailed several herds to the Yukon to feed hungry gold miners.

In 1892 his Calgary plant burned down. He immediately rebuilt a bigger plant, where both cattle and hogs were slaughtered. Of course, one of the Burns enduring trademarks was the Green Shamrock. This emblem was proudly displayed on many of their processed food labels. Burns have always produced a quality product.

By 1912 he had assembled about eight ranches; six of them were big spreads.

In 1913 his Calgary plant burned down again. This time, he built a much larger plant, which he opened in 1914. This plant was still there when I came to Burns in 1950. Several major renovations and facelifts had been made over the years, but it was still the same plant that closed in 1984. It was seventy years old.

In 1931 the city of Calgary held a giant birthday party for Pat Burns. They baked a big 2-ton birthday cake, which they cut into 15,000 pieces. Each piece weighed slightly over four ounces. Everyone wished Pat well. At that party, a message arrived from Prime Minister R. B. Bennett announcing that Pat Burns had been appointed to the Canadian Senate. Thereafter, he was referred to as Senator Patrick Burns. It was a well deserved honour.

In 1938 Senator Pat Burns passed away. Burns' plants had been sold to other interests before he passed away. A few of his ranches had also been sold. There were still several good ranches left that continued to operate as the Estate of Burns Ranches. The estate was not fully settled until sometime in the 1970s.

When I started to work at the Calgary plant, there were still plenty of employees who remembered Pat Burns personally. So I heard a lot of stories—some maybe slightly exaggerated. Burns owned seven plants at this time. They were located at Calgary, Edmonton, Regina, Prince Albert, Winnipeg, Kitchener and Vancouver. In the 24-year period that I was with Burns, four more plants were purchased. They were located at Lethbridge, Medicine Hat, Brandon and Toronto; however, Burns Vancouver closed in the early '60s.

Many of Burns' earlier traditions and methods were still employed. They had a stable of horses used for feeding cattle, making short deliveries, and doing other chores. Forty percent of the cattle and about 50 percent of the sheep and hogs arrived at the plant by rail. The rest of the stock was delivered by small trucks or bought at the Stockyards where many of them had arrived by rail as well.

Burns' plant and the Calgary Stockyards were located on an old flood plain in East Calgary not far from Stampede Park. The wells were shallow and produced an abundance of very good water. A packing plant needs lots of water. Burns used to flush about three-quarters of all their manure down the city storm sewers. Can you imagine what a stir that would cause today?

Aerial view of Calgary Stockyards and Burns, 1950.

The presidents of Burns, in the 94-year period they operated out of their Calgary headquarters, were as follows: Pat Burns, John Burns (Pat's nephew), R. J. Dinning, Mr. Munn, Mr. Kelly, Mr. Hill, Mr. Klasing, A. J. E. Child, and John Nielsen.

The following people were at one time or another in charge of the livestock-buying operation at the Calgary plant: Pat Burns, Billy Bannister, Leonard Gates, Fred Watson, Mickey Dirrane, Sonny Gray, Bill Aubrey, Leonard Friesen (myself), Pat Collins, Albert Bethal (briefly) and David Shantz.

There were also dozens of plant managers and beef managers, many of whom I knew. I haven't listed them, since I am sure I would miss some. A few are mentioned later in this book in the character sketches.

Burns was a pioneer company in Calgary with a long tradition. Most of the employees were very loyal. I knew quite a few who retired after working for Burns for forty or fifty years. Burns' fortunes started to sink in the mid-'50s. The Company got quite stagnant in spite of employee loyalty. There was a lot of deadwood—in other words, people who produced very little. Also, some of their methods and equipment were quite antiquated, and things were needing repair.

In 1962 things came to a head. At this point, a "hotshot" from Ontario by the name of Hill, along with his associates, took over. He made some radical changes—not every one for the better. He had turned the Atlantic Sugar Company around; however, even though the principles of running a packing plant may be the same as running a sugar factory, the methods you have to employ are quite different.

Before it could be decided whether Mr. Hill could turn the Burns fortunes in the right direction, he passed away. At this time, one of Hill's proteges, by the name of Klasing (an American), took over. From there on, things deteriorated pretty fast.

Then, Mr. Child came on the scene. He arrived at Burns with a wealth of experience and expertise. He had been a vice president with Canada Packers in Toronto but left them to become president of Inter-Continental Packers in Saskatoon. From there, in 1966, he came to Burns Calgary where he became the President and Chief Executive Officer. He was given an option to purchase Burns' shares. He exercised that option almost immediately. Howard Webster and one other person from Eastern Canada were the other two major shareholders. A. J. E. Child ran the whole show. After Mr. Child took over Burns, things changed fast. It was like a sleeping giant waking up. He made numerous changes in personnel as well as to the mode of operating. He moved the Company's operation into the 21st century, and it did not take long for it to show on the balance sheets.

In 1970 Mr. Child opened the Burns corporate office in downtown Calgary. He was the CEO and appointed John Nielsen president. Eventually, Mr. Child and his partners bought out the other shareholders, and they made Burns a private company. The stock is not listed on any exchange.

Today Burns employs about 3500 people across Canada. They do over a billion dollars' worth of business a year. They have a large processed meats business and have hog killing plants in Edmonton (the old Gainer's plant) and Winnipeg. At Lethbridge, they still slaughter cattle.

Mr. Child, at age 85, is still the CEO of the whole Burns operation, which includes the Scott National Fruit Co. and several other subsidiary companies. Ron Jackson is President of Burns Foods (1985) Limited, and Larry Harding is President of Burns Meats Ltd. The Burns' enterprise has always been very civic-minded. The Company under Mr. Child's direction has carried on this longstanding tradition.

The Burns organization is still very active in community affairs. For the past 15 years, Burns has purchased a chuckwagon canvas at Stampede Park. Every year thousands of people see the Burns wagon race at the annual ten-day Calgary Exhibition & Stampede held in July. Burns' participation is a very fitting tribute, since Pat Burns was one of the four pioneer cattlemen who, amongst themselves, backed the first Calgary Stampede in 1912 for $100,000. The other three backers were George Lane, A. E. Cross and A. J. McLean.

In 1990 Burns Foods held a picnic at Heritage Park to celebrate their 100th Birthday. During the year, they held a number of picnics right across Canada to celebrate the special occasion. They also celebrated by being one of the three major sponsors of the "Hooves of History" video chronicling the fund-raising Cattle Drive 1990 organized by the Canadian Rodeo Historical Association. During this three-day event, donated cattle were trailed from Sibbald Flats to Cochrane Main Street. The CRHA auctioned the cattle and presented the funds to The Western Heritage Centre Society to assist with building the Western Heritage Centre on the Cochrane Ranche Historic Site.

In 1995 Burns Meats became a major sponsor of the Cannons' baseball team in Calgary. Consequently, the Foothills Stadium was recently renamed Burns Stadium. I think that was great idea.

The foregoing is just a brief sketch of the Burns story. In recent years, a number of changes, including the sales of some divisions, have taken place. It would be out of order for me to comment on these changes, since I do not know all of the details. One thing I know, Mr. Child is a very intelligent civic-minded executive who is highly respected in the business community.

Arthur Child at the Burns yards, 1967.

When I started working for Burns in January of 1950, my goal was to become a cattle buyer—a goal that I achieved with the encouragement and help of two people, namely, Mickey Dirrane and Dutch Ryder. On the road to becoming a full-fledged cattle buyer, I encountered a lot of little hurdles, one of which was working seven

112

days a week on many occasions. There were things like unloading and loading cattle, hogs, and sheep as well as strawing cars, watering, gathering, and sorting thousands of cattle, plus several years of buying hogs and sheep at the Alberta Stock Yards. I also bought some cattle off trucks. I started to buy cattle full-time at the Stockyards in 1955. I had literally served a five-year apprenticeship.

In 1967 I left Burns to become a partner with Henry and Jim Bridgewater. In 1970 I went back to Burns as their livestock manager and later became general livestock manager. In 1974 I left Burns again to take over the order-buying division of Bridgewater Livestock, and I renamed it Friesen Cattle and Properties Ltd. We operated at the Stockyards until 1986. Then my wife, Edna, and I moved to Colorado. For several months each fall, from 1986 to 1989, I came back to Calgary to "order buy" cattle for my longstanding customers. So, all in all, I was at Burns and the Stockyards from January 1950 to December 1989—forty years.

The following is what a typical day's work was like at the Burns livestock department in the early '50s. On an average, in the livestock division, there were about 17 people employed: four cattle buyers, one sheep and lamb buyer, one hog boss (hogs were all bought rail grade), one scalehouse bookkeeper and weighman, three livestock office clerks (no computers those days), two feedmen, one handyman, two nightmen, plus three to five flunkies (I started as a flunky), who helped wherever needed—the latter all hoping to become cattle buyers. Ambitious employees arrived at seven o'clock; the others arrived at eight o'clock.

The first order of business was to unload the livestock from the rail cars which had arrived overnight. Hogs were put on water only, because they were always slaughtered that same day. Sheep and lambs were usually put on feed and water, because we only slaughtered sheep once or twice a week. The cattle were sorted, priced and placed on feed and water. Nearly all the cattle prices were decided after they arrived at the plant. Some of the big strings of cattle had been bought and priced in the country, either by a Burns buyer or an agent. Those loads were easy to handle, since they required no sorting, just a "catch weight" to see what the shrinkage was. All this activity was usually finished by noon.

Meanwhile, two cattle buyers had gone to the Stockyards to purchase more cattle. On most mornings, there were some direct off-truck cattle to be bought. At the same time, hundreds of hogs arrived off-truck. They had to be tattooed and killed that same day. If they were held over till the next day, the packer had to pay a "shrink" penalty, since hogs were rail graded. Burns always had about 1,500 to 2,000 cattle on hand. About one-third of them were destined to be shipped to the Vancouver plant. Feeding all these cattle was quite a chore. We mostly fed them cut feed with some grain in it. This work was all done with a team of horses. Cattle that were only there for one or two days before slaughter were fed hay. When the sale was over at the Yards, around 3 p.m., the boys had to go over there to collect the day's buy.

Once or twice a week, we loaded a train load of cattle, hogs, and sheep to ship to the Vancouver plant and occasionally to the Kitchener plant. This was done between 4 p.m. and 6 p.m. The train pulled out around seven o'clock at night.

Generally speaking, everyone got along; however, once in a while, a problem arose. Often, it had to do with the promotion of someone to a cattle-buying position. Sometimes, the hopeful future buyers felt bypassed. Life can be cruel.

Another issue was pay discrepancy. Only about four or five were members of the Packinghouse Union. The rest were on a weekly salary, which ranged anywhere from $40 to $100 a week. I started at $55 a week in 1950. My salary rose fairly rapidly in the next five years. We were always paid in cash. Yes, cash—in an envelope—every Thursday afternoon. Everyone's salary was very secret; however, it did not take a genius to figure out approximately what each one received. The lower paid ones often complained about the higher paid ones not doing their share of the work. The full-fledged cattle buyers very seldom watered or loaded cattle, but they did a lot of the sorting when time permitted. I enjoyed sorting cattle, especially if I had a good man working the gate.

The Burns Yards had about 104 cattle pens with catwalks over them, which came in very handy when looking over the cattle that were on hand. The only catwalk that had a hand rail was the main one. One Saturday afternoon, I was there looking down at some cattle in Pen 103. There was no one else around. It was in the early spring and we had not gotten around to cleaning that pen so there was still about 18 inches of sloppy manure in it. Suddenly, without warning, the brittle old plank I was standing on, snapped. I landed in that sloppy muck flat on my back, just missing a cement water trough with my head by inches. That soft manure saved me from getting hurt, since underneath that manure there was 18 inches of cement.

Needless to say, I was a mess. With no other clothes along, I scraped off the worst of it, then crept into my car and went home. My wife is used to almost any smell or mess, since handling cattle often entails this, but, on that particular day, she could not believe her eyes. I looked like I had lived in a sewer for the last year. A good scrubbing with soap and water and I was as good as new. Incidents similar to this were not uncommon around the Yards.

I enjoyed working for Burns. I felt they treated me very fair, even though I received no severance pay or gifts when I left. I did not expect anything because I resigned to go on my own, which is something I have never regretted. Although I must say, I missed the old Burns gang with whom I had shared a lot of fun.

CHAPTER VII

CHARACTER SKETCHES

The pages that follow cover some 625 brief biographical sketches of persons who worked at or spent a lot of time around the Calgary Stockyards from January 1950 to December 1989. I knew every one of these people. Of course, I knew some much better than others. These "sketches" are written from my perspective in my vernacular. If some others had written this, they might have had a totally different view or slant about these individuals.

You will notice some sketches are much longer and more detailed than others. This is for two reasons: First, some people were much more dominant in the everyday activities at the Yards. Second, I had a lot more contact with certain individuals in business, and even socially.

One thing for sure, I have not written anything with the intent to hurt anyone's feelings or to put anyone down. I left a few "pimples" about people's characteristics and idiosyncrasies—which we all have. To do otherwise would make this very bland and boring reading.

I have avoided the personal marital problems or extramarital affairs that were quite common at the Stockyards, just as they are in all sectors of society today.

I do mention some drinking and gambling addictions. This was a reality every day at the Yards. It was pretty well taken in one's stride as part of the hazards of the livestock industry. I do not know of any drug abuse. If there were some cases, I was not aware of them.

We were one big family, even though we had very different backgrounds and lifestyles. I can honestly say I got along with everyone. Oh sure, we had our little quarrels and differences of opinions at times, but then, doesn't every family? Like you sometimes see on a pen or paddock at the zoo: "THIS ANIMAL HAS NO KNOWN ENEMIES," that is how I felt. To my knowledge, I had no enemies at the Yards.

I do touch on some of the religious beliefs. I must say we were quite a diverse bunch of individuals. There were Catholics and Jews and about ten different Protestant beliefs—and maybe others. The people were anywhere from very conservative to very liberal or from nominal to evangelical. When I mention "born-again" Christian, I am referring to what is generally called a conservative evangelical. I happen to believe and belong to that category. I must hasten to add, this does not mean I am more important to God than those who believe otherwise. God cares for and loves all people. One thing I observed at the Stockyards was the fact that there were very few atheists—maybe a few agnostics. Belief in God is very widespread in the ranching and farming communities. Maybe it is because they live so close to nature.

There are four more things I want to explain: First, the characters listed in this book are the people, as I stated earlier, who spent much or most of their time at the Stockyards. A problem with this list is that maybe I have left off some names. If I have, believe me, it was not intentional. I talked to a number of my peers from the Yards to try to ensure that everyone was included. In spite of this, I am sure a few have been missed. If you are one of those people, please forgive me—I tried my best. Also, if your name is misspelled, please forgive me, I was not able to trace everyone. An error that I hope I did not make is to have stated that someone is deceased when, in fact, that person is still alive and kicking.

Second, the Alberta Stock Yards Co., over the years, had quite a large turnover of personnel. Some worked there only for very short periods. Many of these will not appear in this book. There were also a number of women who worked at the Bank of Montreal. I got to know a few of them; however, many of them I knew only by sight. I did not even know their names. Sorry ladies, your names are not mentioned in this book. The same applies to the majority of the waitresses in the Stockyards Cafe, although I do mention a few of them. Both the bank and the restaurant had a large turnover of staffs. In the forty years I was there, I estimate that at least 150 different women worked for those two businesses.

Third, there were thousands of faithful producers and patrons who sold and sometimes bought cattle at the yards—several generations of the same families. Those people are not listed. I could not begin to name all of them. Even if I tried, many would be missed, so the list covers only the names of about 625 people instead of 6,000 or more.

Fourth, another group of people not included on this list are the truckers, who originated a distance from Calgary, but hauled a lot of cattle to and from the Stockyards. There again, I found it impossible to think of all of them. I knew at least 100 truckers, but the names of many have slipped my memory. In the old days, the '50s and '60s, before all the surrounding auction markets came into being, trucks came to Calgary from all directions. Some of the locations that come to mind are: Airdrie, Bassano, Bowden, Brooks, Calgary, Camrose, Carbon, Cardston, Carstairs, Claresholm, Cochrane, Consort, Coronation, Cremona, Crossfield, Drumheller, Fort Macleod, Hanna, High River, Innisfail, Lacombe, Linden, Medicine Hat, Milo, Nanton, Okotoks, Olds, Pincher Creek, Ponoka, Red Deer, Rimbey, Stavely, Stettler, Strathmore, Three Hills, Vulcan, and dozens of other locations.

One more thing I must explain: Right from the inception of the Alberta Stock Yards Co., in 1903, until the Burns plant closed in 1984, the two outfits had a very close relationship. I worked for Burns over a twenty-four-year span. During that time, I spent the bulk of my time at the Stockyards representing Burns. So, I'm taking the liberty of including many of the people I worked with at Burns. Even though these people seldom went to the Stockyards, they were an important link in the livestock chain.

Here then are the people who inhabited the Stockyards—plus a few from Burns. This covers the forty years I was at Burns and the Calgary Stockyards.

BOB ABBOT set up a hat shop in the Calgary Livestock Exchange Building in the mid-'80s. He is an expert hat man. He can make them, shape them and clean them. I do not know a whole lot about Bob's past; however, I do know he was a good hand, having worked on several B.C. ranches as a cowboy. In the summer of 1989 he sold the shop to Lace Noyes.

DAVE ABRAHAMS was raised in eastern Alberta. As a young man, he was a good bronc rider—the late '40s and early '50s. Rodeo prize money in those days wasn't what it is today. I don't think he won any great amounts of money, but he put up some good rides.

Dave bought a place just north of Balzac on the east side of Highway 2. There he built a feedlot for 800 to 1,000 head of cattle, which was a fair size in the '50s. From the highway, you can still see his Double Y brand (Ⅺ) on a building there. Dave was a staunch Adams, Wood & Weiller customer. He bought mostly short-keep steers from 800 to 1,000 pounds. The bulk of his fat steers were sold back through the ring. Every once in a while, I would purchase several hundred head directly from him. I was working for Burns at the time.

It's been a number of years now since Dave passed away. He left his mark in the cattle business. If he were living today, he would be astonished to see all the large feedlots operating in Alberta. He was one of the pioneers in this industry.

WALTER ACTON was raised in East Calgary. He worked for Katchen Bros. as both a beef manager and a provisions manager for a number of years. I have seldom met a man who was as fast and accurate with a pencil as Walter. This was before calculators and computers. Quite regularly, Walter bought all the hogs at the Stockyards. This was much to the dismay of the larger packing companies who were always seeking to suppress the hog market because they didn't want to have to pay too much for their direct hogs. Walter got involved for a while with Alberta Western Beef at Medicine Hat and stayed there until Burns bought the plant in 1972. Last I heard, Walter was working for a packer in Toronto.

BILL ADAMS, or "Dollar Bill" as we used to call him, liked to come to the Yards to shoot the breeze with the boys and pick up a few cattle. He was a hard worker. He owned several trucks, which he kept busy hauling gravel, rock, dirt or whatever needed hauling. Bill had a place on the west side of Calgary. After he sold that place, he bought a farm at Carstairs. He is a good operator and feeds and trades quite a few cattle. His main haunts are the Olds and Innisfail auction markets. He often works the ring for them, especially at Innisfail, Alberta. I always enjoy a visit with Bill. In some ways, we are the same; in other ways we are quite different.

HARVEY ADAMS was born and raised in Missouri. When he came to Canada, he settled at Tofield, Alberta. In 1919, he, along with Henry Weiller and Roy Furgeson, started a livestock commission firm at the Calgary Stockyards. Over the years, he built up a large clientele. He was hardworking and honest; the customer always came first.

Harvey must have shaken a million hands in his lifetime. Somebody once said: "If Harvey had a dollar for every hand he shook, he would be worth a million dollars." And, maybe he was. I remember, when I first came to the Yards he shook my hand many times. His eyesight was starting to fail, but his mind was keen.

During the Dirty Thirties, things got pretty tough. I was told Harvey even rode a streetcar to work. He stuck with it. When World War II came along, he was going great guns again, and after the War things went really well.

Yes, Harvey Adams left a great legacy for his family and friends to follow.

ART ADAMS was Harvey Adams' son. Art was involved at the Yards from a very young age. Gradually, as Harvey got older, Art took over. When I arrived at the Stockyards in January 1950, Art was running the outfit.

Art was a bit of a playboy. He loved golfing and partying; however, when it came to business, he was as straight as an arrow. Everybody knew Art was a good cattleman. He treated everyone the same. It didn't matter if you had one cow or a thousand cows, he always did the best he could for you. Art shipped thousands of cattle to St. Paul and other U.S. destinations. He also shipped a lot of cattle to Eastern Canada.

Art never really drew a salary. He more or less went to "Fergie"

(Roy Furgeson) in the Stockyards office whenever he needed some money. Getting rich was not one of Art's goals. On several occasions, he borrowed twenty or fifty dollars from me and others because he forgot to get some money from Fergie. He always paid it back in the next day or two.

Art died very suddenly between Christmas and New Year's in 1967. He was fifty-six years old.

JIM ADAMS is a son of Art Adams and grandson of Harvey Adams. Jim spent some time at the Yards when he was still in school. When Art passed away in 1967, Jim and his brother, Pete, along with Roy Furgeson, took over the firm. Jim was always a very honest, straightforward kind of person. He and Pete did a good job of operating the family firm. Sometime in the mid-70s, Jim became a born-again Christian. He stayed around the Yards for several more years. Finally, he decided to start a Christian book store in Calgary called *The King's Corner*. He and his wife are still operating it today.

PETER "PETE" ADAMS is the oldest son of Art Adams and is a grandson of Harvey Adams. Pete, too, was around the Yards a lot as a youngster. After completing high school, he went up north to work on the oil rigs. He soon decided he would rather be in the cattle business, so, at age 19, he started with AWW. He learned the business from the ground up.

After Art passed away in 1967, Pete and his brother, Jim, together with Roy Furgeson, took over. Pete operated a very good business. He was considerate and honest, just like his father and grandfather before him, and he was always easy to get along with.

Pete also bought and shipped thousands of cattle. Many of them went to McIntyre's in Ontario. Pete and McIntyre were both third-generation cattle people doing business the same as their forefathers had for over sixty years; however, something went wrong. McIntyre went broke and left Pete "holding the bag" for a lot of money. It was amazing how seldom a thing like this happened, but every once in a while it did.

When we reorganized at the Stockyards in 1981, Pete was one of the partners. The others were Stan Denoon, Cecil Barber, J. C. "Red" Wheatcroft, Eric Tribble, Sonny Gray, and me. Pete left the Stockyards in 1984 and went up to the Peace River Country.

Hughie Kane and Pete Adams enjoy one of the favourite pastimes at the Yards.

LAURA ADAMS (nee Gardiner) is Pete Adams' wife. She clerked for the auctioneers at the Yards for many years. Laura and Pete fully supported their son, Larry, in his rodeo endeavours, including such trips as travelling 900 miles to Douglas, Wyoming, to attend High School Rodeo Finals. I'm sure Laura is still doing the books for Pete's cattle operation in the Peace River area.

LARRY ADAMS is a son of Pete and Laura Adams, grandson of Art Adams and great-grandson of Harvey Adams. Larry was raised around the Yards since his parents both worked there. After finishing high school, he came to work for his dad at the Yards.

Larry was a saddle bronc rider. He went to several high school rodeo finals in the USA. He has also been to the Canadian Finals Rodeo (CFR) in Edmonton in the novice saddle bronc competition.

One incident that I am sure Larry will never forget is the time he bought a calf at the Stockyards for about $30,000. What happened was, we were holding some special opening ceremonies that included special sales of individual animals. Proceeds were to go to the 4-H of Alberta. The first calf entered the sale ring. The bidding was fast and furious. The animal was being sold by the pound. The price got

123

higher and higher. Bruce Flewelling was doing the auctioning. Bruce stopped and said: "Do you guys realize how much money this comes to?" Then he started to auction again. Shortly after that, he knocked it down to Larry for $30,000. It only took Larry a few moments to realize that he had miscalculated the end figure. The ring was full of people—a lot of dignitaries and government people. What now? Well, I was president of the market at the time so I called some of the government and 4-H people together and explained the error. I told them that Larry figured the price was around $3,000, not $30,000. They were all very gracious and said they understood. They were quite happy to receive $3,000. Larry, if you or your parents read this, please do not be offended. We all make mistakes. All's well that ends well. It was unique at the Yards. We operated as a family—when one hurt, we all hurt.

For a number of years, Larry and his dad order bought cattle in the Peace River Country. I understand Larry works with his father-in-law in the horse business these days.

DR. GEORGE ADLEM was in charge of the Federal Health of Animals Division at the Stockyards for a number of years. He was a redheaded, pipe-smoking, easygoing kind of person. He was a great friend of Geoff Parker's. Dr. Adlem went to New Zealand in the early 1950s where he became the head of the Health of Animals Division. As far as I know, he still resides in that country.

RICHARD ADRIAN was beef manager at Burns for several years. A. J. E. Child, CEO for Burns, brought Richard up from Saskatoon where he had worked for Inter-Continental Packers. Last I heard of Richard, he was running a home-freezer meat operation and doing well.

JACK ALLAN came to Calgary from western Saskatchewan. He worked at Burns for over forty years: first, in the plant; then, as an assistant to Art Wimble, who was in charge of the hogs in Burns' yards. Jack loved to talk, and this often got him into hot water. It really didn't bother Jack, he just shrugged if off. He was a lifelong fan of the Saskatchewan Roughriders and the Brooklyn Dodgers. Also, he was a very loyal member of the Meat Packers' Union. Jack passed away recently at the age of 76.

JOHN ALLAN worked for the Alberta Livestock Co-op for many years. After they folded, he came to work for the Health of Animals Division, testing cattle. I can still see John as he walked very erectly, usually with a cigarette in his mouth. He was known around the Yards as "Hobee." I'm not sure where that "handle" came from. I think Chris Jacobsen hung it on him and it stuck. Last I saw of John, he was still with the Health of Animals Department.

DON ALLWELL was a freckle-faced, good-natured individual. He worked for the federal government grading division. He graded thousands of cattle that I had bought while at Burns. He was a very fair grader. Don left the government a number of years ago and went to work for the Saskatchewan Wheat Pool, cattle division, in Regina. Last I heard, he was the head honcho there.

ROLAND AMERY was a real gentleman cattleman from Crossfield, Alberta. He fed nothing but the best. He was a lifelong

Roland Amery and Ken Denoon, December 1972.

customer of Parslow & Denoon. Vern McRae used to buy most of the cattle that Roland fed. Roland sold all his fat cattle through Parslow & Denoon. He would order the trucks out early in the afternoon. The cattle would be sold sometime in the forenoon the next day. He really believed in giving good weighing conditions; consequently, his cattle always brought top dollar.

Roland and his brother, Fred, came here from the state of Washington. Their father originated out of Missouri. Since Roland lived in Calgary, he spent a lot of time at the Stockyards. It would be hard to find a more honest man. Those of us who knew Roland well had a great deal of respect for him.

BILL AMERY is Roland Amery's son. He, too, fed cattle at Crossfield using more or less the same program as his dad. He didn't feed quite as many, but he did a good job on the ones he fed.

One year, Bill asked me to buy a 4-H steer calf for his son. It was his son's first year in 4-H, so Bill asked me to buy a nice "gentle" British breed of calf. He told me it didn't really matter if his son won or not. "It's his first year," Bill said, "so, I just want him to have a gentle calf." So, I bought him a nice gentle Hereford calf.

The next June, I was judging the Calgary 4-H Show at the Stampede Corral. About halfway through the show, just as a new class was being led into the ring, there was a sudden loud clatter down where the steers entered the ring. A steer spooked when it stepped onto a wobbly piece of plywood that was laying at the entry gate. The steer knocked over the boy leading it and stepped on him. To my horror, it was Bill's son leading that "gentle" steer. Luckily, he wasn't injured very seriously. Let me tell you, I felt really bad about it.

In his younger years, Bill was an avid skier. He sure enjoyed going to Sun Valley, Idaho. He and his wife live in Airdrie.

GEORGE ANDERSON hails from the Hussar country of Alberta, where he still lives and runs a farm and cow-calf operation. He loves black cattle.

George started to auction cattle at a tender age. He was an auctioneer at the Lloydminster Stockyards for about five years. Then he started selling at purebred sales, which he still does today. Between his farming and auctioning duties, he spends a fair amount of time at the yards. He has filled in at the Calgary market for a number of years.

It was actually through George that I began to write a cattle column in the magazine, *Beef Today,* back in 1975. Rod James was starting this new livestock paper, and he happened to mention to George that he was looking for someone to write a column about the commercial cattle business. George said to him: "I know the man who can do it: Leonard Friesen." Shortly thereafter, Rod phoned me and we set up a luncheon date at the Stampeder Hotel. Rod, George and I met and discussed what we thought the column should consist of—and I said, "Sure, I'll take a shot at it and write the column." In those days, it was twice a month; well, I have been writing a regular column, "*Cattle Call,*" for twenty years, now. Thanks, George.

JOHNNY ANDERSON was born and raised at Stavely, Alberta. His parents were friends of Danny McDonald's. As a young man Johnny came to the Yards to work for Paul & McDonald.

Johnny was one of those innocent looking people. Even if he was guilty about something his pale-blue eyes and blond-curly hair made him look like an innocent three-year-old.

Often, Johnny worked the gate from the ring to the weigh scale. He did a pretty good job, but, in spite of this, the boys liked to give him a hard time, in a good-natured way.

Unfortunately, Johnny was a little too friendly with certain distillery products. Eventually, he left the Stockyards. Last I heard, he was running a secondhand store in Stavely. Johnny was a good guy, but as the saying goes, he was his own worst enemy.

DICKIE ANDREWS had a ranch in the Porcupine Hills of Alberta. He loved to come to the Calgary Stockyards to gamble. Every year he brought his calves to Paul & MacDonald. On the day they were sold you could bet your bottom dollar a big craps or poker game would take place in P&M's back office. "Rodeo Dick," as the boys called him, passed away about fifteen years ago. I had coffee with him in Claresholm a few weeks before he died.

DR. GORDON ARMOUR was the head veterinarian for the Health of Animals Division at the Stockyards for a number of years. "Gordie" or "Doc," as he was called by his friends, was a very sociable person. He didn't miss too many so-called do's. He was very reasonable to deal with. I'm not sure where Doc went after he left the Stockyards.

FRANK ASKIN worked in the AWW office for several years. He was an accountant. I really did not know him very well, but they tell me he did a good job. Frank and his wife operated a beauty salon on the North Hill. Maybe they still do, I am not sure.

ALFIE ATKINS was a little Englishman who always had a straw in his mouth. His speciality was trading in milk cows. In those days, (the early '50s) many farmers still milked a few cows. The Stockyards did not receive many milk cows (except used-up ones); however, once in a while, one would show up. Andy had several people watching for a cow for him. I only once sold him a cow. Andy passed away at least thirty-five years ago.

BILL AUBREY was the livestock manager at Burns Calgary from 1964 to 1970. He was transferred to Calgary from Winnipeg. Prior to that he was a cattle buyer at Burns Edmonton. After he left Burns Calgary, he joined L.K. Ranches at Bassano. Several years later, he seemed to disappear for a while. Last I heard, Bill was selling cars in Edmonton.

DWAYNE AUGER is a good-natured character. These days he is a roofer in Camrose. I still remember when Dwayne and a buddy of his arrived at the Calgary Stockyards. They slept in a haystack across the road from the Stockyards for several nights until they collected some pay. Dwayne is affectionately known as "Bearman" by his friends and he has lots of them because he is a very friendly person.

STAN BALLARD was general sales manager for Burns. He was also the plant manager in Calgary for a while. He sold a lot of beef, and, in this way, I considered him a friend to the cattle industry. He is now retired from Burns. Stan is very devoted to his church. He is also Gideon. These days, in his retirement, he enjoys an odd game of golf and other activities with his friend Art Moore, who was the canning manager at Burns for years.

128

CECIL BARBER was born and raised in Cheadle, Alberta. He is a man of few words, but a good cattleman and manager. He sold cattle at the Stockyards ever since he was old enough to operate his own outfit.

In 1958 Cecil and Doug Keer bought out Jimmie Paul's share of Paul & MacDonald. They operated this partnership for a number of years. After Danny MacDonald passed away, Cecil bought out Danny's share, and, when Doug Keer passed away, Cecil became the sole owner.

In 1981, along with the other principals at the Yards, Cecil became a partner in the Calgary Public Livestock Market Ltd. In 1986 he became the lone survivor of the original seven. Will Irvine then joined Cecil. Shortly thereafter, Cecil sold his share out to Don Danard.

Cecil has many other interests besides the Stockyards. He operates a very successful farming and feedlot operation at Cheadle, Alberta. He also owns a ranch at Claresholm. He was the president of Western Feedlots at Strathmore and High River for many years and is still on the board of directors. He is also a Shriner. He rode in the mounted patrol for a number of years.

Cecil feeds a lot of cattle at Western and he buys nothing but the best in feeders. He is very well informed on the cattle industry and attends most of the meetings pertaining to cattle organizations such as, The Western Stock Growers' Association, Alberta Cattle Feeders, Auction Markets, etc. Some people call him "The Little Giant" of the cattle industry.

GEORGE "GEORDIE" BARKS worked for the Alberta Stock Yards. He was a very dependable sort of chap. He liked kids and often had some candy for them. These days, kids should not accept candy from strangers; in those days, nobody thought a thing about it. I am sorry to see such a change in our society. George was a good fellow.

BRIAN BARNETT came to Calgary from southeastern Saskatchewan. He worked for Burns Calgary for a while and then went on his own, order buying. He encountered a bit of a financial problem along the way. (Who hasn't?) But, he is back on track order buying again. These days, he works with the Stockyards at

Mr. and Mrs. Brian Barnett

Another first at the Calgary Public Stockyards

At 6:30 pm on Saturday, October 21st, 1978 a "first" took place at the Calgary Public Stockyards. Judy Paulsell, secretary for Salers association and Brian Barnett, Burns Foods Ltd. cattle buyer exchanged wedding vows in the stockyards sales ring.

The ring was beautifully decorated for the occasion including green and yellow streamers, hay bales, colored commission jackets, old fashioned antique country fixtures, and sheaves of grain all placed to create a beautiful setting.

Justice of the peace, Patricia Harrington; the groom, Brian, and Dave White, the best man, stood patiently awaiting the arrival of the bride.

On the briede's arrival, the band, the Country Travellers played and sang the popular tune, "Devoted to You".

Judy looked radiant in a soft green gown and holding a bouquet of white carnations, red roses and miniature sheaves of grain, was given in marriage by Mr. Hughie Kane, a cattle buyer for Parslow and Denoon. Wilma Bertsch was Judy's maid of honour.

A beautiful ceremony for a delightful couple.

We wish all the best for them in the future.

The ceremony was followed by a dance and mid-night lunch at the Ramsay community centre.

Brian and Judy Barnett, 1978.

130

Strathmore. He is also an auctioneer, although he hasn't done much of it lately. Brian and his wife had a very unique wedding—they were married in one of the sale rings at the Calgary Stockyards.

VAL BARRON came to Calgary from Bassano, Alberta. He had several cattleliners, plus an office in the Exchange Building. He was a very congenial sort of person. After about ten or twelve years, he disappeared from the Yards, and I really do not know where he went. Val hauled quite a few cattle for our outfit, Friesen Cattle Co.

ALBERT BARTON worked for the Alberta Stock Yards in various capacities. For many years, he was the janitor and maintenance man. He was very obliging. One of his daughters married Vern McWaters.

JOHNNY BARTON, Albert Barton's brother, also worked for the Alberta Stock Yards for a long time. He took Nick Burok's place at the branding chute. He branded thousands of cattle for our outfit.

Johnny also used to castrate feeding bulls for whoever needed the chore done. These bulls usually weighed from 700 to 1,000 pounds; and, occasionally, up to 1,100 pounds. One day we gave Johnny an order to castrate about 15 bulls for us. He found the pen number where the bulls were located. The count checked out, but the bulls looked awfully big to him; however, he decided to castrate them anyway. When he told us about this, we were aghast. He had castrated some big bologna bulls that we were assembling to ship to the United States. Somehow, the pen numbers had gotten mixed up. These bulls weighed from 1,500 to 2,200 pounds. Since we couldn't ship them in that condition, we sent them to our feedlot near the Calgary Airport to heal. Amazingly, none of them died.

When Johnny left the Stockyards, he moved to B.C.; but, I understand, he has now moved back to Calgary.

NORMAN BASCHON (not sure about the spelling of his last name) worked for CIL. He loved coming to the Yards to mingle with the boys. After he left CIL, he opened up a courier business. His office was in the Livestock Exchange Building. His son worked with him. This gave Norm some spare time, so he clerked for the auctioneers for several years as well. Norm is a friendly sort, the kind of person who gets along well with people. He had quite a large family, either eight or nine children. I think, these days, he is more or less retired.

JACK BATES was raised just east of Calgary. His brother, Chuck, still lives on the home place. Jack worked for AWW for many years. He was a good hand. With Jack around there were very few mix-ups. I'll never forget Jack telling about the time he and his wife Barbara took their children on a trip to California one summer. They had no air-conditioning in their car, which wasn't uncommon in those days. Jack said they nearly perished from heat while driving through the desert areas. They were sure happy to get back to good-old-cool-Calgary. For many years now, the Jack Bates family has owned and operated a holiday ranch for children. It is called Bates Bar J Ranch and is located northwest of Cochrane. They also raise registered Paint horses. Jack passed away a few years ago.

JACK BEACHAM worked for the Alberta Stock Yards for many years. He was a very dependable, hardworking person. He was always on the move. For a long time, he supervised the loading and unloading of railroad stock cars. I can still see Jack striding down the alley with his cane hanging on his arm.

JIM BEAL is Jim O'Gryzlo's son and Bill O'Gryzlo's brother. The reason his name is Beal is because he belongs to a religious group that believes in changing their names—so he became Jim Beal. He worked for the Alberta Stock Yards Co. Jim was a honest worker, and it was easy to visit with him. In his youth, he was a good boxer. These days, he is a freelance writer.

BUD BECK was an office manager and later a plant manager at Burns. Bud, Bill Wiles, Harold Hanna, an accountant, whose name I have forgotten, and I, once spent five days in the Seattle, Washington area. We were negotiating the purchase of a packing plant and feedlot (Auburn Pack) for Burns Foods. The deal never materialized. I, for one, thought it was not a good bargain as the feedlot and cattle were way overpriced and the plant was outdated and rundown. As it turned out, I was right, because the plant was condemned by the United States Department of Agriculture six months later. I have lost track of Bud Beck.

JOE BECK worked for Burns as a teamster. He fed the cattle that Burns kept in their Yards prior to slaughter. It was not unusual for Burns to have two or three thousand cattle on hand in the 1950s. We used to ship ten to fifteen carloads of cattle, plus hogs and sheep, to Burns' plant in Vancouver every Friday. Joe was a big, slow-talking, friendly person. He was a good teamster.

HENRY BELKIN was one of our Jewish friends. He was in partnership with a man by the name of Mayland. They owned Union Packing on Nose Creek. A little while before I came to the Stockyards, he split up with Mayland.

For many years Henry bought cattle at the Stockyards. He custom killed them, then sold the beef to local stores and restaurants in Calgary. The Calgary Stockyards never received a lot of veal calves. Henry always bought the few that showed up. Price was no object. Nobody could buy them away from him.

One thing Henry always demanded was to balance the scale before weighing anything he bought, even if it had just been balanced on the previous draft. I can still hear him calling out: "Get a balance down dar."

Henry always wore thick glasses, since his eyesight was not the best; but, in spite of this, he always drove a car. One weekend, Henry and his wife drove to Banff. (He loved the hot pool.) On their way home, they stopped at the Park Gates. They got out to go to the washrooms or something. When Henry came back to the car he assumed Mrs. Belkin was in the car with him, so he drove off. He didn't notice she wasn't with him until he was almost to Cochrane, some 40 to 50 miles down the road. He rushed back to the Banff Park Gates and there she was waiting for him. I don't know what transpired after that!

Henry moved to the Coast where he and his son owned a large box-making factory. As far as I know his son still owns it.

FRED BENNETT was a cattle feeder from Airdrie, Alberta. In the 1950s and '60s there were about twenty small feedlots, handling 500 to 1,500 head, scattered around the outskirts of Calgary. Quite a few of them were within the city limits. Burns Ranches operated the biggest one with a capacity of about 8,000 head. Fred was at the Yards nearly every day buying short-keep feeders. He was a very careful buyer. His brother, Cliff, was there once in a while, but not as often as Fred.

KEN BENNETT came from Winnipeg, Manitoba. He was a cattle buyer for Katchen Bros. When they sold out to Canada Packers, he stayed on as a buyer. When Canada Packers bought Red Deer Packers, he became the head buyer there. Ken was the nervous type. He often chewed his nails and constantly adjusted his glasses. Ken passed away several years ago.

HENRY BERG worked in the plant for Canada Packers, then he switched to livestock where he bought cattle for four or five years. A number of years ago, Henry moved to Grande Prairie to operate a butcher shop, which he still operates today. Henry liked to fish.

LEIF BERG came from an old ranching family at Patricia, Alberta. There were a number of boys in the family. I think, nearly all of them went to university, which was quite unusual in those days. Leif's brother, Roy, was a professor at the University of Alberta in the Faculty of Agriculture and Forestry for years. I think he is retired now. Leif was a government grader for quite a while in Calgary. He did a good job. For the last few decades, he has worked in Edmonton as a supervisor of the grading system. Leif is a real gentleman.

TOM BERGER is the son of Jake Berger, who was a good customer at Calgary for years. I really do not know Tom very well. I did see him working at the Yards in the late 1980s, mostly in the fall. The boys tell me he is a good hand. I always enjoyed visiting with Jake when he came to town from his ranch at Nanton.

BOB BERGEVIN worked for the Alberta Stock Yards. He did some auctioneering too, although not at the Calgary Stockyards. I understand Bob owns a Turbo Station. He is also a good rodeo pick-up man.

BOB BERTRAM worked for the Alberta Stock Yards most of his life. For many years, he was a yard foreman. Bob was a good worker and expected the same from the men who worked for him. He could get quite testy at times, but, in spite of this, he always got the job done. Bob was a boxing champion in his weight range. He was quite a small man; however, I never heard of anyone around the Yards who ever tested his boxing skill in a real fight. It has been a number of years now since Bob retired.

MIKE BESCO worked for the Alberta Stock Yards as a hayman (feeding hay to cattle). He was big and burly and could handle two to three bales at once. Often, he worked in bars as a bouncer. I, along with a lot of other people, always made sure we stayed on the right side of Mike.

ALBERT BETHEL was born and raised at Maple Creek, Saskatchewan. His ancestors were Basque sheep people from Spain. Albert worked for Burns as a cattle buyer for several years. He was the head buyer for a short period after Pat Collins went to work for Dvorkin's, and before Dave Shantz came down from Edmonton. When Albert left Burns, he went to work for XL Beef. After a few years there, he moved to Edmonton to start his own order-buying business. He is still there today. Albert really likes to keep fit, so he often jogs. "How are you making out, Albert, with all that snow up there?"

BILLY BETKER came to Calgary from Yorkton, Saskatchewan. He worked for Union Packing, which belonged to Swift Canadian. From there he went to work as a cattle buyer for J. C. Wheatcroft. He worked very closely with Roy Gilkes. I ran into Billy several times in the Billings, Montana area. We were both there to buy U.S. cattle to ship up to Canada. Billy was a good-natured redhead. We were all stunned, when, one morning, at age 42, he suddenly passed away from a heart attack.

ALEX BEVERIDGE was only around the Calgary Stockyards for a few more years after I arrived in January 1950. I don't know much about Alex' background, but he was in partnership with Irish Johnston. They owned Producers' Livestock Commission Firm. Alex stayed in their office most of the time and did his work very diligently. He also looked after the firm's hog and sheep interests. Alex was kind of a gruff sort, but I think his bark was worse than his bite.

ALFRED BILBEN lives just north of the Calgary Airport. He spent a lot of his time at the Yards. Years ago he used to come there to buy feeder pigs. Alfred is the only man I know who could out-wait Cliff Green. Cliff had certain prices on various bunches of feeder hogs. Alfred, in his slow drawl, would say to Cliff: "That's too high." Next day Alfred would come back with the same scene. This would be repeated several more times. After about a week, Cliff would weaken and sell to Alfred at his price. The Bilbens feed out large numbers of cattle at different feedlots. Alfred isn't exactly hurting financially.

GRANT BILBEN is Alfred Bilben's son. Grant surfaced at the Stockyards in the 1980s buying cattle for their operation. I thought he did a good job—sometimes, maybe, a little too cautious. The Bilbens also have a purebred herd of Herefords. You can see them along Highway 2 as you leave Calgary, when travelling to the north.

PHIL BISCHOFF lived at Stettler, Alberta. He was a cattle dealer who sent a lot of cattle to Burns when Mickey Dirrane was in charge. Phil was not around the Calgary Stockyards very much, but he was often at Burns. Bill Collins, the calf roper and horseman, was a good friend of Phil's. It was through Phil that Bill brought some cattle to Burns. Phil was a very calm, reflective person who did not make too many false moves.

BERT BISHOP was an old, skinny cowboy when I came to the Yards. For many years, he had hired out to various people to trail cattle to the Stockyards on horseback. This practice more or less had ended by the end of World War II. I can still see Bert with his red neckerchief tied around his neck, his worn cowboy boots, and a somewhat crunched hat. I can imagine him, as a young man, looking like Little Joe the Wrangler in that old Texas ballad.

HAROLD BISSEL came from Viking, Alberta. He was a nightman at Burns Livestock. From there he went to work for Adams, where he stayed for many years. Harold is a real western cowboy-type. He used to ride saddle broncs and rope calves. He does excellent leather work and has made belts for many people, including me. He is also very good at mounting horns. You might run into him wherever there is a gathering of old cowboys. Harold is a very slim, quiet individual, but, he really comes to life when the topic is about cowboys or the Old West. He lives in northeast Calgary.

GERRY BISSEL is Harold Bissel's son. Gerry worked for Producers' Livestock for a few years. He is very outgoing and easy to talk to. When Gerry left the Stockyards, he got involved in several ventures in the sales field. He owned and operated some kind of a disposal outfit at one time. I think Gerry is kind of semi-retired these days.

JIM BLAIN worked for the Alberta Livestock Co-op. He was a top hand. He performed the same good job day after day. He always had a cane hung over his arm ready for action. Jim was a straight-shooter, but his brother, Bob, was a different kettle of fish. Bob was one of the few people who left me hung up owing a few funds. Jim did not approve of some of his brother's dealings, but there was not much he could do about it. I always appreciated Jim, but somehow I have lost track of him.

FRED BLAZENKO came from the Crowsnest Pass area. He was an accountant and bookkeeper for P&D for most of his life. "Freddie," as he was known, had an opinion on every subject: sometimes right; sometimes wrong. (Like most of us.) He always wore suspenders. He liked to play pinochle with the boys. After P&D closed, Freddie kind of semi-retired. He still does the books for the Three Brothers Restaurant, which is located in the North Hill Shopping Centre.

SAM BLYTH was a real good-natured trucker at the Calgary Stockyards. He and Elwin Jackman worked together most of the time. They hauled thousands of cattle to the Yards as well as across the country. They each could haul about a dozen fat steers on their "body-job" trucks. When Sam was younger, he was a good cowboy and a good horse breaker. He worked for several ranches, including the old Virginia Ranch north of Cochrane, where they raised polo ponies during the late 1920s and early 1930s. Sam was everybody's friend, and it was a pleasure to do business with him.

BOB BLYTH is the son of Sam Blyth. Bob started working for the Alberta Livestock Co-op as a young man. After some years, he became their head salesman. He operated the sale ring. He always put the cattle producers ahead of the buyers. In other words, he was tough to get a deal from for the buyers. He would pass a lot of cattle out, no sale. The Co-op always gave good weighing conditions. This resulted in more money per pound, alive, which looked good for the producer—at least on paper.

Bob moved with the Co-op to the Agri-Mart near the Calgary Airport. When it folded, he went to work for Kerrs as a fat-cattle buyer. Now, he was on the other side of the fence. He soon found out what it felt like when people like Roy Gilkes and others passed cattle out that he was the high bidder on.

Bob also operated a feedlot close to the Airport. It was pretty successful.

Bob's favourite sport and pastime is running hunting dogs. He has good dogs and travels all over North America to dog trials. He likes to go down to Georgia and Alabama, especially in the wintertime. Bob's favourite expression was: "Why wasn't I born rich, instead of so good looking?" Bob resides in Calgary.

PHIL BOISVERT worked for the Health of Animals Department at the Stockyards. He wasn't exactly overworked. He seemed to have a lot of time for hobbies. Phil was an expert locksmith. There wasn't a lock made that he could not open without a key. It was lucky that he was an honest man. Phil was 100 percent on the up-and-up, and he did not use his skill for illicit purposes.

DALE BOLTON came from Nanton, Alberta, where he still resides and raises Salers cattle. In the late 1970s and early 1980s, when the Salers Association of Canada had an office in the Exchange Building, Dale was their secretary-manager. He is a knowledgeable cattleman, rather on the quiet side. Dale and Frank Whitham, from Kansas, and I partnered on a Salers bull calf that Dale had raised, named Pathfinder. We sold him at the Denver Fat Stock Show. We did okay on him—he brought $40,000.

EDDIE BOWLEN came from an old Alberta pioneer family. His uncle, J. J. Bowlen, was a big horse dealer who ended up being the

Lieutenant-Governor of Alberta. The J. J. Bowlen Building in Calgary is named after him.

Eddie was one of the great horsemen. He broke and trained horses at many places, including the New England States in the USA. While there, he was employed by some very prominent horse people. Eddie was the 1923 and the 1928 Calf Roping Champion at the Calgary Stampede.

For the last twenty-five or thirty years of his life, Eddie was a trucker at the Yards. Between Eddie and Tom Gerlitz and Blyth and Jackman, they must have hauled over 200,000 steers from Burns Ranches to the Calgary Stockyards.

Eddie was a very good man—what I would call a real gentleman. He was very agile even up to eighty years of age. He and his wife Toddles retired in Calgary. Eddie passed away about ten years ago.

Eddie's son, Jay, ranches northwest of Cochrane. I do some business with Jay. He is a chip off the old block. At one time, Jay was a quarterback with the Calgary Stampeders.

AL BOYCE worked for the CPR as a shipping clerk. Whenever a person shipped a load of cattle from Calgary to anywhere in North America, Al was the man he had to deal with. I can still see him, with his cigar clamped between his teeth, looking at me over his glasses. He also had a very successful sideline business. He owned a car spring plant in competition to Standen's Limited. When Al left the CPR, he went to operate his spring business full time.

ARCHIE BOYCE was not related to Al Boyce. Archie lived at Olds, Alberta. When the Stockyards changed from private treaty selling to the auction method, he was one of the people they employed. That was in 1951. Later on, he, along with the Rosehills, started the Olds Auction Market. These days the Olds Auction Market is operated by the Rosehills and Harry Drever. For many years, Archie was one of the auctioneers at the Calgary Bull Sale. He had a booming voice and hardly needed a microphone. I had a lot of good visits with Archie. He loved to talk to people. The Calgary Exhibition & Stampede named the Archie Boyce Pavilion in his honour. It was well deserved. When Archie lost a son to polio, he bought an iron lung and donated it to the Red Deer Hospital in the hopes that someone else's child could be saved. Archie was well into his eighties when he passed away. He was a credit to the auctioning profession.

JOE BOYCO originally came from Blaine Lake, Saskatchewan. He owned a little packing plant just south of the Stockyards. He had been with the Health of Animals Division in Swift Current, Saskatchewan. Joe used to custom kill cattle for various people. He also killed some for himself that he sold around town. He then switched to killing horses, which he did for a number of years. The horse meat was shipped to France by aeroplane.

Joe told me an interesting story one day. There was a rich German by the name of Von Maffei who had a big place northwest of Airdrie. This guy was a real flake. (I know, firsthand.) At any rate, one day, Von Maffei's hired man delivered two choice grain-fed steers to Joe's plant for custom processing. This is what the instructions were: kill the steers, age the beef, cut the hind quarters into portions for Von Maffei's guard dogs, then cut the front quarters for the hired help. I guess he wanted his dogs to be in top condition to attack any intruder.

A few years ago, Joe visited us in Colorado. As far as I know, he still owns the plant, although he isn't killing horses anymore.

RUSS BOYER came from Drumheller, Alberta. He worked for P&M for many years. He was as quick as a cat on his feet. Often, he worked the gate in the sale ring. There was no one better than Russ for that job. After he left the Stockyards, he went to work for XL Beef where he worked in the cattle receiving and holding area. Russ was a top-notch boxer in his weight division. Over the years, the odd person challenged him, much to their regret two black eyes later. He wasn't very big, but, believe me, he was fast. Another thing about Russ, he always kept his car sparkling clean.

RUSS BRAMAN (not sure I've spelled his last name correctly) worked for the Alberta Stock Yards. He was always on the job. Russ was the same person every day—no mood swings. He was easy to visit with. I really have no idea where Russ is these days.

HENRY BRIDGEWATER came to Calgary in 1959 from Yorkton, Saskatchewan. He had been buying, selling, and dealing in cattle for years. As a young man, he owned and operated a butcher shop at Bredenbury, Saskatchewan. He shipped a lot of cattle to Winnipeg.

When Henry came to Calgary, he liked what he saw and decided to start an order-buying business. This was not easy to do. A person had to be accepted by the Calgary Livestock Exchange and obtain a federal license. Henry is a patient man, and, eventually, they granted him a license and the privilege to operate on the Calgary market.

Henry Bridgewater conducting a bit of cow business at the Yards.

Red Wheatcroft had been operating an order-buying business at the Yards ever since W. J. Johnstone departed ten or twelve years earlier. Red wasn't exactly delighted to have Henry for competition. Red was a big operator. He shipped thousands of cattle East, besides doing his local business. To start with, Henry's business was relatively small. It was too costly for Red to run Henry off by bidding everything up in the sale ring, so, they more or less agreed to an unspoken truce, (a little uneasy at times).

While I was working for Burns and buying cattle at the stockyards, Henry and I got acquainted and became good friends. In May of 1967, Henry phoned me one night and asked if I would be interested in becoming a partner with him and his son Jim in their order-buying business. He made me such a good proposition that I couldn't resist. I was assistant livestock manager at Burns at the time. The next day, I handed in my resignation; however, Burns needed me for another six weeks because the Canada Packers workers were on strike and Burns had doubled their cattle kill. So, I stayed on with Burns till the beginning of July. During the second week of July, my wife, Edna, our children and I packed up and headed for Expo '67 in Montreal. When we came back around the first of August, I immediately started with the Bridgewaters.

Before I go any further, I want to mention the two people who influenced me most in the cattle business: one was Mickey Dirrane, who hired me at Burns; the other was Henry Bridgewater, who became my partner. Mickey was a hard-drinking crusty Irishman. He was a great cattleman. I learned all the fundamentals about buying and handling cattle working with him for six years. At that point, Burns and Mickey parted company. Mickey died shortly thereafter. Henry taught me how to conduct business: "Stay calm, analyze the situation, then make your move." Henry seemed to have a sixth sense about when to stay in and when to get out.

As soon as I was settled in with the Bridgewaters, the beef orders started to pour in. I could hardly believe it. We shipped cattle to 15 or 20 different packing plants in Canada and the USA. In those days, Calgary was a big market for fat cattle.

We shipped cattle to the following plants: Burns Brandon; Burns Winnipeg; Burns Kitchener; Intercon Red Deer; Intercon Regina; Pacific Meat, Marpole, B.C.; CDM Lethbridge; Dee's Beef, Guelph, Ontario; Amour, Spokane; HH Packers, Yakima, Washington;

Flavorland Inc., Fargo, North Dakota; Black Hills Pack, Rapid City, South Dakota; Landy Packing, St. Cloud, Minnesota, plus some to California, Nebraska and Toronto.

I made more money with Henry in six months than I made at Burns in two years—in other words—four times as much. Believe it or not, it got better.

Henry and I also used to play the stock market—mostly penny stocks, but often bigger ones as well. In 1971 our pipe-smoking finance minister, by the name of Edgar Benson, slapped on a capital gains tax. This basically ended the stock market business (at least for a while).

Henry and Jim and I owned a farm at Delia, Alberta. We also owned Diamond Five Cattle Feeders. Later on Will Irvine and my son Lee became partners in Diamond Five Feeders as well.

About 1972 Henry and Jim started to deal in land around Calgary, subdividing it into acreages. I was a partner in the first two ventures. They made good money, but since I was handling the cattle dealings, I didn't contribute much to the land business.

In March of 1974, Henry and I, by mutual and friendly agreement, split up. Jim had left the cattle business earlier on. I got the cattle dealership all by myself and Henry and Jim continued with the land business.

I have written a lot about Henry, but I have only scratched the surface. I could write a whole book about him and my business relationship with him in the past thirty-five years. We are still the best of friends, and we socialize together quite often.

JIM BRIDGEWATER is Henry Bridgewater's son. He spent several years in Edmonton, where Bridgewaters had an order-buying business at the Stockyards. In the late 60s, Jim came to Calgary to join us at Bridgewater Livestock. Will Irvine, who worked with Jim in Edmonton, came down to Calgary and joined us about two years later. Jim had a very alert mind and could see even bigger opportunities in land development than there were in the cattle business. So, he left and went into the land business with Henry's blessing. Henry and Jim developed a lot of acreages and other properties in the Calgary area as well as in Phoenix, Arizona. Jim was a partner and the major driving force in building an upscale senior citizens' home in Calgary. He and his wife reside in Calgary.

RON BRIDGEWATER is also a son of Henry Bridgewater and brother of Jim Bridgewater. Ron worked mostly at the gatehouse in summers and on weekends while attending university. He graduated and was admitted to the bar as a lawyer. A number of years ago, he moved to Ontario where he is still practising law today. I'm sure Ron still remembers the cold winter nights when trucks would line up to unload cattle for the next day's sale.

ROY BROMLEY, ex-hockey player and ex-city policeman, was hired by the Packers as a "watchdog" on overcrowding and overloading livestock trucks at the packing plants as well as the Stockyards. He also checked for bedding in trucks and made sure there was enough cover to prevent the livestock from freezing in cold weather. Roy was a reasonable man, but he could get tough when he had to. He always had some costume jewellery to sell as a sideline. I've lost track of him.

PADDY BROWN was a brand inspector at the Stockyards for quite some time. After Paddy left the brand office, he took on the position of secretary-manager for the Canadian Rodeo Cowboys' Association—a position which he held for a number of years. Paddy was a good saddle bronc rider in his day.

Paddy worked with Bill Wearmouth when they demolished the old Stockyards Exchange Building in 1966. I am sure Paddy had some good memories about that place as the walls came tumbling down. Wearmouth also demolished the Stockyards' pens and sheds on the west side of Portland Street in 1981. I don't think Paddy helped with that.

These days, Paddy is involved with the Canadian Rodeo Historical Association. He is a well-liked, soft-spoken individual and is a credit to the cowboy fraternity.

In 1994, Paddy was honoured as a "Pioneer of Rodeo" by the Calgary Exhibition & Stampede.

RAY BROWN, or "Brownie" as he was always called, was a good worker with a violent temper. He had served in the Army. For many years, both before and after the Second World War, he worked for Adams, Wood & Weiller. He was usually in the back sorting cattle. Every once in a while, Art Adams would have him in the ring moving

144

the cattle around. If Ray thought the cattle were not bringing enough money, he would rant and rave, cussing every buyer in the sale ring seats. You could literally see the fire flying out of his eyes. In spite of all this bluster, I often had good conversations with Ray. He really wasn't that bad beneath the surface, he just felt he had to express himself in a forceful way. The last I heard of Brownie, he was somewhere in the Windermere Valley in B.C.

SLIM BROWN was no relation to Ray Brown. Slim, whose real name was Herman, came to Calgary in the 1930s from the Saskatoon area. He was kind of a freelancer. Sometimes, he worked at the Stockyards for short periods; then, he would move onto something else—often a local feedlot; quite often, he would help out at Dave Abrahams' feedlot.

For many years, Slim was a horse dealer at the Yards. For a long time, he worked with Bill Perry. When Bill passed away, Slim went on his own.

Slim often brought our sale tickets from the sale ring, while the sale was still in full swing. One Christmas, my wife thought we should give him some goodies. So, she made up some home-baked treats for him. He accepted the gift all right, but, after that, no more tickets for us. I guess he felt we were getting too chummy with him. He basically was a loner.

For years, Slim lived at the King Edward Hotel on 9th Avenue. He always walked to work. This was a fair distance. I can still see his long strides with his shiny brown leather jacket. (He wore that jacket whether it was 80 above or 30 below.) Slim never married, and, to my knowledge, never went back to his home in Saskatchewan. Maybe he did once or twice in fifty years.

Slim either said nothing or just kind of grunted a greeting. Every once in a while the mood would hit him and he would talk nonstop. He observed everything that went on around the Stockyards. He also held some pretty strong opinions on just where our society was headed. A horse kicked Slim while he was loading it and he died shortly after that.

CHARLIE BROWNFIELD was a cattle buyer for Swift Canadian. He was an easygoing individual. Having worked for Swift all his life, he was one of the few buyers who bought both cattle and hogs and sheep at the same time. Some people started at the hog and sheep scales then graduated to cattle, but Charlie often bought cattle in the morning, then he would match for hogs and sheep at 1 p.m. If he did not buy any, which happened quite often, he would go back to the cattle sale. Charlie also looked after Swift's "thru-billed" livestock. He developed some joint problems in his hands and legs but, in spite of this handicap, he always got the job done. He transferred to Lethbridge where he worked until he retired.

LAWRENCE BRUCE came from Forestburg, Alberta. He is the father of Winston and Duane Bruce. Lawrence was a good cowboy. In his heyday, not many broncs could unload him. He always kept some bucking stock on hand and that's why his sons turned out to be good bronc riders. Lawrence was a brand inspector at the Yards until he passed away. Lawrence was a really nice man. I used to love visiting with him. In the early 1960s, when Winston was cutting a wide swath, both here and in the USA, Lawrence kept me updated on Winston's performances at various rodeos. Winston won the world saddle bronc title in 1961. Sometimes, I used to see Lawrence in the bank when he was depositing some of Winston's winnings into Winston's account. Yes, Lawrence Bruce was a credit to the rodeo world.

DUANE BRUCE worked for the Alberta Stock Yards for a little while. He is a son of the late Lawrence Bruce and brother of Winston Bruce, who is the rodeo manager for the Calgary Exhibition & Stampede.

Duane was a very good saddle bronc rider. I am sure he has many buckles and trophies to show for it. I am quite a rodeo buff, and, in my humble opinion, Duane often did not get marked as high as I thought he should.

For many years now, Duane has operated his own tinsmithing and furnace business. He has done some work for us. He keeps busy and does a good job. Duane is very involved with the old-timers' rodeos. It is nice to see someone with the dedication to rodeo that Duane possesses.

RICHARD BUHLER was a fine looking young man when he came to Calgary. He came from the Handhills, Alberta. I am not sure if he was born there, but I know he worked on a ranch there. Richard was a brand inspector at the Stockyards for a long time. He was transferred to Medicine Hat as a brand inspector a number of years ago. I heard he had become a born-again Christian. Richard still lives in Medicine Hat.

MERV BURKE from Yorkton, Saskatchewan, was a friend of Henry Bridgewater's. Merv used to run the Saskatchewan Wheat Pool Market at Yorkton. After Merv moved to Calgary, he set up a little feedlot east of the Airport where he fed cattle for several years. He bought most of his feeders at the Calgary Stockyards.

NICK BUROK came to Canada from the Ukraine, I think. He had quite an accent. He ran the branding chute at the yards. I must say, he was rough and ready. He had those enormously big dehorners and it did not matter how thick or hard the horns were, he would give them one big squeeze and blood would be spurting all over the place, including on himself. By the end of the day he looked like a Roman Gladiator. I never did, and still do not, like dehorning big cattle. It should be done when they are calves. Nick retired and I lost track of him.

TOM BURTON was a horse dealer. He was only there briefly, after I came to the Stockyards. I know in the early days he traded a raft of horses.

ROBIN BURWASH was raised at Airdrie, Alberta. In fact, his mother, Vi, resides only a mile from our place. For several years, Robin worked for the Alberta Stock Yards in the fall of the year during the rodeo slack season.

Robin is one of Canada's most famous rodeo personalities. He has been the Canadian Bareback Riding Champion four times. He went to the National Finals in Las Vegas a number of times. Twice he was reserve World Champion Bareback Rider. Twice he won the $50,000 prize money at the Calgary Stampede. Robin hung up his bareback riggin' at the end of 1994. I am sure Robin is going to be inducted into the Rodeo Hall of Fame one of these days.

These days Robin and his wife and daughter reside at Okotoks, Alberta, where they raise cattle.

Calgary Stampede, 1989. Robin Burwash spurs Guilty Cat to a showdown-winning ride for $50,000 in the bareback event.

ARCHIE BUSHFIELD had a place on the north side of Calgary. Now, there is a golf course where his original buildings used to be. There are a lot of Bushfields residing just north of Calgary and around the Balzac area. Archie spent a lot of time at the Yards. We bought quite a few cattle for him. Several other people did as well. He is not hurting too much financially. I think the cattle are just sort of a pastime or tax shelter—maybe both. He loves auction sales and does not miss too many. Archie was a pretty fair saddle bronc rider in his day.

DORA BUTCHER worked in the office for Bridgewater Livestock. She was there when I joined the firm. Dora was very meticulous in her appearance and work. She would turn the office upside down in order to discover how come she was out a penny when she balanced the books at the end of the month. Of course, she always put the office back in order. There was no "almost right"; it had to be 100 percent correct. Dora married a chap by the name of Stan Butcher. I think they still reside somewhere in the south side of Calgary.

KENT BUTTERFIELD comes from the famous rodeo family at Ponoka, Alberta. His dad, his uncles, and his cousins are all top hands in the rodeo business. Kent, or "Fingers" as he was known at the Yards, was a good calf roper himself. He worked for J. C. Wheatcroft for several years. He is quiet and likeable. At the present time, Kent and his brother own a ranch at Big Valley.

LEROY "ROY" BUTTS came from Wainwright, Alberta. He was the nightman at Burns for several years. When Clayton Williams passed away, Roy took his place. Roy's job consisted of doing the basic bookwork in the cattle scalehouse. He also weighed cattle and sometimes bought cattle right off the trucks arriving at the plant. He stayed with Burns till they closed shop at their Calgary plant, at which point, he retired. Roy often enjoyed talking about his family. He also composed songs and wrote music. He had his own little band as well, and they played at a lot of parties and dances. Also, Roy has attended more funerals than any person I have ever met. He now resides in Bowness, which is now part of Calgary.

RONNIE BYERS worked for Parslow & Denoon for many years. He was a good judge of cattle and liked being in the business. He used to trade a few cattle on the side. He often took calves over to the MacLean Auction, which was located in East Calgary and often referred to as the little "World's Fair." A sale was held there every Saturday. At one time, Ronnie had a drinking problem. (This was not unusual at the Stockyards.) Finally, he quit completely, like a lot of others did. He left the Stockyards a number of years ago. He bought a place not too far from Lloydminster, where he still operates today.

BILL BYMA came from Holland in the early 1950s. Bill knows cattle well. When he first arrived, he worked for Bob Smolkin's Nose Creek Feedlot. After several years, he went to work for Jack Leavitt at Hubalta in East Calgary. He stayed there quite a while and really learned the business. Then he rented a place southeast of Shepard where he started to feed cattle on his own. This often brought him to the Stockyards. He sometimes went to Edmonton to purchase cattle as well. Occasionally, he bought cattle from his neighbours for Burns. Eventually, Bill bought a place at Carseland where he continued to feed cattle. He fed cattle for us on several occasions. Later on, he relocated and built a nice house and feedlot west of Carseland. Some years later he sold out because all their children had grown up and gone. My hat is off to Bill and his wife, Tina. They raised a good family, and they are all doing well. Bill also served as councillor for Wheatland County.

JIM CALDER came to Calgary from Regina where he had worked for the Saskatchewan Wheat Pool in the cattle division. He worked for the Alberta Stock Yards. He was a tall thin man who knew his job. Every once in a while, he would get into the rum. (He loved rum.) I have lost track of Jim.

JIM CAMMAERT grew up in Rockyford, Alberta. The Cammaerts were longtime Shorthorn breeders. Jim worked for P&M at the Yards for some time. He was a bit of a daredevil. I have seen him run on the backs of a bunch of cattle crowded in the ring. Sometimes he rode a cow into the sale ring. If there was a prize for the most improved calves in the last ten-year period, Jim would stand a good chance of winning. He went from the bottom end of the scale to the top end. His calves today (1995) are some of the best in the country. Jim was a good bareback bronc rider, until he got seriously hurt in an industrial accident. Today, he is involved with some kind of show and movie promotion business. I understand he is doing well in this venture. That little "goatee" of his and the way he dresses makes him look like the great showman from another era, Buffalo Bill Cody. I enjoy visiting with Jim. He is always upbeat.

BOB CAMPBELL went to work as a young man for Tom Farrell, who was the manager of Burns Ranches. Bob stayed there till his retirement. He was the manager of Burns Ranches Feedlot in Bonnybrook, south of the Stockyards. It was the largest feedlot in Alberta till about the mid-60s. For many years, Burns Ranches shipped from 100 to 200 fat steers every Monday morning. Bob always sold them through the Alberta Livestock Co-op in Calgary. Burns Ranches fed a lot of good British cattle as well as a large number of Holstein steers. The Holsteins came from markets like Edmonton, Prince Albert, or Saskatoon. Calgary never was a big market for selling Holstein feeder steers although, from time to time, some would show up. Bob and his wife have retired to Carstairs.

JOHN CAMPBELL never did handle or feed a lot of cattle, but, for years, he often came to the market. I think he liked rubbing shoulders with cattle people. He was also in the real-estate business. I suppose being at the Yards gave him the opportunity to contact people about real estate. John lives on a neat little place just north of Calgary off the Symons Valley Road. I once sold him a manure spreader.

DARYL CARLSON is from Pincher Creek, Alberta. He still ranches there. For many years, Daryl was the secretary-manager of The Western Stock Growers' Association. They had an office in the Exchange Building. Daryl is a good-natured person, easy to get along with.

ED CARR, along with a partner, bought out Eamor Trucking. Their office was right across the hall from our office in the Livestock Exchange Building. We gave them a lot of business. Ed was the office manager and dispatcher. When things were slack, he often strolled into our office for a visit. He was a chain smoker—I never saw him without a cigarette in his mouth. Unfortunately, this finally claimed his life. Ed was a good man to do business with.

TIM CARROLL was a friendly person. I really don't know much about Tim's background. I first became aware of him when he was running the J.C. Wheatcroft Feedlot, just south of Midnapore on the west side of Highway 2. After Tim left Wheatcroft, he went to work for the Alberta Stock Yards. He was a reliable employee, who always did his job well.

DR. GARY CARTER was a veterinarian with the federal government. He had a place south of Calgary just east of the Okotoks turnoff. The Mestons own it today. Gary was a genuinely nice person. He always tried to accommodate you no matter what the situation. Gary had a fairly severe case of sugar diabetes. I am not sure where he is these days.

JOE CASEY, or "Windy Joe" as he was sometimes called, was a real live character. He came from the Maritimes as a young man and had a small place south of the Ogden district. He used to feed a few cattle. According to Joe, they were always the best no matter what their quality.

Dale Christiansen said to me one day: "Did you ever see Joe's place?"

I said, "No, I haven't."

"It's worthwhile seeing," Dale said. "If you fly over it in a small plane, it looks like somebody flew over it with a big plane, about three thousand feet up, loaded with every type of junk imaginable, then opened up the hatch and let it fall, scattering it all over the place."

Regardless of Joe's ways, he could help pass the time of day when he sat beside you in the sale ring. He also had sulky racehorses. Although I did not follow the sport too closely, I think he did come up with a few winners.

Joe passed away a number of years ago.

JIM "DEAK" CASSIDY was a cattle buyer for Canada Packers. He also worked for one or two commission firms at the Yards. He was a good hockey player and a true sportsman. Deak was named Calgary's "Sportsman of the Year" in 1984 by the Calgary Booster Club. He and his wife, Marjorie, reside in northwest Calgary.

PAT CASSIDY was raised in East Calgary. He was a hog and lamb buyer for Canada Packers. He also bought some cattle. Pat was a friendly sort. He developed a debilitating disease some years after he left CP. I'm not sure what eventually happened to him.

BILL CHESNEY was a brand inspector for a number of years. Bill was a very tall and lean man, who went about his business very matter-of-factly. I think Bill came to Calgary from the Medicine Hat area. His son, Bill Jr., is a fieldman for Bow Slope at Brooks. Bill Sr. passed away some years ago.

GEORGE CHESSOR was a government grader at the Yards for years. I think he came from the Lacombe district. I do know he is the uncle of Bruce and Murray Flewelling. George was a fine man and did a good job as a grader. He loved to play pinochle. He was transferred to Lethbridge a number of years ago. He retired from the government and still lives in Lethbridge.

JOE CHESTER came from Winnipeg, Manitoba. He worked for Canada Packers. Joe's name used to be Joe Chicowski but he changed it to Chester. In those days, Canada Packers liked to have a very Anglo-Saxon image, not like today, when names are really quite irrelevant. Joe was always known as "Chic." He was a teller of tall tales and was a wild man. His eyes always looked like he had had a rough time the night before. Chic, like most people, had a good side to him. He was a very aggressive buyer. He went back to Winnipeg for his vacation one summer and, while either going there or coming back, he died in a car crash.

A. J. E. (ARTHUR) CHILD is the Chief Executive Officer for Burns Foods (1985) Limited. He was never around the Calgary Stockyards, but he sure was very much in evidence around Burns.

Formerly, Mr. Child was a vice president at Canada Packers in Toronto. From there he went to Saskatoon where he was the president of Intercontinental Packers. When the opportunity presented itself in 1966, he came to Calgary to take over Burns Foods, which was floundering very badly at the time.

It did not take Mr. Child very long to turn the fortunes of Burns in a profitable, positive direction. He is a very intelligent, disciplined, hardworking man and he expects the same from his employees.

I had left Burns in 1967 to join the Bridgewater organization. Three years later, in 1970, Mr. Child made a very generous deal with me to come back to Burns. So, I went back to Burns as Calgary livestock manager; however, I still retained my interest in Bridgewater Livestock.

A. J. E. Child

After several years, Mr. Child and a few of his key people moved uptown to Burns' new corporate offices. Shortly thereafter, I was appointed general livestock manager for all Burns' plants in Canada. John Nielsen was Burns' vice president, and he moved into Mr. Child's former office.

I did enjoy the head office. But, in March of 1974, I decided to resign to completely take over the order buying division of Bridgewater Livestock. I made it part of the Leonard Friesen Cattle & Properties Ltd., a company which I incorporated back in 1967.

I flew with Mr. Child on Burns' corporate jet on several occasions. I must say, I enjoyed our conversations. He is not only a good businessman, he is also well versed in all areas of life. He reads a lot. At the age of 85, Mr. Child is still going strong at the corporate office. A lot of restructuring has taken place around Burns since I left in 1974.

EION CHISHOLM is well known in the cattle industry. He was the founder of Western Feedlots, is a past president of The Western Stock Growers' Association, and has had many other involvements concerning the cattle business. I first got to know Eion when he was the secretary-manager of The Western Stock Growers' Association. They had their office in the Livestock Exchange Building.

Eion and a few friends of his started a little feedlot along the Bow River west of Bowness called Pyramid Feeders. I was working for Burns at the time and purchased some cattle from them. Later, Eion and a group, including the McKinnons, Cec Barber and others, built a feedlot at Strathmore called Western Feedlots. They also have a lot at High River. Over the years, we bought cattle for Eion, bought cattle from Eion, and fed thousands of cattle in their feedlots. Eion was the manager and he assembled a good crew. I can't mention all of them, but a few that were and have been there a long time are: Bill Hartall, cattle manager, cattle judge and all-around PR man; Ray Wegner; Dale Cockx; and Ralph Sietz. Dave Plett is the present manager of Western. Eion is still on the Board of Directors.

Eion still order buys cattle for some of his friends and feeds cattle for himself. He is a credit to the cattle industry. He is 100 percent honest in all his dealings. He was inducted into the Agriculture Hall of Fame in Alberta in 1993. He lives at Okotoks.

DALE CHRISTIANSEN lives at Carseland, Alberta, where he was born. He was at the Stockyards for a number of years. He worked for the Health of Animals Division. The Christiansens raise good cattle and have always supported the Calgary market.

Dale was also a top-notch bareback bronc rider until he injured his arm and had to give it up. He married a girl from Wheatland, Wyoming. He met her when he was going to college down there. My wife and I usually stop at Wheatland for a night or sometimes lunch at Vimbo's Restaurant on our way to our ranch in Colorado. While there, I'm always reminded of the Christiansens.

Dale told me a funny story that happened to him one day. He and his future wife and several other people were heading to a rodeo in Fort Collins, Colorado. They were a little behind schedule. Dale came to a red traffic light and looked both ways—no cars coming, so he sailed through. The same with the next red light, but, sure enough, there was a patrolman around the corner. He pulled Dale over, walked up to his window and said, "Didn't you notice the red light you just went through?"

Dale put on his most innocent look and said, "What red light?"

By this time the patrolman got pretty upset and pointed to the lights on the corner and said, "When that light is red, you stop!"

"Oh," Dale said, "I didn't know that. Where I come from in Canada we don't have electricity, so I didn't know what those lights were for." Believe it or not, the cop bought the story. He lectured Dale for about five minutes about driving and traffic lights, then let him go without giving him a ticket.

Dale is very honest; however, he enjoys an odd prank or joke.

Calgary Stampede, 1973. Dale Christiansen aboard Cindy Rocket.

DR. JOHN CHURMKA is the head vet of the Health of Animals Division in Calgary and has been for many years. I think he originated from Brooks, Alberta. He is a very decent and competent person. Everybody likes him. I have had many good chats with him.

BILL COATES came to Calgary from Saskatchewan where he had farmed. He worked for the Alberta Stock Yards for quite a few years. He was what they called the weighmaster at the hog and sheep weigh scale. One time he got badly injured by a bull at the Yards. He recovered, but always had a limp after that. I don't know where Bill went after he left the Yards.

IAN COBURN came from Prince Albert, Saskatchewan, where his dad was an Indian Agent till he got killed. Ian was and still is with the Health of Animals Division. He is a pleasant fellow who seems to enjoy his work. Ian is a good horseman. If you need a horse, look him up. He lives in the Balzac area.

BILL COCHRANE was a crusty Scotsman, who was a sheepman at Burns Calgary. His boss was Mickey Dirrane and they were good buddies. Bill got transferred to Burns Lethbridge where he was both a sheep and cattle buyer. He never got married. Bill could really quote the Bible, but, by all appearances, he did not live by its rules. During the last few years of his life, he suffered a lot because of very bad feet.

FRANKIE COCKX came from Strathmore, Alberta. His dad, Cornie Cockx, bought and traded cattle in the Strathmore area for years. Frankie won the boys' steer riding at the Calgary Stampede in 1957. When he got a little older, he went with Harry Vold and tried his hand at bullfighting. Frankie did this for a while; then decided to take an auctioneer's course. Shortly after that, he appeared at the Calgary Market as a regular auctioneer. He was one of the youngest men to ever auction at the Yards. He was there a long time and did a good job. Then, something happened that happens to a lot of people. He got nipping a little too regularly. In time, he got really ill and partially lost his voice. I am sure Frankie doesn't mind me telling about this, since he is very open about it. Anyway, he got married, and between his new wife and his strong will to quit, he finally beat the problem. It's great to see Frankie back up on the auction stand. His voice isn't quite as strong as it used to be, but he still does a good job.

Frankie took over the Wainwright Market a few years ago. He is still there, doing well.

MASON COCKX is the youngest of the Cockx boys. He came to the Stockyards to work for J. C. Wheatcroft. Mason also did some auctioning at the Yards. After several years, he left the Yards and joined forces with Teske Auctions, where he still is today. In 1967 Mason won the Boys' Steer Riding at the Calgary Stampede—ten years later to the day that his brother, Frank, won the title. Mason got to be a good bareback bronc rider and steer wrestler. He still jumps on a few, but he has hung up his bronc spurs. It is always a pleasure to have a little visit with Mason.

BILL COLLINS came from Stettler, Alberta. He moved to Edmonton and finally to Calgary. When Bill was young, he was a friend of Phil Bischoff's. It was Phil who introduced him to Burns. As a consequence, Bill bought a few cattle in the country from time to time and hauled them to Burns.

Bill was the Canadian Calf Roping Champion four times. He also is one of the best cutting horse people in Canada. He has 12 Open Cutting Horse Championships to his credit. He was inducted into the Canadian Rodeo Cowboy Hall of Fame in November of 1994. He breaks and trains horses and judges lots of horse shows in Canada and the USA.

Bill broke a horse for me once. He said the horse was very cold-backed and hard to break. I believed him, because this horse unloaded several people rather suddenly, including Will Irvine, in the Okotoks arena. We, and many other people from the Yards, have supplied cutting cattle for shows where Bill was in charge. These days, Bill operates Rocky Ridge Stables owned by Bill Nilsson.

JACK COLLINS was the accountant at the Burns livestock office. He had been with Burns since back in the days when Pat Burns still played a very active role. Jack was an O.K. guy, but he could get a little cantankerous once in a while. One day he got into an argument with a man from the main office while on the phone. The office was about 500 yards away. Suddenly, the man slammed down the receiver and, a few minutes later, he walked into Jack's office and punched him right on the nose. Jack sprawled backwards on the floor. The pipe he always had in his mouth clattered onto the floor along with his glasses and his dignity. Would you believe, in those days, nothing ever came of an incident like that? It was all in a day's work. Jack retired four or five years after I arrived at Burns.

PAT COLLINS is not related to Bill Collins or Jack Collins. Pat was raised in Calgary. He started to work for Burns about twenty-seven years ago: first, in the office; then, in the livestock department, where he became a cattle buyer. When I went to Burns' head office, he took my place as livestock manager. After several years, Dvorkin Meat Packers made Pat an offer he could not refuse, so he went there as a cattle buyer. He became their head buyer. When Dvorkins closed the plant, Pat went to work for XL Beef as a cattle buyer, where he still is today.

Pat and Will Irvine and my son Lee all worked for me in their early careers. They are all the same age. I am proud to have had a small part in their training as cattlemen. Pat is a real gentleman. He is a credit to the buying profession.

Pat and his wife, Joanne, and their four daughters live northwest of Okotoks where they run a few cows. They also have a team of horses that they hitch to either a wagon or a sleigh so they can enjoy rides from a bygone era.

GARTH COLPITTS is a government grader. He is a very knowledgeable and consistent type of person—someone you can depend on. He is always willing to help or answer any questions regarding the grading system. Lately, he has been involved with the ultrasound reading of fat cover. He is still with the department in Calgary in the uptown office.

MAX COLPITTS is Garth Colpitts' cousin. Max came from New Brunswick as a young person. This may explain why he was a committed liberal. Even when the name liberal was a swear word in the West, Max never wavered; he just did not like Tories. Max was a government grader for many years. I considered him one of the best. He was fast and fair and knew what he was doing. He went from the Calgary Stockyards to XL Beef where he was their head buyer. Max had a mink and fox farm on the side, and when he left XL Beef, he went fur farming full time. I did quite a lot of business with Max. We used to get into some very hot arguments (nearly always political), but we always parted friends.

HUGHIE COLVILLE is a very quiet, good-natured chap who liked to come to the Yards to buy or sell a few cattle. These days, he goes to most of the sales north of Calgary. Hughie is an honest man who would hurt no one.

BOB COMFORT was a cattle dealer from Creston, B.C. He shipped quite a few cattle to Calgary. He always came along and often stayed for two or three days. He liked mixing and visiting with other cattleman. Occasionally, he would purchase some cows to ship back to B.C. He was a very easygoing individual. It was never his goal to corner the market, he plain liked buying and selling cattle. Bob passed on a number of years ago.

KEN COOPER spent his entire working career as an accountant for the Alberta Stock Yards Co., in the Calgary office. He was a quiet, competent individual. He always minded his own business and never made any negative waves. I often talked to him, but I cannot recall any specific incidents that relate to him. He was always well dressed and exuded a gentlemanly image. Ken was one of the nice guys. People enjoyed working with Ken.

WARREN COOPER was known as "The Voice of the Calgary Stampede." He lived at Nanton, Alberta, all his life, where he operated a ranch.

When the auction method of selling cattle first started at the Calgary Stockyards, Warren came down to take his turn as an auctioneer. He did not sell at the Yards for very long; however, he did auction for many years for the community auctions in southern Alberta—including such places as Pincher Creek, Whisky Gap, Pakowki, and Cardston.

I loved to sit and visit with Warren. He had such a dry humour and slow drawl. He took you back in history, which reminded me that, I too, had descended from early pioneer stock. My dad and mother were born at Morris, Manitoba, in 1881 and 1884, respectively. They homesteaded in southwestern Saskatchewan in 1906.

The last time I heard Warren auction was at the Round-up Cattle Show in Calgary in 1977. (I wish I had taped it.) He sold the live carcass steers in the "Calcutta," which supposedly was illegal betting—we could not do it the next year. I remember what Warren said: "We are selling these steers by Quebec rules"—a bit of a slam to La Belle Province, but nobody seemed to mind.

Warren Cooper was truly a son of the West.

DON COPAS was a brand inspector, who hailed from the Stavely country. He was a tall cowboy-type who did his job on a daily basis with very little fanfare. Don knew how to use a rope and ride a horse. I have kind of lost track of him.

GEORGE COPELAND came from Kindersley, Saskatchewan, where he was engaged in farming. After he came to Calgary, he became a brand inspector at the Yards. Several years later, he went to work for Dvorkin Packers as a cattle buyer. George could cover a lot of country in short order. I am not sure how many speeding tickets he got, but he must have had some. At any rate, he got the job done and bought a lot of cattle. When Dvorkins closed shop, George moved to Crossfield, Alberta. Maybe he lived there before they closed, I am not sure. I understand George works for the City of Calgary in the summertime and looks after a skating or curling rink in Crossfield in the wintertime. He likes playing the stock market. Like the rest of us, he wins some and loses some—but, that's the game.

RICHARD COPITHORNE was a rancher who ranched west of Calgary in the Springbank district. He came from pioneer ranching families on both his father's and mother's sides. His mother was a McDougall from Cochrane. Richard spent a lot of time at the Calgary Stockyards. We (Friesen Cattle Co.) used to buy some cattle for him. For the last number of years, he bought the cattle himself. He and his son, Roger, set up a brokerage office in the Livestock Exchange Building sometime in the mid-'80s. It was located right across the hall from our office. They traded in various commodities as well as some stocks. Richard died an untimely death in the fall of 1991.

ROGER COPITHORNE is Richard Copithorne's son. Roger is a soft-spoken young man with high ideals. After he and his dad closed shop at the Stockyards, Roger went to work for Canada Packers in the brokerage division. When Canada Packers phased out their meat-packing operations, he went to work for Midland Walwyn as a stockbroker. I set up an account with him and did a little trading. He left there and I think he is still involved in stocks in some capacity.

TOM COPITHORNE is Richard Copithorne's brother, and Bob McDougall is his uncle. Tom is a free spirit and enjoys life. He owns a ranch west of Calgary. In the mid-'80s, Tom teamed up with Ronnie Ward to start an order-buying business. Their outfit is usually referred to as "C and W." They handle quite a lot of cattle every year. Tom is a good steer wrestler on the pro rodeo circuit. Occasionally, he travels to the USA to compete in some of those big winter rodeos. He has enjoyed good success in the sport.

Tom Copithorne in action.

KEVIN CORNFORTH came from Guelph, Ontario. He was with Hartford Insurance Co. in Saskatchewan for quite some time. When Keith Harrison retired from managing Hartford Insurance in Calgary, Kevin came to take charge. I know Kevin a little bit but not too well; however, the boys tell me he is a super nice guy. He is fair and will help you in any way he can. I hope he sticks around a while longer. Maybe I will get to know him better.

TERRY COURTS was an English chap who worked in the office for the Alberta Stock Yards as a bookkeeper. When we reorganized things in 1981, he became our accountant. Sometime after I left the Company, Terry had a difference of opinion with the new management and they parted company.

LOU COVE worked in P&M's office for many years. She was very efficient. She had a smile and a friendly word for anybody that came into the office. She always had a well-groomed, neat appearance. I hope Lou is enjoying retired life.

MELODY COWPER-SMITH is our daughter. She only worked in our Friesen Cattle Co. office for short periods. Melody has a very outgoing personality. She is everyone's friend. These days, she and her husband, Bruce, and their two teenage children live in Red Deer, Alberta, where Melody is a schoolteacher. She teaches kids that require special help. Bruce heads up a family counselling service called Hope Centre.

We also have another daughter. Her name is Dee. She never really worked at the Yards, but I can't resist telling about the day she was born. It was a Sunday in 1955. Early in the afternoon my wife said she was feeling some contractions. On that particular Sunday, it was my turn to load up a "double-deck" of lambs to ship to Vancouver, so my wife and I got into the car and drove over to the Burns plant. When we got there, her contractions were coming a little closer together. She told me there was still a little time before we would have to go over to the Holy Cross Hospital, which was not far away. Needless to say, I rushed and loaded those lambs in record time. When I got back to the car, it was high time to head for the hospital, which we did, also in record time. Dee was born shortly thereafter. Even to this day my wife sometimes reminds me of the day it was more important for me to supply Vancouver people with fresh lamb than it was to hold her hand and await the arrival of our baby. These days, I would opt for holding her hand. Dee and her husband, Roger, have four lovely children.

MARY CRAIG hailed from Ponoka, Alberta. She started working for J.C. Wheatcroft when she was approximately eighteen years of age. She was an attractive girl with red hair. She drew a fair bit of attention from many of the opposite sex and, over the years, she dated several of them. Mary was very competent and she was a good office manager. She had to be, because Wheatcroft handled a huge volume of cattle in those days. If you knew what you were doing, you did not cross Mary up. She was not bashful to give her opinion of you. As a whole, though, she got along well with people. I never had a skirmish with her.

JO-ANN CROOK is Charlie Kennedy's niece. She worked in P&M's office for many years. She has been working with the Stockyards since 1985. She still does books for Cecil Barber. Jo-Ann is a quiet, soft-spoken person. She is extremely competent, pleasant and easy to get along with. If you phone her about something, she is very polite and accommodating. She always does her best for every customer.

TOM CROW worked for XL Beef for quite some time. From there he went to Western Feedlots in Strathmore. Since the mid-'80s he has been a brand inspector. Tom is a real nice fellow, who always does his best. When he was younger, he was a pretty fair saddle bronc rider. He still participates in wild cow milking competitions. Tom is not very big, but he is all man.

CYRIL CURRAN came from Ireland. He started out in Toronto. From there he went to Lethbridge where he was the head buyer for CDM (Canadian Dressed Meats). Cyril never was a regular at the Calgary market. He blew in every once in a while to stir things up. From Lethbridge he went to Red Deer, where he order bought and traded cattle. For a while, he was involved with his brother, Herb, at the Lacombe market. From Red Deer he went to Veteran, where he ran the Veteran Auction Market. Cyril's career has had its ups and downs and sideways bounces—just like a stray football. I will say this, he knows cattle. It's his overenthusiasm that gets him into trouble. Sometimes, Cyril did a little steer wrestling to work off some energy. Today he is in the insurance business at Carstairs. I know, because we are one of his customers.

DEAN CURRANS, I believe, came from Carstairs, Alberta. If not, I know he was around there for a while. He was a cattle dealer.

Sometime in the late 1950s or early 1960s, he teamed up with Irish Johnston, who operated Producers' Livestock at the time. Dean used to, what we called, "bird dog" cattle in the country and he usually found some. He also worked the sale ring for Irish. Things didn't go too well for them; so, one day, Dean decided to end it all and took his own life. He was found in a stock car behind Burns. One of Burns' men, who did not know him, rushed in and told us about a body in a boxcar. I went out and there was Dean. I can still feel the shock that overtook me when I saw him. One wonders why these things have to happen.

ARCHIE CURRIE was the barn boss at Burns. He loved horses, especially teams. He was one of the men who knew Pat Burns well. I am sure he hitched up many a team for Pat or Pat's driver. Archie retired several years after I came to Burns.

DORIS CUSHNUK worked in AWW's office for many years. She was a very nice lady. She knew her job and did it well. I often visited with her. When AWW closed shop, she went to work for XL Beef in the livestock office. Doris is now retired and I wish her well.

MERV DAHL came from the Spruce View country west of Innisfail, Alberta. He worked for P&D and, later on, for Canada Packers. Merv was a heavyset individual, who liked to party with the boys. He had quite a few buddies he used to hang out with. In the end, it affected his health—sad to say, but the party was over.

NORMAN DALSTRO is a real gentleman. He used to own the Virden Valley Ranch south of Hanna. He always sold his calves at the Calgary market. After he sold the ranch, he came to Calgary as a brand inspector. For quite a few years, he was the head inspector. He recently retired from the job. It was always a pleasure to do business with him. Norman is a top-notch curler. He also loves horse racing, but, I hope, in his retirement, he will concentrate more on curling than on horse racing. Please do not take offence Norman, I'm only kidding.

DON DANARD is the son of the late Don Danard of Edmonton. Don Sr. was well known in livestock circles. He worked for

Lee Williams for years, then started his own commission firm. Don Jr. arrived at the Calgary Stockyards just a few years before the Calgary operation was shut down (in 1989) and moved to Strathmore. He is an excellent businessman. He and Will Irvine, along with their crew, are doing a fine job at Strathmore. Their live receipts are good. They also sell large numbers of cattle on the computer system. I find Don a very congenial person. He is on the quiet side, but he can deliver the goods. Don also has interests in racehorses, some of which win more than just pocket money. Don's wife, Sue, helps out with some of the office work these days.

WALTER DANCOCKS worked for Producers' Livestock at the Yards. In fact, I think he was a partner with Alex Beveridge and Irish Johnston. At any rate, Walter looked after their sheep and hog operation. He always looked a little out of place at the hoghouse. He wore pretty fancy duds. His dress shoes were always polished. He looked more like a car salesman than a hog salesman; and, that's exactly what he did when he left the stockyards, he became a car salesman for Maclin Ford. Walter always felt bad that a beautiful girl like Rita Hayworth married an ugly little European. But, beautiful women marrying ugly men, and handsome men marrying ugly women, is as old as time. Anyway, who knows what beauty is? It is in the eye of the beholder. Walter passed away a number of years ago.

BUD DAVID is either an uncle or a cousin to the two Davids that race chuckwagons. Bud worked at Burns for a long time: first, in the plant; then, in the livestock department gathering and yarding cattle. Sometimes, he worked at the hog scales. Bud was a good-natured character. He loved to wrestle and fool around. One day, he tackled me in the cattle scalehouse. I was about twenty-five years old, weighing approximately 235 pounds. I didn't have the middle I've got today. I was in pretty good shape and maybe I got a little lucky. At any rate, I grabbed him, lifted him up and dropped him, rear-end first into a large garbage barrel. He sank right down with his legs solid on one side and his back on the other and he could not move. It looked kind of comical to see his head and feet sticking out of that barrel. I tipped the barrel over and pulled him out. He was a good sport and did not get mad. After that he gave me a wide berth whenever it came to horseplay.

IAN DAVIDSON was the head buyer at Canada Packers for many years. To some people, he was like Howard Cosell—the man people loved to hate. He was really not all that bad, but he was 100 percent a Canada Packers' man. This often rubbed his competitors the wrong way. I sat beside him in the sale ring for many years. There was not much give to the man. On the other hand, that was his job. Some days Ian would not say ten words; other days he was quite talkative. Danny MacDonald and Ian had more than one skirmish. Ian liked to buy cattle direct in the country. Danny hated that, thus the conflict. When Ian retired, he asked me for a job as a cattle buyer. I had to turn him down, because I didn't think he would fit into our operation. Ian was called "The Duke," a name that Ken Whitley hung on him.

TONY DAVIDSON was a skinny little Irishman who loved to talk about Ireland. For many years, he worked in the livestock department for Burns. Sometimes, it was not too clear just what Tony's job was. One thing was for certain, you could always count on him walking across the catwalk with some papers in his hand. He was some kind of market reporter. I'm not sure if he really knew who he was reporting to. He also billed out the hogs and cattle that we shipped out to other plants, mainly Vancouver. When Tony passed away, I took over his billing-out duties along with my cattle buying.

DOUG DAVIES was a foreman at Burns Ranches for a number of years. When he left Burns Ranches, he came to the Stockyards where he drove a truck for one of the big cattleliner outfits. After a while, he got his own truck. Doug was a super nice guy. It was a pleasure to do business with him. He had very dark whiskers, which he shaved off, but he always had what you would call a "five o'clock shadow." I haven't seen or heard anything about Doug for several years.

BRUCE DAVIS came from Acme, Alberta. He worked with the Health of Animals Division. He had a bit of a bark, but his bite wasn't too serious. He sort of headed up the laymen in the department. Of course, the real head honcho was always a veterinarian.

RAY DAVIS worked in the office for P&M. Once in a blue moon, he would help them in the alley. Ray was a very easygoing sort. I had a lot of visits with him. He had a place south of Calgary on the west side of Highway 2, just a little past the weighscale that used to be there about five or six miles from the city limits. I have often wondered what happened to him.

TED DAVIS is an affable Englishman who lost his accent and sounded just like the average Canadian. He has been involved with the medicine end of the cattle business ever since he came to Calgary. I visited a lot with Ted, but, somehow, I never quite knew what his role was in the medicine business. I know he imported certain products from the USA. He was probably what you could call a distributor. For several years, he was involved with Dr. Bernie Tonkin, who was a vet. I always enjoyed having coffee with Ted. We would discuss almost any topic. He had a wide range of knowledge.

VIC DAVIS worked for the Health of Animals Division. He was an easygoing, big man. For some reason, he developed some serious health problems. I am not sure if it was for health reasons or not, but he moved to the Peace River country. Last I heard, he was still up there.

WAYNE DAYE came from Ontario. He has adopted western ways and culture 100 percent. He looks like he belongs in John Wayne movies. He was with the RCMP for some time. He spent some of that service as a stock detective. He then became a brand inspector at Medicine Hat. From there he was transferred to Calgary as district supervisor, a position he still holds. Wayne, if you happen to read this, please forgive me if I have your career slightly mixed up. I know you were an RCMP officer, but maybe that was after you were a brand inspector at Medicine Hat. Wayne likes horses and riding. That is what built the West. He is easy to visit with and you may do so if you go to any of the markets that operate in his area.

TOMMY DEAKIN was the assistant killing floor foreman at Burns. He used to come down to the livestock department to shoot the breeze with us. He knew, and could do, every job on the killing floor. He was easy to get along with. He worked for Burns forty-nine or fifty years.

STAN DENOON is the son of George Denoon Sr. who came to Calgary from Peterborough, Ontario. In 1915, George Denoon Sr. and Vern Parslow started the livestock commission firm of Parslow & Denoon at the Calgary Stockyards. George Denoon passed away in the fall of 1949. At that point, Stan became a partner with Vern Parslow and his son, Bud Parslow. Parslow & Denoon had a lot of loyal customers, such as Roland and Bill Amery, Tom Mathews, Terry Giles, Dick Havens, plus many others.

Stan is a very honest person. I always found him really fair in all his dealings. He always had a good crew in his employ; one that really stands out in my mind was Vern McRae. I sat beside Vern in the sale ring for at least twelve years.

Stan, along with many others, including me, found the early- and mid-'80s pretty tough going. When Stan left the Stockyards, he and his wife opened up a very successful ice cream and candy store in Bragg Creek. He still does a little cattle business with some of his connections in the USA. Those of you who know Stan should drop in and visit him sometime.

NORMAN DENOON is Stan Denoon's son. I know Norman when I see him; however, I do not know him very well. He sometimes worked for his dad in the summertime. Norman is an intelligent, alert type of person. He went into the oil business and it is my understanding that he has done very well.

GEORGE DENOON JR. is the son of Stan Denoon and a grandson of George Denoon Sr. who was a legend in the cattle business. George Sr. was usually referred to as Father Denoon. George Sr. passed away several months before I arrived at the stockyards, but I heard many stories about him. George Jr. worked for his dad for a number of years. At one point he got involved in a meat market, but, like some of the rest of us, he found the competition a little too tough. He managed a ranch in B.C. for a while. It is my understanding he is working in the oil industry with his brother, Norman. George is a good-natured individual.

KEN DENOON is a son of Billy Denoon and cousin of Stan Denoon. Ken was raised at Nanton where his dad and, later, his brother, Gordon, operated a butcher shop and meat market. Here, Billy Denoon used to hand out free wieners to youngsters. They made the best bacon in Canada. I know, because I bought it quite often from Gordon. They shipped bacon all over the country.

As a young man, Ken came to Calgary to work for Parslow & Denoon. He was a salesman in the old private-treaty days. He then got into dealing and feeding some cattle on his own. He also owned some valuable property where Canyon Meadows is today. He progressed into the real-estate business, setting up an office in the Exchange Building. He continued to feed some cattle.

He and his wife moved to Vernon for several winters. In the end, they decided Calgary had a sunnier climate and stayed here.

DAVID DENOON is the son of Ken Denoon. David is a very pleasant young man. He was never really in the cattle business; however, he did spend some years in his dad's real-estate business, which was located in the Exchange Building. I always enjoyed my conversations with David.

RENNIE DESCHAMPS was born at Val Marie, Saskatchewan. He left there when he was about fourteen or fifteen years of age and came to Alberta to work on ranches. He was employed by Burns Ranches under Tom Farrell in the Brooks area. I think he was the foreman. What I do know is that not too many people crossed Rennie up when he was a young man. Rennie was not to be trifled with, as several people found out.

Rennie was actually a very nice man and got the job done. I dealt with him in trucking for years and found him very accommodating. After he came to Calgary, he went into the trucking business for himself. I think he had only two liners but he hauled a lot of cattle. He did not lose too much time on the road. He really "dangled" with those trucks. It was not unusual for him to travel 75 or 80 miles an hour with an empty truck—and only a little slower when it was loaded.

For the last few years, Rennie has been a little stove up. He was a great friend of Cliff Vandergrift's. He used to buy a few cows for Cliff.

LARRY DESCHAMPS is Rennie Deschamps' son. He was a good trucker, like his dad. Larry is a blond-haired, easygoing young man. I have lost track of him. I am sure he is doing okay.

LEONARD DESMET lives at Strathmore, Alberta. When he was a young fellow he worked for P&M one fall. One day Jimmy Marsh told Leonard and Ronnie Ostrim that he was collecting 25 cents from each employee to keep the boot wash operating. The boys were young, new employees then, so they each gave Jimmy 25 cents. The next week Jimmy told Leonard it was his turn to go collect the 25 cents for the boot wash—so Leonard went collecting. It did not take him long to learn he had been had. Leonard still runs some cows at Strathmore.

RALPH DEVER came to Calgary from Montreal, Quebec. Harry Feldman brought him here as a cow buyer for Rocky Mountain Packers. Harry built that plant and eventually sold it to the McKinnons, who renamed it XL Beef. After Feldman sold out, Ralph went to work for Lakeside Packers where he still is a cow buyer for them. (This company is now owned by Iowa Beef Packers, IBP). He bids on fat cattle at feedlots. I have never really visited much with Ralph. One thing I do know, he is a good cow buyer and does a good job for the Company.

JIM AND KEVIN DICKIE were two Scottish lads who forsook the bonny hills of heather in Scotland to take up residence in the Chinook country of Alberta. They both worked for the Alberta Stock Yards Co. These really nice young men had one small vice—they liked the horse races. Jim was killed in a parachute accident at Beiseker several years ago, and I have lost track of Kevin.

MICKEY DIRRANE, or the "Irishman" as we called him, was the livestock manager at Burns from 1936 to 1956. He hired me in January of 1950 for a three-month try out. I stayed for a span of twenty-four years. I learned about the cattle business from many people. In my opinion, I learned the most from Mickey. He really knew cattle and how to handle them.

Mickey had a big following. He had a large number of people who bought and shipped cattle to Burns. One was Augie Sauer.

Augie would run a lot of cattle on cover-crop in southern Alberta. They all ended up at Burns. He used to operate out of Calgary, then he moved to Medicine Hat. Some of Mickey's other followers were: Andy Goun, Claresholm; the Burtons, Claresholm; the Streeters, Stavely; Bert Uttley, Big Valley; Teddy Gardiner, Stettler; Phil Bischoff, Stettler; and Johnny Wilson, Jr., Innisfail.

Then there were the shipping associations: Bow Slope, headed up by Carl Anderson; Mountain View Co-op, up the north line and headed up by a chap named Esperson; the Blindman Valley Co-op; and many others.

These cattle, hogs and sheep arrived by rail—some from as close to Calgary as Crossfield. It was common for us to unload whole train loads of cattle and hogs and some sheep. We slaughtered a lot of them at the Calgary plant, but many of them were shipped to our other plants, especially Vancouver, which relied almost entirely on livestock shipped from Alberta. The train always had to make several "spots," since there were not enough chutes to unload the whole train at the same time. Mickey presided over the whole operation.

Mickey had a drinking problem. That is putting it bluntly, but it was a fact. He would be okay for a long time, then "bingo" he would fall off the wagon. When he was sober, he was a great guy, but beware when the drinking binge took over. He would fire people, then hire them back when he sobered up. I got fired once. It only lasted about five minutes. Here is what happened: There was an old Scotsman who looked after the sheep at Burns. One day, old Pete said to me, "Do you want a newborn lamb?" (We lived on an acreage out by the Calgary Airport.)

I said, "Sure." The lamb had no value as its mother, along with some other old ewes, was destined for slaughter. To this day I do not know for sure who told Mickey, although I have a pretty good idea.

Mickey asked me, "Did you take a lamb home yesterday?"

I said, "Yes, I did."

"Who told you, you could have it?"

"Pete Murry . . . because it was of no value to Burns, it would just die."

Mickey kind of glared at me and said, "Pete is not in charge here, I am. You are fired!" (He was quite drunk.)

"O.K.," I said to him, "If that's how you feel, I guess I am finished."

A few more things were said and Mickey suddenly realized how foolish the whole thing was, so he said to me, "Oh, forget it, you can stay." (The lamb became a real pet to our two little boys.)

Not long after this incident, my dad dropped over to Burns for a visit. He was talking with Mickey. I was a little distance away. I overheard Mickey say to my dad, "Mr. Friesen, you sure raised a good son." (He was sober.)

In 1956 Mickey took his own life. He slid into the Bow River when it was in flood. I will never forget Mickey. He taught me a lot of valuable things about the cattle business. It is a real shame that, over the years, liquor has decimated a lot of good men.

DICK DIRRANE is Mickey Dirrane's brother. Dick worked at Burns for a number of years. Maybe I used the word "work" loosely. He was just the opposite to his brother Mickey. Dick was allergic to work. He would much sooner sit and visit. He liked to tell stories about when he was in the Army. After work he always hoisted a few at the Shamrock Hotel.

TOM DOHERTY was a CPR inspector. He was a tall, skinny man. He was always very well dressed. One day, we heard Tom had passed away. You can imagine the surprised look on our faces when he walked into our office the next day. False rumour! I am not sure what happened to Tom after he retired.

LAWRENCE DUFFIN came to Calgary from Delburne, Alberta. He was a yardman and rookie cattle buyer at Burns in the early '60s. I always liked Lawrence and kind of took him under my wing. I didn't really do that much for him, but I always tried to encourage him. When Sims built a cattle killing plant in Red Deer, Lawrence saw an opportunity to work for them. He asked me what I thought he should do. I said to him, "You are young and have a little experience, why not take a shot and take the job." He did.

Several years later, Intercontinental Packers Limited bought out the Sims plant. Lawrence stayed on with them as a cattle buyer. After a while, they transferred him to their Regina plant where he was the head buyer. While he was in Regina, I order bought quite a few cattle for him. After Lawrence left Intercontinental, I hired him back on a part-time basis. He bought fat cattle for Burns and feeder cattle for his own customers. When Burns closed the Calgary plant, Lawrence went completely on his own. He is doing very well. I always enjoy a visit with him whenever I meet him.

BILL DUGGAN worked for the Alberta Livestock Co-op for many years. In his youth he chauffeured Pat Burns and Charlie Duggan (a partner of Pat Burns) around the country. Charlie was Bill's uncle. Burns owned about ten ranches; some of them were big: the Bar U, the C.K., the Flying E, the Reid Ranch, the Bow Valley, and quite a few others. This job gave Bill a chance to see a lot of country and a lot of cattle. Bill was a good market analyst for the Co-op. He knew every man, woman, child and their dog. People did listen to what he had to say about their cattle marketing strategy. When Bill was sober, he was a real gentleman; but, sometimes, he had a little problem with liquor. At those times, he could get difficult. Bill is still with us, and I do not wish to embarrass him. He really is a good man. Bill is a devout Catholic. He and his wife raised a good family. Their son is a priest.

JOE DUGGAN lives at Camrose, Alberta. He is Bill Duggan's cousin. Joe handled a lot of cattle. A big percentage of those cattle ended up at the Calgary Stockyards. He always shipped to P&M. Frequently Joe shipped four or five liner loads of cattle to the market each week. He owned about a half a dozen cattleliners. Joe loved race horses. He owned a number of them and did very well with them. Joe liked to party, so whenever he hit the Yards, which he did for ten years (late '50s to late '60s), the party was on. Joe is a good-natured person. I am sure he is still enjoying life.

WILF DUNSMORE was the head grader for the government when I arrived in Calgary. I remember him as a very austere man with his clipped mustache and erect posture. He looked more like an army general than a government grader. One thing about Wilf, he was a very fair man and made sure the graders under him did a good job.

BILL DURNO was a horse dealer and auctioneer. He sold at the Calgary Bull Sale for many years. By today's standards, he would not be rated very high, but in his day he did a decent job. Bill was very foul-mouthed. I know people who knew him when they were kids forty years ago. They still remember his cussing.

ED DUVALL was a slender little man who worked for Union Packing. After they shut down the plant, he went to work for the Alberta Livestock Co-op. He assisted Ook McRae with the hogs and sheep. I am not sure what color his wife's hair was, but I do remember Ed saying he liked women with black hair much better than those with brown, red or blonde. Ed also said that, in his garden and lawn, there was not one single weed, not even quack grass. If he had been with us here west of Airdrie, I think the quack grass would have got the best of him. It's like hair on a dog's back on our place.

DAVID "DAVEY" DVORKIN was a free-spirit type all his life—he loved to party, he loved the ladies, and he loved to gamble. I knew Davey very well. I sat next to him in the sale ring for years. He would arrive in the morning sometimes looking pretty jaded. I'd say, "What happened, Dave?" He would give me that mournful look and say, "I blew my brains out last night." What he meant was, he'd lost a lot of money gambling—and gamble he did—be it poker, craps, horse racing (usually through a bookie) as well as most of the sporting events in Canada and the USA. He must have won sometimes; however, he didn't say much about that. But, he sure told the whole world about his losses.

Davey liked to sing. I think he learned that talent in the Synagogue as a young boy. He was nine or ten years old when they came to Canada from Russia. He had no accent. One "ditty" that he often sang went something like this: "If the rain makes the flowers so beautiful, why don't it rain on you?" Plus many others. Sometimes, when someone had just told a story or a joke, Davey would say to them: "You should be on the stage." Then, after a brief pause, he would add: "The first stage out of town."

For years Dave and his brother Harry Dvorkin bought cattle, which they had custom killed. Then, they sold the meat around the City. Sometime in the 1960s, they built their own plant south of the Calgary Stockyards. Here they developed a large business, which did quite well over the years.

Once, Davey broke his arm and it was in a cast. He was quite superstitious and did not want anybody to autograph it, as is often done. One day, he dozed off at the sale ring. On an impulse, I signed "Jane Fonda" on his cast. After a while, he woke up and glanced down and saw what I had written. Well, he really exploded. He didn't give me a chance to say anything. The next day, he would not talk to me; in fact, he completely ignored me for three months.

One day I noticed Davey sitting alone in the cafe, so I went over to him and said, "Davey, I am sincerely sorry for writing on your cast. I didn't know it would bother you that much." He grabbed me and tears welled up in his eyes. He said, "I accept your apology, Texas." He always called me "Texas." (He said I was big, big.) After that, everything was back to normal again.

Another time, I came into the cafe in the morning when Dave was having breakfast, bacon and eggs. I said to him, "Davey, you are not supposed to eat pork." He looked me right in the eye and said, "This is not pork; this is bacon."

We had a condo in Phoenix, and, one winter, Dave rented a condo right close to ours. We moved in different social circles; however, we often met him and his lady friend at the swimming pool.

One day, we invited Dave in for breakfast. I think she was sleeping in. At any rate, he was there alone visiting with my wife and me. We got to talking about the Bible. Dave said he believed the Old Testament, but not the New Testament. So, I got out a Bible and proceeded to read excerpts from the New Testament as they related to the Old Testament. Dave became very interested. We must have talked and read in the Bible for over an hour. You see, the Jewish people do not believe that Jesus was the promised Messiah. They are still waiting for Him to come. I don't think we changed his belief, but we sure got him thinking.

I often thought the boys at the Stockyards would have found it hard to believe that Dave Dvorkin and I examined the Bible together. The last time I saw Davey, he was not very well. Nobody around the Stockyards will ever forget Davey Dvorkin.

HARRY DVORKIN was Dave Dvorkin's brother. Harry was a solid citizen and a good businessman. He did not have too many of Davey's wayward ways. After Harry and Dave built their packing plant, things really got rolling. They had some good people working for them such as Johnny Robinson, (who supervised the construction and the initial operation of the plant), Harry's son Norman, Larry Farrell, and many others. Harry was not afraid of work. When they first started out, he would give his men a hand in the beef coolers in the mornings, as well as sell beef, then go buy cattle. By 4 p.m., he was back at the plant doing whatever needed doing. After he got things organized and had hired some good key people, he backed off a little. During the last few years of his life, he, more or less, just looked after the purchasing of cattle, which is a big key to any plant's success. Harry died a relatively young man.

BARNEY DVORKIN is Harry Dvorkin's son. Barney worked at the family packing plant. I am sure he did a good job. After hours, he was a song-and-dance man, much like his Uncle Dave. Barney always appeared to be happy, as though he did not have a care in the world. I heard he is quite a family man these days.

NORMAN DVORKIN is also a son of Harry Dvorkin's. Norman is a very aggressive individual. When he was fourteen years old, he used to buy and sell hogs and calves at the MacLean Auction Market on Saturdays. As soon as Norman finished school, he went to work at his dad's and uncle's packing plant. It did not take long till he was in charge of selling beef. Norman was considered one of the best beef salesmen in the industry. After his dad passed away, he took over the operation. I had no way of knowing, but it was pretty obvious the Dvorkins were making a lot of money. They ran a very efficient operation.

One day, Norman phoned me. "Leonard," he said, "we have just too many cattle bought. Would you like to take over 200 steers, east of Carstairs?" He went on to say, Davey would run me up there to have a look at them. Soon, Davey showed up in his new Lincoln and away we went. This was about the middle of February. It was a mild day, but there was still a lot of snow around.

We were about a quarter of a mile from the place when we got hopelessly stuck in a snowdrift. Of course, we had no shovel, so I walked up to the buildings, but there was nobody home. I spied a big tractor sitting in the yard. I walked over to it and climbed into the cab. The keys were in the ignition. There was even a logging chain on the floor. I am not much of a machine man, but we needed a pull out of the drift so I thought I would give it a try. The tractor started immediately and, after fiddling around with the gear shift, I got it moving. Away I went to pull Davey out.

I attached the chain to what I thought was a good solid place. I then proceeded to pull Davey out. I pulled him out all right, but, unfortunately, a large portion of the frontend parted company with the rest of the car. I felt awful, but Davey didn't seem to mind. He was glad to be out. (He must have had insurance coverage.) On the way home, all he talked about was how fantastic I was because I knew how to start that big tractor and "pulled him out." Incidentally, I bought the steers. They were good Char-crosses. The market moved up and we made a little money on them. Norman is still in Calgary, and I am sure he is still involved in some business ventures.

HYMIE DVORKIN, Sol, Tony and Yale Dvorkin were brothers. Hymie was Harry's and Dave Dvorkin's uncle. Hymie had been a cattle dealer at the Stockyards ever since he first came to Canada from Russia in about 1928. He worked in the Burns plant for a short period. He soon decided it was easier to handle live cattle than dead ones. He said he sold some cattle to Pat Burns personally, which was quite unusual, since Pat Burns had turned over the purchasing of cattle to a man by the name of Billy Bannister in about 1910.

Often, Hymie told me about the horror of communism when they took over in Russia. He said he saw lots of bloodshed. He was very happy to come to Canada.

When I first came to the Yards in January 1950, there were about 25 or 30 Jewish cattle dealers at the Yards. Hymie was the last of this group. He was around the Yards for well over fifty years. Not too many of the young Jewish men took up the centuries' old tradition of trading cattle. They became doctors, lawyers, hotel owners, and the like.

SOL DVORKIN was also a cattle dealer. I did not know him very well. He passed away many years ago.

TONY DVORKIN was a fairly tall, slender man. He, too, was a cattle dealer. I had a lot of conversations with him. He was a levelheaded man and didn't get nearly as excited as brother Hymie did when his cattle made or lost money. Tony passed away many years ago.

MORTON DVORKIN was Tony Dvorkin's son. Morton also was a cattle dealer. For years, he bought big bunches of cattle out in the country and sold them through Parslow & Denoon. It was not unusual for Morton to bring in several hundred head at a time. As more auction markets were built in the country areas, the country buying got less and less. Finally, Morton quit the country buying and went to work as a cattle buyer for Dvorkin Packers. He continued to feed some cattle, I think mostly for tax reasons. Believe it or not, I bought quite a few feeder cattle for both Morton and Hymie. Morton passed away quite suddenly.

YALE DVORKIN, like his three brothers (Hymie, Sol, and Tony), was a cattle trader. He was small in stature. He did not operate on a large scale; however, he was one of the last Jewish dealers at the Yards. He was there nearly every day. He took life as it came.

RAY EAGLESTON was born and raised in Calgary, Alberta. He worked for the Alberta Stock Yards most of his life. He is a good-natured type of person. Maybe that's because he never married. Ray was what we called a weighmaster. In other words, he weighed the cattle after they were sold. As far as I know, Ray still lives in Calgary.

REG EALS was an old-time horse dealer. He was a little hard to understand when he talked. I think it was an English accent. It always sounded like he had his mouth full of marbles. Reg liked big draft horses. He also took an odd nip, which did not improve his speech. Reg was a good friend of Sonny Gray's. Sonny knew him from the time when Sonny was a kid in East Calgary.

GEORGE EAMOR came to Calgary from Vulcan, Alberta. He was one of the first people to have a cattleliner in the province. He was a very aggressive individual and wasn't bashful when it came to soliciting business. Eventually, he owned 13 cattleliners. They were small compared to the pots and triple-axle rigs that we have these days; however, they were a big step up from the "body-jobs" common in those days. George ran a good outfit. He had some excellent drivers. He sold out to Ed Carr and Associates. Not long after that, he passed away.

DR. BRIAN EDGE is the son of Irene and the late Dave Edge. The Edges are pioneer ranchers in the Cochrane area. Brian is carrying on the ranching tradition. He raises some of the best commercial cattle in the country. His heifers are in big demand for replacements. Brian was a vet at the Yards in Calgary for many years. Now, he's at the Yards in Strathmore. A few years ago, when we were operating in a big way, Brian did most of our work. He tested thousands of our cattle that were going to the USA. He also preg checked our cows. Brian also does a lot of work at Stampede Park as well as at the Calgary Bull Sale. He is also a good horse vet.

DON EDGE is not related to Dr. Brian Edge. Don was a brand inspector at the Yards for a few years. He ranches a few miles northwest of Cochrane. He raises a few buffalo.

Don Edge in the steer decorating event at the Calgary Stampede, 1956.

Don is involved in quite a few community affairs. He is one of the people who helped organize the Pine Slopes Ranchers' cattle sale at Water Valley. He was also a councillor for the Municipal District of Rocky View No. 44 for nine years.

It's always a pleasure to visit with Don. He has lots of friends. Like all good cattlemen, he has an opinion on most subjects. He also likes rodeo. His specialties were steer decorating and steer wrestling. He continued to wrestle steers at the odd old-timer rodeo until he was fifty.

Don's wife, Dorothy, typed this book on her computer. I do not want to embarrass her, but I find her very pleasant to work with. Both Don and Dorothy are very hospitable people. We see them quite often these days and it's a pleasure.

Don's brother Norman was a good bull rider. He ranches, judges some rodeos, and works with the movies. Their sister Edith also ranches. She was the Calgary Stampede Queen in 1953. Frank, the youngest of the Edge family, moved to the USA many years ago.

LYNN EDGE is a son of Norman and Claudia Edge and a cousin of Dr. Brian Edge. Lynn is not related to Don and Norman Edge. Lynn was a friend of Norman Denoon's. Lynn only worked at Parslow & Denoon for a few summers. Lynn's brother Barry is a good calf roper. Barry went to the Canadian Finals several times. Their dad has many trophy saddles plus other trophies. He won several bull and bronc riding titles at the Calgary Stampede in the late 1920s and early 1930s. I have lost track of Lynn. He was a bright young man, so I am sure he is doing okay.

RUSTY EDWARDS was born and raised in Winnipeg, Manitoba. He was a cattle buyer at the Burns plant in Winnipeg. He was transferred to Edmonton where he was the head buyer for Burns. In the early 1960s, he was transferred to Calgary where he became the general livestock manager. He had ten plants under his jurisdiction. After about seven or eight years, he was transferred back to Edmonton. Rusty retired in 1970. Shortly thereafter, I became the general livestock manager for Burns. At one time, Rusty was a top-notch baseball player—not quite major league—but very good. He was an interesting person. He was the type of man you either liked or didn't. I did not always agree with Rusty; but, in the end, I always got along with him. He passed away a number of years ago.

ART EDWARDS is Rusty Edwards's son. Art was born and raised in Edmonton. He worked for Burns Calgary as a rookie cattle buyer. He was transferred to Burns Edmonton as a cattle buyer. When the Edmonton plant closed, Art moved to Saskatchewan to manage a feedlot. I think he is still in Saskatchewan. Art is married to Charlie Monroe's daughter, Kathy.

GUY ELLIOT was raised in the Calgary area. He is Bruce Flewelling's stepson. Guy started to work at the Stockyards in Calgary. He is still with them in Strathmore. I have talked to Guy a few times, but I really do not know him very well.

CARMAN ELLIS lived in the Calgary area all his life. He farmed for years in the Chestermere Lake district. He was related to another pioneer family in the area, the McElroys. Carman was a good businessman. He always arrived at the Yards in a big shiny car. He nearly always smoked a cigar. He liked to buy good cattle just like the McElroys did. They always bought the best. Carman owned several sections of grass, south of the Spy Hill Jail on Calgary's north side. He bought the land from Burns Ranches. It used to be part of the C.K. Ranch. In the early '60s, we leased two sections of grass from him. Our cattle did very well on that good native grass. In the mid-60s, he built a nice house on his ranch. In 1962, he offered to sell those two sections of grass to us for $300 per acre. We did not buy them. Today it's worth about $50,000 an acre. Carman moved to Calgary several years ago and lived there until he passed away.

CECIL EMBREE lived at Hanna, Alberta. He was what could be termed as an old-time cattle dealer. He liked to buy, sell, and trade anything that moved. He often came to the Stockyards, which was part of his trading territory. Cecil liked to get into poker games with the boys. He wore diamond rings and good clothes. For many years, we lived next door to his son, Cliff. Cliff was in the trucking business. Cecil's grandson, Rod, was a disc jockey for several different radio stations, including CFAC.

MORRIS ERICKSON was a brand inspector. He came to Calgary from Saskatchewan. Morris is what I would call a good guy. He is quite a horse breaker and trainer. Even as a brand inspector, he did this as a sideline. Morris is now retired, but I think he still works with horses in the Airdrie area.

DON EVANS was born and raised just north of Calgary and west of Balzac. The Evans family are old-timers in this area. They were some of the first people to grain-feed cattle. Don is an order buyer on the market. He also feeds quite a few cattle. I still remember Don as a young boy. He used to come to the market with his dad, Jack. His uncles, Buster and Doug, were there quite often as well. The Evans family has always been very involved with 4-H beef clubs. Don and his brother, Harold, and their sister always showed good cattle. Now, Don's and Harold's children are showing 4-H steers. Over the years, the Evans family has won many ribbons in 4-H competitions. A number of them have had grand champions. Don is also involved with the Calgary Feeders' Association. He is a good operator. As for his dad, Jack, they do not come much better.

DR. JACK EVANS is not related to the Balzac Evanses. "Doc," as we called him, was the head government veterinarian at the Burns plant in Calgary for years. I spent a lot of time visiting with him. He was very soft-spoken, but a great story teller. He was tough, but fair in all his dealings. As often happens, the good die young. Doc Evans was not very old when he died of a heart attack.

RUDY EVENSON originally came from Saskatchewan. Rudy was a brand inspector for many years. When Harry McWilson got promoted to regional supervisor, Rudy took over as the headman at the Yards. He could be sticky, but I always found him fair. In fact, I got along real well with him. Rudy used to rope calves. He made some very respectable runs. I saw him rope many times. Now that he has retired, he still team ropes, often with his wife or father-in-law, Bob Winthrop. Rudy and his wife live at Millarville.

TOM FARRELL, or "Tommy" as he was usually called, was a nephew of Pat Burns. Tom went to work for his Uncle Pat as a young man. After gaining some experience around the plant and the livestock department, he was promoted to manager of Burns Ranches. Tom could be tough, but fair. He was in charge of a large operation. Burns Ranches owned a number of ranches. Can you imagine putting up all that hay, then wintering and calving out thousands of cows, plus grain-feeding a lot of cattle? No wonder Tom sometimes had a short fuse.

Tom Farrell and John Harper doing a little reminiscing.

Hired help can make or break any operation. Tom was determined for it not to break the outfit he operated. There are dozens of stories about Tom. Cliff Vandergrift told me quite a few. He used to put up hay for Tom on a custom basis. Tom would test you pretty good. If he decided you were doing a good job, he was one of the easiest people to work for.

Cayley, a small town just south of Calgary, used to have a big stockyard for shipping cattle out by rail. One day Burns Ranches' cowboys were bringing a big string of wild range cattle to Cayley for shipping. Just as they approached the railroad track, the steam engineer blew his whistle. Well, you should have seen it. There were cattle going in all directions. The cowboys tried to hold them, but it was a lost cause.

Tom was sitting in his vehicle a short distance away, and he lost his cool. He couldn't fire the engineer because he did not work for him; however, he could, and did, fire every cowboy that was there working for him. In retrospect, it doesn't seem very fair, but nobody ever said being a real cowboy was easy.

I am not sure who gathered the cattle. I suppose there were many cowboys available in those days, probably some local ranchers who could use a few days' work.

Mickey Dirrane, who was a close friend of Tommy's, told me a lot of stories about him. Apparently, Tom used to say: "The weather determines whether you are a good rancher or not." Tough winters, spring blizzards, and summer droughts all help to decide how much success or failure you have in the ranching business.

I talked with Tom every once in a while. I never worked for him, since the Burns meat-packing plant and the Burns Ranches split up in 1938. I worked for the Burns packing division.

Yes, Tom Farrell was a feisty individual, but he did a good job as a cattleman and manager in the transitional period from large scale ranching to today's more confined intensive type of operations. Burns Ranches' fat cattle were all sold through the Alberta Livestock Co-op at the Calgary Stockyards.

Tom passed away a number of years ago. He left his mark on the cattle industry.

LARRY FARRELL is a son of Tom Farrell and grandnephew of the legendary Pat Burns. Larry was one of the best cattlemen around the Stockyards. He started to work there when he was quite young. During his lifetime, he worked for several outfits. One thing was certain, Larry always did a good job. He worked for the Alberta Livestock Co-op and the J. C. Wheatcroft Co. For some periods, he was on his own, often working closely with Adams, Wood and Weiller.

185

Sometimes, Larry bought a lot of cattle for Burns Foods. He was also a shareholder in Alberta Western Beef at Medicine Hat. For a number of years, he was in charge of Dvorkin's cattle buying operations. When he retired from Dvorkin's, he order bought cattle for a few more years. I hope I am not wrong when I say he is now semi-retired.

There was a time when Larry had a bit of a problem with liquor. To his credit, though, he overcame this many years ago. He also liked to gamble. One thing for sure, he always paid up and left no debts.

Larry and his wife, Joan, raised a very fine family.

MIKE FARRELL is also a son of Tom Farrell, brother of Larry, and grandnephew of Pat Burns. Mike went through school and became a lawyer. He eventually became a Crown Prosecutor in Calgary. Mike kind of liked the livestock business, so he got himself a place just east of Calgary where he raised a few cattle and some sheep. I think he sold some lamb and mutton to ethnic people in Calgary. Mike used to come to the sale ring, usually wearing a tam. He would sit there for hours, often reading a book or some other material. He was not as feisty as his dad or his brother. He seemed to enjoy his lifestyle. I have not seen or heard about Mike for a number of years.

HARRY FELDMAN lived in Montreal and operated a large meat market there. The reason I have him in this book is because, for many years, he spent a lot of time around the Calgary Stockyards.

Harry procured most of his beef right out of Calgary. He bought mostly cows. He custom killed them at the Burns plant. I know he got a good deal at Burns. For many years, before Mr. Child took over Burns, the Company had a hard time coming up with a profit from Harry. I feel free to say this now, but custom killing cattle for Feldman or anyone else was not the answer. It used to really bug me when Burns' own cattle were held back for slaughter while custom cattle came first. Let me assure you, when Mr. Child came on the scene things changed. All the cattle we slaughtered were ours and never mind the custom cattle. The result? We started to show profits.

Getting back to Harry, he was a character in his own right. He had the typical Jewish accent of his generation. With his eyes rolling expressively and his arm gesturing, he completed the image of a New York comedian.

A number of people worked for Harry as cattle buyers. Here are some of them: Abe Green, Mel Morrison, Ken Jones, Ken McLean, Murray Myers, Ralph Dever, and Irish Johnston.

At one point Harry tried to hire me. I had a meeting with him in the Palliser Hotel. I think this was after Murray Myers died. At any rate, he offered me big money. He had already built his own plant here called Rocky Mountain Packers. He wanted me to take charge of his buying. I felt somewhat flattered; however, I declined, since, at that time, I was on my own at the Stockyards and, bluntly speaking, was making gobs of money. That all changed in the 1980s, when I lost gobs of money.

Harry finally sold his plant to McKinnons, who renamed it XL Beef. As far as I know, Harry spent the last few years of his life in Florida.

LES FERGUSON came from Saskatchewan. He worked for the Alberta Stock Yards. He often worked in the gatehouse. Les was a very friendly person who always gave it his best shot. I don't know where Les is these days, but I am sure he's doing O.K.

ED FINLEY was a government meat grader for a number of years at the stockyards. I considered him a good grader. When Ed first started, we still had the old grading standards. The cattle were not ribbed. The grader would grade strictly by eye. The grades for steers and heifers were as follows: Red, Blue, Standard, Commercial, and Boner. "Red" was considered the best, even though, by today's standards, it was way too fat. "Blue" was the next grade, which was really more desirable, but brought less money than a "Red." "Standards" and "Commercials" were leaner still. Often they were Holsteins. Well, you see it was this way, when Ed graded the cattle in the cooler, he came up with a lot of Blues. (He was ahead of the times.) This led to the boys nicknaming him "Eddie Blue." After the grading systems were changed, the Blues actually were the top carcasses, either A1 or A2. The old Red became A3 and A4, or less desirable. Ed was transferred to the interior of B.C. I think he is grading fruit and vegetables. Eddie Blue was an okay guy.

LARRY FIRMSTON works for the United Farmers of Alberta (UFA) in the livestock medicine division. For a few years, he had an office in the Exchange Building where he sold medicine. As a matter of fact, we took over his office after he moved out. Larry can be found with his cattle-medicine-chest-on-wheels at almost any function where cattle people gather. For years, his "spot" at the Calgary Bull Sale has been a favourite gathering place for cattlemen. In 1992 he won the Rosie Nystrom Memorial bronze sculpture. It is an "all-around congeniality award" as follows: (1) the recipients will have the ability to get along with all kinds of people, (2) they will display a good working attitude, and (3) they will have the ability to boost the morale of their colleagues. Nice going, Larry.

KEN FISHER worked with the Health of Animals Division. He was a strong, stocky individual. He came from Rocky Mountain House. Ken was a good steer wrestler. To the best of my knowledge, he is back at Rocky.

LEROY FLANDERS worked for Paul & MacDonald for several years. He did a good job. He was always on time and stayed until the work was done. He left most of the partying to his co-workers. When Leroy left P&M, he started his own feed business. He has a place just off Highway 2, east of Okotoks. He bales a lot of hay and straw, then sells it to customers. When we (Friesen Cattle Co.) owned a ranch at Stavely, I often bought feed from him. To start with, Leroy worked with his dad. I think he is completely on his own now. He also runs a cow herd.

DICK FLEMING was a brand inspector for a long time. He was easygoing. He liked to visit and knew a lot of stories about the old days. Before he became a brand inspector, he worked for Burns, feeding cattle in the Yards with a team of horses. As brand inspector, I think Dick enjoyed throwing a rope better than he did throwing feed to cattle. Can't say as I blame him. Dick passed away a long time ago.

BRUCE FLEWELLING came from Lacombe, Alberta. He has been at the Stockyards since he was sixteen years old. I remember the first day he was there. When I left Burns to drive home after work, I saw this skinny kid walking down the road. I stopped and asked him if he needed a ride. He said, "Sure." I asked him what he was up to. He told me he started to work for the Alberta Stock Yards that day. My next query was: "How come you ended up at the Stockyards?" He informed me that George Chessor was his uncle—thus the Stockyards contact.

Bruce did not stay with the Alberta Stock Yards Co. very long. He had other ambitions, so he went to work for Canada Packers as a rookie buyer. After a few years, he decided to go brand inspecting. While working as a brand inspector, he practised auctioning.

When the opportunity came up, Bruce tried out for a job as an auctioneer on the market. The commission men liked what they heard and hired him. Bruce never went to auction school, but in my and many others' opinion, he is as good a commercial cattle auctioneer as we have in Canada. I know Bruce enjoys the auctioning profession and the people around the Yards; however, if the truth were known, his first love is rodeo.

For many years now, Bruce has been one of Canada's best pick-up men. I've watched him many times. He is good! He always rides good horses. He knows what kind of horse will do the job and that is what he gets, then trains it.

Our youngest son, Trent, who went to Olds College, had great respect for Mr. Flewelling, as he called him. Trent was a green saddle bronc rider. Bruce also has some bucking horses, so once a week in the wintertime, he goes up to Olds to buck some horses and pick up the kids learning the sport.

One day, Trent drew a horse that basically just raced around the arena. Bruce finally got him off. Bruce told me later what Trent said: "My dad would have kidded me about being a jockey."

Bruce is a late bloomer in the wild cow milking contest, but he is making up for lost time. In the last seven years or so, he has won the wild cow milking trophy twice at the Calgary Stampede. He has also won the Canadian title four times, including last year (1994).

Bruce and his wife, Iloe, live in a log house, south of Strathmore. He has been a source of some information for the writing of this book. He likes people and history. Iloe shares Bruce's love for rodeo and knows the sport well. She is a timer at many of the rodeos where Bruce picks up.

Bruce and Iloe are very hospitable people. A top-notch young

Australian bronc rider by the name of Glen O'Neill has made his home at Flewellings' for the last year and a half.

Bruce still auctions at the Calgary Stockyards-Strathmore. In the summer he picks up at a lot of rodeos. I think he will still be picking up when he starts to receive his old age pension. Of course, that's still a long way down the road.

Bruce Flewelling and Gary Remple picking up at Handhills Stampede, 1994.

MURRAY FLEWELLING is Bruce Flewelling's brother. Murray, too, has been around the Stockyards a long time, I would guess, for at least thirty years. He worked at the Yards for a while, then went to work for J. C. Wheatcroft. In 1981, when we reorganized the market, Murray came to work for us. He now works at the Calgary Stockyards-Strathmore with Will Irvine and Don Danard.

Murray is what you'd call a real nice guy. He is well liked by farmers and ranchers. He has a really pleasant personality, plus a good knowledge of cattle. He can also auction, but has chosen not to do it. Murray did auction quite a bit when he worked for Wheatcroft. For some reason, he preferred the cattle business on a person-to-person basis rather than as an auctioneer.

Murray has an unbelievable memory for people and their names. He is something like Bill Duggan used to be. He knows every man, his wife and children and their pet poodle, by name.

Murray did not follow his brother Bruce into the rodeo game; however, he is a rodeo fan and knows a lot of the cowboys that compete. Murray is a real asset to the cattle industry.

HELEN FOCHUK worked in the office of the government grading service for years. She was a very helpful, friendly lady and had a good rapport with the other women in the Exchange Building.

IAN FORBES was a bank manager for the Bank of Montreal in the Exchange Building. He got along fine until the tough times hit in the early 1980s. Up until that time, anybody could get all the money they needed; then, when many people had large loans and the interest rate shot up to 23 percent, the roof fell in. It wasn't really his fault, all the banks were calling in their loans. Ian retired from the bank and I have never heard what happened after that.

DORIS FOSS worked in our office. She was a very efficient person. She got the job done with a minimum amount of fuss. About a year before she started to work for Bridgewater Livestock, she and her two small sons were involved in a bad car accident. Doris was seriously injured. After a year or so, she had pretty well recovered, although she still suffered from some of those injuries. Doris's niece, Mary, also worked in our office awhile. She was a very cute redhead. Mary turned all the young men's heads in the building. She was not available for dating, since she was already married to a young man by the name of Eric whose last name slips my mind. I have not seen or heard of Doris Foss for many years.

LOU FOWLER was a sidekick of Archie Currie's at Burns horse stable. Lou always wore high top boots and breeches and looked like he should be driving the Queen of England around in a horse-drawn carriage. He, too, remembered Senator Pat Burns. Lou, like Archie, was one of the last people from the horse and teamster era.

JIM FOWLIE was a horse dealer. He often worked in conjunction with Alex Watson. Jim was a very calm man. He never got angry, at least, not so as you could notice it. He had a very strong English accent. I am sure that he was not a remittance man, although he talked exactly like those chaps did. Jim died many years ago.

DWAYNE FRIESEN is not related to me. It seems like quite a coincidence that Dwayne's dad was also a cattle buyer. His dad came from Torrington, Alberta. He moved to Lloydminster, Saskatchewan, where he was a cattle buyer. Dwayne's dad was killed in a car accident when Dwayne was just thirteen years old. He decided he wanted to be a cattle buyer too. I am not sure exactly where he worked before he came to Burns, but I do know that Bill Aubrey hired him as a cattle buyer in the late 1960s; and, when I came back to work for Burns in 1970, Dwayne was working there. He worked as a cattle buyer under me for three years. After I left Burns to go on my own, he only stayed on a little while longer. From Burns, he went to Thorlakson's feedlot at Airdrie, Alberta. Some years later, he had a heart attack and his health is not as good as it could be.

Dwayne still lives at Airdrie. He is one of the people that took time to drop me a line encouraging me to write this book. Thanks, Dwayne.

EDNA FRIESEN is my wife and the mother of our children: Leland, Ward, Melody, Delight, Graham, and Trent. She was a schoolteacher in the Swift Current area of Saskatchewan. We were married on November 16, 1946. I came to Alberta and scouted the land in Calgary from October to December 1949 and bought a house in southwest Calgary. I went back to Saskatchewan to pick up Edna and our two-year-old son, Leland. We moved to Calgary in January 1950. I started work at Burns that same month.

For the next twenty-one years, Edna more or less stayed at home raising our six children. In addition, she did volunteer work at our church. She also ran a hardware store that we owned for about two and a half years, 1958-60. In 1971, she came to work in our office at the Stockyards. She was there till we closed it in 1986. At that point, we moved to Colorado. In 1987, 1988 and 1989 we were only around the Yards for two months in the fall of the year.

Leonard and Edna Friesen at Banff Convention, 1978.

Edna, like a lot of women, is very perceptive. She has a lot of intuition and could often sense a problem before I was aware of it. She is very open and honest in all her dealings with people. She is a very competent businessperson, especially in matters pertaining to office management and sales. She is a born salesperson. We did very well in that little hardware store. Her dad was a good merchant and so were a few of her uncles. I guess she inherited some of that skill. Yes, Edna is a very special lady. I should know, I have lived with her for almost fifty years.

Edna is also a very modest person and does not want me to brag about her too much in this book. Let me assure you, she deserves a lot of credit for the wonderful family we raised—also for putting up with all my wandering around and involvement in the cattle industry. She sometimes claims that, in my life, cows come ahead of her. Let me set the record straight, once and for all—she comes ahead of all the cows!

JIM FRIESEN is my nephew. He is the son of my oldest brother, Dave Friesen. Jim moved to B.C. as a child: first, to Trail, B.C.; then, to the West Coast. He always wanted to go back to the prairies, so, in 1951, he came to Calgary. He went to work for the Stockyards and stayed there quite a while. Then he got a job at Canada Packers in the livestock department. Somehow, it did not quite work out the way he had hoped, so he moved back to B.C., this time to Revelstoke. He married a girl from there by the name of Ilene Tucker. Jim worked for B.C. Power at Mica Creek. He is now retired in Revelstoke.

JOE FRIESEN is also my nephew. He is a brother of Neil Friesen. Joe was raised in Saskatchewan. When he completed school, he came to Alberta and worked for us at the ranch at Stavely. By this time, Neil was at Airdrie. Joe also worked for the Stockyards for several years. He then went to work for Alta Genetics: first, at their Crossfield place; then, for the last few years, at their Bearspaw location.

Joe reads cattle extremely well. I have sorted cattle with him many times, and it's a pleasure; he makes very few false moves. He is also a good horseman, and he has a lot of patience, which is essential when you break and handle horses.

Joe, too, is a good artist. Like his brother, Neil, he doesn't draw or paint much these days, but he is very capable. He has two brothers and two sisters. They are all artists and so was their father, Nick. As for me, I can't even draw a stickman.

Joe is married to the former Brenda Lamb from Claresholm. Her grandfather, Joe Lamb, hauled thousands of cattle to the Calgary Stockyards. He also drove a team of Highland steers with a big horn span in the Calgary Stampede parade for a number of years. Brenda's parents still farm and ranch at Claresholm, Alberta.

LELAND FRIESEN is our oldest son. These days, he is usually called "Lee." Even though we lived in the City, he was exposed to the cattle business from a toddler on.

Leland graduated from high school in 1965. He went to seminary college in Vancouver for one year. He then attended the University of Calgary for four years. He graduated with a Bachelor of Education degree in 1970. During his seven years of high school and university, he worked part-time at Canada Safeway as well as at the Calgary Stockyards and at Burns.

On January 1, 1971, Leland left for the Fiji Islands where he

194

taught school for one year. That summer my wife and I went to visit him in Fiji. We were amazed he could actually converse with the Fijians in their language, although he taught them in English.

On January 1, 1972, Leland and his brother, Ward, went to New Zealand. Lee had various jobs there. He met and married Lisa Evans, a girl from Auckland. In March of 1974, Lee and Lisa and their baby son, Daun, came back to Canada. They moved to our ranch at Stavely where they stayed for three years. They enjoyed the ranch, but it wasn't the most productive place in the world. At that time, our order buying business was in high gear, so it was mutually decided he would come and join us in Calgary.

Everything went well for a few years, then things got rough. We were feeding a pile of cattle in the early 1980s when the fat cattle market literally collapsed. We lost millions, but that's another story. By this time, Lee and Lisa had four children, so Lee went back to teaching school. He did not mind teaching, but his heart was in the cattle business. So, when Cargill built a packing plant at High River, Lee applied for a job as cattle buyer, and they hired him. He has been with them from the day they opened the plant in June of 1989.

Lee is a very friendly person, and, I know, as his father, I may have a biased opinion, but I have never met anyone who doesn't like him. Lee and Lisa have always been involved in church activities. They attend the Baptist Church. They built a new house west of Airdrie last year. They like the country.

Lee also judges quite a few 4-H shows these days. Again, in my humble opinion, he is a good judge of cattle. I know Bill Hartall and some other cattlemen think so too.

NEIL FRIESEN is my nephew. He is the son of my brother, Nick Friesen. Neil was born and raised in Saskatchewan. After high school, he came to Alberta and worked for us at our ranch at Stavely. After seven years at Stavely, we transferred him to our place west of Airdrie. Neil helped to build a feedlot there. After it was finished, he more or less operated it on a day-to-day basis.

Neil may not move as fast as some people, but he is very steady and dependable. About seven years ago, he went to work for the Calgary market. He is quite mechanically inclined, which is a good asset around a market. There is a lot of equipment to keep in running order. Presently, he is the yard foreman at Strathmore.

Not many people know this, but I am going to let the cat out of the bag. Neil is a good artist. I wish he would do more drawing and painting. He is good. I know, because we have one of his pictures hanging on our wall.

GRAHAM AND TRENT FRIESEN, our youngest sons, never officially worked at the Stockyards, but they both spent a lot of time there helping us move or sort cattle. Often, in the fall, when we had late Friday sales, they would come there after school, also on Saturday mornings. Sometimes they went to the country with me to look at cattle. Graham was somewhat older than Trent—so, first, it was Graham for a number of years; then, it was Trent in later years.

Graham got into the sign business. He operated that business for many years, but he always maintained a keen interest in cattle. He has often helped me with our cattle. He also has cattle of his own.

Trent also liked cattle and horses. He passed away suddenly in a motor vehicle accident a mile and a half from home on May 28, 1990. Trent enjoyed riding saddle broncs, which he did in college. He was a fine young man and our family will never get over losing him.

WARD FRIESEN is our second son. He, too, worked at the Stockyards and at Burns in the summertime as well as on weekends. Ward found the Stockyards very interesting. He was a good student, so, in his third year at University, he wrote an essay about the subculture of the Stockyards. I think it was in his sociology class that he wrote this essay. He received an "A" grade for that effort. So, actually, I am the second member of the family to write about the Stockyards.

Ward graduated from the University of Calgary in 1971 with a Bachelor of Arts degree. He then went to the Fiji Islands where he joined his brother, Lee, for a few months; then they both went to New Zealand. Lee got married and settled down, but Ward went on travelling.

Ward was in Australia for quite a while. Some of the jobs he had over there were: fixing typewriters in Sydney, picking apples in Tasmania, working in a packing plant in Brisbane, and I don't know what else. From Australia, he went to South East Asia. In a three and a half year period, he visited some 63 countries, including places like India, Nepal, Indonesia, and Malaysia.

In 1975 Ward came back to Canada. He worked for us on the ranch at Stavely for a little while. Then, he went to Carlton University in Ottawa where he earned his master's degree. Next he went to London, England, where he got a job in the New Zealand Embassy. After one year, he went to New Zealand where he began his doctoral studies at the University of Auckland. He wrote his thesis on the Solomon Islands where he had spent a considerable amount of time.

Meantime, Ward married a New Zealand girl by the name of Mary Ann Crick. They decided to do the same thing as the Joe Clarks did. She retained her maiden name. Hence, any mail to them is addressed Crick-Friesen.

BOB FULTON had a farm and feedlot at Indus, Alberta. He was a very good friend of both Cec Barber's and Danny MacDonald's. Bob was around the Stockyards a lot. He liked to hobnob with cattlemen. He sold all his cattle through P&M. Danny MacDonald was a good auctioneer. Whenever he sold Bob's cattle he was in top form. Danny squeezed every dime out of the buyers for the Fulton cattle. Bob's father was in the oil business. Bob leaned more toward agriculture. He was a fellow Shriner with Cecil Barber. He was the Grand Potentate of the Shrine once.

ROY FURGESON was with Adams, Wood and Weiller at the Stockyards for at least sixty years. He started with Harvey Adams in 1919. Roy was a partner in that firm. I am not sure exactly what percentage he owned. Roy ran a very tight ship in the office. He did not spend any money unnecessarily.

Art Adams used to tell me that most of their office equipment should be in a museum along with Roy's long black overcoat. Be that as it may, Roy did a good job when you consider the characters he had to deal with. Most of them had to have advances before payday. Often, their previous paycheques had been spent at the beer parlours in the Shamrock and National hotels or, sometimes, at the racetrack. In spite of their wayward ways, the boys did a good job for AWW, so Roy went along with them on the advances. They usually had to listen to a lecture on how to take care of their finances, but next week they would be back.

Also, Roy was a Commissioner of Oaths. He signed quite a few papers for me. We had a retirement party for Roy at the Palliser Hotel. He passed away a few years later.

BILL FURGESON is Roy Furgeson's son. Bill is a tall, easygoing person. He worked in the alley for AWW for many years. Bill is a likeable person. I often felt that he was misunderstood by his fellow employees. In those days, there was very little tolerance for anyone who was not a dyed-in-the-wool cattleman or, at least, rough and ready. He did not fit either one of these descriptions.

Bill was very talented in electronics and gadgetry. When we reorganized in 1981, we hired him to look after the electronic and mechanical end of things. He only stayed for two years. He recently told me those were his most enjoyable years in the thirty-six years that he was at the Yards.

Bill is also an excellent photographer. He has many pictures that were taken at the Stockyards. He also has a moving picture of the demolition of the old Exchange Building as well as the construction of the new one. For a number of years, Bill and his wife had a place at Chestermere Lake. They moved back to Calgary several years ago.

ART GALARNEAU was raised in the Finnigan country of Alberta. He was a brand inspector at the Stockyards. Art was a very slender man. I can still see him walking down the alley with his rope slung over his shoulder. Art, and his brothers, Albert and Fred, were top-notch rodeo cowboys. Art and Albert were both good calf ropers, extremely fast. Albert won the Calf Roping Championship at the Calgary Stampede several times. Art was very "sudden" as well, but he never won Calgary. In their younger days, they both rode saddle broncs. Fred was a good saddle bronc rider as well. Art and his wife, Leona, were killed in a car crash about twenty years ago. They left six children. The oldest girl, Mary Ann, was about twenty years old at the time. Between the older children and their uncles and aunts, they managed to raise the younger children. Even twenty years later, our hearts go out to them.

FRANK GALICK was the killing-floor foreman at Burns for at least four decades. He was efficient and tough. Like his assistant foreman, Tommy Deakin, there was not a job Frank could not do. He liked visiting with us in the livestock department. I guess it gave him the chance to get away from all the blood and guts. In the '30s, during the Great Depression, jobs were very scarce. If Frank had somebody working for him that was slacking off or not doing a very good job, he would ask that man to come with him to look out the window. Right below them, just a little to the west, was the office where people lined up to apply for a job at Burns. Candidly, Frank would say to the man: "See all those people looking for work? Well, if you don't smarten up and shape up, that's where you will be. Now make your choice."

EARL GALVIN came from Moose Jaw, Saskatchewan. After becoming an auctioneer, he worked at Amarillo, Texas, for a while. He then came to Calgary where he worked as an auctioneer with Harry Hays. Eventually, Earl purchased the MacLean Auction Mart in East Calgary. A few years later, he sold it and came to the Stockyards as an auctioneer. He was there for about ten years. Earl used to say: "It doesn't matter where you start the cattle; it's where the price ends up that counts." While he was at the Yards, he and his family built up a good auction business, which they operated in the evenings and on weekends. Earl sold cars, machinery, household goods or anything else that was for sale. As time went by, they concentrated more and more on sales of antiques; in fact, they became experts in that field. They had a large clientele for both selling and buying. They brought in many antique items from Great Britain and other places. Earl is getting on in years. Last time I heard about him, he and his wife, along with their son, David, are still going strong.

MR. GARDINER (no relation to Clem and Teddy Gardiner) was a bank manager for the Bank of Montreal at the Yards. His first name completely escapes me. I must have asked a dozen of my old buddies if they knew his first name. All of them gave me the same answer: Oh, they knew him well; however, none of them could remember. Anyway, I borrowed some money from him. He had a very intimidating manner. (Don't most bankers?) Actually, he was a good man, was quite big and wore horn-rimmed glasses. He did a good job of keeping that (sometimes) rowdy bunch in check.

TEDDY GARDINER was a brother of the legendary Clem Gardiner from Pirmez Creek. Teddy lived at Stettler, Alberta. He spent a fair amount of time at Burns. He was a close buddy of Mickey Dirrane's.

Teddy was as close as I ever got to meeting a real bonafide old-time cattle buyer. In fact, I think he had a hard time adjusting to buying cattle by the pound, rather than by the head. All those cattle that were trailed up from Texas to Kansas were sold by the head. This method of buying cattle persisted in this country right up into the 1930s. Many of the Jewish cattle buyers continued to buy cattle by the head until the late 1950s. Today only bred cows and heifers, as well as baby calves, are sold by the head.

Incidentally, I sold my first two yearling steers by the head. The year was 1941. Pete Perrin, who at that time was the foreman at the Matador Ranch on the South Saskatchewan River, bought them. He paid me $65 apiece for a total of $130. I guess it worked out to about 9 cents a pound. Not bad, when you consider that, just a few years previously, we only got 5 cents a pound for two- and three-year-old steers that we shipped to Winnipeg. That sale for $130 was pretty heavy stuff for a fifteen-year-old boy in 1941. Several years ago, when I was judging cattle at Agribition in Regina, Pete told me he still has the receipt I gave him for those two steers. My brand was 7H, right hip. Our family brand was diamond dot (◊), right hip.

Sorry for wandering away from the Teddy Gardiner story. When I think about the old days, I get carried away. Teddy shipped a lot of cattle to Burns. I always liked it when he came around. I felt like I was rubbing elbows with a man from an era that was fast slipping away from us.

WHITE GARRIES came from Bentley, Alberta. During World War II, he was in the Air Force. White was a very competent man. He was the office manager for the Alberta Livestock Co-op from right after the War until they closed their Agri-Mart operation near the Calgary Airport. The Co-op not only handled a lot of cattle, they also were the biggest handlers of hogs at the Calgary Stockyards. They looked after a lot of shipping association hogs. White kept everything in order. The Co-op did well until their venture crashed at the Airport. White and his wife have experienced several tragedies. Twenty-four years ago, they lost a son in a motor vehicle

200

accident. He was only twenty years old. They also lost a daughter, aged 31. The Garries are enjoying retired life these days.

IVAN GARRISON was the head government meat grader. He took over from Wilf Dunsmore. Ivan was much more outgoing than Wilf. He loved to visit. You felt that if you had an opinion on a matter pertaining to grading, he would listen to what you had to say. Ivan was fair with everyone, including those who worked under him. He retired about thirty-five years ago. I never heard anything about him after that.

MAURICE AND SHIRLEY GASNIER bought the Stockyards Restaurant business from a Hungarian couple whose names escape me. Shirley actually was the person who ran the restaurant. She was a small vivacious woman. As the saying goes "there were no flies on her nose." She ran a pretty good show; however, the number of customers had been shrinking for several years before they took over. There were two reasons: First, the cattle receipts had declined and, also, a lot of farmers sent their cattle to market with commercial truckers. Second was the fact that many new cafes and restaurants had opened up on 9th Avenue and in the Bonnybrook industrial area, just south of the Yards. At any rate, Shirley finally closed shop and that was the end of a restaurant at the Yards. A year or so later, the Yards closed and moved to Strathmore.

ANDY GAUN was a skinny Irishman. If you wanted to get ahead of him on any deal, you had to get up before breakfast. He lived at Claresholm, but came to Calgary a lot, especially to Burns. He was another one of Mickey Dirrane's pets. Andy sent Mickey quite a few cattle. I think Andy came out ahead more often than Mickey. Andy kept on buying and trading cattle till he kind of faded away.

HARRY GEDAGER was a cattle dealer. He was one of the last half-dozen Jewish cattle dealers who operated at the Yards. He was a very excitable individual—nothing calm about Harry. He always reminded me of a cat or a dog, whose tail had just been stepped on accidentally—rather snarly. Fortunately, his bark was worse than his bite. He bought a lot of cattle from the Hutterites. I have lost track of Harry.

201

DANNY GERLITZ lives on Highway 2, northeast of Okotoks, Alberta. He spent a lot of time at the Yards. He liked to come there to buy cattle for his little feedlot.

One day, he bought some high-priced Limousin heifers of mine that the vet had tested "open" (non-pregnant). There were about a dozen in the package. Well, you should have heard the ribbing he gave me, four of them were pregnant. He never let me forget it. I won't mention the vet, only to say it was <u>not</u> Dr. Brian Edge.

Danny liked to race pony chuckwagons. He travelled all over the country with them. He was one of the chuckwagon judges at the Calgary Stampede for many years. Finally, it came my turn to rib him. I was a partner in an outfit called "Elkwater Ranches." For four years in the early '80s, this ranch bought a canvas with Edgar Baptiste as the driver. He had fast horses, but he always picked up a lot of penalties, so whenever I met Danny I would say, in my most serious manner: "When are you going to stop picking on Edgar and quit giving him all those penalties?" Of course, I was just kidding; but, a few times, I think Danny took me seriously. Maybe in the back of his mind, he was thinking he had been too tough.

I have not seen Danny for quite a while.

TOM GERLITZ may be related to Danny Gerlitz, but I am not sure in what way. Tom was a real solid, dependable person. He trucked around the Yards for as long as I can remember. He had what we called a "body-job." He could haul about 12 fat steers. Tom never seemed to be in a hurry, but he always got the job done. He was one of those nice guys who is hard to write about. He never rocked the boat. Tom passed away a number of years ago.

LAWRENCE GIBSON had a stockbroker's office in the Exchange Building for several years. I bought and sold quite a few stocks through him. So did many others. We did not always hit the jackpot, since many of those penny stocks were pretty volatile. Lawrence was very knowledgeable about stocks. In spite of this, he could not outsmart the promoters on the Vancouver Stock Exchange. They sold him—and many of us—on some real dud mining stocks. In my humble opinion, the Vancouver Exchange is a disgrace to Canada. They have tried to clean it up several times without much success. Lawrence was very involved with the big white cattle from Italy, the

Chianinas. They were new to Canada and made a few waves. I found the breed rather interesting myself, especially if they were crossed with Angus. I don't know where Lawrence went after he closed his office.

DAVE GILCHRIST was the foreman for the Alberta Stock Yards when I first came to the Yards; and he was for quite a few years after that. He came from Scotland and, let me tell you, his speech had more of a Scottish accent forty years later than it did the day he landed in Halifax in 1910. You had to listen to him very carefully—he sounded like he had his mouth full of porridge.

When Dave stepped off the boat, he asked the first Canadian he met: "Do you have a government in Canada?" When the person replied, "Yes," Davey said, "I'm agin it."

I had a lot of good visits with Dave, including an odd debate about Americans. You see, Dave was anti-American, to the extreme. When he got going on that subject, he would tap his cane on the cement alley so hard that he would almost injure his hand. I always stuck up for the Americans.

Dave was a very nice man, even though he was a bit of a character. He never married. He passed away a long time ago.

TERRY GILES was born and raised at Shepard, Alberta. I also knew his dad, Jack Giles. Jack used to sell his cattle through AWW. His brand was Circle J (⌀). His son, Merv, still uses that brand. Terry was a Parslow & Denoon customer.

When distillery soup became available, Terry and Merv used vast amounts of it in their feedlot south of Calgary near the Bow River. I bought quite a few of their steers directly from them. They would weigh anywhere from 1,200 to 1,500 pounds. After they sold out at Shepard, they both bought places west of Airdrie.

Merv lives close to Cochrane. His miniature eight-horse hitch is very popular these days. He and the hitch attend many fairs and participate in all the local parades as well the big one, the Calgary Stampede Parade, every July.

Terry likes good cattle and buys nothing but the best. He has won a lot of ribbons at the beef expo sponsored by the Calgary Exhibition & Stampede every summer. He also owns a large arena where the boys can test their skills in cattle penning and team roping.

ROY GILKES came to Calgary from Winnipeg-Brandon where he had been a cattle buyer for Canada Packers. He went to work for J. C. Wheatcroft in the early '60s. Roy is a good cattleman. When he and Wheatcroft teamed up, it was pretty formidable competition. For a while, Roy spent a lot of time in the Medicine Hat area. Wheatcroft was one of the major shareholders in Alberta Western Beef.

To this day, there are very few people, if any, who can out-figure Roy when it comes to reckoning the average weight of cattle in the sale ring. He is also a very accurate counter. He has paced up and down in sale rings ever since I have known him. There is not much that escapes Roy. When I watch him walk back and forth, he reminds me of a timber wolf locked up in a zoo.

Roy was a good buyer when they were in the order-buying business. When they became a commission firm, he was a tough salesman. It was hard to buy cheap cattle from him. Of course, that was good for the producers. When we reorganized the market in 1981, Roy was our general sales manager.

Roy likes to hoist a few once in a while. One day, we had a little blowup and he and the market parted company. After about a year, he resurfaced as an order buyer and has been at it ever since. To his credit, he holds no grudges and is on good terms with everybody. Like myself, and many others, he has mellowed with age.

I know Roy does a good job for the people he buys for. Another good point about him, in my opinion, is that he is completely honest and above board. I always enjoy a little visit with him, especially when we reminisce about bygone years.

ALEX GILLESPIE was an Irishman that made good in Canada. He started out by working for Pat Burns as a teamster. He then got himself a little place and started feeding a few cattle. He was shrewd, and pretty soon he expanded. He bought several ranches, some on his own and some with partners, namely, Lee Williams, Harvey Adams, and maybe there were a few others. He also got involved in the oil business. I think he only had limited success in the oil venture.

Alex had an office in the Exchange Building. He and a few of his cronies played cards there nearly every day. I think it was rummy. He always wore a hat and smoked a pipe. He was a man that

250 years of good living

From left to right, Eddie Bowlen, Alex Gillespie and Tom Gerlitz.
Three well-know gentlemen who have participated for many years
at the Calgary Livestock Market.
Eddie Bowlen was a long-time rancher, a trucker, horseman
(former winner of the Calgary Stampede calf roping contest);
Alex Gillespie, a former rancher who owned one of the first
feedlots in the Calgary area; Tom Gerlitz, a long-time trucker
to the Calgary stockyards.

A fine trio!

could not be bluffed too easily. If he had cattle to sell, time was of
no essence: "If I don't sell them this week, maybe I will next week or
next month"; this was his philosophy.

Alex was a great friend of Davey Gilchrist's, Mickey Dirrane's
and Lee Williams'. Alex' son Delbert still owns and operates one of
their ranches at Finnigan, Alberta.

BILL GILLESPIE is a son of Alex Gillespie's. Bill operated his dad's place just south of the Stockyards. It was kind of a cattle boardinghouse. Many of the people from the Yards, including us, had cattle at his place, sometimes for short periods, sometimes for long periods. It was a very handy place to keep cattle, and Bill did a good job looking after them. It was not unusual for us to have 200 or 300 hundred bred cows there. We would sell them to people in small lots. When Deerfoot Trail was extended south, Bill sold out to the City of Calgary. I haven't seen or heard about Bill for quite a while.

CRAWFORD GILLESPIE is also a son of Alex Gillespie's. He worked for the Alberta Livestock Co-op with Ook McRae for several years at the hog and sheep scalehouse. Crawford was a nice chap, but his interests did not lie in livestock, but rather, in cars and trucks or anything mechanical. I have lost track of him.

CLARENCE GINGRICH was born and raised east of High River at Mazeppa, Alberta. He was a brand inspector at the Yards. He could be very blustery, but underneath he was a kind man.

Clarence liked rodeo. For many years he had his own string of bucking horses. He also was a good pick-up man. He picked up at the Calgary Stampede for a lot of years. He absolutely loved it. I liked rodeo too, so I talked to him quite often about the sport.

One day, I asked Clarence the age-old question: "Who do you think was the best saddle bronc rider ever? Was it Pete Knight, Carl Olsen, Casey Tibbs, Bill Linderman, Leo Watrin, Marty Wood, Kenny McLean, Jerry Ambler, or Winston Bruce?" He had picked up all these cowboys at one time or another. He looked at me, and, without a moment's hesitation, he said, "Kenny McLean." In his opinion, nobody could equal Kenny in reading what a horse would do next. He could get on the rankest horse and make it look easy. He may have been right. Kenny McLean won two world titles. If he had liked travelling better, he probably could have won five or six.

Clarence had trouble with his legs when he grew older—maybe, too much rodeo. He passed away about ten years ago. We went to his funeral in High River. I never saw so many old cowboys gathered in one place. His wife, Betty, is a wonderful person. She still lives in High River.

KEN GINGRICH is the son of Clarence and Betty Gingrich. Ken did not take after his dad in the rodeo business. He worked for the Alberta Stock Yards. Later, he got a job with Henry Bridgewater. This was before I joined Henry. I still feel kind of bad about what happened. Ken was hoping to become a cattle buyer, so Henry let him buy a few once in a while. When I joined Henry, Ken quit. I was an experienced cattle buyer and I had been at it for about fifteen years. There were two sale rings. Henry bought in one and I bought in the other. I guess Ken thought there was no room for him. I am sure we could have used him. Several years later, we hired Irish Johnston. Then we transferred Will Irvine here from Edmonton, and, in 1977, my son Lee came with us as well. When the Co-op started the Agri-Mart, Ken opened up a restaurant called the Horned Heifer. I ate there several times. It was a good place. He also did a lot of catering. Last I heard, Ken was working at the Calgary Airport.

GERRY GOING came from Ontario on a harvest excursion as a young man and he never went back. There are three men in Alberta who came from Ontario, but, to see and talk to them, you would swear they had been born and raised on a big cattle ranch in the Foothills: They are Wayne Daye, brand inspector; Ian Tyson, composer of songs, country singer and cutting-horse man; and Gerry Going, auctioneer, rancher and horseman. Please don't take me wrong, Gerry, I think you are a great asset. We are proud of you as a western Canadian.

Gerry was an auctioneer at the Stockyards for quite a few years. About 1959 or 1960, he and George MacLean opened up an auction market at High River in the old airport hangar. I was at their first sale and many more after that.

Gerry has owned several large ranches. One is at Black Diamond and one is in the Arrowwood country. He excels in raising quality horses. Gerry keeps a fairly low profile. I very seldom see him. When young, he was a good boxer. Even when he got older, he kept himself in good shape.

MARY GOLL was a buxom blonde who worked in the office for the Alberta Stock Yards in the old Exchange Building. If she ever lacked dates it was not because of unwilling men. She had a way of turning men's heads. I am sure she did a good job in the office or

Charlie Kennedy would not have had her there. I have no idea where she is or what happened to her. She probably married and raised a family and lived happily ever after.

JOHN GOWANS worked for Swift Canadian all his life: first, at Moose Jaw; then, Edmonton; and finally, Calgary. He truly was a nice man—a real gentleman. I first met John in Moose Jaw, about 1947. I was there with my uncle John, my dad's brother, with a load of cattle. Uncle John trucked a lot of cattle to Moose Jaw, which was about 120 miles from our place. This particular load, he sold to Swift. The buyer was young black-haired Jack Gowans. You can imagine my surprise when I met him, some thirty years later, when he came to Calgary. The young black-haired Jack had turned into a somewhat older and somewhat grey-haired man by the name of John—not Jack. We had a few good laughs about it. He remembered my uncle John really well. Uncle John passed away peacefully at the age of 104 years 9 months on March 4, 1993. John Gowans passed away very suddenly in 1990.

ART GRAMS worked in the gatehouse for the Alberta Stock Yards for quite a few years. Art was an easygoing person. He always reminded me of the country and western singer, Don Williams—kind of a casual look. Art retired about ten years ago. As far as I know, he still resides in the Bowness district of Calgary.

SONNY GRAY was born and raised in East Calgary. He had hung around the Yards for as long as he could remember. Sonny joined the Canadian Army during World War II and was overseas for several years. After the War, he went to work for Burns as a cattle buyer. In 1956, he became the head buyer for the Calgary plant. In 1963 he was transferred to Winnipeg. He was only there a short time. He left Burns and came back to Calgary, where he went to work for P&M.

It was no secret that Sonny had a drinking problem at this point in his life. Danny MacDonald has to be credited with giving Sonny several chances to hold down a buying job with them. He fell off the wagon a few times, but Danny always took him back. Finally, Sonny kicked the habit, and, for the last twenty-five or thirty years of his life, he was cold sober and never took a drink. A real credit to him.

Sometime in the mid-1970s, Sonny left P&M and started his own order-buying business. He and his son Scott had an office in the Exchange Building. They built up a good business, having several large feedlots as customers. Sonny was a very close friend of Augie Sauer's. Augie was from Medicine Hat and Sonny did a lot of business with him.

Sonny was not a very talkative individual. He more or less minded his own business. He could sit at the sale ring for hours and never change expression. Because of this, a few people, in a good-natured way, referred to him as "stoneface." Sonny was a good judge of cattle. He liked to buy the good ones. For the last few years of his life, he had a health problem. By this time, Scott was pretty well running the outfit.

Sonny passed away in 1992.

SCOTT GRAY is Sonny Gray's son. Like his dad, Scott was around the Stockyards at a young age. After completing school, he joined his dad in the order-buying business. They moved a lot of cattle and, after about ten years, Scott took on a lot of the responsibility of running the business.

Scott is a very fussy buyer. He usually likes to take one or two head out of nearly every package that comes through the ring. Because he purchases quite a lot of good quality cattle, the markets usually comply with his request. I, as well as several other buyers, often request a few head out as well. In the USA, the cattle are not sorted nearly as well as they are in Canada. Some markets will take a head or two out once in a while; however, for the most part, you have to buy whatever they chase into the ring. Sometimes they are not very uniform. It took me quite a while to get used to the system.

Back to Scott. Since his dad passed away, Scott has been on his own. He buys at several markets as well as in the country. He lives in Strathmore. His dad lived there as well for the last few years of his life.

ABE GREEN, or "Whispering Abe" as we sometimes called him, was around the Stockyards most of his life. He was a Scottish Jew—quite a combination. He was a good cattleman, but he found it hard to trust very many people. I liked to visit with him; maybe it was because he was such a unique character. With Abe, everything was a secret. He would cup his big hand to the side of his mouth and whisper in your ear. Bob Smolkin told me about the time he and Abe were going to a cattle sale at Whisky Gap, which is close to the Montana border. While they were driving through some desolate country with only himself and Abe in the car, Abe looked around to see if there was anyone nearby. Of course, there wasn't anybody within ten miles of them. Abe then leaned over towards Bob and whispered some important matters concerning the cattle business.

Abe was Harry Feldman's right-hand man in Calgary for many years. If any of you readers are interested in knowing more about Abe Green, give Mel Morrison a call, he worked with Abe for several years. Mel has a good sense of humour about it.

Abe passed away about twenty years ago.

CLIFF GREEN worked for AWW all his life. I think he started with them shortly after they opened in 1919. He was their hog and sheep salesman. As the saying goes, there were "no flies on Cliff's nose." He knew the business from the ground up.

When I was a rookie at Burns, I seldom bought hogs; however, I often bought lambs at the scalehouse. In those days, the early 1950s, there were still a lot of sheep in Alberta. Cliff sold quite a few lambs. Let me tell you, they were never easy to purchase from him. He was 100 percent for the producer.

I'm not sure why, but Maule McEwen always called Cliff "Gandhi." Maybe it was because Cliff did not give in too easy when it came to trading hogs and sheep.

Cliff was quite a gentleman. He was always dressed clean and tended to business while some of the other boys were playing cards. They used to call the hog and sheep scalehouse "The Den of Iniquity."

To my knowledge, Cliff never told anybody his age. I know he was getting on in years. He looked after himself, so he did not look as old as he actually was. He and his wife liked to take winter holidays. As soon as he was back, he was raring to attend to business.

Cliff passed away quite a few years ago.

BOB GREEN was a son of Cliff Green's. He was employed by Canada Packers. He worked with Graham Jones in the livestock department in Edmonton for eight years. He bought cattle for three or four years. When Bob left Canada Packers, he went to work for Neon Sales and Service in their sales division. He stayed with them for thirty-two years, until he retired. I might also add that he, too, worked at the Stockyards every summer when he was in high school. Bob and his wife are good Christian people. They raised two fine children. These days, Bob spends quite a bit of time on the golf links.

GLEN GREEN was Cliff Green's youngest son. He worked at the Stockyards for many years. Glen always was a good worker. He had a small farm at Millarville. Glen passed away from lung cancer in 1980. He was forty-five years old. He left a wife and three children. Sometimes, these things are hard to understand.

TONY GREEN was Cliff Green's oldest son. As a student, Tony worked at AWW at the Stockyards every summer. He worked as a salesman for Canada Packers in Edmonton for ten years, then transferred to Calgary. Tony was a born salesman. He had a good personality. In February of 1978, he died in a plane crash at Cranbrook, B.C. The plane hit a snowplow on the runway during a raging blizzard. If my memory serves me correctly, only six passengers and one crew member survived. There were 49 people on board. Tony had four children. How tragic his loss was for his family.

FRED GROSS had a body-job truck at the Stockyards for years. He was a fairly hot-tempered person and had red hair. He was a good trucker. If you stayed on the right side of him he would really look after you. He disappeared from the Yards many years ago.

GARY GUICHON is a brand inspector. He came to the Calgary Stockyards ten or twelve years ago. He was pretty tough to start with, but time has mellowed him. At the present time, he is the head brand inspector at the Stockyards in Strathmore. He is a good farrier and does a good job in both professions.

DON GUNDERSON and his brothers, Maurice, Gene, Wally and Roy Gunderson, all worked at the Yards. Don worked for

J. C. Wheatcroft for a number of years. He is a soft-spoken individual. He always did a good job without making too much noise. He likes cattle. He and his wife live on their place at Water Valley where they run some cows. It is my understanding that they have bought a place up north.

MAURICE "MORRIS" GUNDERSON worked many, many years for AWW. He did a good job for them. He was always on the move, there was not a lazy bone in his body. He was a nice man. We all hope he enjoyed some retired life at Water Valley. In the last few years, Maurice had lung problems. He was a heavy smoker, but I am not sure if that had anything to do with his health. On September 28, 1994, at age 64, he passed away at Sundre and was buried in the Water Valley Cemetery.

EVELYN GUNDERSON is the wife of the late Maurice Gunderson. She is a very capable lady. She clerked for the auctioneers for many years. Needless to say, she did an excellent job,—not many errors when she was up on the stand. These days she is semi-retired and has looked after Maurice's needs. Like always, she will have done a good job. Evelyn and Maurice raised five fine children.

GENE GUNDERSON is Maurice Gunderson's brother and is a half-brother to Don, Wally, and Roy Gunderson. Gene worked for AWW whenever he was not on the rodeo trail. He was a very good bareback bronc rider. In 1955 he won the Calgary Stampede in that event. As was the case for so many rodeo cowboys, especially in those days, Gene had some besetting sins. He liked to party and that costs money. It also involves a fair bit of tippling. Usually, by the time he hit the Yards, he was broke. He put the "touch" on quite a few of the boys, including me. He paid me back, so he does not owe me a dime. Gene was very personable and easy to visit with. Last I heard, he lived at Kinsella, Alberta.

ROY GUNDERSON worked for P&D one summer when he was sixteen years of age. He worked in the alleys and helped sort cattle. Young Roy hangs his hat at Connor Creek, Alberta, where he is a supervisor with the Department of Agriculture on the Provincial

Grazing Reserve. He likes doing leather work and makes saddles in his spare time.

WALLY GUNDERSON worked for several of the commission firms. In 1973 he came to work for me at Friesen Cattle Co. He bought fat cattle for Burns and feeder cattle for us. He is a very quiet type, not real aggressive, but competent. After he left us, he went to work at the ranch at Hanna owned by the Calgary Stampede. He stayed there for a number of years. He has an infield job at the Calgary Stampede every summer. Wally likes rodeo. These days, he lives at Water Valley and works for the Olds Auction Mart on sale days.

LESTER GURNETT worked for P&M for a long time. Many years ago, he took an auctioneer's course. He auctioned for P&M till we reorganized the market. He then worked for the Calgary market as an auctioneer. I consider him a good auctioneer. From a buyer's

Lester Gurnett on Vold's Powder River, Ponoka Stampede, 1972.

point of view, I think he hangs on too long; however, that's good for the cattle producer and that's what it's all about. He solicits a lot of cattle for the Calgary Stockyards-Strathmore. He also order buys cattle.

Lester was raised around Youngstown, Alberta. He took to rodeo like a duck takes to water. His event was saddle bronc riding. He made some outstanding rides; he has quite a few buckles and trophies to prove it. He has been to the Canadian Finals; on several occasions, he was in the crying hole, eleventh spot. Only the top ten qualify for the CFR, which is held every November in Edmonton. Since he hung up his bronc spurs, he now judges at a number of rodeos.

Lester and his family live north of Airdrie where he raises a few sheep. He is not the only cowboy doing that. I stopped in at Chris LeDoux' place at Kaycee, Wyoming, and he, too, raises sheep. Chris is a country and western singer and a former World Champion Bareback Bronc Rider.

JOYCE HABER came from Strathmore, Alberta. She worked in P&M's office. It just so happened that her office was located across the hall from the brand inspector's office. Working in the brand office was a tall cowboy brand inspector by the name of Hank Pallister. Pretty soon, romance blossomed and, in due time, Hank and Joyce got married. After several years, Hank was transferred to the Brand Department Headquarters in Stettler, where he was the man in charge. Joyce started a health food store in Stettler, Alberta. At the time of writing, she still owns it. Hank and Joyce are fine Christian people, and they are very involved with a church in their community. Joyce and Hank created a plate commemorating the Alberta Stock Yards, 1903 - 1989.

BRIAN HALL worked briefly for the Alberta Stock Yards in the late '80s. Brian's dad, Archie, came to the Yards a lot. These days, I meet Brian and Archie at the Strathmore market quite often. For as long as I remember, Archie was always trading a few cattle. They have a place just east of Calgary.

RUDY AND TILLY HAM came from Germany. They were the first proprietors of the cafe located downstairs in the new Exchange Building built in 1966. Before they came to the Stockyards, they had operated a restaurant uptown for several years. They were very frugal, but put out good food at reasonable prices. The restaurant was a great meeting place, especially at noon. Some days the place was absolutely packed. The boys liked to tease Tilly. She was a good sport about it. In fact, anybody that could not take a joke or suffer a prank once in a while did not survive at the Stockyards. If they did, they had to be miserable. Rudy was a more serious type and he pretty well looked after things in the kitchen while Tilly tended the front till. Eventually, they sold out to a Hungarian couple whose name completely escapes me. I do remember the man's first name was Ted. I have lost track of the Hams.

BETTY HAMILTON came from DeWinton, Alberta. She is a real nice person. She used to waitress in the Stockyards Cafe. When it closed, she set up shop in a little room on the ground level of the sale ring. She was one of the most accommodating people I have ever met. She served coffee, soft drinks, sandwiches, and chocolate bars. When the sale was on, there was nearly always a small lineup to buy some refreshments and snacks. Several times during a sale, she would come into the sale ring to serve coffee and donuts or whatever anybody wanted. It was always done with a smile. Betty raised a fairly large family, mostly on her own. She knew what work and hardships were. When the Stockyards closed, we had a farewell night at the Sandman Inn. We honoured Betty that night with a big bouquet of flowers in appreciation for her work and good service at the Calgary Stockyards. I think Betty still lives in East Calgary.

VIC HAMMILL was born and raised in Calgary, Alberta. He went to work for his Uncle Ot Hammill, who had a commission firm at the Stockyards before I came along. I think Vic also worked for several other people at the Yards. When I got to know him, he was a freelancer. He bought and shipped a lot of cattle to the USA, mostly to Billings, Montana. The results were mixed. I know for a fact, many times, he took a real shellacking. I am sure there were times when he did okay. At one point Vic and Jimmy Paul opened up a feedlot south of the Stockyards where they fed distillery soup. This venture did not last too long.

Vic was a playboy type. He was always dressed to the T. He almost looked out of place with his fancy duds. As far as I know, he did not do much work in the alleys. He was a friend of Art Adams'. They loved to golf together. Vic owned a golf driving range where the Chinook Shopping Centre is located today on Macleod Trail.

When Vic went to a restaurant or night club, it was steak and lobster— or maybe, even, caviar and champagne. He was not cheap. He was easy to converse with. His dad owned Hammill Motors. I guess Vic enjoyed the better things of life, early in his career.

BILL HAMPSON worked for Burns as Calgary sales manager. The reason I included him in this book is because he sold a lot of good Alberta beef that came through the Stockyards. The first time I met him was before he was promoted to manager. He was a salesman marking beef in the cooler for his customers. As a cattle buyer and, later on, as a livestock manager, I had a lot of dialogue with Bill about beef. The theme was "Let's Move It."

HAROLD HANNA was the general feed manager at Burns. Before that, he had worked for several feed companies, including XL Feeds at Bassano. Burns fed cattle in several lots around southern Alberta. Once in a while, Harold and I would take a tour to check things out. Harold was a good travelling companion. We had a lot of discussions on many topics. When I was in Burns head office, I was located quite close to Harold's office. In the course of a day, I would get three or four memos from Harold. That was his way of communicating. As for myself, I would much sooner use the phone. It's a good thing we are not all the same; it would be a dull world. When Harold left Burns, he went to work for the Alberta Government in the Farm Credit Division at Camrose.

DR. MORRIS HANSON was a vet around the Calgary Stockyards as well as the Stampede Park. He was considered to be a very good vet, especially for horses. Morris also fed some cattle. At one time, he was involved with Meyers' feedlot at Houghton, Saskatchewan. He had a place west of Cayley as well. It was always a pleasure to pass a little time conversing with Morris. He was interested in all phases of the livestock industry. Just by coincidence, Morris' mother, a dear old lady, lived next door to a house we owned in Riverside. We never lived in that house, but our daughter and son-in-law did. I am not sure what Morris is up to these days.

HENRY HARDER was a cattle buyer for Swift Canadian. He came from Edmonton, where he had also worked for Swift. I never met Henry's father, but I was told he was still ramrod-straight from being in the German Army in World War I. He, too, worked in the plant in Edmonton.

Henry was a good cattle buyer. He must have bought cattle at the Calgary Yards for at least thirty years. In the 1950s and 1960s, he always went to the Bow Slope sale in Brooks on Thursdays. Often, he would have his two little dogs with him. Henry nearly always bought in the P&D and Co-op sale ring.

Henry enjoyed a drink once in a while. He retired about fifteen years ago and has since passed away.

JOHNNY HARPER was a Scotsman, who sometimes was a sheepman and sometimes a cattleman. He wasn't exactly a blockbuster in either profession. Johnny liked to rub shoulders with greatness, but somehow the prize always escaped him. Some of the more successful cattle people enjoyed his company, so it worked out for everyone.

GORDIE HARRIS worked for the Alberta Stock Yards for many years in various capacities. I think it was when Woodward Thompson retired that Gordon moved into the office. For the last few years before he retired, he operated the truck wash at the Yards. Gordie liked to visit. He seemed to have more time for that than I did; however, I had many a chat with him. He died several years ago.

MIKE HARRIS was the head honcho of the government graders in Calgary. He was born and raised at Blaine Lake, Saskatchewan, Jack Horner's hometown. (Jack Horner was a former Alberta MP, Crowfoot riding.) Mike was very fair in his approach to grading cattle. On several occasions, I was not satisfied with the grades at Burns, so I went to Mike and told him. He immediately dispatched several graders to go and have a look. Usually, they upgraded a few carcasses, but not many; however, the next day, the grading always improved. I thank Mike for that.

Several years before Mike retired, he bought a place west of Airdrie. He and his wife still live there. In 1978, we bought some property almost next door to them. In 1989 we built a log house on our land, so now we are close neighbours.

When our son, Trent, passed away in 1990, Mike and his wife were some of the first people to come and see us. They are good neighbours, even though, in this rushed day and age, we do not see them very often. The Harrises and ourselves have big families with lots of grandchildren, who keep us pretty busy.

Mike and his wife and family are devout Catholics and attend Mass in Airdrie.

WAYNE HARRIS worked for the Alberta Stock Yards. Wayne was a very pleasant fellow. He always did his job without any fuss. Long before mustaches became popular, he always wore one. Wayne and his wife owned a little place south of Midnapore on the west side of the Highway. His wife came to the Stockyards quite often to pick up a few calves. She did her own buying, which was unusual in those days—not many women bought cattle in the sale rings. Wayne retired some years ago. I think he is still with us.

KEITH HARRISON was the manager of Hartford Insurance Co., Calgary office, for a lot of years. He was a well-known person and was very sociable. He liked to play pinochle with his buddies, including Cliff Vandergrift who always called Keith "Cocky." Keith did a good job with Hartford. There were times when he got tough on claims. Usually the animals in dispute had died of natural causes, which meant they were not eligible for collecting insurance. Keith retired about ten years ago. He and his wife own a motorhome and, in the summer, they use it often.

BILL HART worked for the Federal Health of Animals Division at the Stockyards. Bill was an innovative person and liked a challenge. So, when the importation of the "exotic" cattle from Europe got started in late '60s, he saw an opportunity. He left the government service, and he and his wife, Stella, were the first people to set up a "bull stud station" in the Calgary area. The dairy people in B. C. had already been using artificial insemination for many years. The Harts called their operation Prairie Breeders. They also owned a ranch in the Hanna area. At one point, Bill got into the selling of "natural" beef. He passed away quite a few years ago.

BOB HARTELL was born and raised at Strathmore, Alberta. He became a brand inspector at the Stockyards in Calgary in the late 1980s. He is still with the brand department in Strathmore. Bob's dad, Jack, was a good rodeo cowboy and so was Bob. He was a bull rider and steer wrestler. I think he also rode bareback horses. In 1975 he was the all-around champion cowboy of Canada. He broke his wrist riding bulls and it never healed properly, so Bob had to give up the competition, but not his interest in rodeo. Bob was easy to work with and was very obliging. His nickname in the rodeo world was "Hog." He now owns Hoggy's Bar in Strathmore.

SYLVESTER HARVEY managed the office for Parslow & Denoon and really knew his stuff. He might find running an office a little more difficult these days, though. The reason I say this is because he never hired any women. I think he thought the Stockyards was no place for a woman. It's true, at times, the language used by certain individuals would curl your hair and make a sailor blush. Sylvester, himself was quite a prankster, although his language was okay.

One day Sylvester saw an ad in the newspaper. The ad was about a certain breed of tomcat standing at stud, fee $10 or whatever. Sylvester phoned the number. A very dignified, polite lady answered the phone. Sure enough, the tomcat was available if he had a willing female cat. Sylvester did not even own a cat. He discussed the whole business, pro and con, for about five minutes. Then, he politely ended the whole conversation by saying: "I'll have to think it over."

I'm sure those who knew or worked with Sylvester Harvey will never forget him. He had a striking appearance with his heavy mop of white hair. He passed away a number of years ago.

NORMAN HAUGAN came from Aden in the extreme south of Alberta. He was a cattle buyer for Canada Packers. He was a low-key type of person. He thought things out before he moved. I think he did a pretty good job for CP. I know one thing for sure, he was a 100-percent Canada Packer's man, just like Ian Davidson used to be; however, Norman was much mellower than Ian. Norman became the head buyer in Calgary—a job he held for several years before CP closed down their killing operation in Calgary. After that, he transferred to Lethbridge where he was a cattle buyer. When CP got out of the killing business altogether, Norman retired. It is my understanding that he does some work for the Vanee boys these days.

GAIL HAVARD worked at the Bank of Montreal for a while. She left the bank and went to work for the Alberta Livestock Co-op. She was a very pretty girl, which did not go unnoticed by Bruce Flewelling who courted and married her. They had two lovely daughters. As so often happens these days, the marriage ended in divorce. I am not sure where Gail lives at present. I hope things are going well for her.

DICK HAVENS farmed and ranched at Madden, Alberta. He was a staunch customer of Parslow & Denoon's. He came to the Stockyards a lot. I think Stan Denoon and Dick were in on a few deals as partners. Dick was a top-notch bareback bronc rider in his day. He often was a finalist at various rodeos. In 1959, he won the Canadian Bareback Championship, and, in 1961, he was the All-Around Champion. Dick's son, Raymond, has pretty well taken over the operation at Madden. Dick and his wife, Claire, are enjoying semi-retired life in Crossfield. Dick likes to go to rodeos as well as the auction markets, where he still purchases some cattle.

ROY HAXTON was a beef manager at Burns Calgary. He was a very tall and handsome man with black hair. His dad, Jim, and his brother, Jimmy, also worked for Burns. Roy was a good beef salesman. Burns transferred him to their Kitchener plant in Ontario, but his wife refused to move there for at least two years. She finally weakened and joined her husband. Can't say I blame her for not wanting to exchange Calgary for Kitchener.

CLIFF HEAL came from Delburne, Alberta. He liked dealing in cattle and hogs. Usually, the Calgary Stockyards was his final destination. Cliff was a very erect, concise person. He was all business— buying, selling, trading, and trucking. This is what he liked, and did. I have lost track of Cliff.

EDITH HECK was the first woman beef grader in Calgary. I did not know her very well. I think she did a pretty good job; however, for some reason—maybe Cupid—she did not last very long. Edith ended up marrying a butcher that worked at XL Beef. I hope they lived happily ever after.

DAVE HEDLEY worked for the Alberta Livestock Co-op: first, in the office; then, for a number of years, in the alley, penning cattle.

I first got to know Dave when he was an employee with Ashdown's Hardware in their wholesale warehouse. He worked at the front desk. I used to pick up a lot of orders from there in the days when my wife operated a hardware store. One day, he asked me if there were any job openings at the Stockyards. I happened to know that the Co-op was looking for help. He applied and got the job.

After working several years around the Yards, Dave became sort of a mascot. Everybody liked him, but for some reason the boys liked to pull off a joke or prank at his expense. He was a good sport and took it all in his stride. Sometimes he lost his temper, but not very often. He was not a very big man, but when he got mad, he seemed twice as large as he was.

After Dave left the Yards, he went into food catering for a while. He also worked as a security guard in a large office tower in downtown Calgary, and, on the side, he kept busy with his secondhand (collectibles and antiques) store on Macleod Trail South.

I liked Dave and always enjoyed a visit with him. We both have quite a few opinions on a number of subjects.

CASPAR HEIDRICK was not at the Stockyards very long. His first love was trucking, and, as far as I know, he is still at it. He was a very pleasant fellow.

WENDALL HEIDRICK and Caspar Heidrick are brothers. Wendall worked for the Alberta Stock Yards for years—in fact, most of his life. He was a good man with equipment and worked as a foreman for a long time. If you played ball with him, he played ball with you. When the Calgary Stockyards moved to Strathmore, Wendall stayed on in Calgary to look after the Livestock Exchange Building for Marathon Realty.

RUSS HILL worked for the Alberta Stock Yards for several decades. He was a good worker, but it was advisable to stay on the right side of him. I always did. Russ liked the country. On his days off, weekends or holidays, he would work for Pete Morison or the DeWitts at Airdrie. In fact, it was Russ who told me one day to contact Denver and Dallas DeWitt because they wanted to sell their place. I was not interested right then; but, about six months later, I did get in touch with them. Sure enough, we bought their place in 1978. There is a hayshed on our place that Russ helped build. I see Russ once in a while. He seems to be enjoying retired life.

HANS HINDBO lives at Spruce View, Alberta. Hans was the supervisor for the Raven Feeders' Association in the Innisfail area. He was not a fixture at the Yards, but he did buy a lot of cattle there— often, through our firm. Hans is a real gentleman. He came from Denmark as a young lad. He has had a full life. He wrote three small books about his life's experiences and they are very interesting. Hans is retired now and lives at Dixon, Alberta. Later in the sketches, I mention two other Feeder Association supervisors, Gerry Mooney and Stan Rock.

DON HOCKLEY came from Maple Creek, Saskatchewan. He was a brand inspector at the Stockyards. After Rudy Evenson retired, Don became the head brand inspector. His first day on the job, I had a terrible run-in with him. He was throwing his weight around a bit. (A new broom sweeps clean.) I won't go into details about our problem, but to this day I know I was right. Lest you get the wrong idea, I actually liked Don and still do. After that one incident, we got along just fine.

Don did like the horse races, which he attended on a regular basis. I do not know whether he made or lost money, but, knowing what the odds are, it probably was the latter.

Don's dad worked for the PFRA out of Regina. I often saw him at bull sales. He bought a lot of good bulls for the PFRA pastures.

Don is presently a brand supervisor in central Alberta.

JIM HOGG came from Endiang, Alberta. He went to work for the Alberta Livestock Co-op when he was sixteen years old. He arrived at the Stockyards a few months before I came to Burns. The first time I saw him was in February of 1950. He came to Burns with Lee Teasdale to pick up some cattle that Lee had bought from Mickey Dirrane.

Jimmy spent a lot of years sorting cattle for the Co-op at both the Stockyards and, later, the Agri-Mart. For a number of years, Vern

Scoun, Bill Duggan, Jimmy Hogg, Don Richie, and, sometimes, Chris Jacobsen went to Brooks to operate the Bow Slope sale on Thursdays. The boys sometimes referred to Jimmy and Don as the Katzenjammer Kids. After the Agri-Mart closed, Jim came back to the Stockyards to order buy cattle. He bought quite a few bulls to ship. For several years, Jim bought big buckskin steer calves to ship to Quebec. I was buying the same type of steers, so, at times, we heated the market up pretty good.

Jim likes to take the odd nip. He is a carryover from the old school. He still attends the sales in Strathmore. He has been around for forty-five years. If he lives as long as his dad did, he may be around for another forty-five years. Good luck, Jim.

BOB HOLDGATE was a brand inspector. He liked visiting slightly better than brand inspecting. I am not saying he was not a good inspector, but he did cut a few corners, especially on cold winter days. Bob always wore a big cowboy hat. He coiled his rope in a bigger circle than most ropers do. He always had a story to tell. As far as I am concerned, Bob never lost his cool or messed us up. He retired a number of years ago and has since passed away.

PETER HOLT worked in the office for Parslow & Denoon. He took an interest in life. He would sometimes pick your brains for ideas on how to make an extra buck. He also liked to get into card games with the boys. He was a friendly sort and knew everybody around the Yards. I understand Peter is in the garbage disposal business these days. That seems to be the trend of the '90s.

ANDY HOOD worked for Burns feeding cattle with a team of horses. When he left Burns, he became a brand inspector. He was quite laid-back, but he got the job done. In many ways, he reminded me of Bob Holdgate, except Holdgate was a better story teller. Andy passed away a number of years ago.

ROY HOOD was Andy Hood's son. He worked for the Alberta Stock Yards for a while. When he left, he went to work for XL Ranches at Bassano. I really did not know him very well. I have no idea what he is up to these days.

CLIFF HOOD was a bank manager at the Bank of Montreal, Stockyards Branch. He was a skinny little guy. Some days he imbibed a little too freely. When he was sober, he was a good person to do business with. I am not sure where he went after he left the Yards.

GEORGE HOPKINS was a likeable redhead who was White Garries' assistant in the Co-op office for years. When George Winkelaar retired, George was promoted to general manager of the Co-op.

Things were going pretty well. The Co-op got good receipts; everything was fine. Then, George, along with some of the Co-op directors, got the idea of building their own selling facility. This idea did not sit well with the Stockyards' general manager Charlie Kennedy, or, for that matter, with the entire Livestock Exchange. It was felt that splitting up the market in Calgary was not a good plan; however, George and his directors were determined to go ahead.

They purchased land on McKnight Boulevard close to the Airport and built what they called the Agri-Mart. Like I said, George was a likeable person; however, he made a few errors. Number 1: He had a falling out with Red Wheatcroft, who had been a big Co-op supporter ever since he opened up his order buying business. Number 2: He made no overture to me, by not inviting me to support their market. I guess he thought I was not a big factor.

As it turned out, we became one of the biggest order buyers in Canada, during the next decade. (That's all history now.) What George did not seem to realize was the fact that, in order for a market to succeed, you have to have a lot of buying power at every sale. Farmers and ranchers are not dumb. They soon figure out which market has the buying power. In those days, not many farmers bought cattle; they were nearly all bought by order-buyers and commission men.

After a few years, they had to give up their dream of their own market. They closed and sold the property. The Edmonton Co-op and the Fairview Co-op closed up as well. George did give it his best shot, but the power of the Calgary Stockyards was too overwhelming.

I have not seen or heard about George for years. I am sure he is doing okay.

RANDY HOPP was a brand inspector who lived at Okotoks, Alberta. His wife worked in the cafe downstairs in the Livestock Exchange Building. One year, Randy and his wife were involved with selecting a rodeo queen for the Okotoks Rodeo. They asked me to be one of the judges. There were seven or eight contestants. The girls were all put through the paces, including horsemanship and personality. The girl I thought should have won, didn't. The other four judges had other ideas. It was neither the first nor last time that I have been wrong. Randy and his wife treated me very well. In my opinion, they did a good job working with those young ladies. I have lost track of the Hopps.

DONALDA HOTOMANIE started to work for the Calgary Stockyards in 1987. She is a competent, pleasant person. She is computer literate. Whenever she is on the auctioneers' stand punching the computer there are very few errors. She works in the Calgary office except on sale days when she does her thing at Strathmore.

PERCY HOTOMANIE worked for the Calgary Stockyards for a about a year in the late '80s. He came from an Indian Reservation by the unique name of "Carry The Kettle" in eastern Saskatchewan. He is Donalda's father.

NICK HUCULAK was a cattle buyer from Burns Edmonton, Alberta. When Edmonton closed, he was transferred to Calgary. In Calgary he bought cattle in the sale ring. He was not what you could call a volume buyer but whatever he bought was usually bought right. When Burns Calgary closed, he went to work for Dvorkin's in the scalehouse. After Dvorkin's closed, he retired. Nick is one of the few people who were on deck for three plant closings. He lives in Calgary.

BILL HUNTER hung around the Calgary Stockyards a lot. I was never quite sure what his occupation was. I know he liked diamond rings. He traded some livestock; however, it seemed his main interests were always somewhere else. He lived in a nice log house south of Calgary. I often wonder what happened to him.

KEN HURLBURT was born and raised at Milk River, Alberta. He always liked cattle, so he went to Lethbridge to get involved with livestock. He got a job with J. W. Johnstone, a big order-buyer headquartered in Winnipeg.

Ken soon decided he liked selling cattle better than buying them, so he took an auctioneer's course. This gave him the opportunity to sell cattle for community auctions in southern Alberta. For many years, he also sold the Walsh sale, which was headed up by Bert Hargrave. In the late '50s, Ken auctioned at the Calgary market. Then, in the early '60s, he teamed up with Ted Nichols and, I think, one other partner. They then built and opened up the Fort Macleod Auction Market.

For many years, the Fort Macleod Auction Mart sponsored a cattle show called the "Little Royal." It was a good show. I judged it for five consecutive years. I was sorry when they discontinued it. They had a single steer class as well as pens of steers and heifers. I also felt bad when the Calgary Round-up Show was dropped.

In 1982 Ken and his partners built the Highwood Auction Mart at High River. You have to hand it to Ken, he is a good promoter. He also has some very solid people working with him: his son Brant Hurlburt, Bob Dyck, Frank Noble, Harvey Bourassa, Kirk Williamson, Bill Perlich as well as many other good people. I think the experience Ken gained at the Calgary Stockyards helped him a lot, later in his career.

Also, Ken was the Conservative MP for Fort Macleod for at least two terms.

BOB HURST worked the night shift in the Burns livestock department. He was a son-in-law of Archie Currie's. Bob liked to talk—anytime, anywhere. There was very little in this world he had not tried one time or another. I have no idea what he did after he left Burns.

INAMASU BROTHERS—there were five of them: George, Jim, Albert, Pat, and Harry. They operated the Stockyards Cafe in the old Exchange Building. Their father had immigrated to Canada from Japan as a young man, and the boys were all born in Canada. Their dad had cooked on a few big ranches. I think he cooked on one of Burns' big spreads, among others. After that, he opened up a

226

restaurant in the old Alberta Stock Yards Hotel, which was demolished long before I came to the Yards. He then started the cafe in the basement of the back end of the Exchange Building. The boys grew up around the Stockyards. They took over where their dad left off and ran a really good restaurant. They were fast, the food was good, and the price was right. George usually worked in the kitchen. Jim and Pat kind of alternated. Albert did the table waiting and ran the cash register. Harry was very seldom there.

The Inamasu boys liked racehorses—they always raced a few. They had a place southeast of the City where they kept them. Harry looked after the horses at home and at the track. They did not get rich with the horses, but I know they produced a few winners.

There was one little incident in the cafe I will never forget: I often went in there for coffee. (They made really good coffee.) One day I went into the cafe and as I was walking to my table I noticed the big coffee urn had the lid off. For some reason, I looked inside and there was a whole bunch of egg shells laying on the bottom. I was so shocked that I ordered another drink instead of coffee. I have since heard that egg shells do enhance the taste of coffee and that it is a fairly common practice.

I have lost touch with the Inamasu brothers. I think only two of them are still with us. They were a great asset to the Calgary Stockyards.

BILL INVERARITY has a place a little northeast of Calgary. He has been around the Yards for a long time. He feeds and trucks cattle. His truck is one of the so-called body-jobs still in the business of hauling cattle. He also order buys cattle and attends pretty well every sale at Strathmore. Bill is a good man. Occasionally, he stays in the pub a little too long. At those times he can cause a few waves. He is a good trucker—very dependable. One day, not too long ago, somebody cut him off as he was barrelling down the Deerfoot Trail. He had to take the ditch. His truck flipped over and about twelve big steers were "home-on-the-range" in the City. Bill was not hurt, and he knew somebody would round up the steers. His main concern was his dog, Hoot. Luckily, like his master, the mutt was located and well. Bill and Hoot are still in business.

WILL IRVINE was born and raised in Calgary, Alberta. He is a very special person to my wife and me. He worked with us for about fifteen years, and even though we had four sons of our own, he seemed like a fifth son.

Will started to work at the MacLean Auction Market on Saturdays when he was about twelve years old. After he finished high school, he went to work for Canada Packers. He was only there about six months. At that point, Henry and Jim Bridgewater hired him. Bridgewaters opened up an office in Edmonton and Jim and Will ran the operation. In 1968, Jim came back to their Calgary office. Will stayed in Edmonton for a few more years. In 1971 we closed our Edmonton office. Will then joined us in Calgary. About a year later, Jim left to go into real estate. In 1974 Henry turned his share of the business over to us. From March 1974 to the spring of 1977 Will and I held the fort in the cattle-buying department.

In 1977 my son Leland came on board in Calgary. He had been on the ranch at Stavely from 1974 to 1977. From 1977 to 1981 Will, Lee, and I worked together in the order-buying business.

In 1981, when we reorganized the market, Will went to work for us as a country representative for the market. It so happened that I was president of the market. After several years, Will had the opportunity to work with the Canadian Simmental Association—a challenge which he accepted. He was Canadian fieldman. By all the reports I heard he did an excellent job for them. (I heard this from other people, not Will.) So, all together, Will had a close association with us for a period of fifteen or sixteen years.

When he left the Simmental Association, he came back to take over the Stockyards along with the sole remaining partner of the original seven, Cec Barber. Will introduced computer cattle selling to western Canada.

In his travels with the Simmental people, he met Jim Wideman from Kitchener, who was selling fat cattle by computer. Will liked what he saw and secured the franchise for western Canada. It has proven to be a success. They have sold hundreds of thousands of cattle by that method in the last seven or eight years. One reason things have gone as well as they have, is because Will is a knowledgeable cattleman. He is honest, personable, and a hard worker.

This may be hard to believe, but Will and I have never had a major disagreement. We always discussed everything in a very open way.

Will, like Lee and I, is a born-again Christian. But, that doesn't make any of us perfect people—far from it. We have lots of faults and problems, but our strong belief sure does help us in our daily lives and interaction with other people.

Will, like many of us, has quite a temper. To his credit, he usually controls it, but there have been a few occasions when it got away on him. I am proud to have been associated with him in the cow business as well as socially. Will's favourite expression, when things go wrong—as they sometimes do—is: "Oh, filth!"

On July 1, 1993, Will took over the Edmonton market. He ran a good operation. As the proverbial saying goes, he was busier than a one-armed paper hanger. He would either drive or fly up to Edmonton on Monday mornings. After three hectic days up there, he would return to Calgary on Wednesday evening. On Thursdays and Fridays he was at Strathmore. He kept this pace up for one year. At that point, he sold the Edmonton operation to Ted Wood. Will stayed on to manage the market for another six months. After that he returned to "Cowtown" permanently.

Will, Don Danard, and their crew run a good show at Strathmore.

BEVERLEY IRVINE is Will Irvine's wife. She came to the Stockyards after Will left the Simmental Association to become a partner with Cec Barber in operating the market. Bev is very sharp with figures and computers. She is the office manager at Strathmore and does a good job. There is not much that escapes her. Several years ago Will and Bev adopted a baby girl—a real cute little thing. Sometimes Bev brings her along, but, oftentimes, she leaves her with a sitter. Bev also likes dogs; she has several of them. She came from Ontario originally, but now she is a dyed-in-the-wool Westerner.

ELWIN JACKMAN was a trucker at the Stockyards for years. He worked very closely with Sam Blyth. Elwin was a small man with a big heart. He could also do a man's job on anything he undertook. I talked with him quite often—this was about thirty-five or forty years ago. Elwin passed away many years ago.

LINDA JACKSON was a short-term brand inspector who worked at the Yards in the late '70s. She was the first and, I think, the last lady brand inspector. Linda was a really nice person; however, she failed to mention that she was pregnant. After three months, the evidence started to show. On most jobs this is no big deal these days. But, roping snuffy cows to clip for brands is not exactly a job for somebody who is a candidate for the maternity ward. So the brand department and Linda parted company on good terms. I haven't a clue where Linda is these days, but, with her get-up-and-go, I am sure she is doing okay.

PETER JACKSON was a flamboyant Irishman that hit the Yards like a storm. Actually, he worked for Calgary Packers. After he left there, he worked for P&M. Peter lived life in the fast lane. His main hobbies were women, wine and fast cars. He could also spin yarns. Ireland must be a pretty good country. They have exported a lot of characters to Canada and the U.S. Boston and New York City are loaded with their descendants and all of them are proud of their heritage.

MURRAY JACOBS was an auctioneer from Edmonton. In 1951 the Calgary market switched from private treaty selling to the auction method. They had to find some good auctioneers. It so happened that Murray was willing to come to Calgary and was a good auctioneer; however, after several years, he yearned for Edmonton. (Hard to believe!) So they exchanged—Murray went back to Edmonton and Vern Scoun came to Calgary. Maybe it was a good deal for both parties since Vern turned out to be an excellent auctioneer. I saw Murray once or twice after he went back to Edmonton, but I have lost track of him.

CHRIS JACOBSON came from Brooks, Alberta—the home of many Scandinavian people. Chris always went by the name of "Whitey." He had light blond hair like his Viking ancestors. He worked for the Alberta Livestock Co-op as a cattle buyer. He had good connections at Brooks and other areas in that east country. He was a good friend of Jim Wilfley's. Jim was the founder of Lakeside Packers and Feeders. Whenever the Stockyards' gang planned a social event or party, you could bet your bottom dollar that Hughie

Kane and Chris were on the committee to put it all together. This included golf tournaments. Chris stayed with the Co-op till they closed the Agri-Mart. Since then he has worked with the Rimbey market. Now, he order buys some cattle on his own.

GEORGE JAMISON worked in the office for Parslow & Denoon for many years. He was a workhorse and stuck around till the work was done. As a lifelong confirmed bachelor, hours did not mean much to him, since there was no little lady waiting for him at home.

George was a sincere, good man; however, he had one flaw—it was next to impossible to read any figures that he wrote down. He worked with and wrote figures most of the day, every day. I often wondered how the accountants, who did P&D's tax returns, ever figured out what he had written.

George's dad also was an accountant and worked at the Yards on occasion. One day, George told me he had suggested that his dad buy a TV. This was in the days of black and white television. Color TV would be available in a few years. Mr. Jamison Sr. looked at George in his most serious manner and said, "I am going to wait until color TV is available before I buy one." His dad was ninety-six years old at the time.

George liked to get together with his bachelor friends, Bill McRae and George Johnson, for an evening of cards and story swapping.

George passed away about twenty years ago.

HARVEY JAMIESON worked for Burns and still does. He fed cattle in the Burns Yards for a while before he was promoted to salesman. He turned out to be a good one, so pretty soon they promoted him to account executive. This meant he dealt with the big accounts such as Safeway, Loblaws (in those days) and Calgary Co-op Stores. Harvey is still involved as one of the key people in the Burns Distribution Centre, just south of where the Stockyards used to be located.

MARK JENKINS came from Stavely, Alberta. His parents had a ranch west of our ranch. He used to work for P&M during the winter. In the summertime, he was busy with his racehorses. He also had some kind of executive position with the racing commission in Alberta. He was a good-looking, easy-to-talk-to individual. I was shocked to hear of his early death.

MARY JENSEN was a very vivacious, petite lady with black hair. She worked in the office for the Alberta Stock Yards Co. She spoke in a very cultured voice and looked like the high society type. We did not move in her social circles. It was my understanding underneath the veneer there was quite a party girl. She did a good job for the Stockyards and stayed until her retirement about two and a half decades ago.

ALVIN JEWELL was a fixture around the Yards. He was a wheeler-dealer, as was common in the old days. He moved a lot of cattle from market to market. The old High River Market was a favourite hangout of his. He owned a place not too far from there, near the Highwood River. Alvin was a happy-go-lucky kind of guy. He had an answer for everything. His son was a jockey for a while, then he got too heavy and had to quit. Alvin died in a car crash a number of years ago.

ERIC JOHNSON started coming to the Stockyards in the mid- to late-'80s. He is a cattle dealer and order buyer who lives at Didsbury. Eric is a good-natured chap and likes to shoot the breeze with his buddies. He is easy to spot with his big black cowboy hat. We are almost shirt-tail relatives. His mother is a sister of my cousin's son's wife. (Both my cousin's son and his wife have passed away.) The future looks good for Eric.

GEORGE JOHNSON was a trucker at the Yards for many years. He was an easygoing, good-natured man. Maybe that's because he never married. He never got rattled, no matter what the situation; he just went on about his business. He hauled thousands of cattle to and from the Yards. He also liked racehorses. (This was very common around the Yards.) George passed away some years ago.

LORNE JOHNSON was raised in the Hanna country. For several years he worked for AWW. When he left the Yards he went to work for Western Feedlots at Strathmore. For a few years, he ran the calf lot just west of the main feedlot. When he was young he did some calf roping. In later years he had draft horses. He often competed in horse-pulling contests. I have lost track of Lorne.

LYLE JOHNSON was a trucker around the Yards. He owned a body-job, which he kept on the move six days a week, sometimes seven. I don't know where he went after he left the Stockyards.

IRISH JOHNSTON was a big ruddy-faced Irishman. He came to the Stockyards in 1923. He was involved with various people and firms. Some of his associations that I am aware of are: Adams, Wood and Weiller as a salesman; Producers' Livestock as owner and auctioneer; Harry Feldman as a cattle buyer; and Bridgewater Livestock as a part-time buyer and cow seller. We used to sell a lot of bred cows. Irish had some other connections in his early years at the Yards, but I am not certain what they were.

Photo by Bridgewater.

"Man, that's an awful lot o' beef," Northern Packers buyer "Irish" Johnson seems to be saying, as he poses with a pair of hefty visitors to the Calgary Yards. The steers that Irish, and fellow buyer Mel Morrison, were admiring were two of the heaviest cattle ever to visit the stockyards, having individual weights of 2,330 lbs. and 2,000 lbs. The blue steer in the foreground — the larger of the two — was five years old. Its companion — carrying an impressive set of horns — was four years old. The animals were produced by Dyck Brothers of Didsbury.

2 HEAD . . . 2 TON . . . NO BULL!

Irish was not the best auctioneer, although he got the job done. He really got tongue-tied when he hit the figure of "66" so we always tried to bid up to 65 and leave him hung up trying to get 66. It was kind of a cruel prank, but boys will be boys no matter what their age. Try repeating "66" in rapid succession like an auctioneer does. It does test your tongue.

Every once in a while an old Holstein dairy cow would make her appearance in the sale ring. Many of the cows had enormous udders. More than once I heard Irish say, "I wonder how many cups of tea her milk has coloured in her life time." If all her milk had been used for that purpose, I am sure the number of cups of tea coloured by her milk would have been about the same amount as the dollars of Canada's national debt these days. Like many Irishmen, Irish liked to tip a few. He had a few favourite watering holes.

Irish was around the Stockyards about fifty years. He and his wife had one daughter. She is married and lives in Spokane. When Irish retired, he and his wife moved to Creston, B.C. That is a lot closer to Spokane than Calgary.

ANNE JONES was Charlie Kennedy's private secretary for a number of years. In fact, she worked there on two different occasions. Anne was articulate and competent. She happened to be a Jehovah's Witness, but this certainly did not interfere with her performance at the office. These days, Anne and her husband are retired and living in Calgary.

CY JONES worked for the Alberta Stock Yards for some years. When they opened up their Lethbridge market, they sent Cy there as the Yards manager. I met him on several occasions, but I really did not know him too well. Like so many unsung heros in the cattle business, Cy did his bit without much fanfare.

KEN JONES was raised in East Calgary. He was around the Yards for as long as he can remember. At ten to twelve years of age, he, along with several other East Calgary boys, started to "muck" the farmers' trucks.

In those days, there were a lot of farmers with small to medium sized trucks, who hauled their own cattle or hogs to either Burns or the Calgary Stockyards. After the farmer unloaded his stock, the boys would offer to clean the straw and manure out of his truck for a small fee—25 or 50 cents. Usually, the farmer said: "Go ahead, but drive carefully." Of course, these boys were all too young for a driver's license, but that didn't seem to bother the boys or the farmer. On more than one occasion, these trucks were taken on "joy rides" after cleaning them. A few times, this little caper resulted in a wreck. To my knowledge, Ken never wrecked a truck.

After Ken grew up, he went into the cattle trading business on his own. For several years, he worked for Harry Feldman as a cow buyer. Those years were the exception; Ken liked working on his own. Along with cattle dealing, he went into the cattle trucking business. He later sold the trucks to Gordon Meston.

As the years went by, Ken gradually got into dealing in what he calls "odd and unusual" livestock, such as llamas, buffalo, and ostriches as well as many other kinds of exotic animals and birds. Every year, he has two sales of these creatures. For several years the sales were held at Red Deer, and for the last number of years at the Daines Innisfail Auction Market.

For some years, Ken had a nice lady by the name of Betty Jones doing his books. She was not related to him.

Ken lives on Highway 27, just south of Highway 1 at the Cheadle Corner. If you glance to the south of Highway 1, you may spot some of those exotic animals in a field close to his house. Different strokes for different folks.

NORM JONES had a real-estate office in the Exchange Building. He specialized in farm and ranch sales. He moved a lot of property. His daughter, Sally, worked with him as a salesperson. She was quite a hustler (in real estate). She knew the business. Norm always walked around as though he was deep in thought—maybe he was. In spite of that, he always had time to stop and chat. Last I heard, he had a real-estate office in Olds.

RON JONES is not related to any of the other Joneses. He works for the Health of Animals Department. He was around the Yards for years. He is low-profile and goes about his job in a matter-of-fact way. He doesn't throw his weight around to cause anybody extra problems. Presently, he is an inspector of farm products at the Calgary Airport.

AL JORDAN was Roy Furgeson's right-hand man in the AWW office for at least forty years. He was a friendly, striking-looking man, with his well-manicured nails and neatly combed hair. He did his job day in and day out without any complaint. I always thought he could have handled a much bigger job but, as so often happens, a person gets in a rut and stays there. Besides, Al liked it at the Stockyards.

HUGHIE KANE was born and raised in East Calgary. As a boy, he spent a lot of time at the old Victoria Hockey Rink on the Stampede grounds. After he got out of school, he worked for the Calgary Exhibition and Stampede. In the late 1950s, he went to work for AWW at the Yards.

Hughie was a very social person. Whenever there were events planned such as banquets and golf tournaments, he was always front and centre. He was good at organizing these affairs. He took a few years off from the Stockyards and, during this period, he and Vic Hammill operated a curling rink in Phoenix. I think they thought that, with so many Canadian "snowbirds" down there for the winter, curling would go over big. Somehow, it didn't work out that way. Even though Vic was a good promoter and Hughie did his part, it just didn't pan out. I know a little about the Phoenix area. We owned a food plant there that should have worked. We lost a million and a half dollars before we locked the doors.

In the late 1970s, Hughie went to work for the Olds Auction. He stayed there till a few years ago when he retired.

HERMAN KARPERIEN came from Holland wearing wooden shoes. He was employed by the Alberta Stock Yards and was a very good worker. Herman came from a very big family. They came to Canada in the early '50s. He was one of the first Dutch immigrants that I met. During the decade of the '50s, thousands of Dutch people arrived in Canada. I know a lot of them. They have been very good for Canada. These people are mostly God-fearing, hardworking, law-abiding citizens. Maybe I have a biased opinion, since my forefathers left Holland (Friesland) in the year 1744. As far as I know, Herman still lives in South Calgary.

KEN KARSTEN SR. and his wife Theresa came to Canada from Holland in the early '50s. Ken worked for the Palmers at Pincher

Creek for a while. Then he started driving cattleliners. When I first met him, he was driving for Eamor's Cattleliners. He always did a good job.

I think it was in the early 1970s that Ken, along with a few other partners, opened up a feedlot at Claresholm called Claresholm Beef Producers. After a few years, he bought out his partners. He runs a good operation. I have fed a lot of cattle at his place. I always liked to visit with him. He is very meticulous; everything has to be in order and cleaned up. Ken's word is his bond.

Ken and his wife are very fine Christian people. They attend a Reform Church east of Granum. We attended their son's funeral at that church. Their son-in-law was the minister. We wish Ken and Theresa the best in the years ahead.

KEN KARSTEN JR. was the son of Ken Karsten Sr. Ken was born in Calgary, but grew up and went to school in Claresholm. After he finished high school, he worked for Burns Calgary in the livestock division for a little over a year. He then went back to Claresholm and joined his dad at the feedlot. Ken was a really nice guy. He was always pleasant and easy to talk to. In my opinion, he was one of our better up-and-coming young cattlemen. Ken passed away in a very unexpected manner in the winter of 1993. Our hearts ache for the family. We lost our youngest son, Trent, in 1990.

MYER KATCHEN, along with his brother, Sam, owned and operated a packing plant they called Katchen Bros. Myer came to the Calgary Stockyards to buy cattle. In the private treaty days, he always got his share. Then when the auction method took over, he was there every day. He was a top-notch cattle buyer. One interesting fact is that in both Canada and the USA the small independent meat-packing plants put a high premium on the purchasing of livestock. Often, as in the case of Katchen's and Dvorkin's operations, the owners themselves bought the cattle whereas, at the multiplant companies, the "wheels" liked to sit in an office, not in a sale ring. Katchen Bros. did very well. It was sometime in the late '50s that they sold out to Canada Packers.

SAMMY KATCHEN was Myer Katchen's brother and partner. He, too, came to the sale ring once in a while, but not nearly as often as Myer. Sam was much more relaxed. He looked after things around the plant.

Every once in a while, Sammy would come to the hog and sheep scale to buy. On the hogs, he was as tough as he needed to be; however, when it came to lambs, he was a "patsy." Cliff Green, Maule McEwen and Ook McRae loved it when Sammy came over to buy lambs. They priced them $2 or $3 over the market and he bought them every time. I would be trying to buy some for Burns, but whenever Sammy was there I went home empty-handed.

After Katchen Bros. sold out to Canada Packers, Sam went into several other business ventures. I never heard, but I am sure they succeeded.

BOB KEDDIE was born and raised in Calgary, Alberta. He is a stepson of Don Stewart, who worked at Burns all his life. Bob was around Burns and the Calgary Stockyards at an early age. He came to work for Burns in the mid-'60s. He started in the livestock department where he became a cattle buyer. In 1970, he was transferred to Brandon, Manitoba, as a cattle buyer. He stayed with Burns until they closed that plant a few years ago.

Bob liked rodeo and contested for a few years. He also liked karate, where he earned a black belt. He has promoted some rodeo activity around Brandon. His sons played pretty good hockey. I don't think they made it to the NHL level. Bob still resides in the Brandon area.

Oh, yes, there is one story concerning Bob I have to tell: One day, at Burns' Calgary plant, a wild steer escaped while being unloaded at the truck chutes. The steer took off into an East Calgary residential neighbourhood. This was pretty dangerous for the people living there. A few of the boys from Burns jumped in a pick-up truck and took off after it. Bob was standing in the back with a lariat. They chased this steer all over the place. Finally, Bob got a chance to throw the rope. He caught the steer in someone's backyard. He was very quick, so he dallied the rope around a medium-sized fruit or ornamental tree. When the steer hit the slack, the tree got jerked out by the roots. Away went the steer—rope, tree and all. After another half-hour, they captured the steer again. This time they held onto him. Burns had to pay lawn and tree damages to at least one resident—I think actually to several.

It was a small price to pay. Someone could have gotten hurt and that would have been a tragedy. All's well that ends well.

DOUG KEER lived at Lyalta, Alberta, where he farmed and fed cattle. In 1958 he and Cec Barber bought out Jimmy Paul, so Doug and Cec became partners of Danny MacDonald's. Doug was a very low-key person. He never caused any ripples around the Yards. He was a gentleman in the true sense of the word. While Danny was rolling the dice in the back room and Cec was contemplating his next move to keep the outfit profitable, Doug was calmly chatting with customers doing his public relations bit. Those three were quite a combination, but they ran a good show. As I have said before, the good often die young. Doug was not an old man when he passed away.

KEER BROTHERS: Johnnie and Bert were Doug Keer's sons. They, like their dad, are fine decent citizens. They still farm and feed cattle at Lyalta. I think they feed some of their cattle at custom feedlots. Both Johnnie and Bert worked in the Yards in the off-season. They did a good job there, just like they do in their farming operation. I see them quite often at the Strathmore market. They are also involved in community affairs. Doug set a good example for his sons to follow.

ALBERT KELLSEY worked for AWW as a cattle buyer. He was not the friendliest sort of man. I got along with him, even though at times it was a little "iffy." There were some people that Albert did not talk to, including Buck Rothwell, Henry Bridgewater and a few others. Albert always had a chew under his lip. This gave him an even more sour look. Vern McRae used to say: "Just think of it, Albert was somebody's beautiful baby once." He was not all that bad, but like most of us, he had some personality quirks. Albert actually was a good judge of cattle. He had his following in such people as Dave Abrahams and Bill Clappison, who owned a meat-packing plant at Haney, British Columbia. Albert died many years ago.

STAN KELLSEY was a cattle dealer from Carstairs, Alberta. In the '50s and '60s, it was common practice to buy cattle in the country, or from some of the auction markets that were springing up. The dealers would then haul them to Calgary and sell them. Stan did a lot of this, and he was very good at it. He had a lot of patience and bought very carefully. In spite of this, sometimes the cattle would lose money. Win or lose, his expression never changed. He was completely calm and unruffled, never complained, and always stood on his own two feet.

In the very early '50s, when I was at Burns, Stan used to haul quite a few hogs to Burns. Sometimes, in the winter, when it was extremely cold and blizzarding and we were short of hogs to kill, we could always depend on Stan to show up with a load of hogs, which would be in a covered truck to prevent frostbite to the hogs. Weather never stopped him; business went on—rain, shine, blizzard or whatever.

Stan was a fine Christian man. He passed away at a Bible School banquet where he was giving a talk. I think he was promoting a steer-a-year project to help the school defray costs. This fine man left behind a good legacy. Not all cattle dealers can be compared to used-car salesmen. Some had a lot of class, and Stan was one of them.

GARY KELLSEY is Stan Kellsey's son. Gary, too, lives at Carstairs. He started out with his dad so I know he had some good training. Gary continued on in the cattle dealing business; however, as the years passed, cattle dealing almost became obsolete. With the advent of the big feedlot, order-buying took over.

For many years now, Gary and his two sons, Raymond and Laverne, have order bought thousands of cattle. They cover at least seven or eight markets—plus country buying. They still haul some of the cattle they buy with their own trucks, but, with the volume they handle, they have to employ quite a few other truckers at times.

Gary came to the Calgary market for a lot of years, often to sell cows and bulls. Like I mentioned, dealing in cattle from market to market was common in the early days.

There was one class of cattle that survived dealing longer than fat cattle and feeders and that was butcher cows and bulls. The packers often had no representatives on the smaller markets. Farmers brought the cows and bulls anyway. Somebody had to buy them. This is where the dealers came in. Calgary always had packer buyers in attendance. Often, the dealer only made enough profit to pay for his trucking expenses. But, this provided a real service to the farmer, saving him from hauling a few head 50, 60 or 80 miles to the Calgary market.

The cattle business can test one's faith at times, but the Kellseys are survivors. Gary and his wife, along with Raymond and Laverne and their wives, are Christian people involved with their local church.

WAYNE KELLSEY is a son of Stan Kellsey and brother of Gary Kellsey. Wayne, too, often came to the Calgary market. Like his dad and brother, he is a dealer and order buyer. Wayne moved to the Ponoka district many years ago. Even after he moved there, he showed up at the Calgary market quite often. Wayne is also an auctioneer and, I might add, a pretty good one. For some reason he does not do a lot of auctioning anymore. Maybe he likes the cattle business better from the other side of the ring. Wayne has experienced some health problems in the last few years.

(L-R) Bob Sievert, Wayne Kellsey and Bruce Flewelling doing a little socializing, 1979.

WILF KELLY worked in the office of the government grading service. He was a very low-key person. He caused no waves. It was quite obvious that he indulged fairly regularly. He used to pick up the scale tickets and sort them for prices. He never hung around—when the work was done, he was gone.

CY KELSON was raised in Calgary, Alberta. His dad had a meat market, so Cy was exposed to the beef industry at a young age. I think it was a Kosher meat market, but I'm not sure. Later on, he worked for Dvorkin's as beef manager. When XL bought Rocky Mountain Packers, Cy went to work for XL Beef as manager.

Cy was a sociable kind, but tougher than whalebone when doing business. I know, because I did some business with him. I am not saying he was not fair, but he did not give you any breaks whatsoever.

At one time, we owned a meat market in partnership with XL Beef and two other partners. It did not pan out. We used to feed a lot of cattle at Western Feedlots in Strathmore. We always put them up for bid and the highest bidder got them. One winter, there was a lot of "tag" on cattle, which is not unusual during some winters. XL were the high bidders on our cattle. After they slaughtered them, they said they had not yielded very well. They were looking for some rebate on the price. This was quite unorthodox since all the other packers also bid on the cattle and the tag was very visible. In a weak moment we gave them a rebate. What was our reward for the next six months? They did not bid on our cattle. I never did figure Cy out on that one.

Cy was good friends with Mac MacKinnon, who was the beef manager at Burns. Mac often had lunch with Cy and sometimes I joined them. We had some very good discussions on many subjects. Cy was what I would call "worldly-wise." He had done a lot of living, but he was a tough customer when it came to business.

In later years, he had some health problems. I think he is okay now.

CHARLIE KENNEDY started out as assistant general manager but soon became general manager of Alberta Stock Yards Co. He worked there from 1938 until his retirement in 1976—about thirty-nine years. He was a good administrator and did not stand for much nonsense in the workplace. Charlie was a very sociable individual, and he and his wife, Marie, attended a lot of social functions.

When I first met Charlie, I thought he was rather aloof. Then I discovered he had what they call "tunnel" vision. In other words, he could only see straight ahead, so if you were to the side of him, he did not see you. This ran in his family; several of his brothers had the same problem.

Over the years, I got to know Charlie and always got along really well with him, but he could be tough when it was necessary. When the Alberta Livestock Co-op decided to move out of the Yards to start the Agri-Mart, Charlie literally saw red. He worked day and night to prevent them from leaving.

It was Charlie's contention that the Co-op had been treated very well by the Alberta Stock Yards Co.; and, indeed they had. He also felt it would be very detrimental to the Yards with the Co-op gone. He did not think that Calgary could support two cattle markets. The Co-op won the first round. After much hassle and red tape, they built their Agri-Mart.

Charlie was not finished yet. The next move he made was to give J. C. Wheatcroft the right to start a commission firm. Wheatcroft had been a Co-op supporter until about six months before they moved out. Red Wheatcroft and Roy Gilkes went after customers and they got them. The other three commission firms also doubled their efforts. As a result, the total receipts at the Yards hardly suffered any loss.

Meanwhile, the Co-op had their problems. They had a big investment in buildings and equipment, including a first-class truck wash that the city made them erect. They also had cattle receipt problems. The diehard Co-op customers stayed with them. They may have even had a few new ones, but their receipts could not support the large capital investment and overhead they had. They gave it their best shot, but it was not enough. They hosted the first Elbow Slope Cattle Sale. I think they had several sales there.

They may deny it, but one of their weak spots was buying power. Things have changed today. They would have lots of buyers. In those days, almost thirty years ago, there were a limited number of volume buyers. Those in this area were nearly all at the Stockyards. This is where Charlie comes back into the picture.

Calgary was a federally licensed market along with about nine other markets in Canada. Those days, under the Ottawa rules, you could only operate a commission firm or order-buying business if you were licensed by them through the market.

In my case—with the Calgary market—what happened was this: I was on good terms with the Co-op boys. Even though their manager, George Hopkins, had never invited me up there, I went anyway. I bought some cattle that were really worth the money. All cattle buyers like cheap cattle, so I went back for more. You guessed it, Charlie heard about it and called me into his office. He kind of glared at me and said, "Did you buy cattle at the Agri-Mart yesterday?

I said, "Yes, I did." Charlie opened his desk drawer and pulled out a document with my signature on it. I had signed it about five years earlier when I got my order-buying privileges on the market. He pointed to some small print and this is what I read:

> "Under this agreement, you as an order buyer on the Calgary market are not permitted to buy any cattle within the city limits of Calgary except at the Alberta Stock Yards."

I looked at him and said, "I never knew this rule existed."

"Well," he said, "you know it now!—and if you ever go up there again to buy cattle I will revoke your license."

Needless to say, even if I was a little annoyed at this rule, I never went back to the Agri-Mart. I never heard, but maybe he had this conversation with a few other people as well. Once the Agri-Mart closed, Charlie returned to his normal routine of running a tight, but fair, ship.

Charlie is a past president of the Calgary Exhibition and Stampede, and is also a past president of the Rotary Club. He had other involvements as well.

When Charlie retired, we had a big farewell party at the Palliser Hotel, which was attended by about 500 people. Gord Rauch organized the whole evening. It was quite an affair. There were the usual cocktails (my wife and I had ginger ale), and then a prime rib dinner with all the trimmings. There was entertainment, plus some presentations made to Charlie and his wife, Marie. Then, finally, the "roast."

Gordon had lined up quite an impressive group: C.N. (Buck) Crump, retired chairman of the CPR; Fred Kennedy, author and older brother of Charlie; Herb Packard, CEO of Marathon Reality; Senator Harry Hays; Don Slinger, president of the National Livestock Markets Association; Stu Eagles, president of Marathon Realty; Jack Isley, president of the Rotary Club of Calgary; Fred Campbell, general manager, Toronto Stockyards; Ed O'Conner, past president of the Calgary Exhibition and Stampede; and yours truly, Leonard Friesen, president of the Calgary Livestock Exchange.

It was a good roast and it was all done in good taste. I have forgotten just about everything I said that night except for this one thing: "Since Charlie Kennedy has been a strong liberal all of his life and has worked so hard, he deserves a good rest and does not want to do any more work for the rest of his life. I therefore, suggest he be appointed to the Canadian Senate immediately." The crowd loved it. There was one man there who could see no humour in it—Senator Harry Hays. So when he got up to say his piece, he started out by saying: "Friesen is out to lunch." (Maybe not the exact words, but close enough.) Then he responded with: "There are only two kinds of people—those that are in the Senate and those that wish they were."

The barbershop quartet, who called themselves "The Stockyards Choir," were Eric Tribble, John Gowans, Romeo Fredette, and Keith Harrison. They were good. They should have turned pro.

Charlie and Marie are presently in a seniors' home. Charlie's sight is pretty well gone, but his mind is still keen.

Charlie and Marie Kennedy enjoying banquet.

BENNY KERR was a cattle dealer turned meat packer. At one time, he owned a store on 9th Avenue called "The Sugar Bowl." For many years, he operated a small abattoir close to the Bow River, just west and north of the present historic site of Fort Calgary. He bought that plant from George Lumbach. Benny and his sons killed cattle there for their own customers. They also custom killed cattle for other people, mostly some of their Jewish friends, including Dvorkin Bros. They sold the plant (I think to the City). Then they built a nice plant, just south of the Stockyards, called Kerr Packers. They purchased the bulk of their beef requirements at the Stockyards. They also bought some at the big feedlots on the bid system.

Benny was physically a small man, but he always tried to stand up for himself. This gave the boys many opportunities to tease him. Sometimes, he would stand up at ringside all excited, shaking his finger at someone or whatever. Invariably, some wise guy would shout to the already standing Benny: "Why don't you stand up, Benny?" (He was about the same height standing or sitting.)

Another trait Benny had, especially back in the days when he owned the abattoir, was whenever an off-quality critter came into the ring, often grain-fed, so its eating qualities were okay, but its appearance might be somewhat ugly, Benny would start the animal as low as possible—maybe, 10 cents a pound. This low price got someone else interested, so the bidding began. It would continue in slow dimes to, say, 19 or 20 cents a pound. That represented about a hundred bids on the animal. The auctioneer often tried to get him to bid at least a quarter each bid, with no luck. Benny would stick to his dime. Whoever was bidding against him knew he would not bid more than a dime at a time, so neither would they.

Benny had a good singing voice; however, he very seldom sang at the sale ring, like Davey Dvorkin did. We used to bug Davey by saying: "It's too bad you haven't got a good voice like Benny's."

Like so many of the characters around the Stockyards, Benny helped us all to pass the time of day. In reality, I think he actually enjoyed some of the good-natured ribbing he had to put up with almost daily.

Benny passed away a number of years ago.

KERR BROTHERS: Allan, Morley, and Alvin were Benny Kerr's sons. I knew Morley and Alvin quite well, since they were around the

Yards a lot. As for Allan, he, too, was there at times, but not as often.

Allan was a good actor so he quite often had parts in plays and productions in the theatre world. With a little break, he would have made Hollywood. He was much better than many of the actors we see parading across our television screens these days. He was a hard worker and generally well liked by everyone. He was kind of the unsung hero who kept things going at the back. You very seldom saw Allan loafing. He was always doing something.

Morley was the plant manager for Kerr Packers. He was in charge of the day-to-day operations. His big account was Safeway. That also probably was his downfall. Safeway demanded nothing but the best quality beef. All the other packers knew that Kerrs had the order, so whenever those top-quality cattle came in the sale ring the battle was on. Kerrs had to pay a big dollar for those cattle. Another factor was that they had to ensure their supply, so they would buy a lot of cattle in advance. These they would store at the Stockyards across the road. That was very expensive in feed costs as well as shrink. Finally they had to close the plant. They were not the only ones to close in Calgary. Union Packing closed about twenty-five years ago. In the 1980s, there were four closures in Calgary: Kerr Packers, Burns Foods, Canada Packers and Dvorkin's.

I have no idea where Morley is these days. I have lost track of Allan and Alvin as well. I'm sure they are making their way, considering their good work ethics.

JANET KIDD was a clerk in the government grader's office. She sorted out the sale tickets and prepared the government market report that went across Canada. She was exactly the same, day in, day out. She was very accommodating if you asked her for information. I hope Janet is enjoying retired life.

JERRY KING worked at Burns as a rookie cattle buyer. Of greater interest to Jerry was riding bareback horses at rodeos. In fact, it was because of this that Burns and Jerry parted company. The Company did not mind people rodeoing; however, they were not too fond of a person doing it on company time. He was young in those days and maybe he did not understand corporation policies. The last time I talked to Jerry was a few years ago. He told me he was operating a riding academy at Bragg Creek. I hope it worked out for him. He really is a nice guy with a beautiful wife and cute, little, twin girls.

GARY KLESSENS was born and raised in Montana. He came to Alberta almost three decades ago. Gary owns a place at Nanton where he has an order-buying station. He moves a lot of cattle. One of his big orders is Lakeside Feeders at Brooks. He has many others as well. When Dvorkin Packers were still operating, Gary bought a lot of fat cattle for them. Larry Farrell and Gary often attended sales together. Larry was Dvorkin's head buyer. Gary was not a steady fixture at the Yards, but he came there quite often. He likes golf and is involved in sponsoring a tournament every year. He also owns a ranch in Montana.

DON KNIGHT is one of the four Knight boys from Strathmore, Alberta. The other boys are: John, Fred, and Pete. They are all in the cattle business. Don is the only one that spent a lot of time at the Calgary Stockyards. He has a truck—one of those long body-jobs. He hauls a lot of cattle, including quite a few for us. He is a good trucker and always goes out of his way to do a good job. He also owns a good cow herd. His calves usually bring top dollar.

TOMMY KNIGHT lives at Alix, Alberta. He is not related to Don Knight. Tommy hauled a lot of cattle to the Calgary Stockyards. He always dealt with P&M. Tom not only hauled cattle, he bought a lot of cattle in the country, which often ended up in Calgary. This practice was very common in the '50s and '60s.

One year our outfit, Friesen Cattle Co., ran some yearlings at Tommy's place. Tom owned a beautiful Palomino horse. One day I asked him how much money he would take for him. He looked me right in the eye and said, "I would not sell him for $5,000." That would be like $25,000 today. Needless to say, I did not buy the horse.

Tom's son, Ken, is an auctioneer. He sold at Ponoka for a while. Then he moved to Winnipeg.

I have not seen Tommy for years. I think he still lives at Alix, Alberta.

DALE KONSCHUK is a brother of Larry Konschuk, who was the Reeve of the Municipal District of Rocky View No. 44 for several terms. Dale worked in the office of the Alberta Livestock Co-op. He did a good job for them. It was not enough challenge for him; so he left and became an electrician—a trade he has worked at ever since. I am sure he is good at it. Dale and my brother-in-law, Orville Peters, were good friends. Orville worked in the Co-op office as well.

FRANK KOOLE owns a number of cattle "pots." He hauls a lot of cattle with them each year. For many years, he hauled thousands of cattle for our company. His wife, Barbara, is the best truck dispatcher in the business. She is fast and accurate—I have never known her to make a mistake. I often would give her a complicated location of where to take cattle. I never had to repeat it to her. She always had it right. At one point, Frank and Barbara left the trucking business to go farming at Arrowwood (that's where Frank was raised). That only lasted one year. They found that trucking was much more to their liking than farming. They have been at it ever since.

DR. DAVE KOVITZ was a dentist, who came from Winnipeg, Manitoba. He married a Calgary girl, Muriel Libbin, who became the chancellor of the University of Calgary.

After the "Doc" came to Calgary, he, along with two other partners, bought out Dvorkin Packers and Centennial Meats. He loved coming to the Stockyards. He would sit in the sale ring nearly every day. He was fascinated by the auction. I guess it was a good break or change from peering into mouths of people who were sitting in his dentist chair.

After Larry Farrell retired from the daily grind of keeping the packing plant supplied with cattle, he went order buying. He bought for a number of people, but the Doc was his big account. The good doctor had gotten into cattle feeding on a fairly large scale. I think that was mainly for tax shelter—but he also enjoyed it. For several years, the Doc went wherever Larry went. He had complete trust in Larry and Larry called the shots, but the Doc just loved going to sales. They went to several other markets besides Calgary.

Several years ago, the Doc's health deteriorated. Things slowed down and he passed away shortly thereafter.

OSCAR KURL was an old-fashioned cattle wheeler-dealer. He was at the MacLean Auction every Saturday. During the week, he hung around the Stockyards looking for a bargain. He was not the last of the big-time spenders. Oscar had a lot of respect for a dollar bill. He had a little feedlot south of the Stockyards, where he assembled some trading cattle. No big volume, but I am sure what he did handle made a profit. I could never figure out why Ronnie Byers was a buddy of Oscar Kurl. Ronnie, too, was a bit of a trader, but he had quite a lot of class. Maybe Oscar did as well, only it was not quite as visible. Oscar has passed on.

ARCHIE LAMONT worked in the office at AWW. He was a tall skinny man with a slight stoop. He often indicated to me that he was rather bored with his job. For some reason, he was not very fond of his boss, Al Jordan. Jordan seemed okay to me, but then I did not work for him. Archie spent most of his life at the Yards and processed hundreds of thousands of cattle that AWW sold for producers. Last I heard, Archie retired and lives in West Calgary.

DANNY LANG came from Swift Current, Saskatchewan. He worked for Burns in the mid-'70s. Pat Collins hired him as a rookie cattle buyer. When he first started to buy cattle at the sale ring, he sometimes sat beside me. Whenever he made a good buy I would encourage him by saying "good eye, kid." After a few years, he went back to Swift Current to join his dad and brothers in the order buying firm they operate. These days, Ed Lang Sr., Danny, and his brother Doug work out of Swift Current. Eddie Jr. looks after their interests at Medicine Hat, Alberta. The Langs handle a large volume of cattle.

ELLIE-MAE LARSON was a waitress in the Stockyards Restaurant. Her real name was not Ellie-Mae, but that's what everybody called her. She had seven or eight children, and, for most of her life, she was the sole bread winner. It is a credit to her that she could do that by working every day instead of taking the easy way out and going on welfare. These days, she has many grandchildren and a few great-grandchildren. Believe it or not, she is still waiting on tables at the Crowchild Inn. We see her there quite often. The last time we were there, she was not there. She had taken a few days off to celebrate Christmas with her family.

JOHNNY LEASK was the happy-go-lucky bossman of the government graders for a number of years. He loved people and life. He always had time to communicate. Johnny was interested in many other areas of life. He is a cousin to the rodeo Leask family at Bottrel. Johnny was a good civil servant, who did his job well. He could identify with live cattle and dressed beef. I was sorry to see him leave. If I remember correctly, he was transferred to Regina.

JACK LEAVITT was a good cattleman. In his day, he bought and sold a lot of cattle. He also owned several places, including one at Nanton. He has a Jewish background and was born in Canada and raised at Rumsey. There was quite a Jewish settlement in the Rumsey area. These people came from Europe shortly after the turn of the century. They were all good cattlemen. Besides Jack, there were Sam Raskin, the Sangas brothers and others. For the last thirty years of his life, Jack fed cattle at Hubalta, just east of Forest Lawn. His old feedlot is covered with houses now.

Jack was a good businessman. His word was his bond. He knew what he wanted and went after it. By that, I mean he had a game plan and stuck to it. He sold all his fat cattle through the Stockyards.

One Saturday, I went to the MacLean Auction Market. (I seldom went there.) On this particular day, they were auctioning off a guitar. I wanted to buy it for our oldest son, Lee, who was about twelve or thirteen years old at the time. There was one little catch: I had forgotten my wallet at home. Jack happened to stand close to me, so I said to him: "Will you lend me enough money to buy this guitar?" "Sure," he replied. The final price was seven dollars, so I was its new proud owner. I paid him back his money on Monday morning. Lee learned to play on that old instrument. Lee still plays the guitar today. "Thanks, Jack."

One day, Jack came into the Stockyards Restaurant chuckling. So, somebody asked him: "What makes you so happy?"

Jack replied, "I just made an easy five dollars.

"Oh, how is that, Jack?"

"Well, Harry Lee hit me up for a ten-dollar bill, and I talked him into taking five."

Jack suffered with sugar diabetes for many years. This finally claimed his life.

HARRY LEE was a blustery character who was around the Yards for years. Some of those years were spent with Producers' Livestock. His language was mostly unprintable. He was also very gullible. The boys used to get a great kick out of telling him false tales. One day, they told him the Canadian Government was recruiting people to go over to Egypt to reshingle the Pyramids because they had sprung some leaks. Harry was ready to take up the challenge. Another time, during the Second World War, when Europe was in a big turmoil and there were invasions and declarations of war by various countries, the boys told him the Dutch had declared war on Holland. Harry did not like that news one bit. He said, "At that rate, we'll all soon be in it."

Harry was quite an imposing figure with his curly hair and ruddy complexion. He was rather intimidating to someone who first met him, but it did not take long for anyone to realize he was actually a "pussycat." He just sort of disappeared from the scene several years before he passed away.

CLINT LEECH liked visiting at the Yards. He dabbled in real estate and a few cattle. He had steely, light-blue eyes like a big time gambler. At one time he owned a small gambling casino in Reno, Nevada. In the end it cost him a small fortune. I rather enjoyed visiting with Clint. He was kind of a unique personality. I have lost track of him.

RON LEHR was a cattle buyer for Burns. After several years he went to work for Red Deer Packers. Ron was a friendly person and easy to get along with. To my knowledge, Ron is no longer in the cattle business. I have no idea what he may be doing these days.

AL LENNOX worked for the J. C. Wheatcroft Co. for a number of years. He was intelligent and always exuded a bit of class. He got along well with his fellow employees. He left the Stockyards and went to work for the Calgary Exhibition & Stampede. It did not take long for management to see Al's potential. He rose from the bottom up. His field was horse racing.

GORDIE LETZ worked for the Alberta Stock Yards for a long time. When he left there, he went into the trucking business. For many more years, he operated out of the Stockyards location. He was an easygoing sort. Rain, shine or snow, he was always on deck. As far as I know, Gordie still does some trucking up north. It seems to me I heard he also had a little farm. He served the industry well.

EARL LOGAN was a teamster for Burns Foods. His job was feeding cattle hay and cut-feed with horse-drawn wagons. For a while, he was Joe Beck's helper. When Joe retired, Earl took over. Earl was not very swift, but if you gave him a job he tried to carry it out to the best of his ability. In the wintertime, he looked like an Egyptian mummy. He had enough clothes on to go on an Arctic expedition. I have no idea where he went after he left Burns.

DON LOVE was a truck driver for Eamor's or maybe Frank Koole. I am not sure which one. I do know, he was kind of a small man with a smile—the type of person you could trust with a load of your cattle.

ERNIE LOVE AND SONS had a feed company office in the Livestock Exchange Building for a number of years. His family are old-timers in Calgary. I always enjoyed visiting with Ernie. He was well informed on most issues. He was a very gentle, but manly, figure around the building with his shock of white hair and good clothes. Two of his sons, Jim and Mike, were in partnership with him and their uncle Jack. The younger Loves were very fine young men. Like their dad, they kept abreast of events as they unfolded. I used to talk a lot with them about the stock market, a subject that has always interested me. Ernie and his sons are still in business, but they moved their offices into southeast Calgary near their plant's location.

JACK LOVE is Ernie Love's brother. He was a partner with Ernie and sons. He appeared to be a little more carefree. Jack, too, was easy to visit with. As he got older, he liked to go to Arizona for the winter. While there, he stayed at a real nice resort. I know, because we went over there one day to see him. Jack liked singing in the United Church choir. He passed away several years ago.

GEORGE LUMBACH was a butcher most of his life. I think he came from Mongolian ancestors. He really knew his business and was a straight-shooter. George used to own a little abattoir down by the Bow River. He also owned a farm west of Airdrie. He sold it to Harvey Alexander. After a number of years, Harvey moved to California. Later on, Harvey sold the farm to John Lee, who still owns it. George died many years ago. He was a good example of what honesty and hard work can achieve in a free country.

LLOYD LUMHEIM worked for the Alberta Livestock Co-op. He always wore oxford shoes in the cattle alleys. Lloyd had a second business venture. He owned a taxi, or maybe two. At any rate, Lloyd did his thing on a daily basis at the Stockyards. At night he hauled people around the City. I am not sure who drove his taxis during the day. They call what he did "moonlighting." There is a lot of this going on to this day.

GORDON LYLE lives at Sundre, Alberta. He was quite a cow trader. He was around the Stockyards on a fairly constant basis for quite some time. He covered a lot of territory as his business grew bigger. I do not want to tell tales out of school, but I heard on pretty good authority that he hit a major wreck. That has happened to a lot of us. He also had health problems. Last I heard, he had more or less overcome both problems. I wish Gordie well.

ED MACAW was the office manager for P&M for a long time. He knew his work well and did an excellent job with some of Danny MacDonald's deals. It was not always easy. Ed was very calm and in control. I often talked with him, but for some reason, I have no idea where he came from or where he went. I do know that while he was at the Stockyards, he was a good asset to P&M's operation.

AL MACDONALD came from the Claresholm-Stavely country. He was Danny MacDonald's brother. Al came to the Yards quite often. When he was younger, he may even have worked for P&M on odd occasions. He was a realtor and, I think, a pretty good one. He was a lot tamer than his brothers, Danny and Roddy. Al also was a first-class golfer, a sport I am sure he still enjoys today.

BILL MACDONALD worked in the Burns livestock paying office. He spent his entire life working for Burns. He was Jack Collin's son-in-law. Jack ran that office for at least four decades. When Jack retired, Bill took over. I got along real well with Bill, but he was not exactly "Mr. Personality." If he did not like you, he could make it tough for you. Whenever someone appeared in the office to receive payment for livestock, he would often ignore their presence for three to five minutes. At other times, he would be quite chatty and affable. Bill retired from Burns and not too many years later, he passed away.

DANNY MACDONALD was born and raised at Stavely, Alberta. He spent his youth in the Stavely-Claresholm area where he knew every farmer and rancher. He took an auctioneer's course about 1950 or 1951. When the auction action started at the Yards in 1951, Danny was there. Shortly after that, he and Jimmy Paul bought out the W.W. Starke commission firm.

Danny was one of the best auctioneers to ever mount an auctioneer's stand, bar-none. Some of today's hot shots would argue that, but, in his prime, I will take Danny. He could read markets and buyers and played his cards accordingly. He was especially good on big loads of top-quality cattle. His face would get red as a beet. In the heat of auctioning, he hardly took a breath. He had what I call total concentration. He did not hang on very long, so you knew you had to bid up if you wanted to own the cattle. I loved buying cattle from him, not because they were any cheaper, but because it was fast and furious action. I bought thousands of cattle from him. If you treated him right, he treated you right.

Danny was pretty much an addicted gambler. Maybe not as bad as Davey Dvorkin, but not far behind. On two or three nights a week, and on Fridays for sure, there were poker or craps games in their back office. At these events, the whisky flowed quite freely. It got very noisy, and, once in a while, slightly violent—but not very often. Danny's partners, Cecil Barber and Doug Keer, did not get involved in those affairs, although Doug liked to play cribbage with a few of his cronies.

Danny also bet on the races. One day he bet everything but the kitchen sink on one horse. Unfortunately, the horse had a bad day and ran out of the money. This did not faze Danny—maybe better luck next time out.

Danny liked to go to B.C. to buy cattle at the Panorama Sale, which included a number of big reputation ranch cattle. One year,

255

they had about 3,000 head for sale at the Douglas Lake Ranch. The auctioneer announced before the sale that the high bidder could take a "lot" of several hundred, or all of them. As it turned out, Danny was the high bidder.

The auctioneer said to Danny, "How many do you want?"

Danny replied, "All 3,000."

The sale had lasted less than three minutes, probably a record in North America—selling 3,000 head in a few minutes.

In those days, there were very few big feedlots. Most of those cattle had to go to farmer feeders who would buy anywhere from 50 to 500 head. Danny only had a few small orders, so, for the next week, he, Cecil, Doug and Russ Phillip were on the phone trying to place all those cattle. They finally got homes for all of them, much to Cecil's relief, since he had to pay for the cattle at the time of Danny's purchase. That is just one little incident. There were dozens of other situations when Cecil had to bail him out.

Danny developed quite a drinking problem, which was no secret around the Yards. He was very open in admitting he had a problem, but seemed unable to correct it.

Danny passed away in his mid-50s in the mid'70s. We went to his funeral. There must have been a thousand people there to pay their last respects. He was the best in his field. He also played hard and, as so often happens, it caught up to him. Danny will always be remembered by all those who knew him.

RODDY MACDONALD is a brother of Danny and Al MacDonald's. Roddy worked at the Yards on several different occasions. His nickname was "Lightning." He got this handle because of his steer wrestling ability—on a given day, he could be as fast as lightning. I said "steer wrestling"—it was actually "steer decorating." Steers used for decorating were much bigger than those used in steer wrestling. The contestant would leave his horse while it was on the dead run, grab the steer by the horns, and then place a ribbon on one horn. This event was a lot more dangerous than it appeared to be. Those big steers often ran right over a contestant.

I don't think Roddy won many titles, but he did win some shows with very fast times. He was somewhat like his brother, Danny. He loved to party. The difference between the two brothers was that Roddy enjoyed fisticuffs more than Danny. Roddy's black eyes were not always from the rodeo action. He was a tough character. In spite of this, he had a big circle of friends. Last I heard about him, he was cooking for a hunting party in the mountains west of Claresholm, Alberta.

AL MACGREGOR was a hog buyer for Union Packing. When Union closed, he came to work for Burns. In those days ('60s and '70s), soliciting hogs was a science. Al was one of the best. He had most of the Hutterite Colonies in his pocket. Burns' hog receipts increased dramatically after he came on board. Al knew every Hutterite in the country. Whenever he went to visit a colony, he made sure he had a big supply of candy with him. These he handed out freely to the Hutterite children. Al has passed away.

DON MACKENZIE came from Mountain View in southern Alberta. He worked in the livestock division of Canada Packers for several years as a rookie cattle buyer. He was a first-class guy. It was almost inevitable that Don would leave and go on his own, and this is just what he did. He went back to the ranch where he and his brother developed one of the best Red Angus herds in Canada.

TOM MACKENZIE was a Scotsman who worked for Burns until his retirement in the early 1970s. He worked for Archie Curry in the delivery and feeding end of things. When Peter Murry retired as the sheep buyer, Tom took over his position. Tom had a different style than Pete, but he was just as good at handling sheep with his dogs as Pete. Tom was not as tough on his dogs as Pete.

One day, I purchased a bunch of ewes on the market. Tom always came over with his dogs to bring them over to the Burns plant. The dogs were very good and we seldom encountered any problems. On this particular day, one old ewe decided to quit the herd. She took off in high gear heading towards the old Exchange Building, the dog in hot pursuit. P&D had their offices in the lower part of the building, sort of a half-basement situation. The windows were at ground level from the outside. On the inside, they were about four feet above the floor. The old ewe saw the window and headed straight for it at a speed that would have been a credit to a Thoroughbred on the racetrack. When she hit the window, there was a terrible crash as the glass splintered into a million pieces. The old ewe flew right over George Jamison's head. He was sitting close to the window. It's a miracle he did not have a heart attack. The ewe raced around in the office scattering books, chairs, papers and stuff in all directions. When I finally arrived in the office (I ran as hard as I could to try and catch up with the dog and the ewe), it looked like a hurricane or a tornado had gone through the office. After a few attempts, I caught the ewe and calm prevailed in the office. George and a few other people in the office were as pale as ghosts—can't say I blamed them.

Tom was an ardent fly fisherman so every Monday we had to listen in detail about his fishing successes or failures. He was a good fisherman, so they usually were success stories.

Tom also was a good family man. He encouraged his sons in any sport activity they engaged in. His son, Bill, played college hockey in the USA, but did not make the NHL. It was pretty hard to make the NHL with only six teams in the league. We held a retirement party for Tom in the Westbrook Hotel. He lives in Calgary.

BUD MACKIE was born and raised in East Calgary. His dad used to own a feedlot south of the Stockyards. Bud was a real easygoing character. He liked to party, and it usually showed the next day. He held various jobs around the Yards. For the last sixteen or seventeen years before his death, he clerked for the auctioneers. He was a good guy in many ways. Even though he made some clerical errors once in a while, he was humble enough to admit to a mistake. This is a good trait in any person, male or female. Some people will never admit to a mistake, even if it is as plain as the nose on their face. Bud was one of "the boys," if you know what I mean.

CHUCK MACLEAN was raised in the cattle business at Picture Butte. His stepfather, Jack Murray, was one of the early large-scale cattle feeders in Alberta. Chuck worked as a cattle buyer for Alberta Western Beef at Medicine Hat. He left them and came to Calgary where he worked for Burns as a cattle buyer. I was his boss for several years. Chuck's wife, Jan, worked at the Stockyards Branch of the Bank of Montreal. When Burns bought Alberta Western Beef in 1972, we transferred Chuck to Medicine Hat where he was a cattle buyer until Burns closed the plant. At that point, he bought a place just south of Bow Island. He has a scale and good corrals, which he uses in his cattle brokerage operation. He order buys a lot of cattle and so does his brother, Mackie, who still lives at Picture Butte. I know Chuck does a good job for his customers. He is honest and is a very good judge of cattle. He also knows all the ranchers and feeders in southern Alberta. In 1994, I had the pleasure of being a judge at the International Livestock Auctioneer Championship competition, along with Chuck, Lawrence Duffin and two Americans.

GEORGE MACLEAN was born and raised in Calgary, Alberta. There was quite a family of MacLeans. I knew Allan, Jack, Don, and George. They were all good stockmen.

All of the MacLeans had a little too much trouble with "John Barleycorn," including George. One day, George quit drinking "cold turkey" and he stayed with it. I never knew him to take a drink for at least the last thirty-five years of his life.

George had a tremendous sense of humour. He had a real quick wit—always in good taste.

George owned MacLean Auction Ltd. He sold it to Bill Renard and Bob McDougall. He then came to the Calgary Market as an auctioneer. I bought thousands of cattle from him. He always had a quip, a joke, or a story. He never seemed to run out.

In 1959 George and Gerry Going opened an auction market in the old wartime High River Airport. I was at their first sale. They had some junk and household items to sell before they sold the cattle. I had no intentions of buying anything except cattle. I went over to where they were selling the junk and household goods. George was fixing to sell a gas freezer—"in good working order." He begged and begged, but could not get a bid, so I bid $20. He worked on it another three to five minutes, but no bids, so he knocked it down to me. I felt quite good about it, because we did not have a freezer and could use it. He then hung a washing machine on me that he advertised as "not in working order" for $5, so now I had a large freezer, plus a washing machine.

While I was standing there pondering how I was going to get them home, a man came along and asked: "How much do you want for the freezer?"

"It's not for sale," I said, "We can use it at home."

"Well," he said, "I came to the sale after it was sold, and I know you paid $20 for it—I will give you $40."

I said to him: "I think it's really worth about $100, but since I have to haul it home somehow . . . and you're offering me a 100 percent profit—I will sell it to you." And I did. (It was still a bargain.)

I put the washing machine in the trunk of the car and took it home after the cattle sale. (I can't remember how many cattle I bought.)

The next day, I took the drain off the washing machine and lodged in there was more money in coins than I had paid for the machine, about $7. That's why the machine was not working. I put it back together, plugged it in, and away it went. My wife used it for two years, then we bought our first automatic washer and dryer. Maybe that is why people hang around auction sales. I had $22 and a free washing machine. Not bad in 1959.

George and Gerry sold out after a few years. George then bought the MacLean Auction back and he and his son, Gary, operated it until George died.

A little while before his death, I visited George in the hospital. Sick as he was, his sense of humour was still good. He also praised the nurses and hospital staff for being so good and kind to him. "As a man lives; so shall he die."

GARY MACLEAN is George MacLean's son. He still carries on the MacLean tradition. He owns and operates the MacLean Auction Market in East Calgary. The "little World's Fair" some of the boys call it. Gary auctioned at the Calgary Stockyards on many occasions, especially in the fall run, or whenever some of the other auctioneers were away on the rodeo circuit. He is a good auctioneer, but he can get tough if he has to. This does happen every once in a while on a Saturday. He has quite a mixed lot of customers, some rather new to the Canadian way of doing business. He does a great job of tuning them in. Gary's brother Dave also auctioned at the Calgary Stockyards on a few occasions. Gary likes horses. When his dad was still alive, the two of them would often drive as far as Edmonton if the right horse was running. For a number of years, he has conducted an annual horse sale at the Calgary Stampede grounds.

Gary MacLean (center), Stampede Park, 1979.

KEN MACLEAN is Don MacLean's son and George MacLean's nephew. Ken clerked for the auctioneers for several years. He was a good clerk, making very few errors, if any. He also worked as a cow buyer for Harry Feldman for several years. Ken had some grass a little way out of Calgary. Every spring, he would buy several hundred top quality heifers. When he sold them in the fall, they always topped the market. Ken was a tall, handsome man with good manners. He did not drink, yet he was a sociable person. I do not know where or what he is up to these days.

DAVE MAILER was born and raised at Cadogan, Alberta. He joined the Canadian Army during World War II. When he came back in 1945, he lived in Calgary for about a year. He then moved to Brooks for three years. In 1951 he came back to Calgary, where he bought some acreage just outside of the City. While living on his acreage, he spent quite a lot of time at the Calgary Stockyards. He was a wheeler-dealer. His specialty was milk cows. He also did a lot of business in B.C. Besides milk cows, he also traded in beef cattle. In the early '60s, he bought a place at Didsbury where he has resided ever since. He still trades cattle. His son, Davey Jr., is a cattle buyer and an auctioneer. These days father and son are often at a sale, each doing their own thing.

BRYAN MANDEVILLE is the son of Harold and Pearl Mandeville from Lethbridge, Alberta. Harold was a good steer wrestler. He won a couple of championships. Bryan followed in his father's footsteps. Maybe it is because of more competition, or maybe he did not go down the road as much, but, at any rate, I do not think Bryan has collected as many trophies as his dad did. Bryan worked for P&M in Calgary for a while. He then went back to Lethbridge. He is still involved with rodeo as a representative for Copenhagen Skoal. I am sure he does a good job for them. He always was a genuine person. He resides in Calgary these days.

FRANK MARION originally came from Saskatchewan. He worked for P&D: first in the country, where they owned several places, then at the Calgary Stockyards, where he worked for a few years. Frank was not a very big man, but he was stout and had a stout heart. Frank's three grandsons, who hail from Wood Mountain, Saskatchewan, are steer wrestlers. Their names are Darby, Darcy, and David Roy. Darby holds the record for the fastest time ever. I think it was 2.8 seconds. Their cousin, Mark Roy, won both the Canadian and World Steer Wrestling titles in 1992. Frank passed away some years ago.

KEITH MARRINGTON is a real fine person. He came West from Ontario as a young man. He spent some time in Colorado at Lamar, not far from where our ranch is located. He is a good auctioneer—a trade which he plied for some years, first in north-central Alberta, then for a while at Didsbury.

I first got to know Keith when he entered the Canadian Auctioneer's Contest at Stampede Park. I was on the committee that sponsored this contest. I was very impressed with his performance, although he did not win. (I was not a judge.) We hired Keith to sell for us on the market. He did a real good job. Needless to say, I was very sorry to see him leave to take a position at the Calgary Exhibition & Stampede as manager of the livestock division.

I have kept in contact with Keith to some degree. I know he is doing a good job for them. I do enjoy visiting with him. I'm sure most cattlemen feel the same about Keith as I do.

CALGARY PUBLIC LIVESTOCK MARKET LTD.

Leonard Friesen, President of Calgary Public Livestock Market Ltd., is pleased to announce that Keith Marrington has been appointed Head of our new Special Sales Division.

Keith brings to CPLM a long association within the Cattle Industry but in addition brings extensive experience in Farm Machinery, Consignment and Pedigree Livestock Sales. Keith will also be assisting in our Company's day-to-day Livestock Operations.

For all your Sales Needs — Contact Keith or any member of our Sales Staff at:

Feb. 1985

CALGARY PUBLIC LIVESTOCK MARKET
LTD
YOUR KEY TO LIVESTOCK MARKETING
2635 Portland Street Southeast
Calgary, Alberta T2G 4M8

Alta. Toll Free 1-800-372-9586 or (403) 234-7429

Keith Marrington

Keith Marrington, February 19, 1985

JAKE MARSHALL was a bit of a character. In fact, he reminded me a little of "Jake" in the movie "Lonesome Dove"—a pretty good guy—but he could get into trouble. Jake was a brand inspector for a while. He then took an auctioneer's course. When he came back, he tried out selling on the market. I don't know if it was nerves or what, but his performance fell short, so the commission men did not hire him. Jake then went to Winnipeg where he tried out and succeeded. He sold cattle on the Winnipeg market for years.

JIM MARSH SR. came from Ireland as a lad. He lived in East Calgary where he and his wife raised a family of 12 or 14 children. Jimmy worked for the CPR all his life. He was what they called a "car knocker." He also built a lot of double-decks. This consisted of building a deck in a railroad car so that twice as much stock could be loaded in each car. At first, they were only built for hogs and sheep, but, in the late 1950s, when the railroad came out with larger and higher ceilings in stock cars, they could also be double-decked for cattle. Each regular shipper could own his own double-deck cars. We only owned four of these. J. C. Wheatcroft owned a whole passel of those double-decks. Jimmy also slatted cars in the wintertime. Jimmy was a fine gentleman. I really liked him, and so did everybody else. I never got tired of his stories. He also owned some racehorses. He and his boys did a good job with them. They produced quite a few winners. Jimmy lived to a fairly old age.

JIM MARSH JR. is a son of Jimmy Marsh Sr. He was raised in East Calgary about four blocks from the Stockyards. He had hung around the Yards ever since he was a child. Jimmy worked for several outfits. I think he started out with AWW.

In his younger days, he was quite a terror when he teamed up with Buck Rothwell and Len Rowland and a few other characters around the Yards. There was not much that they would not do—especially when they were drinking (which was most of the time). As they got older, both Jim and Buck completely gave up on alcohol. This, plus maturity, really tamed them down.

Like his father and his brothers, Jim liked race horses. He was involved with them one way or another most of his life. For several years, he worked for the notorious racehorse man, Mickey MacDonald: first, west of Calgary; then, at Mickey's ranch at Lathom, near Bassano. That's where the famous racehorse, Count Lathom, got his name.

When Jim left MacDonald, he went to work for Rivercrest Ranches at Okotoks. I was a 20 percent shareholder in Rivercrest Ranches, but that's another story. When Jim left Rivercrest, he went to work for P&M where he stayed until he retired.

Late in life, Jim married Babe Yates who was involved with the call girl industry. His first wife had passed away several years previously. Jim died under very mysterious circumstances.

MARSH BROTHERS: Charlie, Bob, Billy and Jim Marsh Jr. are brothers. At one time or another, they all worked at the Stockyards.

Charlie was a hockey-goal judge at the Stampede grounds for years. He also was a timer at the racetrack. On his off days, he helped his dad, Jim Sr., slat railroad cars. Bob was, and maybe still is, a racehorse owner and trainer. He is a very knowledgeable horseman. Billy was a jockey and a good one, but, as happens to many jockeys, he had a weight problem. He spent many hours sweating off pounds in a steam bath. He is one of the few men who rode in a horse race at the Calgary Stampede and rode in the saddle bronc competition the same afternoon.

JOHN MARTHALLER could be what you called a fast-moving trucker. He was an affable sort of person, always friendly. He owned his own rig; in fact, I think he owned two of them. I have no idea what he did after he left the Stockyards, but I am sure he is doing all right.

TOM MATHEWS was closely associated with Parslow & Denoon. He fed cattle and sheep, a little west of Calgary. In fact, that land is now all developed. It was located just west of the Sarcee Trail across from 12th Avenue SW. He also had some land on the east side of Sarcee Trail north of 17th Avenue. I bought quite a few lambs from Tom. Maule McEwen was his agent. Tom enjoyed life. He told me one day, he liked buying things for his wife. He said it had cost him several double-decks of lambs, but she was worth it. Tom passed away many years ago.

DAVE MATTICS was a beef manager at Burns. For a beef manager, he was extremely easy to get along with. I have lost track of him.

JIM MAY was a clerk in the brand office. He was very crippled with arthritis. He always had a positive attitude, even though he found it tough to walk. Jim was everyone's friend. I am not sure what happened to him after he left the Yards.

FRANK MCCURDY came from eastern Canada. He worked for Union Packing as a cattle buyer for some time. After that he kind of freelanced around the Yards. Frank was a short, stubby man who liked to smoke cigars. When he talked, he kind of mumbled somewhat similar to Lester B. Pearson (a former Prime Minister of Canada).

BOB MCDOUGALL is the son of the late Dave and Annie McDougall. He was raised on a cattle ranch northwest of Cochrane. Bob spent quite a bit of time at the Yards as well as at other markets. He has been a dealer all his life and really enjoys the cattle business. For several years, he was a partner with Bill Renard, and they owned and operated MacLean Auction Ltd., in East Calgary. Bob also lived in Montana for quite some time. At the present time, he ranches northwest of Cochrane.

BRIAN MCELROY came from Lethbridge, Alberta. His dad and uncle were some of the first people to own cattleliners. It was a tossup who was first, the McElroys or George Eamor from Calgary. Brian was with the government grading service. He always did a good job. You could not sway him much. He always stuck to his guns. As far as I know, he is still with the government.

WAYNE MCELROY is Brian McElroy's brother. He, too, came from the Lethbridge McElroy pioneers, who were in the cattleliner business. He works for the federal government grading service. He is very competent at his job. I suppose that is one of the reasons why he is the head grader in the Calgary region. It's easy to visit with Wayne but, like a lot of good men, it's not easy to change his opinion on anything. That's okay, especially if his opinion is correct on most issues. He is located in their uptown office, since they closed down the office at the Stockyards.

MAULE MCEWEN was a hog and sheep salesman for P&D for over fifty years. As a young man, he worked for Bill Renard. Renard was the boss of the horse division of Hart Parr Tractor Company. It was Maule's job to pick up and halter-break horses that the company had taken in trade for tractors. For many years, Maule was a partner with P&D on a place on Highway 22. It was called "Stream Camp Ranch." Maule is still enjoying retired life on his place near of Midnapore. His daughter, Carol, is married to Lorne Wells.

DAVE MCGRAW worked for the Alberta Stock Yards at the gatehouse for a while. I have no idea where he came from. I do know he was a good musician. He loved playing music at dances and other functions. When Dave left the Yards, he went to work for Union Packing where he became a cattle buyer. When Union Packing closed, he went to work for Burns. He bought a place at Spruce View, west of Innisfail. He covered central Alberta for Burns. Dave was a good man, but he was very secretive. He often whispered information concerning people's cattle, even if the owners were miles away. I actually was his boss when I was the head buyer at Burns. I will tell you one thing: Dave never hurt the Company. What he bought was bought right. He did not steal the cattle, but he always made sure the weighing conditions were right. Dave was a very devout Catholic.

FRANK MCINENLY was born and raised at Arrowwood, Alberta. He became an auctioneer at a young age. He sold at the Yards occasionally when one of the other auctioneers was absent. He sold at Stavely for a number of years and sold at Balog's Market, Lethbridge for several years. These days, Frank runs an auction service from his place near Vulcan. He holds quite a few horse sales, as well as farm and other sales. Frank is an honest, straightforward individual. It is always good to visit with him. He has an active mind and has lots of ideas. Just lately, he and Gary Jensen bought the Stavely Auction Market.

MAC MCKINNON came from P.E.I. I think he worked for Canada Packers in Toronto before he came to CP Calgary. At any rate, he was their beef manager in Calgary. Around 1970 he left CP and joined Burns: first, at Canadian Dressed Meats (CDM), Lethbridge (owned by Burns); then, Burns Calgary. He arrived at Burns Calgary the same week that I went back to Burns as livestock manager.

Mac is a jumpy sort, but a good man. We had a run-in about the second week we worked together. It was regarding the management of personnel. After a slight shouting match, we both settled down and worked out our differences. After that we were buddies.

Mac stayed at Burns about three years. He left there and

became beef manager for Lakeside Packers at Brooks. Some years later, he left Lakeside and worked for Dvorkin's. He was not there too long when he packed in the beef business and went to work in real estate.

I really liked working with Mac. It did not matter what I bought, he could always find a home for it. When Western Feedlots first went to the bid system, Mac and I would plot our bids. It was absolutely amazing how many cattle we bought for a nickel or dime over our competitors. I'm sure it still goes on today.

JIM AND ISABEL MCPHERSON purchased the Calgary Livestock Market Journal from Gordon and Dorothy Rauch. They ran a good publication; however, things were changing fast in the cattle industry. After the reorganization of the Calgary market, the Journal more or less folded. The McPhersons had other publishing interests, which covered several breeds of cattle. They moved out of the Livestock Exchange Building and into the Stockmen's Memorial Building on 32nd Avenue NE. The McPhersons are very nice people. I hope their other endeavour worked out well for them.

CALGARY LIVESTOCK MARKET JOURNAL MANAGEMENT CHANGE
Gordon Rauch (left) sells to Jim McPherson (right), June 1978.

BILL MCRAE was a real character. He was raised a block from the Stockyards. I really regret that I did not interview him in more detail about the Yards before he passed away. He spent his whole life there except for a short stint in the Army, which he hated. When I came to the Yards, he was the hog and sheep salesman for P&M.

Bill was a great story teller with a dry sense of humour. He always had a chew of tobacco in his mouth, but this never interfered with his story telling, except for an odd spit.

Bill never married. One of his favourite expressions, when things weren't going too well, was: "It could be worse, a man could be married."

(L-R) Bill McRae, R. W. Furgeson, Maule McEwen, 1979.

One day he told us he only knew of one person that was ahead in horse race betting. The person he was talking about was a widowed lady who had never bet on a horse in her life. She happened to read in the paper about a horse that had her maiden name. It was entered in a race at Stampede Park. She was so fascinated with this coincidence that, on the day of the race, she

269

called a cab and went down to the track. (She lived on Scotsman's Hill.) She found the wicket where they took the bets. She placed a $2 bet on that horse to win. It was what they called a "long shot." That meant nothing to her, she didn't know what a long shot was. Once in a while a long shot wins and that's exactly what happened. It won! The payoff was $50. She collected her money and took a cab home. She never bet on another horse race in her life. Her profit was $48, minus cab fare. According to Bill, she is absolutely the only person who made money on racehorse betting, because she never bet again.

There are dozens of other stories that Bill told. Some I have forgotten; others are not too good for mixed company.

Bill passed away a few years ago.

GARY MCRAE is a son of Chris McRae, who had worked for Burns for fifty-one years. Gary is also a nephew of Bill, Ook, and Vern McRae. Gary worked as a scaleman at the hog and sheep scalehouse. He was very good-natured. I have no idea where he is these days.

OOK MCRAE is a brother of Bill and Vern McRae. Ook was what I call a nice guy. I have no idea where the nickname "Ook" originated. I suppose as a child, he pronounced a certain word as "ook." At any rate, the name stuck. Ook was a hog and sheep salesman for the ALC. He was good at his job. He treated everybody fairly. If a young new buyer arrived on the scene, Ook was inclined to help him rather than take advantage of his inexperience. Whenever I bought hogs and sheep from him, I felt that he had given me a fair deal. He did not play games like some of them did. Ook was a good family man, and he was always dressed clean and neat. He passed away at a relatively young age.

RON MCRAE is also a son of Chris McRae and brother of Gary McRae. Ron worked for the Alberta Stock Yards for several years. Eventually, he went into the trucking business, hauling cattle. Ron was a nice man, but somehow he got tangled up with the wrong companions. This got him in trouble with the law. After that he straightened right up. Like most McRaes, Ron liked race horses. Last I heard, he was involved with the racehorse industry.

VERN MCRAE, or "the Senator" as the boys called him, was a real philosopher. I know, I sat right next to him in the sale ring for at least a dozen years. His brothers were Bill, Dunc, Chris, and Ook McRae.

Vern had a lot of "sayings." I remember many of them to this day, three decades later. Here are a few examples: "The money will run out before the cattle will." In other words take your time, there are more cattle where those came from. Another saying was: "If you make a mistake buying cattle by paying too much money, just make sure it's on some good quality ones." When talking about the way some people used to live, Vern would say: "They are trying to live a champagne life on a beer salary."

Vern was a good judge of cattle. The cattle he purchased were bought with care. He was one of the mainstays for Parslow & Denoon. He had a flock of loyal customers, including such people as: Roland and Bill Amery, Tom Mathews, and L.K. Ranches. (After Vern passed away, L.K. Ranches switched to P&M.) His main beef customer was Pacific Meat owned by Jack Diamond at the West Coast. Vern shipped him thousands of cattle. As far as Jack was concerned, Vern could do no wrong.

Vern also loved the races. Jack Diamond happened to own a racetrack at the West Coast, so every summer Vern and his family would vacation at the Coast where Vern attended the races with Jack. Vern always went to the track at Stampede Park when the races were in Calgary. He had a lot of patience. If there were eight races, he would often only bet on one or two. If he couldn't select a horse that looked like it could win, he did not place a bet. He is probably one of a few people who may have been on the plus side on his betting activity. Vern was a big guy who looked like a man with authority, hence, the handle, "the Senator."

Vern developed bone cancer. They had to amputate one leg. He came back and worked for a short while. Then the cancer spread and he passed away. I think he was fifty-six years old at the time. Vern will always be fondly remembered by his family, friends, and business associates.

VERN MCWATERS came to Calgary from western Saskatchewan. I think his dad managed a community pasture. Vern went to work for Canada Packers as a nightman. It did not take long till he became a junior buyer. He was very aggressive; however, in spite of this, I will never forget the first day that CP sent him over to the sale ring to buy cattle. He was so nervous he shook like a leaf. Each time he bought a few cattle, his hand shook so bad he could hardly write them down on his buying card. In about three months, this nervousness had completely dissipated and he was actually overconfident. In other words, he rated himself a little higher than his actual ability.

After a few years, Vern left Canada Packers to work for J. C. Wheatcroft. Then he left there and went to work for Henry Bridgewater, or maybe it was the other way around. I know he worked for both Bridgewater and Wheatcroft. Big deals never scared Vern, but they did Henry, especially if they happened to lose a bundle of money.

After a while, Vern departed for Lethbridge where he worked for someone else. From there he moved to the US: first, to Nebraska; then, to Dodge City, Kansas, where he passed away a young man.

I talked to several Americans and they all told me the same thing. Vern was a good cattleman, but his gambling and finances had him in constant trouble. Whisky and gambling have ruined a lot of good cattlemen over the years.

HARRY MCWILSON is a gentleman. He was raised around Calgary, Alberta. His stepfather was a horse trader, so he got a lot of horse savvy from him. As a youngster, Harry led or trailed a lot of horses to and from Calgary. For a number of years, he worked for the Dominion Bridge Co., in East Calgary. He never lost his interest in cattle and horses. When Harry left the steel business, Jack Short hired him as a brand inspector. Harry was good at his job, so when Jack retired, Harry became the head inspector at the Yards. Later they promoted him to regional supervisor, a position he held until his retirement some years ago. For a while, Harry and his wife lived on a farm east of Didsbury. They sold that and moved to Airdrie. They both enjoy square dancing. Whenever I meet Harry, he seems to be enjoying life, which is great in your old age.

GORDON MESTON FAMILY are in the cattle trucking business. Gordon's wife, Frances, is the dispatcher. Both of their sons, Randy and Scott, drive trucks. Gordon came from Saskatchewan a number of years ago. After they were in Alberta for a few years, Gordon bought Ken Jones Trucking. Gordon had a slow start, since some of the trucks were not the greatest, but he persevered and expanded. Today, he has a fleet of state-of-the-art trucks. They haul feeders, fats, hogs or whatever livestock is transported. They also haul to the USA. The Mestons have a nice place in the country about ten miles south of Calgary. They own a small but good herd of cows. They are good truck operators.

BILL MIDDLETON was raised in Calgary, Alberta. He was a brother of Sonny Gray's wife, Laura. Bill was in the Second World War where he got seriously wounded and ended up with a steel plate in his head. His health was always somewhat fragile after that. In spite of this, Bill operated his own cattle truck at the Stockyards for many years. He hauled a lot of cattle for us. He was a good-hearted soul and always did his best. Bill never married. He passed away a number of years ago.

JACK MILLER was born and raised at Lethbridge, Alberta. He worked for the Alberta Stock Yards in Calgary for many years and still works for the Calgary Stockyards at Strathmore. He always gives it his best shot. He branded thousands of cattle for us and, of course, for many other people as well. Jack's eyesight is not as good as it could be, but, somehow, he manages to do a good job yarding cattle. Jack is everyone's friend. He has enjoyed single bliss all his life.

VERN MILLER is Jack Miller's brother. In the early 1950's, Vern rode bareback broncs at rodeos. After a brief stint working at the Calgary Stockyards, he went to work for Canada Packers as a cattle buyer. He had a lot of customers in the country. On several occasions, I pulled into people's yards to buy, and I was informed that Vern bought all their cattle and that was that. After Canada Packers ceased operations, Vern retired. These days he does some order buying. From what I have observed, he does a good job for the people he buys for. Vern and his wife have a place just a little northeast of Calgary.

WALTER MILLER was probably the last of the freelance cowboys to operate around the Calgary Stockyards. If there were any cattle to be moved by horseback, Walter was your man. Virtually no cattle were trailed to the Yards after the Second World War, except for a few from the small lots in Bonnybrook, just south of the Stockyards. Every once in a while, somebody would hire Walter to move some cattle within the Stockyards. From the extreme east side of the Yards to the extreme west side, it was almost half a mile. I am surprised that more horses weren't used to move cattle around the Yards. Walter Miller and Bert Bishop were the last of the real Stockyard cowboys. Dave Wheatcroft was the last brand inspector to use a horse. I think Walter must have passed on by now. If you haven't, Walter, please forgive me.

BILLY MILLS came from the Oyen country of Alberta. First, he worked for the Alberta Stock Yards; then, he worked for J. C. Wheatcroft. He got along well with everyone. I understand Billy works for a gas company these days.

CHRIS MILLS is an Englishman with a dry sense of humour. He has been involved in cattle politics ever since he arrived in Canada, some thirty-five years ago. He has been secretary-manager for the Canadian Cattlemen's Association and has acted as an advisor and consultant to a number of other cattle organizations. He is a quiet man who does his homework. When the mood strikes him, he can take a strip off somebody he considers to be out of line. Chris is very perceptive and intelligent, but rather hard to get to know on a personal basis. I used to visit him when he had an office in the Exchange Building at the Yards. I will hand it to him, he had good insight on the state of our industry at any given time. Chris lives on an acreage northwest of Okotoks. I'm waiting for him to write a book about the cattle business in Canada over the last four decades.

BOB MILTON often worked for the Alberta Stock Yards or J. C. Wheatcroft in the summer seasons. He was an excellent golfer. These days, Bob is a salesman for a meat company.

DAVEY MILTON is Bob Milton's brother. Davey was a local boy who worked for J. C. Wheatcroft. Later, he was nightman for the Alberta Stock Yards. Everybody liked "Milty," as the boys called him.

He was a very laid-back, easygoing person. His fellow workers always liked to tease him. Davey was a good sport and took it all in his stride. He is also a good golfer, maybe not quite as good as his brother Bob. Last I heard, Davey lives at Bragg Creek, Alberta.

HARRY MITCHELL was born and raised on a ranch at Maple Creek, Saskatchewan. There were quite a few Mitchells in that part of the world. All of them were ranchers and cattlemen. Harry's uncle Henry, who retired to Medicine Hat, Alberta, was quite a character. He always used to say: "The best way to ranch is to buy yearlings in the spring, summer them on grass, sell them in the fall, and winter the money." I liked that. That's mostly what I do these days.

Harry moved to Lethbridge, Alberta, where he worked for Burns as a cattle buyer. After some time he was transferred to Burns Calgary. Harry and I worked the two Calgary sale rings for several years. He is a nice guy with a good eye for cattle; however, he is extremely cautious. His volume was sometimes low, but whatever he bought was worth the money.

He quit Burns and went to work for CDM Lethbridge. Lo and behold, in a few years, Burns bought CDM and Harry was back working for Burns. Jimmy Thompson was the head buyer for CDM. When Jimmy passed away, Harry became the head buyer. He held this position until he retired. Harry lives in Lethbridge.

CHARLIE MONROE was employed for many years by Swift Canadian at Lethbridge, Alberta, and other locations. After several decades with Swift, he switched to Canada Packers in Calgary. I sat beside him in the sale ring for several years. He was an easygoing person. He knew cattle, but he was not nearly as aggressive as some of the other CP buyers. Charlie's attitude was that there were lots of cattle for everyone.

Charlie bought a new car every year whether he needed it or not. He used to jokingly say to me that it saved him the trouble of getting his old (one-year-old) car serviced for the winter.

In the early '70s, Charlie got a job with an American packer. He worked out of Spokane. He really liked it and worked there till he passed away. His daughter, Kathy, married Art Edwards. Charlie was married to a very nice lady whose ancestors came from Iceland.

HENRY MOON and his family were Korean folks. They bought the Stockyards Restaurant from Rudy and Tilly Ham. The Moons ran a good show. The quality of the food was good, and so was their service. After a few years, they sold out to a Hungarian couple, whose names slip my mind. I know the man's first name was Ted. After a few years, Ted and his wife sold out to Maurice and Shirley Gasnier. I have lost track of both the Moons and the Hungarian couple.

GERRY MOONEY is an order buyer who lives at High River, Alberta. He spent a lot of time at the Yards, especially in the fall. He has been the supervisor for the Little Bow Feeders' Association for almost as long as I can remember. Gerry doesn't get too excited, but he keeps plugging away. He is still actively buying cattle. These days, he sometimes travels to sales with Eion Chisholm, another old-timer. Gerry retired from the Feeders' Association in December 1994.

DR. DON MOORE operated a vet clinic at the Stockyards for over three decades. Don knows his profession well and has many loyal customers. His brother, Doug, is also a vet. In 1993, Don built a facility on Highway 2 between Calgary and Balzac. He has seven associates working with him.

PETE AND GLEN MORISON from Airdrie, Alberta, are brothers. They are longtime cattle people, who spent a fair amount of time at the Yards. They fed quite a few cattle. Bill Morison, Pete's son, often auctioned at the Yards as a spare. Glen and his son, Stewart, still operate a feedlot three miles west of our place. They are good cattle people and good neighbours. We have fed quite a few cattle at Stewart's feedlot and he does an excellent job. Stewart serves on the Board of Directors of the Alberta Cattle Commission.

LAWRENCE MORISROW came from Rimbey, Alberta, where he owned a hotel. He got into the oil business, among other things. In other words, he was a promoter. He also fed cattle on his place south of Calgary, which was called Zeus Farms. He was a great buddy of Danny MacDonald's. I got several hot stock tips from Lawrence. One stock called Cadillac Mines made a fair bit of money for us. He was big in Plains Petroleum which also did well for us. Some of the best beef I have ever eaten was served at his place. It was pit barbecued. My mouth still waters when I think about it. I have completely lost track of Lawrence.

MEL MORRISON, or "Melly" as he was known, worked for AWW as a cattle salesman and buyer for about fifty years. Melly is a good story teller. In fact, I phone him every once in a while to pick his brains about the Stockyards era before I arrived there. He did take a short leave from AWW to manage the cattle operations for the Co-op on the Lethbridge Market. When he came back to Calgary, he brought quite a few orders with him from the Lethbridge area. He bought a lot of cows for Harry Feldman. He could imitate Harry to a "T." Feldman was full of those old-fashioned Jewish sayings and expressions. To hear Mel repeat them with gestures and all was quite funny. Recently, Mel had a knee replacement and he is doing well. These days, he is enjoying retired life with his wife.

NEIL MORRISON is a grandson of Harvey Adams and he is Mel Morrison's nephew. Neil worked for AWW for several years. He was an O.K. guy, but he really wasn't a cattleman. He was a good car salesman. It so happened that he was married to Sam Parkinson's daughter. Parkinson owned Calgary Motor Products. When Neil left the Yards, he went into the car business for himself.

SAM MOSESON was an easygoing likeable Jewish cattle dealer. He travelled the country. His volume wasn't real big, but he always made a living. His goal was not to get rich, but to enjoy life. Sam always had a cigar in his mouth and a friendly word for everyone. Several months ago, I noticed in the Calgary Herald that Sam had passed away. In his obituary, he was described as a man who cared for others. I agree with that statement.

BOB MOWAT (sons were Gordon and Bill) was a cattle feeder in the Forest Lawn area. Bob worked for the CPR as a conductor for almost fifty years. He had quite a few days off the job, so he got involved with feeding cattle. He fed cattle for himself, Jack Leavitt and the Dvorkins. We also fed quite a few cattle at his place—in fact, I still feed a few head at his son's feedlot these days.

Bob liked to visit. I always enjoyed his conversations. He was very good friends with Jack Leavitt and travelled with him quite often. As his boys got older, they took over. Gordon and his family still run the feedlot. Bill is manager of a feed supplement company.

Bob and his sons are straight-shooters. Bob's wife was also a very fine lady. They did a good job feeding cattle. Many years ago, when they were still in Forest Lawn (they have since relocated to Langdon), I had one steer that gained five pounds a day over a hundred-day feeding period. He went from 900 up to 1,400 pounds. He was a tall, rangy Shorthorn. That's still a record for me.

BILL MURRY was the beef manager at Union Packers for many years. He originally came from Winnipeg. After Union Packers closed, Bill took over the management for beef procurement at Centennial Packers, who custom killed their cattle at Century Packers.

When I was at Bridgewaters, we bought cattle for Bill. They had to meet exact specifications: right quality, right grade, right yield, and right weight. We mostly bought Hereford-Charolais crosses weighing from 1,100 to 1,175 pounds, A1 and A2. Bill was very fussy, but he did an excellent job for Centennial. He always talked, acted, and dressed like a gentleman.

These days, Bill is retired and enjoys life with his wife. Recently, they took a trip to England.

PETE MURRY was a Scotsman who worked for Burns as a sheep buyer. Pete really knew sheep. He was also super good with Border collie sheepdogs. When he first arrived in Canada he worked as a sheep herder on a sheep ranch north of Maple Creek, Saskatchewan. Pete was not bashful to voice his opinion. Often his language would have been more appropriate at a lonesome prairie sheep camp than in mixed company. Pete also liked to hoist a few at the Shamrock Hotel, but he was a good family man. The Murry's had three daughters. Pete passed away about 35 years ago.

MURRAY MYERS came from Winnipeg as a cattle buyer for Northern Packers, which was owned by Harry Feldman. Murray was a good buyer. He had years of experience in Winnipeg, which is a tough place to make a living. Bobby Wolfe, who worked for Burns in Winnipeg, used to tell me that if you could make it in Winnipeg you could make it anywhere in the world. Murray looked impressive with his white hair and clipped mustache. Wheatcroft and Murray weren't exactly buddies. At times, this caused quite a stir in the sale ring, and many a producer reaped the benefit of higher prices for their cattle when those two were feuding. Murray passed away very suddenly from a massive heart attack.

RITA NELSON was a black-haired lady who worked for AWW in the office for a number of years. She had beautiful penmanship. You have heard the expression "a ladies' man"; well, she was what you'd call "a man's lady." She liked the boys; most women do. The difference was, she admitted it. She had a number of children that she supported while working every day. By now, they must all be grown up. I wish Rita well.

ANDREW NETT was a good friend of Mickey Dirrane's. Andrew lived at Milk River. He shipped a lot of cattle to Burns in the early '50s. He was an easygoing, pipe-smoking man. He had immigrated to Canada from Switzerland sometime after World War I. Ken Hurlburt, who also lived in Milk River, told me that Andrew was an excellent skater. He could glide past young people who were thirty years younger than himself. Andrew passed away many years ago.

FRED NEWCOMBE used to be the secretary-manager of The Western Stock Growers' Association. They had their office in the Exchange Building. Fred did a good job. He was always working away at something—no time to stand and stare. Last I heard, Fred, who is in his early nineties, is still active in a variety of interests.

BUCK NICHOLS is the son of Ted Nichols. For years, Ted worked for Burns as a cattle buyer. He left Burns to go to Lethbridge as an order buyer about a year before I started to work for Burns in 1950. Buck worked for the Alberta Stock Yards. He was a fairly heavyset lad who did a lot of work. He had a fairly short fuse; but, five minutes later, he was your friend again. I kind of lost track of Buck. I'm sure he is doing okay.

MORY NICKLESON worked at for the Alberta Stock Yards in Calgary for a little while. He also worked for Don Danard and Will Irvine at the Didsbury Market, which closed several years ago. Mory was a very obliging type of person.

JOHN NIELSEN was a Dane who came to Canada as a young man. He went to work for Canada Packers in Toronto in the sausage kitchen and worked his way up to management. He left Canada Packers to manage Alberta Western Beef at Medicine Hat. From there he went to work for Mr. Child at Burns Calgary, where he became a vice president. John is an impressive looking man with olive skin and black hair. He is an excellent dresser. He also knows the corporate jargon. When I went back to work for Burns in 1970, John became my boss. I actually liked working for him. He was quite blunt and so am I, but we got along really well. After he left Burns, he went to the USA to manage a meat operation. Several years later, he came back to Canada. I am not sure what John is doing these days, but I am sure he is still dabbling in business one way or another.

GEORGE NIES was the beef manager at Burns when I started there in January 1950. He was very concise, no in-between with him. If you did a good job, he told you. If you didn't, he told you as well. He ran what I call a tight ship. I had a lot of respect for George. I was sorry to see him leave when he got transferred to Kitchener, Ontario, as plant manager.

ERNIE NOBLE was an Irishman who never married. He owned land and operated a feedlot on Nose Creek. Ernie was a good operator and always knew the right time to sell his cattle. He could really read markets. Ernie had one slight problem. Every once in a while, he would imbibe till he was right out of it. After about three days he would be back somewhat jaded, but ready to do business. This would happen about half-a-dozen times a year. Ernie was well liked by everyone. There were many people at his funeral, including three lady friends from bygone years.

BILL NORRIE and sons operated trucks, just south of Calgary at Red Deer Lake, Alberta. Bill and his wife also operated an interesting little country store on Highway 22. They had a bulk fuel business as well. Bill was a big strong man. He could lift a barrel of fuel like it was a bag of popcorn. One day, he fell off a load of hay and really injured his back. Physically he was never the same. Bill's boys, George and Jim, have carried on the family trucking business. They are good men, just like their father. Over the years, they hauled thousands of cattle to the Calgary Stockyards.

LACE NOYES is a lady who hails from the cow country of Wood Mountain, Saskatchewan. In the summer of 1989 she bought the Calgary Hat Doctor shop from Bob Abbot. She came there five or six months before the Stockyards relocated to Strathmore. She is still at the hat shop in the Livestock Exchange Building, and she does an excellent job cleaning and blocking cowboy hats. At one time she did some barrel racing. Iloe Flewelling is her aunt.

GEORGE O'BRAY was a character born and raised in Calgary. In his lifetime, he tried quite a few things, such as racehorses and a feedlot on Nose Creek, and he was the owner of O'Bray's Auction Mart, which is now MacLean Auction Ltd. George was a practical joker who liked putting people on. It was all in fun. He was actually a nice person. I'm not sure I should print this, but I will: His registered brand was 2 lazy 2P (2₂P). George sold the market back to MacLeans (original owners) and sort of semi-retired. He passed away a number of years ago.

JIM O'GRYZLO worked for the Alberta Stock Yards. For a long time, he was the janitor of the Livestock Exchange Building, and he kept everything in good shape. Jim also kept a little beer on hand downstairs in case some of the boys developed a thirst when the outlets were closed.

BILL O'GRYZLO is a son of Jim O'Gryzlo and brother of Jim Beal. Bill was a steady hand. He also worked for the Alberta Stock Yards for many years. He was a scaleman at the sale ring and a good one. There were very few errors when Bill was operating the scale. He was pleasant to have around, always courteous. He was friends with a few people at the Yards, but did most of his socializing away from the Stockyards. When the market was reorganized in 1981, Bill left. I understand he managed a Dairy Queen for several years, after which he retired.

LES OLSEN is an order buyer from Airdrie, Alberta. He was involved with the Airdrie Market while it operated. He calls his company "Lesnor." Les started to buy cattle at the Calgary Stockyards in the 1980s. He may have bought some earlier than that, but that's when he started to come on a more regular basis. Les is a careful buyer and likes quality cattle. Several years ago, he and his wife spent some time in Phoenix. So did we. We had them over to our condo for a visit. Les was also involved with the Provincial Cattle Dealers' Association for several years.

DON OLSEN was a tall, well-maintained bachelor, who lived in the Windsor Park district of Calgary. He worked for the Alberta Stock Yards. For the last number of years, he was in charge of releasing cattle. I don't think he ever made a mistake in his count, even if it meant counting them three times. When Don released cattle, I knew the count was right. I appreciated that. Don always wore gloves, and I mean always, whether it was ten below or 100 above. I am not sure why. Maybe he had a germ fetish like Howard Hughes. Don did a good job, and I hope he is enjoying retirement.

ROCKY OSTRIM is a brother of Ronnie Ostrim, who was a Canadian Steer Wrestling Champion. Rocky jumped on a few himself. He was raised at Carseland, Alberta. For many years, he worked for the Health of Animals Division. He tended to business. As far as I know, Rocky is still with the government.

RONNIE OSTRIM worked for AWW for several autumns. He lives at Carseland where he operates a first-class feedlot. Ronnie was a good steer wrestler. He has been to the Canadian Finals in Edmonton a number of times. In 1975, he was a Canadian Steer Wrestling Champion.

BILL OTTEWELL was a dapper little man, who looked more like a gentleman estate-owner than a cattle buyer. For a number of years, he was a buyer for Burns Lethbridge. He was very cautious and didn't get much of a volume going. He left Burns and disappeared for a while. When he re-surfaced, he came to work for P&D. Bill conducted himself in a very respectable manner; however, he never really hit his stride again as a cattle buyer. He passed away many years ago.

BRYAN PAGE came from Medicine Hat, Alberta. He went to work for Alberta Western Beef. When I became the general livestock manager for Burns, he was on staff at our Medicine Hat plant. Burns purchased Alberta Western Beef in the fall of 1970. Eventually, Bryan left the company and went to work for J. C. Wheatcroft in Calgary. After several years with J.C.W., he left it to become the head buyer at XL Beef. When he left there, he went to Arizona where he took on a Grandma Lee's Bakery and Eating Place franchise. After a few years he came back to Canada. I am not sure what he is up to these days. Bryan is a very personable man and was generally well liked.

JOHN PAHARA was a rough and ready cattle buyer and feeder from Coaldale, Alberta. He came to the Calgary market quite often, and when he did, the bull market always took a jump. He was hard to outbid on either feeding or slaughter bulls. He bought other cattle as well and always cleared through P&D. When John was young, he was a boxing champion. I do not think he ever held the Canadian Heavyweight Championship, but he was right up there. In the early 1980s, when many of us lost millions feeding cattle, John Pahara, John Vanderheyden and I did a half-hour program with the CBC on the plight of the industry. I don't think it did any good, but at least we got to speak our piece. John was missed on several markets after he passed away a few years ago.

LARRY PALATA had an Italian background, as his name indicates. He came from Toronto where he and his brother operated a packing plant and meat business. Larry never had an office at the Yards but for several years he spent a lot of time around there. He cleared his cattle through Parslow & Denoon.

Larry was a colourful character and wore very flashy clothes right from his purple shoes on up. He was a heavyset man and always smoked a cigar, which was about 12 inches long.

It was always rumoured, but never proven, that Larry had some Mafia connections. In fact, he sued the Lethbridge Herald for a story they did on him referring to those connections. He won the court case, so we will give him the benefit of the doubt and declare those rumours as false; however, Larry had several other court cases regarding business transactions that he did not win. To be fair with the man, he paid all his bills at the Stockyards and, as far as I know, left owing no one any money.

When Larry was rolling on the market, he was good for the producer. He bought lots of cattle—the bigger the cattle, the better he liked them.

At the World Auctioneer contest held in Calgary in 1977, Larry bought two loads of our steers that weighed over 1,400 pounds, which was way too heavy for our local packers those days. He paid a pretty good shot for them—I appreciated that; in fact, that is the last time I saw Larry. He was easy to visit with, but like so many people with good personalities, he somehow had a penchant for choosing the wrong path. But then, I am not perfect, either—are you?

HANK PALLISTER was ranch-raised in the Foothills, southwest of Calgary. His father was an old-time cowboy. Hank inherited a good portion of that love of the western way of life. In the early 1950s, he came to the Stockyards as a brand inspector. Hank always did a good job. It seemed like he was born with a rope in his hand. He was at the Yards approximately twenty years.

In about 1970 or 1971, Hank was promoted to the head supervisory position for the province of Alberta. His office was located in Stettler. He loved his job. Hank literally knows every brand in Alberta especially the old ones. Once the computer age arrived, it was easy for him to keep track of every brand.

Hank was very cooperative with the Calgary Stampede when they had their "brand" sale of cattle wearing old-time brands. Many of these brands had been registered when Alberta was still a part of the Northwest Territories.

Several years ago, in Stettler. I gave a talk at the United Church. They had kind of selected me as "Cattleman of the Year." At any rate, after the meeting was over, Hank and his wife, Joyce, invited me over to their house. We had a good visit. I will never forget the old revolving table they own. It came from an old ranch kitchen—I think maybe the 44 Ranch.

Hank is retired these days. He sometimes writes a column for *Alberta Beef*, entitled *"Smoke From The Branding Fire."* I find him very interesting. He knows more about brands than any other person in Alberta.

The commemorative plate (front).

The Alberta Stockyards

The Alberta Stockyards served as a landmark in east Calgary where it was established as a shipping point for range cattle going to Eastern and European markets. For many years the cattle sold here set a market value for other cattle traded throughout Western Canada.

The multitude of people who knew the premises as a place of employment, business, and friendship, were devoted to the success and purpose of the livestock industry. This souvenir plate is dedicated to these same people in memory of the stockyards which have now disappeared.

The brands were selected at random to represent some of the pioneer families who were responsible for the development of the livestock industry in southern Alberta.

Poem by H. G. Pallister.   Photo by Joyce Pallister.

Additional plates are available by mailing $24.00 to cover cost and postage to:

Memory Lane Souvenirs
Box 1594, Stettler, AB. T0C 2L0

The commemorative plate, (back).

BOBBI PREMAK was the wife of Bill Premak. She worked in the office of P&M. She was a very pleasant and competent person. She raised a fine son by the name of Don, who presently lives one mile from our place at Airdrie. Bobbi passed away a number of years ago.

BILLY PARKER was a grandson of Colonel Parker, one of the original Mounties who came to Fort Macleod, Alberta, in 1874. Billy was raised in southern Alberta. He was in the forces during the Second World War. When he came home, he went into the hotel business.

At age 42, Burns hired Billy as a livestock buyer at Lethbridge. Around 1960 they transferred him to Calgary where he continued as a buyer. In 1970 he was transferred to Medicine Hat as head buyer. A year later, he was back at Burns Calgary where he stayed until he retired. As far as I can ascertain, he was the only cattle buyer to ever retire from Burns at age 65. The others either died or quit. Tom MacKenzie and Pete Murry also retired from Burns at ages 65, but they were sheep buyers. I guess shepherds are tougher than cowboys. After his retirement, Billy clerked for several years for the auctioneers at the Stockyards.

Billy was a nice, friendly person and was well liked by everyone. When he got hungry, he used to say: "I've got the pork chop staggers." He passed away about twelve or thirteen years ago.

Burns' cattle buyers, (L-R) Bill Parker, Ken Whitley, 1968.

GEOFF PARKER was raised in the Midnapore district of Alberta. He was in the Air Force during the War. When he was released, he got involved in several ventures. In the early '50s he came to work for Burns in the livestock department. I had been there for several years. We became good friends. When Geoff left Burns, he went to work for the Health of Animals Division.

Geoff was a top-notch horseman—Western or English saddle. He played polo, but he also liked western riding. One year, I think it was 1952, Geoff and I, and four other men joined together to form a bareback wrestling team. I don't know how many of you readers have seen bareback wrestling. Let me tell you, it can get pretty rough. We performed for several nights in the old Victoria Arena. This was before the Stampede Corral was built. In those days, they held big horse shows there. So for a little change of pace, they sponsored this wrestling match in between classes. What happens is this: two teams line up facing each other at opposite ends of the arena with six or eight members on each team. They are all mounted on horses, bareback. At a given signal, they charge to the centre of the arena to meet in combat. The goal is to wrestle your opponent off his horse to the ground. If any part of your body touches ground, you are out. There were very few rules. Initially, it is more or less a one-on-one struggle, but, as time goes on, some get eliminated. That means two or three can then gang up on you to pull you off. It gets pretty wild sometimes. You can hang upside down with your feet locked around your horse's neck, or you can lie flat on your stomach with your arms locked around the horse's neck, or you may take off on a dead run to escape your opponents. They can usually corner you.

I remember one night I was the last one left on a horse on our team. The other team still had two riders left on. What happened was, they galloped along side of me, one on each side. They both grabbed me and yanked me forward right over the horse's head. I must have been eight feet off the ground, then I hit the dirt in front of my horse. It reared up and veered right past me. Our opponents won that night.

Geoff owned ten or fifteen acres with a little house on the land. It was located on the west side of Macleod Trail, just south of where Jack Carter Chev-Olds is today. During this period he worked for the Health of Animals Division. After he sold this acreage, he bought a place a few miles northeast of Cochrane. Big Hill Springs starts on the property. Today his widow, Pearl Parker, still owns it. Geoff developed a very debilitating disease which left him incapacitated. He was in hospitals for the last six or seven years of his life. I often visited him in the hospital. He never lost his interest in livestock, especially horses. He passed away a few years ago.

VERN PARSLOW, along with George Denoon, was the founder of Parslow & Denoon in 1915. Parslow was a good businessman; he was maybe a little on the cautious side. Denoon was a good cattleman and deal maker. The two men complemented each other's abilities. Vern was in charge of the office as well as the sheep and hog operation. In the office, he had Sylvester Harvey, and, in the sheep and hogs, Maule McEwen. Vern always knew what was going on. He enjoyed the Yards and it showed. P&D was a very successful firm. Vern's keen interest stayed with him into old age. He finally retired, but all who knew him remember the long-lasting contribution he made to the livestock industry. He has since passed away.

BUD PARSLOW is the son of the late Vern Parslow, one of the founders of Parslow & Denoon. Bud was born and raised in Calgary.

Bud Parslow, on the occasion of his retirement, receives a silver tray from Leonard Friesen, President of the Calgary Livestock Market.

During the War he was in the Air Force. When he came home, he joined his father's firm (P&D). He did some alley work, but most of his time was spent in the office. Bud was always courteous and polite—a real gentleman. He held several positions on the livestock exchange board. His input was always appreciated. When his dad passed away, Bud became a full partner with Stan Denoon. In the early '80s, Bud retired from work. I meet him once in a while, usually with Mel Morrison.

GRANT PARSONS worked for the Alberta Stock Yards. He was probably the best bobcat operator they ever hired. He could move that machine with matchless precision. The boys usually called him "Many Ponies." He was married to a Big Plume girl from the Sarcee reserve. These days, referring to him as "Many Ponies" or the name "Sarcee" is politically incorrect, but this was twenty-five years ago. As far as I know, Grant still resides in Calgary.

GORDIE PASCO came from Saskatchewan. He worked for the Alberta Stock Yards. He was a good worker. These days, you can find him working at Stampede Park. Gordie is well liked by everyone.

JIMMY PAUL came from the Picture Butte country of Alberta. In 1951 he teamed up with Danny MacDonald and they bought out the W. W. Starke Commission Co. Danny was the auctioneer while Jimmy more or less acted as the business manager.

Jimmy used to work the sale ring. Just when a person like myself thought he was doing a great job, Jimmy would walk up to him at ringside and, in a dry voice, would say: "Do you think you'll ever amount to anything?" Even though he said it in jest, as a young man, it kind of deflated your ego.

Before Calgary instituted the Friday feeder sale, we would get gobs of cattle every day during the fall run. The commission men always wanted the buyers to stay late so they could sell as many cattle as possible. Jimmy Paul is the only commission man that used to buy us a steak dinner for sticking around late.

In 1958 Jimmy sold his share of the business to Cecil Barber and Doug Keer. After that he dabbled around feeding cattle stillage soup—plus a few other ventures. Eventually, he moved to the

Okanagan Valley in British Columbia where he purchased and operated a boat marina. Jimmy passed away several years ago.

The name "Paul & MacDonald" is still used today. Cecil Barber owns that company.

JIM PAUL JR. is the late Jimmy Paul's son. He worked for P&M for many years. Jim was a genuinely nice man. I can still see his slight grin as he moved the cattle around the ring. I always thought Jim had a lot of class. I heard recently that he is still at Peachland, B.C., where his he and his dad operated the Marina. His dad passed away a long time ago. Someday, I hope to stop there and see if Jim Jr. is still there.

NELS PEDERSON is an easygoing Dane. He worked for the Alberta Stock Yards as a yard repairman. Nels was not the fastest worker, but he was steady and very dependable. Unfortunately, some of the sturdy bull pens that Nels built were ripped down a few years after he constructed them. When Marathon Realty terminated the lease the Calgary Public Livestock Market had on the Yards, they demolished all the pens, posthaste—just in case someone might have gotten the idea to reactivate the Stockyards. I don't mind telling you that I have very little use or time for the eastern-based Marathon. The history of the Alberta Stock Yards meant absolutely nothing to them. They even destroyed a bunch of records that Eric Tribble had saved. I will never forgive them for that. For a number of years now, Nels has worked for Tom Copithorne.

BILL PERLICH was raised at Picture Butte, Alberta. Joe and Tony Perlich are his uncles. Bill worked for J. C. Wheatcroft for a number of years. When we reorganized at the Yards in 1981, he worked as a country man for the Calgary Public Livestock Market. I was not too happy when he left us to work for the Highwood Auction Market, where he still is today. Now, when I reflect back on it, I guess I can't blame him for making a switch, if he felt he improved his lot. I made a few switches myself. I am sure he is doing a good job for Highwood.

JOE PERLICH came from Picture Butte, Alberta. He auctioned at the Stockyards off and on for several years. Joe was a prince of a man. He was capable and pleasant. I liked visiting with him.

In 1967 Joe and Tony opened up the Perlich Brothers Auction Mart at Lethbridge. For the first year, we sent them many loads of cattle; but, as time went by, they got good receipts without those trading cattle. We always sent them good quality cattle, but did not always make money.

I had the privilege of judging the Lethbridge 4-H Steer Show on three or four occasions. One thing that I always remember is the support Joe Perlich gave to 4-H and the way he talked to those kids when he sold their calves.

Joe developed cancer and passed away at a young age. He was deeply missed by all cattlemen. It is good to see his wife and sons still involved with Tony Perlich in the market to this day.

BILL PERRY came from Quebec. He was a horse dealer and a good one. He was one of the best judges of draft horses in the country; however, for the last ten or fifteen years of his life, he dealt mainly in meat horses. Slim Brown used to work with Bill a lot. Bill was a very calm individual. I think, as an Anglophone in Quebec, he learned it did not pay to get excited. Whenever you visited with him, you had to be careful. Every once in a while, he would let a stream of tobacco juice jet through the air. If his aim happened to be off a little, it could mean a dry-cleaning bill. Bill passed on many years ago.

ED PETERS was a brand inspector. He came from Pincher Creek, Alberta. Ed knew his stuff. He was a ranch cowboy-type of guy. Ed was sociable, but minded his own business. After some years, he drifted back to Pincher Creek.

ORVILLE PETERS worked in the office of the Alberta Livestock Co-op. I know Orville well. He is my brother-in-law, in other words, my wife's brother.

Orville is a quiet, laid-back individual, but his mind is always working. He was at the Co-op a number of years. He may be remembered by some as the blond-haired, blue-eyed chap that could play the piano. When he left the Co-op, he moved to Edmonton where he was a piano salesman. I think he also gave piano lessons. After a while, he moved back to Calgary where he pursued the same field. In fact, I think he met his wife Carol when she took some lessons from him. He always did like music. When he was just a lad, he played in a band in Swift Current, Saskatchewan, for some years.

These days Orville is more or less retired. He and his wife reside in the southern part of Calgary. They raised two fine children: Brent is married and Leanne also recently got married.

LARRY PETHERBRIDGE was raised in Lethbridge, Alberta. I think his dad was a school principal. Larry took to cows and horses like a duck takes to water. He became a good bull rider and went to the Canadian Finals Rodeo in Edmonton several times. Larry worked at Paul & MacDonald for many years. He has a great personality and did a good job for them. After he left, he bought a place west of Bowden where he "backgrounds" and feeds out some cattle. (Another top-notch bareback rider, Allan Thorpe, also has a place in that area. He never spent a lot of time at the Yards, but he loves the cattle business too. In fact, Allan is one of the people who encouraged me to write a book on the history of the Yards.) You do not have to be born on a ranch or farm to be a good cowman. Larry has proved that. A few years ago, he relocated to Barrhead, Alberta.

Larry Petherbridge winning bull riding at the Bruce rodeo, 1969.

RUSS PHILLIP was ranch-raised in the Kamloops country of B.C. He came to Calgary as a cattle buyer for Alberta Meat who had a plant at the West Coast. In 1952 Russ left Alberta Meat and went to work for Paul & MacDonald. He was a good judge of cattle; in fact, he judged a lot of cattle shows. I had the privilege of co-judging several shows with him.

In 1968 Russ left Calgary to open up a commission firm at Lloydminster. He operated there for about seven years. In 1975 the Saskatchewan Wheat Pool bought the Lloyd Yards. Russ left there to work for the Airdrie Auction Market. It only operated for a few years, then they ceased selling, and the property was sold. At this point, he came back to P&M. He was there for several years and then went to work at the Didsbury Auction Market. On his days off, he worked for Harold Evans, a local farmer and feedlot operator. In the late 1980s, Russ went to work for Nilssons at Clyde, Alberta. He only stayed a short while. He retired to Armstrong, B.C.

Russ was a good, honest cattleman who always looked at things optimistically. He had one problem—"John Barleycorn"; but, even when he had imbibed a little too freely, he never became abusive or obnoxious like some people did.

Russ and his wife raised a wonderful family. Their children were all good scholars and took postsecondary education. I think most of them are professionals.

Russ Phillip

It has been a few years now, since Russ passed away. He left a host of friends. I don't think there is a cattleman in Alberta or B.C. who did not like Russ Phillip.

NORA PINTER worked in the office of the Alberta Livestock Co-op. I really did not know her very well. I do know she was a slim, quiet type of lady. One thing I do remember, she used to wear organdy dresses. I am sure she did a good job for the Co-op.

GEORGE PITCAITHY worked for Parslow & Denoon. In the early '50s, he left them to become a hog and sheep buyer for Swift. George coined the phrase "The Den of Iniquity." He always tended to business, even if he did not always agree on the edicts that were issued by Swift's head office in Chicago. All Swift's policies came from the United States. When Union Packers, which was owned by Swift, closed, George got on with the Health of Animals Division. He has been with them ever since.

ALEC PODMOROFF worked for the Alberta Stock Yards most of his working life. He often was in the gatehouse. He was a real gentleman, and was always very helpful. Alec was quite crippled for the last few years, but this did not stop him from doing a good job.

DON PONATH had a place just south of Calgary, Alberta. He was a born trader and dealer who liked challenge. He came to the Stockyards on a fairly regular basis. He dealt almost exclusively with Pete Adams. Eventually, he sold out and headed to B.C. where he continued his involvement in the cattle industry. Don has a brother living in the Cochrane district who has patronized the Calgary market for years.

JOHN POWELL came from Ontario. He could do almost anything when it came to construction or maintenance and was a good man with cement. He helped build a number of places.

John did a lot of work for the Dvorkins at their packing plant. He knew how to operate feed mills or any other equipment that had lots of cogwheels. John was around the Yards a lot, although he never really got involved in the cow business.

I have something in common with John. One day a man surfaced at the Stockyards with a big tear-jerking story about being down on his luck—his children were starving. So, John and I both gave him $200 to buy groceries. Then, later, we really opened up our purse strings and each of us loaned him $2,500 for a total of $5,000, which was to be paid in a short while. This was about ten years ago. To date, we have not received any payment. He was a real con artist, we found out later. Last I heard, he lives at Clearbrook in the Fraser Valley of B.C.

I have kind of lost track of John Powell.

DICK PRATT came to Calgary from Winnipeg, where he had worked at Canada Packers. He also worked in Calgary as a cattle buyer for CP. He was a handsome chap with slicked-down black hair. I do not remember if Dick was married, but when he arrived here, I do know he turned quite a few ladies' heads. I'm sure if he were married, he stayed true-blue to his wife. I better get off that subject in case I step on a land mine! Dick was in Calgary for a number of years. Eventually, he quit CP and went to work for Weiller and Williams in Saskatoon. He was their head man. I am sure he did a good job for them. Over the years, I have met Dick occasionally at conventions. He is always his pleasant self.

BILL PREMAK came from Winnipeg, Manitoba. He worked for J. C. Wheatcroft for a little while, then went back to Winnipeg. It was just as well. He really did not fit in Calgary.

GEORGE PRESCOTT surfaced at the Calgary Stockyards about fifteen years ago. Prior to that, he owned and operated a butcher shop, first in Cochrane, then in southwest Calgary. I can still remember hearing George on the radio announcing his meat specials every Saturday. They sounded like pretty good deals; but, since we always had our own beef in the freezer, I never availed myself of those deals. George started out quite low-key, buying and selling cattle at the Stockyards. In a few years, the momentum picked up and he and his son Terry moved quite a few cattle. These days, they cover a lot of sales in Alberta. The bulk of their buy is cows and bulls. George is well liked and respected in the industry. He is married to Harvey Uffleman's sister.

TERRY PRESCOTT is George Prescott's son. He is a big, likeable guy. He and his wife have a place just outside of Strathmore, Alberta, where they feed cattle, including a lot of bulls for slaughter. Terry buys cattle at auctions and also runs the feeding end at home. When Terry was a steer wrestler, he made some really good runs. These days he is busy tending to business and raising a family.

LEONARD PRESKY lived in Toronto, Ontario, where he owned Prime Packing. He often came to Calgary to buy cattle where his contact was Red Wheatcroft. Red and Roy Gilkes bought thousands of cattle for Presky. One day Leonard went to a horse sale at E. P. Taylor's place. Taylor horses were world-class Thoroughbreds. They sold for big money, so when Presky saw one horse with a bit of a blemish going cheap—$9,000—he bought him. The horse's name was Mosey Dick. This horse went on to win $250,000—not bad money thirty years ago. Presky was hooked. He stayed in the slaughter business; but, from then on, his first love was racehorses. Roy Gilkes told me that Leonard really mellowed after he got involved with horses in a big way. As far as I know, Presky lives in Florida these days, still pursuing his favourite hobby.

LEE PRICE came from Hanna, Alberta. Lee was a good saddle bronc rider. He is a born promoter, so consequently he has been involved in a number of ventures. For many years, he sold real estate around Calgary and throughout Alberta. His company was called Big Country Realty. For a number of years, he had a battle with the provincial government over some land they expropriated from him at Hanna, Alberta, to build an airport. I have not heard what happened. I hope he won his case.

AL PUST worked for the Alberta Stock Yards as a foreman for many years. He was a super nice man, who never got excited. It did not matter if everything had gone wrong, he always stayed his cool, calm self. If there was a mix-up with cattle, Al could always untangle it. He ran a smooth operation, considering all the help that came and went. One reason for the big turnover was that the Stock Yards Co. did not pay very high salaries. When Al retired, we all missed him. He passed away several years ago.

ILERET RABNAY worked in the Burns livestock department for a few years. He originally came to Calgary from Brooks, Alberta. Ileret was a free spirit. He did his job day in and day out in a very nonchalant way. He had a great sense of humour, which was always there whether the sun was shining or not. Last I heard of Ileret, he owned an electrical shop in Lacombe, Alberta.

JIM RAFFAN was raised at Allingham, Alberta. He was an auctioneer at the Calgary market. I always hit it off well with Jim. He was a genuinely nice guy. For several years, he and his family lived on 37th Street SW. At that time, we lived on 17th Avenue SW, so we saw them quite often.

Sometime in the '60s, Jim, along with his partner Billy Thompson, opened up an auction market at Armstrong, B.C. This venture went quite well. After several years, Jim bought out Bill's share. By this time, Jim's son, Don, had grown up. Don teamed up with his dad and things really picked up. Sadly, Jim got cancer and passed away at a young age. Don carried on and today operates a very successful market.

Several times, Don has been the Canadian Champion Auctioneer. In 1994 he also won the International Livestock Auctioneer Championship contest. It would have been nice for Jim to have been around to see his son win this honour. I know Don's mother and family are very proud of his achievements.

BILL RALSTON transferred from Canada Packers Toronto to Canada Packers Calgary. He worked the sale once in a while, but mostly bought cattle in the country. He could cover a large area in a short time. Bill and I did not always see eye to eye. I think the main reason was that he liked buying direct, and I was trying to get the slaughter cattle to come to the Stockyards for public auction. As time went by, we both mellowed a bit. Today, virtually all slaughter steers and heifers are sold direct. When Bill retired from CP, he went to work for Thiessen Bros. Feedlot at Carseland. He has since retired from there as well. I am sure Bill is enjoying a well-earned retirement.

JOE RAPPEL was a beef manager at Burns for a number of years. He was easy to get along with, but he was not the last of the big-time gamblers. In other words, he did not want us to buy any cattle that he did not have a home for in advance. I really have no idea where Joe is today.

SAM RASKIN was raised and lived at Rumsey, Alberta. He was a big-time cattle dealer. He had a good personality—well suited to doing business. Sam had a Jewish background; however, he was considerably different than many of the Jewish cattle dealers that came from Russia in the 1920s. He was born and raised a native Albertan. Size of deals never bothered Sam—the bigger, the better. He was around the Stockyards a lot, especially after he started to court Niva who worked at the Bank of Montreal, Stockyards Branch. He ended up marrying her. Sam passed away a number of years ago. He was a good cattleman.

LLOYD RASMUSSEN worked at Burns as the feedman in their yards. He fought in the Second World War and his mind was not quite right. If you treated him well, he was okay, but if somebody crossed him, he would blow up. I always felt sorry for Lloyd. He served our country and this was his reward. He passed away several years ago.

GORDON AND DOROTHY RAUCH came to the Stockyards in the mid-'60s. Gordon had worked at a newspaper outfit in Nelson, B.C.

The commission men thought they should have a weekly newspaper, so Gordon and his wife came to the Stockyards and started publishing the Calgary Livestock Market Journal. It was quite an interesting little paper with a lot of pictures. It always extolled the advantages of selling your livestock competitively: "Bring them to Calgary. This is where the prices are determined."

Gordon became quite an influence around the Yards. Even though he was actually not a cattleman, he knew what market rules and results were. He and Charlie Kennedy were the main spokespersons for the Calgary Market. For a number of years, Gordon wrote pretty well everything any president of the Livestock Exchange uttered publicly. He was the secretary of the Exchange when I was elected president. That procedure soon changed. Maybe I am too blunt and opinionated, or whatever; but I wanted to, and did, write my own annual reports as well as the agendas for our meetings.

Gordon was a good newspaperman; however, running a livestock market is a slightly different kettle of fish—or should I say beef? In all fairness to Gordon, he was good for the market. He always kept abreast of what was going.

Gordon was also a good artist. He painted some excellent pictures. I think, after they left Calgary, Gordon concentrated mainly on his painting ability. I know he sold some paintings at a fairly decent price.

The Rauchs sold the business to Jim and Isabel McPherson and they operated it for several years. Then they closed shop.

I wish Gordon and Dorothy well in their retirement in beautiful British Columbia.

Dorothy and Gordon Rauch receiving farewell gifts, 1978.

BENNY RAYMOND was what I would call a pleasant Jewish cattle feeder. He was a gentleman and never caused a rift. He always worked hard. Benny's little feedlot was situated just north off McKnight Boulevard in an area that is now covered with houses. He would complete his chores in the morning, then come to the market to see if he could pick up a few bargains. Sometimes, he was covered with dust from the feed he was grinding. Dust or no dust, Benny seemed to like what he was doing. He passed away several years ago.

BERT REA worked at Burns in the livestock department. He was on the night shift for a while receiving livestock. When he worked on the day shift, he often looked after the hog operation. He was a good worker. My advice: Don't cross him—like many of us, Bert had a temper, which was not always even. He had a place just north of Calgary.

GERRY REGIER was a government grader in the Calgary office for several years. He was fair in his grading decisions. At one time, he had a nice piece of land west of Airdrie close to Mike Harris' place; however, Gerry was transferred to Edmonton before he had a chance to build his dream home in the country. As far as I know, he is still with the government in a supervisory capacity.

EDDIE REID is a cattle buyer from Lethbridge, Alberta. Quite often he would come to the Calgary market to liven things up a little. He loved practical jokes and is also a good impersonator. At the Stockyards closing party, Lester Gurnett and Eddie put on a real funny skit pretending they were a couple of Hutterites. Eddie's father, Jim, from Medicine Hat, was also a cattle buyer. Jim and his wife were good friends of ours. Jim was a prince of a man and left Eddie a good heritage. Eddie, too, is a straight-shooter. These days he buys some cattle for XL Beef in the Lethbridge area.

FRANK REID lived at Airdrie, Alberta. He used to feed some cattle. He spent a lot of time at the Stockyards kibitzing with the boys. Most of all he liked to play cards with some of his cronies. Frank was a very thin man, but he seemed to have a lot of stamina. He passed away some years ago. He still has family at Airdrie, including his sons, Ken and Jim, who still feed cattle.

DR. IVAN REID was in charge of the Health of Animals Division at the Yards for a few years. He was a tall, soft-spoken individual. He was very fair in all his decisions. I was sorry to see him leave. He got promoted to a higher position in Ottawa. I met and visited with him on several occasions when I was in Ottawa.

BILL RENARD was a good horseman and feedlot operator. He was at the Stockyards most of the time, although he took time to ride every day. When Bill was a young man, he hauled pipe from Okotoks to the Turner Valley oilfields with horses. He used to tell me the reason he was so strong in his arms and hands was because of driving those four- and six-horse hitches for so many years. Bill also worked for Hart Parr Tractor Co. He handled all the horses they took in on trade. Maule McEwen was one of Bill's understudies. Bill, along with Bob McDougall, owned the MacLean Auction Market in East Calgary for several years. Bill passed away some years ago. He was giving a demonstration on how to load a horse into a trailer to some young 4-H people, and the horse kicked him. Bill died a short time later.

BILL REVELLY worked for Parslow & Denoon. He was the stepson of Pat Burton. Actually, Bill was an American. He was in the U.S. Army in Korea. He could tell some interesting stories—slightly exaggerated, maybe, but interesting. He eventually moved to California.

ELSIE RIDEOUT worked in the Burns Livestock office. In 1975, she came to work in our office at Friesen Cattle Co. She was very efficient and dependable. She worked for us for ten years. One of her great pleasures was playing bridge; in fact, she is so good at it, she now teaches bridge. Elsie still lives in Calgary, close to the Stampede grounds.

DON RITCHIE worked for the Alberta Livestock Co-op for many years. After they folded at the Agri-Mart, Don went to work for P&M. In 1982 he became a country agent for the Calgary Public Livestock Market. As far as I know, he still resides in Calgary.

EFFIE-MAY RILEY was the office manager for P&M. She was a "no-nonsense" lady. With Effie-May everything was done now, correctly, and in order. I really do not know much else about her.

ROY ROBERTS was a laid-back, pipe-smoking government grader. He moved slowly but always got the job done. He would peer over his glasses and make some wise comments on almost any subject. Roy was what I would call an old-timer. I've often wondered what happened to him after he retired.

FRANK ROBERTSON was transferred from Winnipeg, Manitoba, to Calgary, Alberta, in the early 1960s as the head cattle buyer for Swift Canadian. Frank was probably the most gentlemanly cattle buyer to ever set foot in the Stockyards, both in dress and demeanour. He always wore a tie and suit coat along with polished Oxford shoes. He conducted his business with dignity. He was not a snob, just a gentleman. When Frank retired, Jim Thompson took his place, another gentleman, but no suit coat or tie.

JOHN ROBINSON was a packing plant expert. He was one of the main cogs in the Alberta Western Beef plant at Medicine Hat, Alberta. He got along well with Red Wheatcroft. John had a lot of ability. After he left Alberta Western, he went to work for Dvorkin Bros. He kept the wheels going there for a number of years, including some extensive improvements to the killing floor operation. John liked to visit in the coffee shop at noon. He was a cool customer.

LARRY ROBINSON worked with Mr. Gardiner, the manager, at the Bank of Montreal in the basement of the old Exchange Building. Larry got along well with everyone. He had a bit of a gambling habit, but that was not unusual in those days, or today for that matter. I have lost track of Larry.

SYKES ROBINSON came from the Cochrane country. He was a top-notch saddle bronc rider. He could ride with the best, and did. In 1939 Sykes won the Canadian Saddle Bronc Riding Championship at the Calgary Stampede. Sykes worked as a brand inspector at the Yards—a job he did well for quite some time. He then went to work for AWW, where he stayed for many years. I had a lot of good visits with Sykes. He passed away many years ago.

Sykes Robinson

BOB ROBINSON is the late Sykes Robinson's son. Bob, too, was a great bronc rider. He won numerous championships, including the Calgary Stampede. Bob worked off and on at the market in between rodeos. He also was the secretary-manager of the Professional Rodeo Cowboys Association in the U.S. Every December, Bob and a buddy or two would sell Christmas trees in Calgary. We bought quite a few trees from them. Last I heard, Bob lives at Millet, Alberta, which is close to Edmonton. His stepson, Shaun Vant, is a good rodeo cowboy.

STAN ROCK came from Morrin, Alberta. For many years, he was the supervisor for the Drumheller Feeders' Association. This often brought him to the Stockyards. He also fed and handled other cattle. Stan had the misfortune of losing one arm; however, this did not impair his judgement of cattle. He always did a good job. His brother, J. P. Rock, was a very high profile sheepman. Stan passed

304

away in 1977. His son, Andy, is carrying on the family tradition. He is an order buyer and he, too, lives at Morrin.

TOM RODBOURNE was the general feeds manager for Burns. He liked to talk and mix with people and was always very positive in his business dealings. He was always well dressed with a clipped moustache. I am not sure where Tom is these days.

DR. HAROLD ROENISH was a vet who spent much of his time around the Yards. He was a "character" in the true sense of the word. He had plenty of smarts, but he often chose to do the goofiest things—like driving around with a dead pig in the trunk till the odour made him dispose of it. Within a few months a new car was in shambles. He used his car like an army uses a tank. He raised some good Charolais cattle. I wonder what he is doing now.

GUS ROOK worked for the Alberta Stock Yards in the mid-'80s. He was a skinny, blond-haired kid. He had the misfortune of losing his wife from an asthma attack. Gus was an OK guy, but, once in a while, he kicked over the traces: this often involved horses. He would solicit mares to be bred by meat-horse stallions that were waiting in the Yards for shipment to a processing plant. I am sure the stallions enjoyed it; however, those were not really his stallions to use. There was no harm done since those horses were on their way to the happy hunting grounds. As far as I know, Gus still resides in the Calgary area.

BILL ROSE was a big-time gambler and cattleman. He wore good clothes. His hands were soft and they sported several big diamond rings. Bill liked to run cattle on cover-crop in southern Alberta. His brother was a Calgary judge. Needless to say, Bill and his brother did not always see eye to eye. Bill loved to party. One time, when we were in the campgrounds at Banff, he was there also with some friends. They were having roast turkey with all the trimmings. This was in July—not Thanksgiving or Christmas. He insisted we partake, which we did. It was good. About ten years ago, Bill suffered a stroke. Last time I saw him, he was in the Bethany Care Centre. He was not in good shape.

MARVIN ROSE worked for the Alberta Stock Yards in several different capacities, often as a hayman. He was a good worker. His one and only gear was straight ahead at full-throttle.

One Saturday, I happened to be in my office upstairs in the Exchange Building, overlooking the Stockyards. Marvin was cleaning the Yards with a bobcat tractor. He loaded the manure onto a dump truck and hauled it out to a farmer's field. There was nobody else at the Yards and Marvin did not know I was there. As I glanced out of the window, I saw him running to the truck. I kind of wondered what the problem was; there was no problem, he was just in a hurry. When he returned, he was still on the run. There is not one man in 10,000 that would put out that kind of effort when he really does not have to. It's like a plumber charging you less for a job, when it's completed, than what he quoted you in the first place. It just never happens.

At the time of writing, Marvin is still at the Stockyards at Strathmore.

BILL ROSS worked with the government grading service: first, as a grader; then, for many years, as a market reporter for the federal government. He came to the sale ring every forenoon to observe the market. In the process, he would question various buyers on their opinion as to what was happening price-wise.

Bill was notorious for repeating exactly what someone told him. Sort of an instant replay. You might say: "The weather is terrible today." Bill would repeat the exact same words: "The weather is terrible today." Or you could say: "Johnny Anderson's wife had a baby last night," and, he would repeat the exact same words. We used to get quite a kick out of this, and, needless to say, all the buyers would sort of play this little game with him—that is, with the exception of a person like Ian Davidson, who remained all business. His main concern was that Bill should not quote the market too high, which could mean that Canada Packers would have to pay more money for their country cattle buy. Bill never hurt anyone, and he tried to do the best job he could.

Over the years, Bill developed a heart condition that really slowed him up. This finally claimed his life.

SHORTY ROSS worked as a cattle buyer for the Alberta Livestock Co-op. As his nickname indicates, he was a small man. He had a very confident way about his cattle buying and business transactions. He used to buy a lot of bologna bulls to ship to the USA.

In those days, the two sale rings were a distance apart. Shorty always bought in the Co-op and P&D ring. I nearly always bought in the AWW and P&M ring. I was still working for Burns; however, Burns very seldom bought bulls, so, quite often, Shorty would ask me to buy bulls for him, which I weighed to Burns. After the sale, Shorty would send a few of the boys over to pick up the bulls. Burns' pens and the Alberta Stock Yards' pens were connected. Nobody except Shorty and those of us who worked at Burns knew where the bulls came from. Burns often received bulls in carloads of cattle. These we usually sold to him. There was nothing illegal about this. It was just a little unorthodox, since the Co-op often had a representative in the AWW and P&M ring.

For some years, Shorty had an alcohol problem. To his credit, he completely overcame this vice. He passed away when he was in his mid-'50s.

BUCKY ROTHWELL SR. was the father of Bill (Bucky) and Stan (Buck) Rothwell. Bucky senior worked at Burns all his life. He had known Pat Burns very well and liked to tell stories about him. Bucky had quite an English accent and was not easy to understand. Visiting with us at the cattle scalehouse was one of his favourite pastimes. He died a long time ago.

BILL "BUCKY" ROTHWELL worked as a plumber for Burns. You may wonder why I mention him. The reason I do is because he was raised in East Calgary along with his brother, Stan, who worked for Adams, Wood and Weiller. Bill hung around at the livestock scale quite a lot of the time. When things got slack, this was his favourite hiding place. He could fix almost anything, so it was kind of handy having him around. After working for Burns most of his life, Bill left and went to work at Stampede Park. He passed away in Calgary on April 22, 1995, at the age of 77 years.

STAN "BUCK" ROTHWELL worked for AWW for at least forty-five years, maybe more. He, too, grew up in East Calgary. He was literally raised at the Stockyards. He loved the place; in fact, as of this writing, I think he still calls in at the Calgary Stockyards' office on Portland Street on a daily basis.

Buck is a good story teller. Unfortunately, many of them cannot be printed. Buck, Jimmy Marsh, Len Rowland and a few others could dream up more pranks than Carter has little liver pills. Some were funny, some backfired, and some were a little crude. But, on the whole, very few people got hurt by them.

Like so many others in those days, Buck developed a serious drinking problem. Again, like many others, he overcame this and for a quarter of a century he has been dry—like some Texas counties.

Buck likes antiques and has made quite a business out of it. He knows the game well. Antiques are getting hard to find these days—at least, the good ones. He follows up all leads such as ads, garage sales, and estate sales.

Buck is well liked by everyone. If you are interested to know more about the old days in East Calgary and the Stockyards, pay Buck a visit sometime.

KAREN ROWETT worked for Gordon and Dorothy Rauch, helping out with the Journal. She had a very friendly personality whenever I or anyone else talked to her. She was always on top of the world; one of those rare people—always happy. Karen was very active in the Salvation Army. She did not only talk Christian principles, she lived them. Last I heard, Karen was fixing to get married. Lucky man!

DALFAS ROY was an old-time cowboy, turned brand inspector. He was up in years when I arrived at the Stockyards in 1950; however, as a brand reader, he had no peers. Dalfas used to indulge a little too freely on a daily basis, but, no matter how much he staggered, he could read every brand regardless of how obscure it was. He must have had better than 20-20 vision. Dalfas never hurt anybody but himself. He passed away a number of years ago.

MARK ROY only worked at the Yards for short periods. He came from Wood Mountain, Saskatchewan. He was a close relative of Frank Marion, who was either his grandfather or great-uncle. Mark was the Canadian and World Champion Steer Wrestler in 1992. Good luck for the future, Mark.

BUD RYAN came to Calgary from Coronation, Alberta. He and his brother, Lloyd, opened up a Supermarket Grocery store in North Calgary. They sold a lot of meat. Bud would come to the Yards to buy a few cattle and have them custom killed. He would show up wearing a white shirt and bow tie. He looked slightly out of place. After a while the bow tie disappeared. Bud is a laid-back easygoing person. He and his wife liked to take winter cruises. They live east of the Calgary Airport on an acreage that my wife and I used to own. We lived there for two years, 1952 and 1953. At that time, it was a way out in the country. Today, there are all kinds of houses close by.

LLOYD RYAN is a brother of Bud Ryan. When Bud first came to the Yards, Lloyd was busy in the meat department at his store. In time, Lloyd came to the Yards as well. In fact, he became a real regular. He still comes to the market on a regular basis, but Bud quit coming years ago. These days, Lloyd's son, Dale, runs a meat market in the Forest Lawn area. Lloyd has a place just east of Calgary where he feeds a few cattle for the butcher shop and also for resale. He, too, is an easygoing, hardworking person. He likes to visit with the boys.

DUTCH RYDER was a cattle buyer for Burns. He was a good judge of cattle; however, his first love seemed to be gambling. He played cards, bet on horses and all other sporting events. If anyone opened his mouth about a certain team, Dutch would say: "Put your money where your mouth is."
Dutch was instrumental in getting me started buying cattle off trucks at the plant. One day, they were short one buyer for the sale ring. Dutch was buying in one ring. There was no buyer available for the other ring, so he told the boss: "Leonard can easy buy in the ring." I went over that morning, and, just like a rookie on a hockey team, I stuck and became a full-time ring buyer. (In those days, we bought about 85 percent of our cattle through the ring.) Dutch was a good man, but quite moody. Some days he would talk freely, other days he would clam up and not say a word.

Dutch also liked fishing. One day, Tom MacKenzie and Dutch went to the mountains to do a little fly-fishing. They were standing on a gravel bar with their rods. Suddenly, Tom heard Dutch fall on the gravel. He turned around and there was Dutch lying with a heart attack. He was dead when he hit the ground. That was a sad day at Burns.

DWAYNE SAMBELL was a young man who worked for Burns in the livestock department. He started out in the office, then transferred to the Yards. Dwayne was a good-looking, curly-headed blond; however, his knowledge about livestock was somewhat limited. After spending some time at the hog scale, he sort of tired and left for greener pastures. I saw a number of young men start out at Burns or the Calgary Stockyards in the hopes of becoming cattle-buyers. Only a small percentage realized their dreams. There was only room for a certain number of buyers. Some of those who made it did not step aside too often to make room for rookies.

JIM SANDY was a trucker. He hauled a lot of cattle in the late '50s and early '60s. Jim's first wife was Jack Paul's daughter. Jack was a noted purebred Hereford breeder. Last time I saw Jim, he was at a convention in Grand Prairie. He has lived in the Peace River country for years.

AUGIE SAUER was a big-time cattleman and wheeler-dealer. He came from Denmark as a young man. For a number of years, he operated in the Calgary area as a cattle dealer. He always put a lot of cattle on cover-crop in southern Alberta. He was a big buddy of my boss at Burns, Mickey Dirrane. Mickey bought thousands of cattle from Augie. Some of them were Augie's own and some were cattle he bought from other ranchers.

Augie moved to Medicine Hat in the early 1950s where he continued to operate in the cattle business. After Mickey died, Augie started to deal with Sonny Gray.

In his younger days Augie was a good boxer. He had quite a few victories under his belt. It all ended when he fought Spark Plug Boyd from Seattle. Spark Plug made short shrift of Augie. After that he decided to stick to the cattle business instead of the fight game.

Augie was an impressive looking man—well dressed with a ruddy complexion. He always looked scrubbed clean and wore a snap-down cattleman's hat.

Augie hated socialism or anything to do with government. He refused to take any government money. I was told that, after he passed away, his wife found a whole bunch of uncashed old-age pension cheques in a drawer.

Augie was very honest and his word was his bond; however, if he did not like someone, he did not hesitate to tell him. One day, a trucker showed up at his place to haul a load of cattle. It so happened that the trucker had long hair and a leather vest. Augie took one look at him, and, without giving the guy a chance to say anything, he told him to get in his truck and get lost. Nobody with long hair was going to haul his cattle.

Augie passed away very suddenly about fifteen years ago.

BOB SAYERS trucked cattle to and from the Yards for a number of years. Bob also took a shot at the auction business. The last I heard, he had an oilfield firefighting company based in Red Deer. He is Canada's Red Adair.

MARGE SAYERS is Bob Sayer's sister. She worked in Burns' livestock office. She was a very nice person and did a good job for Burns. She was always friendly as well as efficient. She got married and started raising a family. I'm sure she is an excellent wife and mother.

HARRY SCHEINDER was a Jewish cattle drover. He was an excitable character. You could always tell if he was making or losing money on any cattle he was selling through the ring. If he was losing money, the cigar in his mouth would shake like a leaf in a windstorm. It maybe didn't sound very complimentary, but the boys always referred to him as "Lump Jaw" Scheinder. I have no idea why. Harry passed away a number of years ago.

HANK SCHIMPF came from Empress, Alberta. He worked for the Alberta Stock Yards as a gateman for at least twenty years. Even after he came to the Stockyards, he kept his place at Empress. Hank is a genuinely nice person. He always did his very best. Everybody likes him. When the Stockyards first moved to Strathmore, he worked there whenever they needed someone for a day. Hank's daughter, Cathy, often came to the Yards with her dad when she was a young girl. These days she works in the library for the Stockmen's Memorial Foundation in Cochrane. Cathy is a very pleasant lady, who has a genuine interest in our western heritage. She is willing to look up material or help in any way she can. She reminded me of several people whom I had missed in the character sketches. Hank is retired and lives somewhere north of Calgary.

LORNE SCHMIDT came from Beiseker, Alberta. He worked for the Alberta Stock Yards and was a good worker. He had a serious speech impediment which made him seem less wise than he really was. Unfortunately, some of the boys would tease him, which was totally unjustified. I always liked Lorne. He wouldn't harm a flea.

BILL SCOTT was from Calgary, Alberta. He worked for the Alberta Stock Yards. Bill was a bit of an extrovert and the boys had a lot of fun with him because he had a real good sense of humour. One day, he did not feel too well, so he went to the Holy Cross Hospital to get checked out. When he got out of the car, he dropped dead in the parking lot.

LYLE SCOTT was a cattle buyer for Burns. He spent most of his life working for Burns in Regina, Saskatchewan, first as a cattle buyer, then as the livestock manager. When Burns closed their Regina plant, Lyle was transferred to Prince Albert, Saskatchewan. In fact, I was the one who initiated his transfer. Then, when Prince Albert closed, Lyle came to Calgary. He was a nice, easygoing man. He was not about to set the world on fire but he got the job done. Unfortunately, Lyle had a heart condition which finally claimed his life.

VERN SCOUN was born and raised at Acme, Alberta. He moved to Edmonton, where he was an auctioneer at the Edmonton Stockyards. Murray Jacobs was auctioning at the Calgary Yards. One day, with the approval of the commission men, they switched places. Murray went to Edmonton and Vern came to Calgary.

Vern was a very good auctioneer. He was clear, fast and all business. For many years, he would leave Calgary on Thursdays to sell cattle at the Bow Slope Auction in Brooks. The sales were handled by the Alberta Livestock Co-op from Calgary. Vern always drove a big Lincoln. It was not unusual for him to drive at 110 miles an hour—I know, I sometimes travelled with him.

Vern was a brother-in-law of Stan Milner who was the CEO of Chieftain Oil Company. Henry Bridgewater and I used to get firsthand information from Vern about Chieftain stock. On several occasions we made a fair amount of money on that stock. Buy when it is going to go up, sell when it is going to go down. These days, they might call that "insider trading." In those days, the late '60s, I had never heard of insider trading.

Vern's daughter, Dianne Hunter, became a Calgary Alderwoman. When Ralph Klein retired as Mayor of Calgary, Dianne ran for mayor. She did not get elected, but I wish she had. I believe she would have been a good mayor.

After Vern retired, he often went to auction for Jack Daines at Innisfail. Vern passed away several years ago.

CODY SEITZ was a tall, skinny kid who worked for the Alberta Stock Yards. He was a likeable sort. Like the Americans say, "an all-American boy"—well, he was "an all-Canadian boy." He was a good calf roper. As far as I know, Cody still lives in Calgary.

AL SEWALL was raised at Patricia, Alberta. He is a brother of Jim Sewall. When Al first came to Calgary, he worked for CP in the livestock department. He then became a brand inspector. He did this job for a number of years. These days, he works for the Lafarge Construction Materials. Every year during Stampede week, Al has some of the top U.S. rodeo cowboys stay at his place. I think that is a great idea. At one time, Al had a drinking problem. My hat's off to him, he has been dry now for a long, long time. I always like to visit with Al. He is a person you can discuss many topics with.

BUD SEWALL came from a ranching family at Brooks, Alberta. For many years, he worked at Union Packing for A. H. Mayland, as a cattle buyer. When the Union plant was sold to Swift, Bud came to Burns as a cattle buyer. He was a close friend of Mickey Dirrane's. Bud was the only sale ring buyer at Burns who received a commission and not a salary for buying cattle. He got 5 cents per hundredweight, which relates to 50 cents for a 1,000-pound animal or 60 cents for a 1,200-pound animal. If he bought 200 head on a given day, it amounted to approximately $100. This worked out to about three times as much as a salaried buyer received in those days (1950s). Bud was a slight built, but dapper man. He always came across as a gentleman. I was told he cut a fairly wide swath as a young man—whatever that means. He passed away many years ago.

JIMMY SEWALL is a brother of Al Sewall and nephew of Bud Sewall. Jimmy was raised at Patricia, Alberta. He worked for AWW most of his adult life. You could not help but like him. He was a happy-go-lucky person. It was no secret Jimmy had a bit of a drinking problem. It was evident nearly every day. He would sway from side to side as he walked down the alley or when he was moving or sorting cattle. For some reason it did not seem to affect his performance. He actually did a pretty good job. I kind of lost track of Jimmy. I am sure he is still around somewhere. One thing is certain, he never hurt anyone; at least, not on purpose.

Jimmy Sewall and lady friend enjoy a chuckle at AWW's Christmas party, 1978.

CLAUDE SHACKELL was a cattle buyer for Canada Packers. He worked for J. C. Wheatcroft for a little while, then went back to CP. He was a good cattle buyer, especially on cows and slaughter cattle. Claude originally came from Winnipeg. When he was younger he was a top-notch golfer. He was a member of the Wellington golf team. Even after he got older he was a good golfer. There was nobody at the Stockyards in his league when it came to golf scores. There actually were some good golfers at the Yards. Claude liked to take winter vacations in warm climates such as California, Arizona, or Hawaii, where he would play golf. Cancer claimed Claude's life before he had the opportunity to enjoy retired life.

DAVID SHANTZ was a cattle buyer for Burns. He started out as a feed salesman, then transferred to the livestock division in Edmonton. After that plant closed, Dave was transferred to Calgary as the head buyer. When the Calgary plant closed, he was transferred to Brandon as a buyer. After he retired from Burns Brandon, he moved back to Calgary where he lived until his passing several years ago, from a stroke.

Dave was a very good friend of mine. I gave the tribute at his funeral. It was not easy. Two years before Dave passed away, he came with me to our ranch in Colorado. We had a good time together. He thoroughly enjoyed it.

Dave was a great sports fan. Not just one sport, but all sports: football, baseball, hockey, curling, and rodeo (especially chuckwagon racing). Tommy Dorchester was his uncle.

Dave and his wife, Joyce, raised a wonderful family, one son and four daughters. They, too, were into sports such as curling and fastball. His daughter, Penny, won the gold medal for curling at the Calgary Olympics in 1988. Penny's husband, Pat Ryan, has won the Canadian Briar Championship at least twice. He has also won the World Curling Championship. When Dave was young, he played hockey with the Ponoka Stampeders.

Dave was a very loyal friend. I miss him.

ANDY SHAPKA worked for the Alberta Stock Yards. He used to yard cattle behind the Number 2 Scale. Andy was a natural trader so, besides working at the Yards, he traded a few cattle on the side, often at the MacLean Auction Mart. In 1952 when we lived on an acreage by the Calgary Airport, Andy sold a little Jersey cow to me for $65. Six weeks later, I sold her to Alfie Atkins for $135. The moral of the story is that Andy made a few dollars on her and I more than doubled my money. Alfie was sort of a milk-cow trader. He also made a few dollars, plus the people that bought her got themselves a good little family cow which dropped a calf a few weeks later. (Three people made a profit on this cow and no one got hurt. That's free enterprise!) Andy passed away many years ago.

HAROLD SHAPKA is Andy Shapka's son. He, too, worked at the Stockyards for a while. Harold is a nice, soft-spoken man. He and his wife bought a place at Spruce View many years ago, where they raise cattle. Their son, Guy, is a good professional bronc rider. He nearly always finishes in the top ten in Canada. He was a Canadian champion at least once. He also has gone to the National Finals Rodeo in the USA. I am a bit of a rodeo buff, not an expert, but I really like Guy's style of riding. In 1994 he was leading the pack in Canada. Harold is a credit to the cattle and rodeo industries.

HARRY SHEFTEL was a cattle dealer and feeder. He liked coming to the market to buy his own feeders. He also liked going to the country to buy cattle. I went with him a time or two. I enjoyed visiting with him. Like most Jewish entrepreneurs, Harry knew how to make a buck. He and his brothers operated a food market in Calgary. From there they branched into hotels. At one time they owned five hotels.

Harry liked a bargain. (Don't we all?) Sometimes, he got quite frustrated when he was buying or selling cattle on the market. One day, he asked Vern Scoun: "How come, Vern, when I buy cattle from you, you hang and hang before you knock them down to me, and when I'm selling cattle you just dump them immediately?" That really was not the case, but that's how it seems to most of us when our goods are at stake.

Harry passed away some time ago. I believe Leo Sheftel is the only brother left. You can see him in Calgary at the Carriage House Inn, which he operates. My wife and I often go there to enjoy the excellent food.

GEORGE SHIELDS SR. worked at Burns as a handyman. He did not have much formal education; however, this did not prevent him from becoming a good "Mr. Fix-it." He kept everything in good repair. Another job he often did was wash out the pens with a big high-pressure hose. I often saw six to fifteen inches of sloppy manure disappear into the sewer system from George's high-pressure hose. These days that would be a strict "no-no." It was questionable in those days as well; however, the City allowed it to happen up until the 1970s. George died a number of years ago.

GEORGE SHIELDS JR. is the son of George Shields Sr. George Jr. also worked for Burns: first, in the delivery end of things, which sometimes included feeding cattle; then, he transferred to the sales department. George was a good salesman. He has a good personality—sort of everyone's friend. For many years, he was in charge of the parking at Stampede Park. This was a second job which he mostly performed in the evenings. I have not seen George for a number of years.

JERRY SHOEMAKER worked for Burns, first in the office, then in the livestock office. From there he went to work in the plant for a little while. When he left Burns, he became a clerk for the brand department at the Yards. Jerry always had time to visit. At times, his vocabulary was like a longshoreman's or sailor's, but that was not unusual around the Yards. Last time I talked to Jerry, he was at loose ends. I hope he has landed something solid since then.

JACK SHORT grew up in Calgary—one of the originals. For a while, he was one of the poundkeepers in the City; at least, he rounded up stray animals for the pound. In those days, loose animals were not unusual. After some years of catching strays, Jack went to work as a brand inspector at the Calgary Stockyards. His boss was Dave Wheatcroft. When Dave retired, Jack became the head honcho.

Jack was all "WESTERN." He mastered the western slang perfectly. It was always "them" cows, not "those" cows, and "crick," not "creek." One day he complained about the government spending too much money. Like, why did the General Hospital have to build a new tipi? (Nurses' residence.)

Jack was not a very big man. He had a ruddy complexion; but, when he got mad, (which was quite often), he would get as red as a turkey gobbler.

One day, Henry Bridgewater and Jack got into an argument about clipping some cattle, that Henry felt was unnecessary. Jack stood nose-to-nose with him, tapping his cane on the cement. "Henry," he said, "I can shut this whole Yard down if I want to." To that, Henry responded, "Go ahead, shut it down." Jack never did, but he let you know he had the authority to do it, as the head brand inspector.

Jack retired. Then, after several years, he passed away.

BILL SHULTZ was raised in Bowness, Alberta. He became a cattle buyer for Canada Packers. Bill always wore, and still does, a long handlebar mustache. He reminds me of a character from out of the Old West. When Canada Packers closed, Bill went to work for Lakeside Packers. Bill and his wife have a nice place just north of Crossfield.

BOB SIEVERT was a cattle dealer from the Brooks area of Alberta. He "bird-dogged" cattle for AWW for a number of years. This brought him to the Yards quite often. The cowboy hat tilted back on his head made him look like a going-concern cattleman. These days, he represents Bow Slope Shipping at Brooks as a country agent.

DON SILVER was a government beef grader. When I first became aware of him, he was grading beef at Alberta Western in Medicine Hat. When that plant closed, they transferred him to Calgary. Don is a quiet type of person. He goes about his job without much fuss. For a number of years, he was the market reporter, which was part of the function of the federal grading service. Last I heard, Don was grading beef at the Cargill plant at High River.

SHANNON SMITH came from Cremona, Alberta. She was a beautiful, dark-haired, eighteen-year-old when she worked in our office—Friesen Cattle and Properties Ltd. My wife and I really liked her. She was green as far as office work was concerned, but she always gave it her best shot. We were rather sorry to see her leave, but she had other fish to fry. One was getting married. These days Shannon lives at Bottrel with her husband, George Leask, and their three children.

BOB SMOLKIN is Barry Smolkin's father. He was a cattle feeder in the Nose Creek area, just south of the old Union Packing Company. Bob spent a fair amount of time at the Stockyards. He liked to kibitz with the boys. Usually, he smoked a big cigar. He also wore fairly heavy glasses. P&D did most of his buying and selling.

One day, at the sale ring, Danny MacDonald and Bob got into an argument. Finally, Danny jumped out of the auctioneer's stand and came over the cable to punch Bob out. There were several of us close by, so we ended the fight before it ever got started—no damage done. I can't remember, but I am sure by the next day, there was no sign that the two had had any trouble. That's the way it was at the Stockyards: fisticuffs one day; buddies the next.

After Bob quit feeding cattle, I leased his little feedlot for a few years. I never really filled it up. It was just a place to keep a few future grass cattle and cows. I did finish a few cattle there. Once, on a cold March day, I discovered one of the waterers had frozen up. Since there were lots of pens, I just vacated that pen, instead of thawing it out. I completely forgot about it until about the middle of July. When I arrived at the feedlot, the water was spraying like Old Faithful, except it didn't pause in between. That's how long it took for the frost to come out of the ground.

Bob was married to Myer and Sammy Katchen's sister. Last I heard, Bob was in a nursing home.

BARRY SMOLKIN is Bob Smolkin's son. He was university-educated. This was rather unusual for anybody around the Yards in those days, except for veterinarians and the odd other person. Barry was a likeable sort of chap. He wore thick glasses, but this did not prevent him from doing a good job. Eventually, he operated the rendering plant in Bonnybrook, south of the Yards. I believe Jack Diamond from the Coast had some involvement in the venture. I have lost track of Barry.

ELICE SNOZYK worked in the office of W. W. Starke in the late '40s and very early '50s. Her maiden name slips my mind. She is a very nice person, who is friendly with everyone. We got reacquainted with her and her husband a few years ago. They go to the same church that we do.

HAROLD SOPER lived in the Airdrie area. He was a cattle dealer, trader, buyer, or whatever. Harold, like so many in those days (1950), had a bit of a drinking problem. He would disappear for several days at a time. Actually, he was a good judge of cattle. He had a rather comical look about him, but then we can't all be perfect. Harold died some years ago.

MERLE SORENSON worked for the Alberta Livestock Co-op. He always had a cane hung over his arm whether he was working cattle or not. Merle was either a bronc or bull rider—maybe both, I can't just remember. When he left the Yards, he went to work for somebody at High River. His whereabouts today are unknown to me.

DR. LARRY SPARROW was somewhat of a free-spirit type. He was a veterinarian and operated a very good private practice, the Alyth Veterinary Supplies Limited. He was prematurely gray, or should I say white? Every time you met up with him, even if it was daily, he had a new joke to tell you.

The Doc was related to the historical Burns family and was either a nephew or great-nephew of Pat Burns. He spent a lot of time at the Gillespie Feedlot. He really liked being involved in the cattle business as well as with the horse business.

Every year, Larry would mail Christmas cards to his friends and clients. These were always great cartoons that he drew himself. The cards usually carried a subtle message which made people chuckle. I liked visiting with him, which I often did.

Larry passed away a relatively young man.

GARY SPARSHU was raised west of Edmonton. He was with the government grading service in Calgary for a number of years. He was a good grader.

When Gary was in college, he competed in all five major rodeo events. After college, he cut that back to three events—calf roping, steer wrestling, and bull riding. I used to wonder why he chose bull riding over saddle bronc riding. He was a good bronc rider. He posted some good times in the timed events. One day at Ponoka, Gary broke his neck, steer wrestling. He was lucky he survived. He walked around for a long time with a neck collar.

When he left the government, he went to work at Burns as a cattle buyer. From there he went to XL Beef as a cattle buyer. He left XL to operate a place west of Olds where he raised Simmental cattle. He called his company Sunburst Cattle Company. He is also an auctioneer, but does not auction much anymore. I hope things have worked out for him. I always liked Gary.

MIKE SPENCE is Mickey Dirrane's nephew. I knew him around Burns as a fun-loving, little redhead. After he grew up, he worked for the Alberta Stock Yards for several years. He became a cattle buyer for Matt Richmond, who owned CDM at Lethbridge. He worked for a man at CDM by the name of Ayderdice. The two of them cut a wide swath, if you know what I mean. When management changed, Mike went to work for Alberta Western Medicine Hat. I have completely lost track of him.

BILL STAFFORD came from Maple Creek, Saskatchewan. He was a brand inspector at the Yards. Bill was a very likeable man. He was raised in the traditions of the West, where a man's word was his bond. Bill spent most of his childhood and youth with the Gilchrists at Maple Creek. If my memory serves me correctly, he was married to a Gilchrist girl. Whatever her maiden name was, she, too, was a very nice lady. They lived at Cayley. One day they invited us over for a visit and we had a good time. Bill was transferred to Medicine Hat where he passed away at a fairly young age.

W. W. STARKE, or "Bill" as we all called him, came from a place called Spondin, Alberta. I am not sure if it is on the map anymore. It is located north of Hanna, Alberta.

Bill bought out the Cadzo Commission firm in 1944. He operated the W. W. Starke firm till 1951. At that time, he sold it to Jimmy Paul and Danny MacDonald.

For a few years, in the late '40s, Bill took in a partner by the name of Pat Trainor, but they soon parted company.

Bill was a big, rawboned man. He had a handshake that could crush your hand. I am sure that with women, or weaker men, he did not do that; however, with someone like me, he usually did. I always made sure I got a good deep grip on his hand. That way, I could almost hold my own with him. It was all done in fun and no one ever got seriously hurt. I know there were a few people, including me, who had a somewhat painful hand for a day or two.

After Bill left Calgary, he settled in the Okotoks area where he became the supervisor for the Big Rock Cattle Feeders' Association. He was a very patient, honest man, who always did his best for his customers. If he did not like the price of the feeder cattle, he would wait to buy them at a later date. Sometimes, they got cheaper, but quite often, they would go up. Whatever the case, Bill never panicked. There was always tomorrow.

Bill and his wife raised a fine family: Wally, Raymond and Lola. I was quite flattered, when about two years ago, one of Bill's grandsons phoned me asking for advice about moving to the USA. He said that his granddad had told him that if he wanted some good advice about business, to phone Leonard Friesen. I hope my advice to the young man that day turned out correctly. (Maybe, it didn't. I have not heard from him since.)

Bill Starke passed away a number of years ago.

LOLA STARKE is Bill Starke's daughter. She worked in her dad's commission firm office in Calgary. She was a very pleasant person, always easy to talk to. For some reason, I have no idea where she is these days.

RAY STARKE is Bill Starke's son. He worked for his dad for several years. Ray is a fine looking specimen. He did a good job. You could tell he was raised right. He was with the Calgary Police Department for many years. I talked with him on the phone a little while ago. He told me he is enjoying retired life.

KEN STAV was a brand inspector. Ken is a very obliging person. He did a good job. After being in Calgary for a number of years, he went to High River where he was an inspector at the Highwood Auction. Ken is now enjoying retired life.

TED STEVENSON was a Calgary native. He worked for many years as a freight agent for the CPR. When he left the CPR, he went to work in the Alberta Livestock Co-op office. Stevie, as he was called, was a laid-back individual. He was easy to visit with. He was a good asset to the Co-op staff.

DON STEWART was a teamster at Burns. He often fed the cattle, as well as making other deliveries. When all deliveries became mechanized, he became a truck driver. He was a big, good-natured man who always did his job. Don was Bob Keddie's stepfather.

LARRY STIFF was an American who married Rosemary Adams. He worked for AWW for several years. After he left the Stockyards, he and his wife moved to the USA. Last I heard, they lived in Colorado Springs. Larry has become a born-again Christian since I knew him. He seemed like quite an unlikely candidate for this change. One never knows.

SCOTTY AND MURIEL STRACHEN: Scotty, as his name indicates, came from Scotland. He worked for P&M for many years. While there, a romance blossomed between him and Muriel, who worked at the Bank of Montreal in the Stockyards Building. Shortly after they got married they bought a place in the Red Deer Lake district southwest of Calgary. Scotty is a good cattleman. They have operated a small feedlot for many years, and still do. They raised a fine family. Scotland's loss was Canada's gain.

JIMMY SUITOR was sort of the Stockyards' mascot. He was so skinny he had to stand twice to make a shadow. If a cloud passed overhead, he would shiver. It seemed like he did not have enough blood to keep himself warm. He worked with Producers' Livestock for Alex Beveridge and Irish Johnston. When that firm went out of business, he worked for Parslow & Denoon. Jimmy was always on the job, even if the night before he had abused himself with "John Barleycorn." Jimmy was a good person. He would hurt no one, but the boys sometimes gave him a rough time—all in jest, of course. He passed away many years ago.

MIKE SWAGGAR worked for Paul & MacDonald. From there he went to Canada Packers. Mike liked the good life: fast cars, good clothes and whatever goes with that. It is years since I have heard anything about Mike.

MIKE SWAIN is Tim Carroll's stepson. Mike worked for the Alberta Stock Yards often in the gatehouse. He is a good worker and always did a good job. He was what I call a blond-headed kid with lots of potential. I hope he has made use of it.

RUSSELL SWAIN came from Innisfail, Alberta. He was a native Canadian. He worked for the Alberta Stock Yards. Russell's interest in life was mainly chuckwagon racing, which he and his brother, Johnny, did with great success. They won the Calgary Stampede one year. One of Russell's sons was so excited about the win, he ran right out in front of the wagon and was killed. What a terrible tragedy. Russell also liked to play bingo. He is retired and lives in Calgary.

BILLY SNYDER is a cattle buyer from Carstairs, Alberta. It was only in the last few years that Billy attended the sale in Calgary. He usually buys good quality cattle for small to medium sized cattle feeders. When he was younger, he was an excellent hockey player. He and his wife, Judy, are active in the Crossfield Baptist Church.

DON SNYDER is Billy Snyder's brother. Don lives at Ponoka, Alberta. He, too, is an order buyer and cattle feeder. He came to the Calgary sale quite often, especially when he lived at Crossfield, before he moved to Ponoka. Don is quite aggressive in his cattle buying operation. He and his brother Billy, along with Tony Sarestky, operate what they call Cantriex. They are involved in the export of cattle from Canada (mainly slaughter cattle) to the USA. Don and his wife, Hazel, are very much involved with their local church.

BILLY TAYLOR worked at Burns as a nightman in the livestock department. He was married to Leroy Butts' sister. Billy was a bit of a character. Trouble was not unknown to him. When he was young, he was a jockey at the racetrack—never a leading jockey, but pretty good. I often wonder whatever happened to him in the last twenty years.

MERLE TAYLOR worked for the Alberta Stock Yards as a foreman. Before he became foreman, he was weighmaster at the hog and sheep weighscale. He always knew what was going on. If there was a good deal around, Merle would smell it. At one time, he traded a lot of used cars. This helps to keep your senses sharp. Merle was also handy at working with wood. He often drove for Charlie Kennedy, whose eyesight was not good. After Charlie retired, Merle went over there to drive or help Charlie with things. Merle's son, Bob, and our oldest son, Lee, attended Montessori School together in Grade One.

TRETCH TAYLOR came from the Nanton, Alberta. He started out as a brand inspector at the Yards. He was a character in many ways and work was not one of his vices. I know, because Mickey Dirrane hired him after he left the brand department. Tretch could talk up a storm; however, he lacked the action to back it up. He walked very straight with short, jerky, little steps. When you saw him, he always had a cigarette in his mouth. He died very suddenly.

LEE TEASDALE was an American. In the early 1950s, he spent a lot of time at the Stockyards. He had a big ranch in Montana. He also dealt in a lot of cattle. Lee was a big, slow-moving, cigar-smoking man who looked like he knew what he was doing. I will always remember him buying a big black-whitefaced cow that weighed 2,160 pounds. In the early '50s, that was a heavy cow. In those days, very few cows exceeded 1,500 pounds. He took this cow to Montana. He was going to have a little fun with her by taking her to country fairs where people could make guesses on her weight. I am not sure how he made out. He probably made money on her; he did with everything else.

BILLY THOMPSON was an auctioneer at the Yards for a number of years. He was a fun-loving individual.

One day, when the sale ring was full of people, he made sure he had everyone's attention and then doffed his hat to the crowd. As he lifted his hat from his head, a sparrow flew away. He had captured it and placed it under his hat. I am sure he needed a shampoo when he got home that night.

Once in a while, things got a little routine or boring at the sale.

So, one day, Billy and I hatched up a little scheme to liven things up. We pretended to get into a real argument over the sale of a heifer. He knocked the heifer down to someone else and I claimed it was my bid. We started shouting at one another. The final culmination came when we both jumped into the sale ring to fight it out. The rest of the people were aghast at what was happening. We rushed at each other in a fierce manner. It looked quite real, somewhat like pro-wrestling. After a few scrimmages, which inflicted no damage, we threw our arms around each other and laughed. The crowd felt kind of sheepish. They thought we had been serious.

Billy and Jim Raffan bought an auction market at Armstrong, B.C. After some years, Billy Thompson sold his interest to the Raffans. Billy passed away some years ago. I know he had diabetes, but I am not sure if that is what claimed his life.

GEORGE THOMPSON was a "no-nonsense" guy. He was the head buyer for Swift Canadian. George was a company man—100 percent. In those days, all directives for Swift came from the head office in Chicago, and, to George, everything the head office said was gospel. In many ways, George was a gentleman. At times, he was as cranky as a bear with a sore paw. I think it was George MacLean who told me one day that George Thompson was the most even-tempered man he had ever known—always mad! George was an old-time cattle buyer. When the auction method started, he did not really like it, so, quite often, he would vent his anger on the auctioneers, hence George MacLean's comment. George Thompson passed away a long time ago.

GEORGE THOMPSON is no relation to the other George Thompson. George came to Alberta from western Saskatchewan where he worked for Meyers Feedlot at Hughton. Later, he came to Burns to run the Rivercrest Feedlot at Okotoks. I was the head buyer at Burns at the time, so I had the pleasure of working with him. He was an excellent man in the feedlot. Before George came, the sickpen was always full of cattle. He soon changed that. He would rope and treat a lot of cattle right in the pen. This proved very effective. Our death loss decreased dramatically after he arrived. When Burns closed the feedlot, George worked at the Yards as a brand inspector. He had a good sense of humour, which made it a pleasure to be around him. George also worked for Don Cross at Okotoks. If I remember correctly, that was before he came to Burns.

JIM THOMPSON was a cattle buyer for Swift Canadian. He came from Lethbridge, Alberta. When they transferred him to Calgary, he became the head buyer at Union Pack, which was owned by Swift. Jim was a real fine fellow. He became a personal friend of mine. He was capable and honest, which is a good combination.

Jim was a Second World War veteran. He saw a lot of action in the War, but seldom mentioned it. However, he was very easily startled; if there was a sudden noise or bang, he would jump.

One day at the sale ring, the boys got to horsing around. Suddenly, Vern McWaters came up behind Jimmy and dumped a big bucket of water over him. Jim literally went into orbit. He took after Vern in a very serious manner. I still shudder to think what would have happened to Vern if Jimmy had caught up to him. Needless to say, from then on, everyone was careful not to startle Jim.

After the Union Pack closed, Jim went to work as head buyer for CDM Lethbridge, and technically, I became his boss. He did such a good job for us, I never interfered with the way he operated.

After I left Burns, I shipped a lot of cows to CDM (Canadian Dressed Meats). Jim was a good man to do business with.

Jim developed cancer and passed away in his early fifties. It was hard for me when I visited him while he was sick, but he remained his own pleasant self right to the end.

JIM OR JIMMY THOMPSON is no relation to the Lethbridge Jim Thompson. This Jim worked for Canada Packers in Calgary. He was transferred from Winnipeg to Medicine Hat. After working for a number of years at the Hat, he transferred to Calgary.

This Jim, like the other Jim, is a very fine man. He is always cheerful and easy to visit. Everybody likes him.

In 1975 I had already left Burns. I was in Montana buying fat cattle for several plants in Canada. Jim was there buying cattle for Canada Packers. One evening, I met him in the hotel restaurant in Billings, Montana. We discussed our day's buying activities. He told me that he had bought some interesting cattle that day. He went on to say that the cattle were Corriente-crosses that had originated out of Old Mexico. I looked at him in surprise and told him, so had I.

Upon further discussion, we determined that we were talking about the same 400 steers. I had arrived at the feedlot about 2 p.m., and, after looking at the cattle, I bought them from the manager. About two hours later, Jim dropped in to the same feedlot. Of course, I was gone by then. Lo and behold, the feedlot owner was there himself and sold the cattle to Jim for 50 cents a hundredweight more than I had bought them for. Legally, I owned the cattle, but, like most cattle deals, it was strictly word-of-mouth. Since Jim was a good friend of mine and he did not know I had already bought the cattle, I let him have them instead of contesting the deal. The old saying applied—"you win some; you lose some."

When CP closed the Calgary plant, Jim retired. I see him occasionally. He is still the same old Jimmy.

LILLIAN THOMPSON was an older lady who worked in the Alberta Stock Yards office as an accountant. She really knew her stuff—everything had to be right and in order. She dressed very conservatively with no low necklines or bare arms. Usually, her clothes were black or dark blue. She retired about forty years ago.

WOODWARD THOMPSON was working in the Alberta Stock Yards office when I arrived at the Yards. It seemed to me, he must have been there since its inception in 1903. I am sure he hadn't, but he sure looked ancient. He had the most beautiful Old English script handwriting I have ever seen.

LIONEL TIMMINS worked at the gatehouse for the Alberta Stock Yards. Everybody called him Tim. He was ruddy-faced and, pardon me for saying so, a cranky character. If you were in his good books, he was okay, but, unfortunately, not many people were. I used to marvel when farmers would keep coming back with their livestock after taking a good deal of verbal abuse from him. I am sure, like most people, there was a good side to him. He passed away many years ago.

DOUG TINCKNELL was the office manager at Burns. He ran the office like a strict schoolmaster or major-general. He was very competent and tolerated no nonsense; however, when he went on vacation, he let his hair down. I was told by several people that his greatest pleasure was to go to Las Vegas to gamble. This was in the days before it was as common as it is today. Doug is no longer with us.

LLOYD TODERIC came from B.C. He worked for Wheatcroft in the feedlot south of Calgary. After a while, he came to the Stockyards as a partner with Ed Carr. They bought out Eamor's Trucking.

Lloyd was a good man, but somewhat excitable. This quite often landed him in a bit of trouble. One day, he had some fisticuffs with George Syhahada. George weighed close to 300 pounds, but this did not stop Lloyd from taking a poke at him. The fight got broken up before much damage could be done.

Another day, Lloyd and I decided to drive out into the country to look for some cover crop on which to graze cattle. We pulled into a farmyard southeast of Calgary and I stopped the car in the front yard, about 300 feet from the farmhouse. We both got out of the car and walked over toward it. We were about 50 feet from the house, when two big German shepherd dogs came charging at us. Their mouths looked big enough to swallow a calf.

Needless to say, we took off for my car, which was a two-door Buick. I was young in those days and fleet of foot. When I got to the car, I opened the door and dove in, slamming the door shut behind me. Poor Lloyd—he was about ten paces behind me. The dogs were within a few feet of him. Since I had closed the door, he had nowhere to go but onto the roof of the car. The dogs continued to snarl and bark, but they just couldn't jump onto the roof. If my memory serves me correctly, I drove slowly out of the yard with Lloyd perched on the roof.

After a while, the dogs ran back to the house to await their next victims. (The people were not home.) I felt very embarrassed about shutting Lloyd out. On the other hand, if I hadn't closed the door, I am sure those dogs would have ripped Lloyd's leg to pieces before he could have gotten into the car with me. All's well that ends well, but, for the next few years, Lloyd never let me forget that day. I literally sacrificed him to the dogs.

Lloyd moved back to B.C. a number of years ago.

329

DRS. MOE AND BERNIE TONKIN were brothers. Both were veterinarians. Bernie practised at Vulcan, Alberta, for a while. They got quite involved in the wholesale livestock medicine-end of things. These men were gentlemen and easy to visit. Bernie was the more aggressive of the two. The vets were good friends of Ted Davis, who, while not a vet, also handled a lot of wholesale medicine. Moe is still practising veterinary medicine. Bernie recently passed away.

BILL TORME was an American cattle buyer from Spokane, Washington. Bill was at the Calgary market on a seasonal basis for many years. Some people called him a "windrower." In other words, if the cattle suited his orders, he would throw caution to the wind and buy them all. Bill was great friends with Danny MacDonald, Stan Denoon and Pete Adams, plus a lot of other people. Bill liked to party, where he was the life of the party. This included singing ditties; but he was not related to Mel Torme, the famous singer.

DR. FRANK TREVITT was a veterinarian in charge of the Health of Animals Division at the Stockyards. He was an Australian. I had many good visits with him. He was a no-nonsense type of person, but fair. He was a very dedicated Christian who was active in his church.

ERIC TRIBBLE came from Quebec. He is bilingual. He worked for the Alberta Stock Yards as an accountant. When Charlie Kennedy retired, Eric took over as the general manager. In 1981, after the reorganization, Eric became a partner in the new corporation called the Calgary Public Livestock Market Ltd.

Eric and his wife, Dorry, raised three fine sons: Gary, Bruce and Joel. They all three worked at the Stockyards during the summers. I knew Gary the best. He was a very nice young man, whose first love, after family, was flying. My son Lee and I, along with Eric and Gary, flew to Wyoming to look at a ranch we hoped to purchase, but never did. On our way back, we ran low on fuel, so Gary landed the plane at Sheridan for refuelling. It was Sunday evening and, believe it or not, there was no fuel available till next morning, so we had to bed down for the night. This was in 1979. It was on this trip that Eric and I decided it was time to reorganize the Calgary Stockyards. In 1981, we did just that.

Gary got his commercial pilot's license and was looking forward to flying for an airline. On his way home by car, he suddenly passed away from a heart attack. He was forty-two years old. Every once in a while I visit with Eric on the phone. He has given me some good information that I needed for this book.

Eric and Dorry are enjoying retired life these days.

(L-R) Charlie Kennedy, Anne Jones, Eric Tribble, 1979.

SHELLY TRODDEN works in the office for the present Calgary Stockyards Ltd, in their Calgary office. She is an extremely nice person, plus very competent. She handles a lot of the computer cattle selling. Shelly's parents are very good friends of Will Irvine's. I remember, years ago, Shelly's parents coming to the Stockyards with their three little girls. Shelly is a fine Christian lady who is everyone's friend. She is a ray of sunshine even on a cloudy day.

STEVE TUROK worked at the Stockyards as a brand inspector. He came from the Lethbridge area. He was in Calgary for a number of years, then was transferred to Brooks. Steve liked golfing. He was involved in setting up several cattlemen's golf tournaments. I have lost track of Steve.

TED UMPHREY was an auctioneer at the Calgary Stockyards in the 1950s. When he left, he went to Lloydminster where he operated the market for Weiller and Williams. Ted is an aggressive individual, who built up a really good business. He moved thousands upon thousands of cattle, even after he left Weiller and Williams. Ted loves a challenge, which is reflected in his ability to find new customers and hold on to them for repeat business. One of his best clients is Cecil Barber who buys cattle from or through him. Despite Ted's failing health, he still moves lots of cattle. Ted likes sulky horse racing and has been very successful with his horses.

BERT UTTLEY was a cattle buyer from the Big Valley country of Alberta. During my first few years at Burns, Bert was there every week with a load or two of cattle. He was one of Mickey Dirrane's country buyers. Bert was a really good-natured person. I think it would have taken an earthquake to get him excited. He was a bit of a philosopher. He said to me one day that people who run a business into the ground or cannot make a go of it on their own often end up in politics and nearly always get elected. Then they proceed to run the government the same way. Bert has been gone for many years now, but his theory about politicians is right on target.

JIM VANDENBERG was an American from Idaho who decided to set up shop at the Calgary Stockyards. He bought a place at Nanton (Gary Klessens owns it today) and he drove to Calgary to work each day. Jim was quite aggressive in his buying habits—sometimes this works and sometimes it doesn't. In Jim's case, he ran up against a gentleman by the name of Red Wheatcroft. Red was no pushover. He could hold his own anywhere. The result was that Jim ended up with a lot of high-priced cattle. After a little over a year in Calgary, he packed his bags and headed back to the USA.

CLIFF VANDERGRIFT was a "gutsy" rodeo cowboy from Turner Valley, Alberta. After he retired from rodeo, he spent a lot of time at the Stockyards, usually picking up "calvy" cows and sometimes grass cattle.

I always found Cliff very interesting to talk to. He told me endless rodeo stories. Some were a little on the rough side, but mostly they were stories that could be told at the family dinner table. Cliff always called me "the King." During the '70s and early '80s, I was pretty aggressive on the market, so that's what he called me.

Cliff was the Canadian Calf Roping Champion on five occasions. He won 15 Canadian championships in calf roping, wild horse race, and wild cow milking. When he was young, he also rode bulls. With age, Cliff got very heavy, but this did not stop him from team roping. He often mounted his horse from a dock or ramp. In spite of this, he still knew how to rope.

Cliff passed away a few years ago.

(L-R) Lorne Wells and Cliff Vandergrift team roping at Okotoks, 1971.

GILBERT VERRIN was a trucker at the Stockyards for close to forty years: first, he had a body-job; then, he hooked up with Eamor's. Later on, he went back to his own body-job. Gilbert was one of the calmest individuals I have ever met. No matter what the situation, he never got rattled. He always had a grin on his face and it was genuine. He was completely dependable. I know, because he hauled thousands of cattle for us. He was a first-rate trucker.

HERB VICKERS came from Saskatchewan. He was a friend of Henry Bridgewater's. Herb liked coming to the Yards to watch the action and buy cattle that he would feed out close to the Calgary Airport. His other job was delivering milk. When Herb retired, he and his wife spent their winters in Arizona. Herb passed away several years ago.

HARRY VOLD is a colourful auctioneer and a rodeo stock contractor. He sold at the Stockyards for several years. Harry is a very honest person. He does not pull bids out of the air. I enjoyed buying cattle from him.

When Harry left Calgary, he went back to Ponoka, Alberta, where he, along with his brother, Ralph, and Shorty Jones, started the Ponoka Auction Market.

Harry loves rodeo, so he gathered up some bucking stock and started a contracting company. It proved to be a good move. After some years, he turned it over to his son, Wayne, who still operates the company.

Harry moved to Colorado almost thirty years ago. Here he built up a tremendous string of bucking horses and bulls. At one point, he was the largest rodeo stock contractor in the USA. He has sold off some of his interests in the last few years; however, he still contracts a lot of rodeos including the big one at Cheyenne, Wyoming.

Harry's ranch is about 120 miles from our ranch at Kit Carson, Colorado. I meet him quite often at the auction market in La Junta. We always have a good visit—often talking about the good old days at the Calgary Stockyards.

RAY WALDOCK worked in the office for the Alberta Livestock Co-op. He was a big man with a good tenor voice. Nearly every noon hour you could hear him practising his singing. He often sang solos in church. I talked to White Garries about him a while ago. White thought that Ray and his wife had gone to a mission field overseas.

HENRY WALTERS used to own the Imperial Ranch in the Big Valley area. After he sold it, he went into cattle dealing. He moved a lot of cattle from market to market. This worked for a while, then the roof fell in. I am not sure where Henry is today.

LES WARD worked with the Health of Animals Division for many years. He was not a vet, but he was kind of a straw boss. Les would throw his weight around if you let him. Once you knew him well, he could be quite accommodating. He took his work seriously. That is more than could be said for some government people. For some reason, Les had white lips, and it wasn't make-up. He must have lacked blood vessels.

RONNIE WARD was raised at Carseland, Alberta. He went to work for Paul & MacDonald at a young age. From there he went to AWW where he stayed for many years. In 1981, when we reorganized at the Yards, he became a country rep for the Calgary Public Livestock Market. When the Calgary Stockyards closed, he went to Pincher Creek as manager of that market. Eventually, he came back to Calgary and teamed up with Tom Copithorne to operate an order-buying firm. Ronnie and Tom run a successful business. Ron also buys quite a few cattle direct. He has a scale at his place near Cremona. Ron has a real sense of humour and has been responsible for many a good laugh at the Stockyards.

WAYNE WARD is Ronnie Ward's brother. He worked for P&M for a while. I never really got to know him very well. I always thought of him as a good worker who minded his own business. Last I heard, Wayne lived at Rocky Mountain House, Alberta.

ART WARNER was an easygoing type, who liked to visit. He was also a friend of Henry Bridgewater's. Art came to Calgary from the Yorkton, Saskatchewan, area. He owned and operated a feedlot near the Calgary Airport. He spent quite a bit of time at the Yards. He never caused a ripple.

DON WATHEN was raised south of Calgary. He owned a place at Red Deer Lake, Alberta. He was a born trader—horses or cattle—it did not matter as long as he could make a dollar. Don is quite a story teller. For some reason, he knew more about what people were up to than anyone I have ever met. He was also a big rodeo fan. I think, in his youth, he did some competing. Many of his buddies are rodeo people.

ALEX WATSON was a horse dealer or buyer, whichever term you prefer. I think he came from Ontario. Alex was a good judge of horseflesh. He was a very calm, thoughtful individual. Nobody could fool him when it came to horses. Slim Brown worked with Alex for years.

FRED WATSON was the plant manager at Burns when I started there on January 25, 1950. When Leonard Gates suddenly passed away in the mid-'30s, Fred took over as livestock manager. Fred knew nothing about cattle; however, he had some good cattle buyers working for him. One of those buyers was Mickey Dirrane, so, after one year, Fred appointed Mickey as livestock manager and he went back to being plant manager. Fred passed away many years ago.

LYNN WATSON worked in the office at for the J. C. Wheatcroft Co. Ltd. She was very competent, but not very friendly. In 1981 when she came to work for the Calgary Public Livestock Market Ltd., she did a complete turn around. She was still very competent and complemented that ability with an extremely friendly and helpful attitude. She left the company and everyone missed her.

SHORTY WATSON worked for Burns as a teamster. You heard right, a teamster. When I started to work at Burns in 1950, they still did a lot of work with horses; although the deliveries uptown were made with trucks. Eventually, Shorty went to work for Parslow & Denoon. He was there quite a while when he tangled with a bull. It was one of the few serious accidents that happened at the Yards in the forty years I was there. Shorty recovered, but he was never quite the same again. "Shorty," as his nickname indicates, was very small in stature; however, he had a booming voice and had an opinion on just about everything.

MELVIN WATSON was Shorty Watson's son. Melvin, too, worked at P&D. He was a nice kid. He was a good friend of my brother-in-law, Orville Peters. I personally did not know him very well. I do know he never got into much trouble, which was kind of unusual around the Yards.

336

MERVIN WAY was strictly known by the handle "Tex." Maybe this was because he usually wore a black cowboy hat. He idolized the western way of life. He worked at AWW for a number of years. Usually, he and Bill Furgeson were only about 15 or 20 feet apart. I think Bill nearly always walked in front of Mervin. Mervin works at Stampede Park on a part-time basis these days.

EDDIE WEGENER was a trucker from Strathmore, Alberta. He hauled cattle to Calgary for many years. He also hauled a lot of cattle from the XL Feedlot at Bassano. Often, he stopped at the Stockyards Cafe in between loads to shoot the breeze. Eddie is taking it easy these days.

LORNE WELLS came from the Medicine Hat area. He knows how to swing a rope. He was the Canadian Calf Roping Champion no fewer than eight times and runner-up several times. I think he won his first championship in 1958. There is no doubt in my mind he could have been the World's Champion several times if he had competed more in the USA.

Lorne Wells calf roping (time: 11.4) at Lacombe, 1971.

Lorne worked for P&D for many years. He did a good job for them, even though he was a man of few words. After the Stockyards was reorganized, he went to work for the Calgary Stockyards Ltd., at Strathmore. He is still with them today. In my, and many other people's, opinion, Lorne is one of the best cattle sorters in the country. He is also handy with a welder.

These days Lorne is no longer a man of few words. In fact, he is very affable. I enjoy talking with him. He is a true Westerner. We need more people like him.

Lorne is married to Maule McEwen's daughter, Carol. They have one son, Guy.

LEO WENDLING worked in the brand office as a clerk. He was a black-haired, skinny man. Leo always rolled his own smokes. He was easy to get along with and was always willing to look something up when you asked for information about brands. I think Leo came from Medicine Hat. I do not know where he is these days.

FLOYD WEST was a brand inspector at the Yards for a number of years. He is a real gentlemen, who did his job well. At the present time, Floyd and his wife are more or less retired; however, every summer, you can still find Floyd at Heritage Park driving a team of horses hitched to a democrat. He did this work full-time before he retired. The Park could not find a better person for this job. Floyd is a friend to everyone.

DAVE WHEATCROFT was the head brand inspector at the Yards when I came there. All his life, he was a cowboy. He was one of the last inspectors to use a horse on the job. As a rookie at Burns, I was very impressed by Dave's ability with a horse and a rope. His understudy, Jack Short, took over when Dave retired. Dave passed away many years ago.

J. C. "RED" WHEATCROFT is Dave Wheatcroft's son. Red is a colourful character. He went to work at Burns as a young man. He started buying cattle very early in his life. Mickey Dirrane used to tell me that Red was one of his top buyers, but was sometimes a little hard to control; by that, he meant that Red had lots of guts. He would go to the Stavely-Claresholm country to buy a few hundred cover-crop cattle, and, a day or two later, Mickey would receive a call from Red informing him that he had bought five or six hundred head. The cattle usually turned out okay.

When Red left Burns in the late '40s, he went to work for W. J. Johnstone. Johnstone operated out of Winnipeg. In order to cover the West a little better, he opened an office at the Calgary Stockyards. After a few years, Red opened his own order-buying firm at the Stockyards. He blossomed immediately, buying and shipping all over North America. His biggest customers were in Quebec and Ontario.

Red was a major player on the Calgary market for at least thirty years. When the Co-op moved up to the Agri-Mart, Red started a commission firm with Roy Gilkes as his right-hand man. They did a lot of business.

There was a period in the 1960s when Red, along with a few partners, built and operated Alberta Western Beef at Medicine Hat. They gave it their best shot, but found the going very tough. In the very early '70s, they sold it to Burns. After a few years, Burns gave up on it and the plant was closed forever.

Another one of Red's ventures was building double-deck cars for shipping cattle to eastern Canada. He built a whole fleet of them. This enabled him to ship twice the amount of cattle in each car. That really cut down on the freight bills. We also built them, but only four because we did not ship that many cattle east. Ours were CNR cars. His were CPR cars.

When we reorganized the market in 1981, Red became one of the seven partners in the Calgary Public Livestock Market Ltd. After about three or four years there were three of us left: Red Wheatcroft, Cecil Barber and me. Then Red got out. That left just Cecil and me. In 1986 I got out as well, which left only Cecil. That is when Will Irvine came back on the scene.

Red tangled with the odd person over the years, including me. One cannot help but admire some of the risks he took in the cattle business. I have seen nearly every pen across the road filled with his cattle. Then a snow storm would hit but, somehow, everything survived and finally got shipped to its final destination.

I have rambled on quite a while about Red. If the truth were known, a whole book could be written about him. Besides all the above, he also fed a lot of cattle.

In later years, Red spent a lot of time in Mexico. He also built and flew his own aeroplane—in fact, he built several aeroplanes. One day, he showed me a plane that he was building in his garage. It was about three-quarters finished.

These days, very few people from the Stockyards ever see him. I wish him well in his retirement.

HENRY WHITE worked in the office for AWW. He was a little man, always well-mannered, usually smoking a pipe. For some reason, the boys always picked on him, supposedly in good humour. Sometimes, it would get out of hand, then Henry's good manners left him and he got very angry. I used to feel kind of sorry for him.

JACK WHITE was a government grader and a good one. By that, I mean very fair. Jack was a small man with a trimmed moustache. He lived only about a block away from where we lived. I used to see him quite often. In spite of that, I have forgotten what his hobbies were. By the look of his place, I think he liked gardening. Jack died very suddenly about twenty-five years ago.

KEN WHITLEY was born and raised at Alsask, Saskatchewan. He went to work for Canada Packers as a young man. He was with them for at least twenty years. At that point, he agreed to disagree with his boss, Ian Davidson, and this caused Ken to resign. He was immediately hired by Burns in Calgary as a cattle buyer.

For many years, Ken bought cattle for Burns in the Co-op and P&D sale ring. At that same time, I was buying cattle for Burns in the other ring, which featured AWW and P&M. Ken was a good buyer; however, he did not like to do any alley work after the sale in case he got his polished shoes dirty. I know this sounds rather critical, but it's the truth. He ended his cattle buying career with Dvorkin Packers.

Ken had a lifelong battle with the bottle, but he was a very nice person. I liked him. On several occasions I suggested to Ken it would be to his benefit to stop drinking. He would always look at me and say, "I have no drinking problem." Many others also counselled him.

Ken loved trains and railroads. Many times he went for a ride with the engineer in the switching yards behind Burns.

340

Ken passed away at the age of 53. I was at the funeral. I could not help but think of how many good men and women have been ruined by liquor. Ken's wife passed away a short while before he did.

GARY WIENS was a government grader, who did a good job. He bought an acreage west of Airdrie, a mile east of where we live today. He built a good-sized house on this acreage. Later, he sold out to the Burwashes. He was transferred to Edmonton where he is still with the government. Gary was very active in his church.

BILL WILES worked for Burns. He came from Edmonton. When he first arrived in Calgary, he was the beef manager. Soon, he became the plant manager and finally they named him the general beef manager. I worked with him in all three of his capacities. I enjoyed working with Bill. As the beef manager, he was knowledgeable and fair. As the plant manager, he was my boss. We got along great. I became the general livestock manager the same time that he became general beef manager. That made us peers. Our offices in the head office were next to each other, so we had a lot of good visits in between carrying out our duties. When Bill left Burns, he moved back to Edmonton.

JIM WILFLEY is the founder of Lakeside Feeders and Packers at Brooks, Alberta. For many years we never saw him at the Stockyards. After he got his business well organized at Brooks, with capable people in charge, he started to attend quite a few sales himself. He is a sociable type and likes mixing with the boys. Jim loves golf and spends quite a lot of time in Arizona and other sun spots. I met him in San Diego once and in Arizona another time. These days, Jim only shows up at sales on rare occasions.

GEORGE WILKE came to Calgary from Winnipeg as a cattle buyer for Canada Packers. He was truly a nice person. I had a lot of good visits with him. After Ian Davidson retired, George became the head buyer. He was very straightforward and called a spade a spade. George was a Second World War veteran. He married a girl from Scotland. Unfortunately, he passed away at a relatively young age.

CLAYTON WILLIAMS worked at the Burns livestock scale. He was what I would call a preliminary bookkeeper. He kept track of all the incoming cattle. They were all listed on a sheet as to sex, weight and price. A typical rail shipment from the north line would often involve ten different owners. Each of those owners could have a variety of cattle; for example, a bull, two good cows, one canner cow, four 1,200-pound steers, one 950-pound steer, or four 1,000-pound heifers. There were no computers those days, so everything was listed by hand.

Clayton was an easygoing man. Whenever his boss, Mickey Dirrane, got on his case, he shrugged it off like water running off a duck's back.

Clayton was a regular customer at the Shamrock Hotel, and he did not go there to sleep. He often found it hard to stretch his pay from paycheque to paycheque.

Clayton's wife was Bucky and Buck Rothwell's sister. Clayton passed away about thirty years ago.

PAT WILLIS worked in the AWW office. She was there for a long time. Pat was a very congenial person; everybody liked her. I really have no idea what happened to her or where she is these days.

JACK WILLOCKS was a beef manager at Burns. He rose from the ranks. Burns had around 600 people working in the Calgary plant. Only a small percentage worked their way up to management positions. Jack asked a thousand questions about the cattle business. He really had a great interest in doing a good job for the Company. I am not sure where he is these days.

BILL WILSON originated from the Camrose country of Alberta. He worked for Weiller and Williams in Edmonton for a number of years. About seven or eight years ago, Bill moved to the Calgary area. He started to work for Will Irvine and Don Danard shortly after. Bill is a good cattleman. He works as a country rep for the Stockyards at Strathmore. Bill has been involved with the Maine-Anjou breed for a long time. He and his wife and their son, Shawn, are all in the cattle-showing game. They show and sell some of their cattle at the Denver Stock Show every year. Bill is easygoing and ready to visit anytime. The topic is always cattle.

BOB WILSON is an easygoing individual who likes the cattle business. He worked for several outfits during the mid-'70s. For a few years, he was with Hartford Insurance Co. at the Yards. For the last 15 years, he has been with Transcon Livestock Ltd., a purebred sales promotion outfit headed up by Rod James out of Calgary.

DOUG WILSON worked for the Alberta Stock Yards. He is also the fourth generation to have worked for the old Burns Ranches.

Doug loves our western history. Not only does he love it, he does something about it. He salvaged some wooden boards and gates from the Calgary Stockyards before the complex was demolished and took all this stuff to the Burns' Bow Valley Ranch buildings, which have been preserved in their original location, in Fish Creek Park today. He would like to see a complete resurrection of the entire Calgary Stockyards along with an interpretive centre. So would I.

Doug involves himself with a lot of heritage events. In 1993 they held a presentation at Fort Calgary House to honour him. He received a number of plaques and letters including a CANADA 125 medal. He also received acknowledgements from Burns Packers and The Fish Creek Park Society as well as the Fort.

If you are interested in knowing more about Doug, try to get hold of a June 2, 1993 Calgary Herald. It had a nice story on his activities.

FRANK WILSON worked for the Alberta Stock Yards. He was a tall, rawboned man. He knew his job well. He had some connections with the Earl of Egmont at Nanton.

One day Frank and I went to the Earl's ranch. I was going to try and buy some cattle. I agreed to pay Frank a finder's fee. We were cordially received by Fred Percival (the Earl). We visited for a while; then we were invited into the house for lunch. Frank introduced me to the Earl's wife and his grown-up daughter (thirtyish). The meal was okay, but the language those two ladies used would make the most wayward sailor blush. After we had eaten, I thanked them both for the lovely lunch and then stepped out into the beautiful scenery and fresh foothills air. In my humble opinion, there is no better ranching country than the foothills between Calgary and Fort Macleod.

We got into the Earl's station wagon to go look at the cattle.

That was another experience I will never forget. The whole ranch, about 5000 acres, was fenced with industrial-woven steel wire. I think it was about 7 feet high. The cattle were also very interesting. The steers ranged from two to five years in age. They were not really very wild. As we drove among them, they did not spook. The Earl was constantly talking to them like each one was a pet, and they almost were. I rather enjoyed the whole thing.

After about two hours of driving around the ranch, I knew that buying anything there that day was out of the question. I made the Earl an offer that he gently refused. (He did not swear; he was soft-spoken.) After a little more chitchat, Frank and I went home. No money made that day—just a very interesting afternoon. Thank you, Frank.

ART WIMBLE worked at Burns for many years. When I started at Burns, he was in charge of the hog division—a position he held until he retired.

Art was born and raised in Quebec. He came to Calgary as a young man. He was not bilingual; in fact, he was very anti-French.

Art was really quite good-natured, but, when he got upset, he could use language that would make the hair on the back of your neck stand up. If there were any ladies present, butter wouldn't melt in his mouth.

One day Art and another chap were loading some big sows into a railroad car to ship to Vancouver. Art bent down to lift up the tow board. At that precise moment, an old sow decided to go to the washroom. She let a spray of you know what go between the rails of the stock car. It went right down Art's neck. He and his shirt were completely soaked. I won't mention his reaction because it was so dramatic, it defies description.

In the old days, the '20s, '30s and early '40s, there was a race track south of Calgary about halfway between today's Chinook Centre and Midnapore. There was a streetcar line that went to the track. One Saturday, Art Wimble and his buddy, Charlie Freeman, went to the races on the streetcar. That day their luck was not very good. By the time the last race was to be run, they only had two dollars left between them. They had no return fare. After pondering their plight for a few moments, they decided to place the two dollars on the nose of the favourite. The horses charged out of the starting gate; their horse in the lead. They did not have a very good view of the backstretch. As they were anxiously waiting for the horses to cross the finish line, their horse was not there. It had broken its leg in the backstretch. Fifteen minutes later, there were two bedraggled bettors hoofing their way home, about five or six miles away.

Art passed away a number of years ago. He always said he was the only Wimble in Canada. Since he only had one daughter, I guess the name is extinct in Canada, unless some new immigrants have arrived from England in the last thirty years. That is where Art's parents came from.

GEORGE WINKELAAR was the general manager of the Alberta Livestock Co-op. Before he got that position, he was a hog and sheep buyer for Swift Canadian. George was well-known and well-liked. He was a respected member of the livestock community. Under his leadership, the Co-op was very successful. He had wise counsel for anyone visiting him in his office—something I did every once in a while.

Every weekday, George would be on the radio giving a market report, telling what was going on in the cattle industry on that day. People who did not even own livestock enjoyed listening to his comments in that deep voice of his.

George was active in livestock politics. He held various positions over the years, including being a director, as well as president, of the Calgary Livestock Exchange.

George offered me the job of taking over their hog operation in Edmonton. The salary was almost twice as much as I was getting at Burns. I appreciated the offer, but I had to turn it down for two reasons: 1) I did not want to move to Edmonton; and 2) I wanted to stay in the cattle-end of things, not hogs. I had been a hog and lamb buyer for Burns for several years. It was a great day when I was transferred to buying only cattle, although my years of buying hogs and lambs came in handy years later when I became the general livestock manager at Burns. I got kind of side-tracked—now, back to George.

As I stated earlier, George did a good job for the Co-op. His wife, Cath, worked with him in the office for a number of years. Like most wives, she was an asset to the organization. Their daughter, who was a schoolteacher at Brooks, married Jim Graham, who is a very prominent cattleman to this day.

Both George and his wife, Cath, have passed away.

CATH WINKELAAR was George Winkelaar's wife. She often worked in the Co-op office with George. She was a very nice lady; always pleasant and polite. George was a good man. Maybe the old saying applied: "Behind every good man, there stands a good woman." In this case, Socrates' writing did not apply. Socrates once wrote, and I quote: "Every man should marry. If he marries a good woman, he will be very happy. If he marries a bad one, he will become a philosopher and that is good for every man."

RAY WITNEY came from Saskatchewan. He and Henry Bridgewater were good friends. He operated a feedlot east of the Calgary Airport. Ray was a real nice person. He had one weakness—gambling on horse races. In the end, it finished his feeding operation. The cattle could not quite make up for what he lost at the races. Ray passed away some time ago.

PAUL WOO is a government beef grader. He was the only Chinese grader that I ever knew. I am sure there were others. Paul is a heavyset person, which is rather unusual for his race. He is a good grader. A few times I contested his grades, but he was always a good sport about it. Hopefully, we both benefited from those encounters. As far as I know, Paul is still a grader.

MARTY WOOD was an outstanding saddle bronc rider. He was a world champion three different times. He finished in the top 15 for many years. Marty was raised in Bowness (before it became part of Calgary), where his dad operated a riding academy. Marty worked only for a short time for the Alberta Stock Yards Co. I remember him feeding and watering cattle on the west side. He was just starting to compete at rodeos then. He was a slight-built, dark-haired lad of about seventeen years of age. He came on fast, rodeo was his game—and that was the end of his career at the Yards. The last time I saw Marty ride was on a horse called Zone-A-Long at Rodeo Royal in Calgary. I thought he should have won the bronc riding that day, but the judges had other ideas. Shortly after that his bronc riding ended. Last I heard of Marty, he was living somewhere in the USA.

LES WORSDALE was a plant manager at Burns Calgary. He was a small, dapper individual. He was also very capable and was the plant manager at, at least, six different locations. Wherever Les was, the plants made money. He had a knack of getting the best out of his employees. Les was not a livestock person, but he had a good grasp of what was going on. I enjoyed working with him. He was Calgary plant manager when I was in the head office. Even when he was no longer my boss, we enjoyed a good relationship. Several years after Les retired, I met him in Arizona where he and his wife vacationed every winter. He attended one of our food fairs that we held in a hotel at Chandler, Arizona. I asked him for advice on how to make the plant we owned make a profit. He gave me some advice; however, in spite of it, we could not stem our losses. In the end, after losing a bundle, we closed the plant. I have lost track of Les.

ARCHIE AND MAXINE WUDEL operated a beef brokerage office in the Livestock Exchange Building. Before that, Archie worked for Canada Packers, and then for Burns as a beef manager and a plant manager at Brandon, Manitoba. He is very knowledgeable when it comes to the meat trade. He knows every major meat wholesaler and retailer in Canada. Archie is also a hobby farmer. Well, maybe it's a little more than a hobby, since he raises a considerable amount of barley on his farm at Camrose. Archie and his wife are retired these days and enjoying life.

LAWRENCE ZIEGLER was a brand inspector at the Stockyards. He was transferred to Western Feedlots at Strathmore where he worked for some years. He always wore a ferocious handlebar mustache. I heard that Lawrence has become a Christian and he is on a mission field somewhere overseas. I wish him well.

ALF ZIMMER lives in the Shepard district. He has had an almost constant presence at the Stockyards for the last thirty-five years. He is not a big operator, but he is a successful one. Alf loves to visit with the boys and is usually abreast of what is going on in the cattle community.

FRANK ZUKAS came from Europe as a young man, but he never mastered the English language very well. He owned a feedlot near Nose Creek close to the old Union Packing Plant. He fed a pretty good class of cattle. One of his sayings, when it came to buying feeder cattle, was: "You taka dee junk out, you bringa dee junk back." (This was after they were finished.) Frank was a staunch AWW customer. He always had a smile and was clean and neatly dressed. Every Christmas, he put on a big spread at his feedlot. Frank died a number of years ago.

JOHN BLAND never really worked at the Calgary Yards, but he did spend a lot of time there picking up some feeder cattle and visiting with the boys. For a number of years, John was in the Royal Canadian Mounted Police. For several years he was a rider in the famous Musical Ride. These days he has a place at Cheadle, Alberta, where he runs some cows. He and his family also operate a custom fencing company. Nowadays you can visit with him at the Strathmore Yards.

* * * * *

Like I stated at the beginning of the "sketches," some people will be missed. Other names have slipped my mind. These are a few about whom I know very little, so I have just listed their names without a write-up: Helen Belczowski, Frank Carr, Steve Grundson, Hoot Hellergram, Joe Lafluer, John McCaffery, Harvey McEwen, Phil Pust, Mike Rogers, Earl Scheer, Mike Stearns and Wilson Trotter.

Well folks, I hope you enjoyed reading this book as much as I enjoyed writing it. At times the nostalgia of the old Stockyards days almost overwhelmed me. Lord willing, I hope to write two more books. They will cover more of the cattle industry in a general way such as cattle politics, cattle judging, cattle feeding, cattle ranching, and many other aspects of the industry that I have touched on over the years in my "*Cattle Call*" columns.

APPENDIX A

AMERICAN AND CANADIAN TERMINAL MARKETS

To give you an idea of how many US terminal markets were operating in 1914—as recorded—I am going to list them. Strange as it may seem, Chicago, which was the largest terminal market in the US, was not listed in the records. I guess Chicago was not a member of the American Stockyards Association, which was comprised of the following: Union Stockyard Company, Baltimore, Md.; Buffalo Stock Yards, Buffalo, New York; The Cincinnati Union Stock Yard Co., Cincinnati, Ohio; The Cleveland Union Stock Yards Co., Cleveland, Ohio; The Union Stock Yards Co., Dayton, Ohio; The Denver Union Stock Yard Co., Denver, Colorado; Detroit Stock Yards, Detroit, Michigan; The Evansville Union Stock Yards Co., Inc., Evansville, Ind.; Fort Worth Stockyards, Fort Worth, Texas; Port City Stockyards Co., Houston, Texas; The Belt Railroad & Stockyards Co., Indianapolis, Ind.; The Jersey City Stock Yards, Inc., Jersey City, N.J.; Joplin Stockyards, Inc., Joplin, Missouri; Kansas City Stock Yards Co., Kansas City, Mo.; Union Stock Yard Co., Lancaster, Pa.; Los Angeles Union Stock Yards Co., Los Angeles, California; Bourbon Stock Yard Company, Louisville, Ky.; South Memphis Stock Yards Co., Memphis, Tenn.; Milwaukee Stockyards, Milwaukee, Wisconsin; St. Louis National Stock Yards Co., St. Louis, Missouri, National Stockyards, Joliet, Ill.; Union Stockyards & Market Co. Inc., New York, N.Y.; Portland Union Stock Yards Company, North Portland, Oregon; Salt Lake Union Stockyards, North Salt Lake, Utah; The Ogden Union Stockyards Co., Ogden, Utah; Oklahoma National Stockyards Co., Oklahoma City, Okla.; Union Stock Yards Co., Omaha, Nebraska; The Peoria Union Stock Yards Co., Peoria, Illinois; West Philadelphia Stock Yards Co., Philadelphia, Pa.; Mississippi Valley Stockyards Inc., St. Louis, Mo.; Union Stock Yards, San Antonio, Texas; Union Stock Yards Co., Seattle, Wash.; The Sioux City Stock Yards Co., Sioux City, Iowa; Sioux Falls Stock

Yards Co., Sioux Falls, S.D.; Saint Joseph Stock Yards Co., So. St. Joseph, Mo.; Saint Paul Union Stock Yards Co., So. St. Paul, Minn.; South San Francisco Union Stockyards, So. San Francisco, Calif.; Old Union Stock Yards Co., Spokane, Washington; Springfield Stock Yards Co., Springfield, Illinois; Stockton Union Stockyards, Stockton, Calif.; Union Stockyards Co. of Fargo, West Fargo, N.D.; and Wichita Union Stock Yards Co., Wichita, Kansas.

To give you an idea of how many Canadian terminal markets that were operating in those early years, I am going to list them: Montreal Stock Yards, Montreal, Quebec; Ontario Union Stock Yards Co. Ltd., Toronto, Ontario, (owned by the Ontario Government, and the biggest in Canada); St. Boniface Union Stock Yards, Winnipeg, Manitoba; Northern Saskatchewan Union Co-operative Stock Yards, (started in 1919 and closed in 1988 or 1989), Prince Albert, Saskatchewan; Saskatoon Union Stock Yards, Saskatoon, Saskatchewan (later the name was changed to Western Stock Yards); Edmonton Stock Yards, Edmonton, Alberta; and Vancouver Stock Yards, Vancouver, B.C. (closed many years ago).

In later years, stockyards marketing facilities were opened up in Lethbridge, Alberta, (owned by Alberta Stock Yards Co.); Brandon, Manitoba; Regina, Saskatchewan, and Kitchener, Ontario. To my knowledge, the Maritimes had no federal stockyards.

APPENDIX B

TRADING RULES AND REGULATIONS, ALBERTA STOCK YARDS, CALGARY

When the Calgary Livestock Exchange Limited was formed on May 4, 1914, they drew up some by-laws. Over a period of years, these regulations were revised several times. Some of the earlier policies were adopted from many American markets. Some rules were strictly Canadian.

I have in my possession a small blue-covered booklet that set out the trading rules and regulations that basically governed the daily operations at Alberta Stock Yards, Calgary. Unfortunately, it is not dated, but I think it was published sometime between 1914 and 1920.

Here is a exact retype of that booklet:

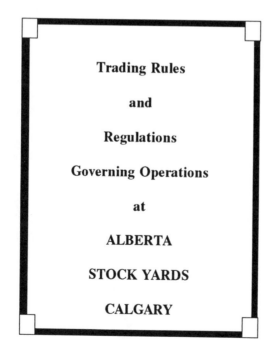

Trading Rules

and

Regulations

Governing Operations

at

ALBERTA

STOCK YARDS

CALGARY

TRADING RULES AND REGULATIONS
Governing Operations
at

ALBERTA STOCK YARDS

CALGARY

•

ARTICLE 1

CATTLE TRADING HOURS AND REGULATIONS

Sec. 1.—The market shall open each trading day at 9:00 a.m. and shall close at 4:00 p.m. with the exception of Saturday, when the closing hour shall be 12:00 o'clock noon.

Sec. 2—The Market shall be officially opened each morning at 9:00 a.m. by the raising of a flag on the Exchange Building and said flag shall be lowered at the close of trading hours.

Sec. 3—When two or more buyers are present in any commission firm's alley at the opening of the market they shall match coins to decide which buyer shall have the preference of trading first with the salesman on cattle deliveries then in the firm's yards. Winner of second and any subsequent turns shall immediately register their order of turn with the salesman.

Sec. 4—All buyers who match for trading positions at the opening of the market, or any subsequent match that day, shall have their positions held for them by the salesman, providing that the buyer is in the cattle yards or his office when his turn comes. The salesman shall take all reasonable means to contact the buyer who matched or some other registered buyer representing the same firm, but he shall not be obligated to wait over ten minutes for said buyer. After expiration of this time the salesman shall be free to trade with the next buyer in order of matching preference.

Sec. 5—Only members of the Calgary Livestock Exchange and regular livestock buyers, who have registered their names with, and been duly approved as such, by the Board of Directors of the said Exchange, shall be eligible to match at the opening of the market for buying precedence.

Sec. 6—It shall be the duty of all regular buyers to register with the Calgary Livestock Exchange, all employees in their employ who are authorized to purchase livestock on their behalf and these employees, after being registered, shall be eligible to match for trading precedence but all purchases made by them shall only be for and on behalf of the buyers who registered their name.

Sec. 7—Cattle arriving at the market after 9:00 a.m. and up until 12:00 o'clock noon can be matched on when two or more buyers are present on their delivery into a commission firm's pens and register their intention of trying to buy that particular consignment and precedence shall be made and held as under Sec. 3.

Sec. 8—Cattle arriving at the market from 12:00 o'clock noon to 1:15 p.m. shall be matched on at 1:15 p.m. and any cattle arriving after 1:15 p.m. and up until the closing of the market at 4:00 p.m. shall be matched on when delivered into a commission firm's pens.

Sec. 9—All matching for cattle trading preference shall take place in the main alley of the commission firm who have the cattle in their hands.

Sec. 10—On each full market day the period from 12:00 o'clock noon to 1:15 p.m. shall be considered closed for any dealing but any salesman who is giving a buyer his turn before 12:00 o'clock noon may complete his dealings with that particular buyer during this period. Similar conditions apply to the closing of the market when the salesman shall have the privilege of completing his trading with a buyer who started with him previous to closing time.

ARTICLE 2

HOG AND SHEEP TRADING HOURS AND REGULATIONS

Sec. 1—Buyers of butcher hogs which have arrived at the market after the close of the previous day's trading or up until 10:30 a.m. shall be matched on at 10:30 a.m. and arrivals reaching the market between the hours of 10:30 a.m. and 1:30 p.m. shall be matched on at 1:30 p.m. Hog arrivals after this hour and up until 4:00 p.m. when the market closes, shall be matched on as separate lots on arrival. On Saturday the first matching shall take place at 9:00 a.m. and any subsequent lots arriving at the market until 12:00 o'clock noon shall be matched for on arrival.

Sec. 2—All feeder hogs, sows, stags, extra heavies, heavies or hogs which in the opinion of the salesman in charge of the sale of same will not receive a Government grade rating of A,B, or C grades, can be traded on any time when the market is open, subject to Sec. 3 or Article 1.

Sec. 3—No trading on hogs or sheep of any grade or classification shall take place between the hours of 12:00 o'clock noon and 1:30 p.m.

Sec. 4—Hours and rules for matching and trading on sheep and lambs shall be the same as contained in Sec. 1 of this Article.

Sec. 5—All buyers who have match for trading preference on either hogs or sheep shall have to notify the salesman in the same manner as prescribed in Article 1, Sec. 4. Hog and sheep salesmen shall carry out the intent and purpose of Article 1, Sec. 4, as same relates to order of preference.

ARTICLE 3

GOVERNING SALES

Sec. 1—In any case where a seller and a buyer do not agree on a price for any livestock and the deal is left unclosed then it shall be considered that any bid or bids made by the buyer are cancelled when he leaves the salesman, unless the buyer makes the stipulation that he is leaving his bid. Any and all bids made during any trading day which are not accepted are considered cancelled when the market closes for the day on which they were made.

Sec. 2—In any case where a buyer leaves his bid the salesman must see that if the stock on which the bid was placed were to be sold to another buyer, there must be an increase in price of not less that 10 cents per cwt. on the total weight of the stock involved.

Sec. 3—When a buyer leaves a bid on certain stock and the salesman has later received a bid only 5 cents better and can get no further raise then the salesman must contact the bidder who left his bid and allow him the privilege of taking the stock at the latter buyer's offer, providing, however, that if the salesman were pricing his stock at a certain figure and the first buyer bid within 5 cents of the asking price, then the salesman would have the right to sell the stock to another buyer at his asking price without reference to the previous bidder.

Sec. 4—In any case where a buyer makes a bid and the salesman allows him to leave and no particular mention was made about the offer and later the salesman finds the bid so made was the best he could get, the stock involved must not be weighed to the party making the offer, unless and until the salesman has contacted the bidder and received his sanction to weigh him the stock involved.

ARTICLE 4

Sec. 1—All persons trading on the Calgary Livestock market at the Alberta Stock Yards whether members of the Calgary Livestock Exchange or registered as buyers, shall be bound to conduct their dealings in conformance with these Regulations and with the Rules, By-Laws and Regulations of the Calgary Livestock Exchange.

Sec. 2—The President of the Calgary Livestock Exchange may on request by a salesman or buyer under special circumstances, grant a special concession for trading after regular hours, but any concession so granted is not to be taken as a precedent on future occasions.

Sec. 3—Only one member of a commission firm or one registered buyer acting for any one firm shall be eligible to match for turn in any one commission firm's alley at one time when the market opens as under these Regulations.

ARTICLE 5

No member or non-member shall be in attendance at the truck unloading chutes or in the vicinity thereof. Stock intended for any buyer or commission firm must be unloaded and yarded for inspection, acceptance or rejection in commission firm's or buyer's pens.

All Rules and Regulations of the Calgary Livestock Exchange relative to buying, selling, trading, or soliciting of livestock at unloading chutes or in the vicinity thereof are hereby rescinded.

The final interpretations of the foregoing Rules and Regulations governing members of the Calgary Livestock Exchange and non-members, shall be subject to the definite and final decisions of the Board of Directors of the Calgary Livestock Exchange. A majority vote of the said Board shall be final and binding on all parties.

The Calgary market was more or less governed by the above rules till 1939. At that point, the Federal Government's Livestock and Livestock Products Act, which had been in place since 1917, was used to enforce the Federal Government's jurisdiction over Canadian stock yards markets. This Act was written by Ottawa bureaucrats in conjunction with the stockyards markets across Canada. It would be boring to reprint that document, so I won't.

APPENDIX C

RULES, REGULATIONS AND BY-LAWS
CALGARY LIVESTOCK EXCHANGE LIMITED

In 1947 the Calgary Livestock Exchange Limited wrote a new green-covered booklet on rules, regulations and by-laws. This book was very comprehensive, containing approximately 12,000 words. It was approved by the Minister of Agriculture for Canada and is dated March 12, 1947.

Here is an exact retype of that document:

Rules, Regulations
and By-Laws

OF THE

**CALGARY LIVESTOCK
EXCHANGE LIMITED**

*

AS APPROVED
BY THE MINISTER OF
AGRICULTURE FOR CANADA,
DATED, MARCH 12th, 1947

MEMORANDUM OF ASSOCIATION

1. The official name of the organization shall be the CALGARY LIVESTOCK EXCHANGE, hereinafter referred to as the "Exchange."

2. The Office of the Exchange shall be located at the Alberta Stock Yards, in the City of Calgary, Alberta.

3. The objects for which the Exchange is established:

   (a) To create and maintain a commercial exchange, not for pecuniary gain, but for the furtherance of all interests directly connected with the buying and selling of livestock at the Alberta Stock Yards, Calgary, Alberta.

   (b) To promote and establish uniformity in the customs and usages of the livestock trade.

   (c) To provide for the speedy adjustment of business disputes among its members.

   (d) To secure to its members the benefits of co-operation for the furtherance of their legitimate pursuits.

   (e) To promote in all respects the interests of the livestock trade in the province of Alberta, and the country tributary thereto.

   (f) To protect members by taking bonds, security affecting insurance, or otherwise.

   (g) To promote and provide for social intercourse among the members of the Exchange; and

   (h) To enact rules, regulations, and by-laws for the purpose of carrying out these objects, and to impose penalties for the infraction of any of the same.

RULES AND REGULATIONS

In the following Rules and Regulations, unless otherwise stated, definitions shall be understood and interpreted as defined in the Livestock Products Act and Amendments thereto.

"The market" shall be interpreted as meaning the "Alberta Stock Yards, Calgary, Alberta.

RULES AND REGULATIONS

ARTICLE 1

Government of the Exchange and Elections

Section 1. The Government of the Exchange is hereby vested in a Board of Directors, composed of a President, Vice-President and seven (7) other members.

Election of President, Vice-President and Directors

Section 2. The President, Vice-President and seven (7) other Directors shall be elected by the members at the annual election to be held, as hereinafter provided, in February of each year.

Election of Committee of Arbitration and Secretary-Treasurer

Section 3. (a) There shall also be elected by the members at the annual election, a Committee of Arbitration consisting of three (3) members. (b) There shall also be elected, by the members at the annual election a Secretary-Treasurer.

Special Committees

Section 4. Special committees may be appointed by the Exchange, by the Board of Directors, or by the President, in such manner and for such purposes as may be determined by the appointing body, and it shall be the duty of every committee so appointed to act when properly called upon. Such appointments shall be revocable at the will and pleasure of the appointing body.

ELECTIONS—Annual

Section 5. (a) The annual election shall be held at the annual meeting in February of each year at such time and place as the Board of Directors may determine.

Postponed

(b) If, from any cause, the election of Officers and Committees is not held at the regular annual election, such an election may be held at any regular meeting or at a special general meeting called for that purpose. Such a postponed election shall not be held, however, until notice of the meeting day on which it is intended to hold such an election, and the fact that it is to be held, shall have been posted on the Bulletin Board of the Exchange for at least fifteen (15) days immediately preceding such meeting. All nominations shall be received and elections held in accordance with the provisions hereinafter set forth.

Special

(c) Special elections shall be held only in accordance with the provisions prescribed in Article Six (6), Section Eight (8); or when, from failure to nominate for any office, no election is held for said office; or if, in complying with the terms of Section Eleven (11) of this rule, no election is declared for any office; and said special election shall be held, in like manner, as a postponed election.

Term of Office

Section 6. The official term of any member elected, at the annual election, shall commence on the first Monday succeeding the election; and he shall hold office until his successor's term officially commences as prescribed in this election.

The official term of any member elected, at a postponed or special election, shall commence on the day succeeding the election; and he shall hold office until his successor's term officially commences, as prescribed in this section.

Qualifications

Section 7. No person shall be eligible to any elective or appointment office, unless he be a member in good standing. No member shall be eligible to hold more than one elective office at the same time; nor shall any member already holding an elective office be eligible for appointment or election to any vacancy which may occur in any other elective office.

Nominations - Withdrawals

Section 8. There shall be posted on the Bulletin Board, by the Secretary, at least fifteen (15) days prior to the annual election a notification that nominations for elective offices are open. All nominations for elective offices shall be made by petition in writing; shall be signed by two (2) or more members in good standing and shall be submitted to the Secretary at or before five (5) o'clock p.m. of the fifth day prior to the annual election.

If any member who is nominated for office desires to withdraw his name from nomination, he must submit such withdrawal in writing, to the Secretary at or before twelve (12) o'clock noon of the day prior to the annual election; and if any member who has been nominated for office has withdrawn his nomination for said office, as prescribed hereinabove, he may have nomination for said office returned to the list, provided such request be in writing and submitted to the Secretary at or before twelve (12) o'clock noon of the day of the annual election.

No member shall be included in the ballot or voted for, unless nominated in accordance with the aforesaid provisions.

The Board of Directors at a meeting held at least four (4) days prior to the annual election, shall certify to the Secretary as to the nomination and eligibility of members to office.

Mode of Voting - Proxies

Section 9. Voting shall be by ballot; and the Secretary shall have ballots printed, showing the names of all members nominated to office, as certified by the Board of Directors. The names shall be in the following order: President, Vice-President, Directors, Committee of Arbitration, Secretary-Treasurer.

Sample ballot papers shall be posted on the Bulletin Board by the Secretary at least three (3) days prior to the annual election.

Each member in good standing is entitled to a vote, and no member shall be allowed to vote by proxy.

Judges of Election

Section 10. Three (3) members, who neither hold an elective office nor are nominated for such office, shall be appointed by the Board of Directors as judges of election, shall receive and count the ballots, and certify the results of the election to the Secretary. Their majority decision, with respect to all improperly marked ballots, shall be final.

Votes Necessary to Elect

Section 11. For President and Vice-President, a majority of all votes cast for each respective office shall be necessary to elect; but for all other elective office a plurality shall be necessary to elect. If any eligible member nominated for elective office shall have no opposition for said elective office, he shall be declared elected "by acclamation," by the presiding officer of the meeting at which the election is held. If any member is elected to more than one office, a majority vote of all members voting at said election shall decide what office the member so elected shall accept; and all other votes cast to elect said member for other offices shall be null and void, but these votes shall be included in the total cast.

Failure to Elect

Section 12. In case of any failure to elect either President or Vice-President on the first ballot, by reason of an insufficient majority, all contestants, except the two (2) receiving the highest number of votes on the said first ballot, shall withdraw; and a further ballot shall be taken on said two (2) contestants who have received the highest number of votes; and balloting shall continue until a sufficient majority be obtained. In case of a tie vote for three (3) or more members receiving the largest number of votes for either President or Vice-President on the said first ballot, a further ballot shall be taken on said three (3) or more contestants; and balloting shall continue until a sufficient majority be obtained.

In case of any failure to elect for other office, by reason of a tie vote, balloting for members so tied shall continue until the tie be broken.

ARTICLE II

Meeting of the Exchange

Annual

Section 1. The annual meeting shall be held in February of each year at such time and place as the Board of Directors may determine.

Regular

Section 2. Regular meetings shall be held once in every three (3) months at such time and place as the Board of Directors may determine, if and when said Board of Directors or a majority vote of members present at an annual, regular or special meeting, deem it advisable and necessary for the proper carrying out of Exchange business.

Special

Section 3. The President and the Board of Directors shall have the respective power to call special meetings upon such notice and for such purpose as they may deem proper. All calls for special meetings shall state the object, time and place of such meetings, and no other business than that for which a special meeting was called shall be considered or transacted at such meeting.

Special—On Request of Two Members

Section 4. Should two or more members submit in writing a request to the President for a special meeting, stating the object for which such meeting is desired, the President shall arrange for the holding of said meeting not less than one business day after the receipt of such notice; and in the interval there shall be posted on the Bulletin Board, a notice calling such meeting and stating its object, time and place.

Quorum

Section 5. Twelve members in good standing at an annual, regular, or special meeting shall constitute a quorum for the transaction of business; but a less number shall have power to adjourn from time to time to any fixed date preceding the next regular meeting.

Place

Section 6. All meetings shall be held with the corporate limits of the City of Calgary in the Province of Alberta.

ARTICLE III

Duties of the President

Section 1. The President shall act as the general executive officer of the Exchange and of the Board of Directors. He shall preside at all meetings thereof, and shall direct their proceedings in accordance with the Rules, Regulations, By-laws, and Rules of Order governing the same.

Must Preserve Order

Section 2. The President shall maintain order and proper business decorum at all meetings of the Exchange. Should any member be guilty of disorderly, boisterous, or offensive conduct while at a meeting, he shall for such offense, be subject to a fine fixed by the President; which amount shall be not less than Five Dollars ($5.00) or more than Fifty Dollars ($50.00); or he may be suspended from all privileges of the Exchange for such time as may be determined by the President; subject, however, to an appeal to the Board of Directors; but pending such appeal he shall, in case of suspension, so remain, if the President decides.

Call Special Meetings

Section 3. The President may call special meetings of the Board of Directors and of the Exchange, subject to the provisions of Article Six (6), Section Eleven (11), and of Article Two (2), Sections Three (3) and Four (4).

Appoint Committees and Fill Temporary Vacancies

Section 4. The President shall appoint all Committees the election of which is not otherwise provided for; he shall fill from among the eligible members, temporary vacancies in elective and appointive offices (except the Board of Directors when acting in an executive capacity) caused by absence, disability, or disqualification; and he shall generally perform such other duties as are usually incident to such office.

ARTICLE IV

Duties of the Vice-President

Section 1. It shall be the office of the Vice-President to perform the duties of the President in case of the absence or disability of the said President; when, for the time being, the powers of the President shall be vested in the Vice-President.

In case of the removal, resignation, or death of the President the powers and duties of said office shall be assumed by the Vice-President.

ARTICLE V

Duties of the Secretary-Treasurer—Secretarial

Section 1. The Secretary-Treasurer, as Secretary, under the direction and control of the Board of Directors, shall keep a record of the proceedings of the Exchange. He shall have the custody of the seal, books, papers, and other property of the Exchange, and under the direction of the President, he shall give notice of all meetings of the Board of Directors and of the Exchange, and shall read at these meetings such records or papers as the presiding officer may direct. He shall conduct the correspondence of the Exchange, attend all meetings of the Board of Directors, Committees of Arbitration and Appeals; also special and standing committees when so requested, shall keep an official record of their proceedings, shall give notice when their services are required, shall issue the necessary notices and papers to parties, and shall deliver copies of all awards or findings.

Certificate for Committees

Section 2. The Secretary shall furnish the chairman of each special committee with a copy of the resolution whereby such committee has been appointed, and shall furnish all members of committees appointed, by the President, by the Board of Directors, or by the members of the Exchange, with official certificates of their appointment. Such certificates so issued shall set out the duties of the appointees and the time for which they are appointed; and shall clearly indicate that such appointments are revocable at the will and pleasure of the appointing body. All certificates shall be signed by the President and Secretary and shall bear the seal of the Exchange.

Notifying Members of Revision of Rules and By-Laws

Section 3. In the event of the repeal, revision, or amendment of an established Rule or By-Law, or upon adoption of a new Rule or By-Law; he shall, within ten (10) days after such action, have the said repeal, revision, or new enactment printed and distributed to each member for record and protection.

Office Hours

Section 4. He shall, if a full time secretary, keep his office open during usual business hours; or if otherwise, he shall make his services readily available during usual business hours, and he shall perform such other duties as are incident to his office or as may be required from time to time by the Board of Directors.

Treasurer

Section 5. The Secretary-Treasurer, as Treasurer, shall collect and receive all moneys due to the Exchange for assessments, fines, fees, or otherwise; shall give his receipt for same and shall, under the direction of the Board of Directors, deposit such moneys at interest in a chartered Bank of Canada to the credit of the Exchange. He shall pay, on account of the Exchange, such moneys as may be directed by the Board of Directors. He shall make a report of receipts and disbursements to the Board of Directors and full reports of same for the year to the said Board at its final meeting in each year. His accounts as Treasurer shall be kept in books belonging to the Exchange; which books shall be at all times open for inspection by the Board of Directors or any member of committee of said Board appointed for such purpose. He shall furnish, as security for the faithful performances of his duties, a bond approved by the Board of Directors, if and when said Board may deem it advisable.

ARTICLE VI

Powers and Duties of the Board of Directors

Section 1. All the business and financial concerns of the Exchange shall be managed and conducted by or under the supervision of the Board of Directors, in accordance with the Rules, Regulations and By-Laws of the Exchange.

Quorum

Section 2. Five (5) members of the Board of Directors shall constitute a quorum for the transaction of business; but a less number may adjourn from time to time to any fixed date preceding the next regular meeting of said Board.

Appointing Delegates or Representatives

Section 3. The Board of Directors shall have the power to select from the eligible members, the delegates and alternates to any convention; also any representative to any conference or meeting at which it shall deem it important that the Exchange be represented.

Appointment of Employees

Section 4. The Board of Directors shall, at the first meeting of said Board succeeding each annual election, or as soon thereafter as may be, appoint assistants as it may consider necessary for the purpose of the Exchange; and it may establish such regulations for the direction and government of such appointees as it may deem proper, and shall fix their compensation and determine by whom the same shall be paid. The term of office of all such appointees shall commence at such time as the said Board may designate, and continue until their successors are appointed and assume their duties. All such appointments shall be revocable at the will and pleasure of said Board.

The Board of Directors shall see to it that all appointees perform their duties faithfully, and may require any or all of them to give such bond or other security as said Board may prescribe.

Notices and Reports

Section 5. The Board of Directors shall cause to be posted on the Bulletin Board for ten (10) days, all appointments of public concern which it shall make, and all revocations of same; and at every annual meeting it shall present to each member present a printed or written report of all receipts and disbursements, properly classified; and an exhibit of financial affairs, property, and general conditions of the Exchange.

Power to Levy Assessments

Section 6. The Board of Directors shall, previous to the annual meeting, and subject to the provisions of Article Thirty (30), make a pro rata assessment on the members; and it shall, at the annual meeting, report to the Exchange, the pro rata amount assessed. It may make such assessments payable in installments and shall fix the time when the assessments or instalments shall be due and payable.

Temporary Absence or Disability of The President and Vice-President

Section 7. In case of absence of disability of both the President and Vice-President, it shall be the duty of the Board of Directors to elect from its number a temporary chairman, who, in addition to his duties as chairman of the Board of Directors, shall also temporarily perform all other duties and exercise the powers devolving upon the President.

Vacancies and Special Elections

Section 8. Should a vacancy occur in any elective office caused by death, resignation, succession, or removal of a member, the Board of Directors shall fill such vacancy for the remainder of the official term from among the eligible members. If, on account of the above stated causes, a quorum of the Board of Directors cannot be secured, a special election shall be held to fill vacancies in all elective offices similar to a postponed election as prescribed by Article One (1), Section Five (5).

To Act As Committee of Appeals

Section 9. It shall be the duty of the Board of Directors to act as the Committee of Appeals.

Meetings of the Board of Directors

Regular

Section 10. A regular meeting shall be held once in every month at such time and place as the Board of Directors may determine.

Special

Section 11. Special Meetings shall be convened upon the order of the President or upon the written request of any three (3) members of the Board of Directors addressed to the Secretary. Such meetings may be called by public notice posted on the Bulletin Board, or by giving verbal or written notice to each member personally through the Secretary or his assistants. If such personal notice cannot conveniently be given to any member of said Board, a written notice left at his usual place of business shall be sufficient.

Place

Section 12. All meetings shall be held within the corporate limits of the City of Calgary, in the Province of Alberta.

Absence of Members

Section 13. Any member of the Board of Directors who shall absent himself from three (3) consecutive regular meetings thereof, without having been previously excused, or without communicating to the President in writing, a good and sufficient excuse for his absence, shall be deemed and taken to have thereby resigned his office.

Meeting Room and Office

Section 14. The Board of Directors shall have the power to provide suitable and convenient Exchange, Reading, and other necessary room and offices for the purposes of the Exchange, and it shall cause the same, when provided, to be kept in comfortable, neat, and orderly condition. It shall have power to make all needful Rules and Regulations in regard to the use of the said rooms, and to enforce the same by the necessary penalties and discipline.

Providing Facilities and Regulations

Section 15. The Board of Directors shall have the power to provide such facilities for the transaction of business as it may deem of benefit to the members and the market; and shall have power to alter, amend, or supplement all such provisions at pleasure.

Interpretation of Rules, Regulations and By-Laws

Section 16. The Board of Directors shall interpret and define the meaning of the Rules, Regulations, and By-Laws, whenever it be necessary for a full and complete understanding, application, or enforcement thereof.

ARTICLE VII

Removal From Office

Section 1. In case any member holding an elective office in the exchange neglects, fails, or refuses to perform the duties of the said office in a proper manner, he may be removed from office.

Procedure

Section 2. A petition stating informally the neglect or complaint, and signed by twenty-five per cent of the total membership in good standing, must be presented to the President or the Board of Directors, who shall call a special meeting of the Exchange within ten (10) days of receipt of such petition, and notice of the meeting stating the object, time and place of the same, shall be posted on the bulletin board.

No meeting shall be held until two (2) days have elapsed after notice thereof, and a copy of the complaint or charge has been served upon the officer so charged. Such service shall be made by the Secretary or his assistants, and may be effective either by leaving the notice of meeting, accompanied by a copy of the complaint, or charge, with the accused personally, or leaving them at, or mailing to, his then or last known ordinary place of business although the accused is not present.

A two-thirds vote of the members present in good standing shall be necessary to make the removal effective.

ARTICLE VIII

Hearing and Discipline

Section 1. It shall be the duty of the Board of Directors to hear and determine all charges of default, misconduct, violation, or evasion of any of the Rules, Regulations, or By-Laws, against any member which directly or indirectly affect any other member of the Exchange; but all cases of disputed claims, or other matters in controversy among members, also among members and non-members, which, in the judgement of the Board or Directors are subject for adjudication by the Committee of Arbitration, shall be referred by the Board to such Committee for determination.

Improper Conduct

Section 2. When any member shall be guilty of improper conduct of a personal character in any of the rooms of the Exchange, or when he has failed or shall neglect or refuse to pay or to settle his legal obligations; or when he has failed to comply promptly with the terms, or shall be guilty of a wilful violation of any business contract, or obligation, and has failed, or shall neglect or refuse, equitably and satisfactorily to adjust and settle the same; or when he has failed to comply promptly with and fulfil, or shall wilfully neglect or refuse to comply with the award of finding of the Committee of Arbitration or of the Committee of Appeals; or when he shall violate or evade any of the Rules, Regulations, or By-Laws; or when he shall be guilty of an act of bad faith or any attempt at extortion, or of any other dishonorable or dishonest conduct; he shall upon admission or proof of such action before the Board of Directors, be, by it, censured, fined, suspended, or expelled (if no specified penalty has been prescribed for said action) as it may determine from the nature and gravity of the offence committed.

In the case of the suspension of a member for failure to pay or to settle his obligations, such suspension shall stand until all such obligations have been paid or settled satisfactorily to the Board of Directors, when application for reinstatement may be considered; and if the Board of Directors shall be satisfied that such failure was merely financial inability or misfortune, such member may be reinstated.

In this rule, the expressions, "legal obligations," "business contract" or "obligation," mean only obligations and responsibilities assumed or contracted in the course of business at the market.

Committee Of Investigation

Section 3. Any member, person, firm, company or corporation, who shall employ a member to purchase or sell live stock at the market shall have the right to demand an investigation by a committee hereinafter provided, of any specific charge or charges against such member for anything done by him in contravention of these Rules, Regulations, and By-Laws, arising out of such purchase or sale, provided such charge or charges shall be made in writing to the Board of Directors.

Investigation of Rumors Of Misconduct

Section 4. Should it come to the knowledge of the Board of Directors in any manner, that an offence against the good name and dignity of the Exchange, or any violation, or evasion of its Rules, Regulations or By-Laws, is alleged to have been committed by any member thereof, the said Board shall cause a preliminary or informal inquiry to be made by a committee of the members of the Exchange regarding such allegation; and if such committee, upon inquiry, is of the opinion that there is reasonable ground for such allegation, it shall so report to the said Board and shall state the offence, violation or evasion alleged, whereupon the member thus implicated shall be notified to appear before the Board of Directors as provided for in Article VIII, Section Six (6).

Charges In Writing

Section 5. All charges made to the Board of Directors against any member or non-member for any default, misconduct, offence, violation, or evasion of any Rule, Regulation or By-Law shall be in writing, shall informally state the default, misconduct, offence, violation, or evasion charged, in general terms, and shall be signed by one (1) or more members in good standing, or by one (1) or more other reputable persons; but the Board of Directors shall not entertain, consider, or act upon, any charge of default, misconduct, offence, violation, or evasion of any Rule, Regulation, or By-Law, unless the party preferring the same shall institute and file with the Board of Directors a complaint in writing, within twelve (12) months from the time such alleged default, misconduct, offence, violation, or evasion shall have occurred.

Notice to the Accused—Temporary Suspension

Section 6. No member shall be censured, fined, suspended, or expelled without a hearing of the charge, or charges against him by the Board of Directors, nor without having an opportunity to be heard in his own defense, except in accordance with Article Three (3), Section Two (2); but in case of a rumor of default or assignment, or complaint in reference to same has been charged against a member, the Board of Directors shall immediately investigate same; and after investigation may suspend said member temporarily until the charge, or charges, against said member have been heard. No hearing shall be held until two (2) days have elapsed after notice thereof, with a copy of the charge, or charges, having been served upon the said member. Such service shall be made by the Secretary or his assistants, and may be effected either by leaving the notice of hearing, accompanied by a copy of the charge, or charges, with the accused personally, or leaving them at, or mailing them to, his then or last known ordinary place of business or his residence. Upon such service the hearing may proceed, although the accused is not present. In case the accuser shall fail to appear, or appearing refuse to substantiate the charge, or charges, the Board of Directors shall determine what action shall be taken in the case.

Members Must Testify

Section 7. In any investigation or hearing before the Board of Directors, or before any other duly constituted committee or other tribunal of the Exchange, if any member, who shall have had notice from the Secretary in writing, or who shall have been cited by the Chairman of any other duly constituted committee or other tribunal of the Exchange to appear and give information, shall neglect or refuse to do so; or, if appearing, any member shall refuse to answer any questions which may by a majority vote of the members present of the said Board, committee or other tribunal, be declared proper and pertinent to the matter under investigation or hearing, he shall, unless he disclose a good and sufficient reason for not answering, be subject to a fine by the Board of Directors or to suspension from all privileges of the Exchange for such period as said Board may determine; such action may be taken by said Board in case of contempt shown by witness before the Board of Directors, or on the report in writing of any committee or other tribunal of the Exchange before which such case of contempt may occur.

Examination of Books and Records

Section 8. In case of any complaints or charges, properly submitted in writing, (see Article VIII, Section Five (5),), the investigation of which necessitates an examination of books and records, the Board of Directors shall have power to appoint a representative outside the Exchange to investigate the books and records of any members, relative to such complaints and charges. On receipt of the written report from said representative with respect to the books and records in relation to such complaints and charges, the Board of Directors shall proceed with the hearing in reference thereto.

Section 9. All books and records of commission merchants, co-operative associations, dealers and order buyers shall be open at all times to inspection and investigation by a Representative of the Minister of Agriculture for Canada.

Legal Counsel Debarred

Section 10. No person shall, in any investigation or hearing before the Board of Directors, or before any committee or other tribunal of the Exchange, be allowed to be represented by legal counsel, but he may be allowed the right to cross-question in his own defence under the jurisdiction of the presiding Board.

Necessity To Censure

Section 11. A majority vote of the members present at any meeting of the Board of Directors shall be necessary to censure or fine, and an affirmative vote of at least two-thirds (2/3) of all the members of the Board of Directors shall be necessary to suspend or expel; and it shall be the duty of the chair to vote on questions of discipline.

Suspended Members Reinstated

Section 12. A suspended member may be reinstated by a vote of the majority of Directors present at any meeting of the Board of Directors, provided notice of application for reinstatement shall have been posted on the Bulletin Board at least ten (10) days prior to the hearing of such application by the said Board.

Expelled Members Reinstated

Section 13. An expelled member shall not be readmitted to membership except in accordance with the provisions governing the admission of applicants for membership.

Disqualification

Section 14. No member of the Board of Directors shall sit as a member of said Board during its consideration of any charge of default, misconduct, violation, or evasion of any Rule, Regulation or By-Law in which he, or the firm which he may represent, is interested directly or indirectly, but his place shall be filled pro tem by another eligible member appointed by the President; otherwise the question of the propriety of any member to sit on the said Board shall rest with the other members of the Board.

Penalties

Section 15. In all cases of default, misconduct, violation, or evasion of any of the Rules, Regulations or By-Laws, for which the penalty is not specifically provided, the Board of Directors shall, at its discretion, inflict such a penalty as it may determine from the nature and gravity of the offence committed.

Section 16. Wherever the penalty of expulsion is provided for in the Rules, Regulations and By-Laws, or imposed by the Board of Directors under its general powers, expulsion shall be understood to mean and to involve the loss and forfeiture of all rights of any description whatsoever. Whenever the Board of Directors shall inflict a fine as a penalty, it shall specify the time in which the said fine shall be paid.

Penalty for Interference with the Application of the
Rules, Regulations and By-Laws

Section 17. Any member who, having consented and agreed in writing to accept and abide by any award of the Committee of Arbitration, (see Article IX, Section Eleven (11),), undertakes or institutes, by injunction or other proceedings in any court, to restrain or otherwise interfere with the proceedings by or before the Board of Directors, or any committee, or other tribunal of the Exchange, or with the force, operation or effect thereof, or who shall in any other tribunal question or attack any award made by the Committee of Arbitration or Committee of Appeals, or who shall institute any suit against the other party to the dispute, or who shall institute any suit against any officer or member for or because of the consequence of any official action taken, or vote cast, or direction given, shall in any or either of said events, and by that act alone, be deemed and taken to have forever and irrevocably resigned and surrendered his membership in the Exchange without recourse, the provisions hereof being declared to be conditions of each membership and of the continuance thereof.

ARTICLE IX

Committees of Arbitration and Appeals

Duties

Section 1. It shall be the duty of the Committee of Arbitration to hear and determine all cases of disputed claims voluntarily submitted for their adjudication by members or by non-members.   All evidence in such cases shall be duly recorded.   In all adjudications the Committee of Arbitration, and the Committee of Appeals hereinafter referred to, shall construe the Rules, Regulations and By-Laws as being designed to secure justice and equity in trade, and all awards or findings shall be made in a fair and equitable manner, and in accordance with the true intent and meaning of said Rules, Regulations and By-Laws.

Privilege to Appeal

Section 2. Any award or finding of the Committee of Arbitration may be appealed, and carried to the Committee of Appeals for review; provided, that notice of such appeal shall be given to the Secretary in writing, within two (2) business days after such award or finding shall have been delivered to the parties in controversy.

Duty of Committee of Appeals

Section 3. It shall be the duty of the Committee of Appeals to review such cases as may be appealed from the Committee of Arbitration and formally brought before the said Committee of Appeals, and its awards or findings shall be final and binding, and shall not be subject to revision by any other tribunal of the Exchange. The said Committee of Appeals shall, however, receive such new evidence as may be offered, and if, in its judgment, evidence is produced which would justify a rehearing of the case by the Committee of Arbitration, it shall remand the case to the said Committee of Arbitration for a new hearing. Should the case not be remanded to the Committee of Arbitration, the Committee of Appeals shall proceed to make a final award or finding based on the records of the Committee of Arbitration.

Quorum

Section 4. Three (3) members of the Committee of Arbitration, and five (5) members of the Committee of Appeals, respectively, shall constitute a quorum for the transaction of business.

Vacancies

Section 5. Should any member or members be absent from any meeting of said Committees, the President may appoint any eligible member or members to act pro tem on the said Committees, in place of those absent.

Members Must Act

Section 6. Any member called upon to act on the Committee of Arbitration of Committee of Appeals and failing to comply with such request, shall be subject to a fine of Twenty-five Dollars ($25.00), unless a satisfactory reason in writing be given to the Board of Directors.

Awards or Findings

Section 7. A majority award or finding shall be sufficient, and each of the above committees shall render its awards or its findings in writing, through the Secretary, within two (2) business days after their decision shall have been made. Such awards or findings shall be signed by the Chairman of the Committee and shall be certified by the Secretary under the seal of the Exchange.

Inspection of Decisions

Section 8. The official record and decisions of these Committees may be inspected by any member in good standing, upon application to the Secretary.

Disqualifications

Section 9. No member of the Committee of Arbitration or Committee of Appeals shall sit as a member of this Committee during its consideration of any matter in which he, or the firm which he may represent, is interested directly or indirectly but his place shall be filled pro tem by another eligible member appointed by the President.

Privilege to Object

Section 10. Neither party to a controversy brought before the Committee of Arbitration or Committee of Appeals for settlement, shall have the right to object to any member sitting on such Committee unless objection is made under Section Nine (9) of this rule; otherwise the question of the propriety of any member to sit on his Committee shall rest with the other members of the Committee.

Agreement to Perform Awards

Section 11. Parties desiring the services of either of the foregoing Committees shall notify the Secretary to that effect in writing, and before the hearing of the case shall file an agreement with him, signed by the parties to the controversy, binding themselves to abide by, perform, and fulfil the final award or finding which shall be made touching the matter submitted, without recourse to any other Court of Tribunal. Any member of a firm, or a representative of a firm, company, or corporation, who is a member of the Exchange may execute said agreement on behalf of such firm, company, or corporation.

Prompt Trial

Section 12. Neither party shall postpone the hearing of a case longer than five (5) days after it has been submitted, unless good cause can be shown therefor, satisfactory to the Committee. If parties to a controversy fail to appear at time set for hearing, or request a postponement, the Committee may insist that the hearing shall take place without postponement. Trifling and unimportant matters shall not be entertained by the Committee of Arbitration.

Cost of Trial

Section 13. Fees and all additional costs that may be incurred in the investigation of claims and grievances, shall be finally paid by either of the parties in the case, as may be decided by the Committee hearing the same, and shall be included in their award or finding.

Non-Members Refusing to Comply with Awards or Finding

Section 14. If any person, firm, company, or corporation, not members, having voluntarily submitted any case of disputed claims to the Committees of Arbitration and Appeals, or either of them, having consented and agreed in writing to be governed by the proceedings and bound by the decisions of the Committees of Arbitration and Appeals, or either of them, as to the disputed claims, shall fail to comply promptly with and fulfil, or shall wilfully neglect or refuse to comply promptly with the awards or findings of said Committees, or either of them, he or they shall be dealt with by the Board of Directors as it may determine from the nature and gravity of the offence committed.

ARTICLE X

Membership

Section 1. Any person twenty-one (21) years of age and of good character and credit, who in the opinion of the Board of Directors has or guarantees to assume sufficient business interest at the market to justify membership, on presenting a written application, endorsed by two (2) members in good standing and stating the name and business avocation of the applicant, may, after notice of such application shall have been posted on the Bulletin Board for a period of ten (10) days, and after a ballot of the Board of Directors has resulted in a majority vote of the total Board being cast in favor of such applicant, be admitted to membership upon payment of an initiation fee of Five Hundred Dollars ($500.00) and the pro-rata amount of the annual assessment or assessments at time of application, or in lieu thereof, upon presentation of a certificate of unimpaired or unforfeited membership, duly assigned and on which notice of application for transfer has been duly posted and the transfer fee paid, as provided in Section Three (3) of this ARTICLE, and by signing on agreement to abide by the Rules, Regulations and By-Laws, and all amendments that may, in due form, be made thereto. Each application for membership shall be accompanied by the said initiation fee and the pro-rata amount of the annual assessment, or assessments at the time of application, or in lieu thereof, by a said certificate of unimpaired or unforfeited membership, duly assigned, and on which notice of application for transfer has been duly posted and the transfer fee paid, as provided in Section Three (3) of this ARTICLE.

No person is eligible to hold more than one (1) membership in his own name and every member shall be entitled to a certificate of membership, bearing the corporate seal of the Exchange, and the signatures of the President and Secretary.

Section 2. Any person whose application for membership is refused, may appeal to the Minister who, upon investigation of the applicant's eligibility may order the Exchange to accept such applicant as a member.

Transfer of Membership

Section 3. Provided there are no assessments overdue and unpaid by him, and no outstanding, unadjusted or unsettled claims or contracts held against him by any member, and provided that his membership is not in any way impaired or forfeited, the member, in whose name a certificate stands, may, upon payment of Fifty Dollars ($50.00) to the Exchange, and after notice of application for transfer has been posted on the Bulletin Board for ten (10) days, assign such certificate to a person eligible for membership, who may be approved by the Board of Directors, after due notice by posting, as provided in Section One (1) of this ARTICLE. The membership of a deceased member shall be transferable in like manner, by his legal representative. Prior to the transfer of any membership, notice of application for such transfer shall be posted upon the Bulletin Board for at least ten (10) days, when, if no objection is made, it shall be assumed that the member has no outstanding claims against him. If any person, firm, company, or corporation shall pay the membership fee of his or its representative or employee, and that fact be shown on the records of the Exchange, the information shall be given by having the said person's, firm's, company's or corporation's name in brackets after the representative's or employee's name in the certificate of membership. However, he shall have no right to transfer the membership; and it shall not be transferable except at the direction of the said person, firm, company or corporation. When the foregoing conditions have been complied with, the President and Secretary shall, upon surrender of the original Certificate of Membership, properly assigned, cancel said Certificate and issue to the person to whom transfer has been made a new certificate, as heretofore provided.

Section 4. No pledge, assignment, or other transfer of a certificate of membership, either by way of security or indemnity, or otherwise howsoever, shall be binding upon the Exchange or have any effect, unless and until the approval of the Board of Directors thereto shall have been first endorsed thereon by the Secretary, and any and all conditions attached to such approval shall have been fully complied with. Should any controversy arise at any time, either as to the right to, or the title or ownership of, or the right to the possession of, any certificate of membership, such controversy shall be determined by the Board of Directors solely upon the information shown upon the books and records of the Exchange. This section shall be printed or stamped upon the back of all certificates of membership and shall constitute a condition and part thereof.

Membership Requirements

Section 5. No commission merchant or co-operative association holding membership in the Exchange shall be permitted to discriminate in rates of charges, or commissions as hereinafter set forth, but this shall not be construed as prohibiting the distribution of patronage dividends.

Representing Persons, Firms, Companies, and Corporations

Section 6. Any person, firm, company, or corporation engaged in the live stock business at the market, may become entitled to the privileges of the exchange, and may be represented in the Exchange by an officer or managing agent, provided such officer or agent shall be a member in good standing (in such case the person, firm company, or corporation represented shall be considered a member); and such privileges and right to be represented shall continue only so long as such person, firm, company or corporation shall comply with all the Rules, Regulations and By-Laws.

Every person, partnership, firm, company, or corporation operating as commission merchant or merchants under the Rules, Regulations and By-Laws shall register a statement with the Secretary giving his or its business title or legal name; and if represented by an officer or managing agent, advice to that effect shall be given promptly; the same shall be done when any change takes place.

Voting Power

Section 7. Each membership shall, subject to Article One (1), Section Nine (9), entitle the holder thereof while in good standing to a vote.

Cancellation of Membership Certificates

Section 8. The certificate of membership of a member who has been expelled, and also a certificate of membership which has been forfeited, shall be cancelled upon the records of the Exchange.

Redemption of Membership

Section 9. When the Board of Directors shall have been given satisfactory proof in writing, of the death of any member in good standing, owning a membership in his name, said Board of Directors, if and when so requested and with the consent of the personal representative, executor or administrator of the said deceased member, after notice of same has been posted on the Bulletin Board for at least ten (10) days, and upon surrender of the Certificate of Membership, is hereby empowered to determine, redeem, cancel and retire the membership of such deceased member, at a fixed sum of One Hundred and Fifty Dollars ($150.00), provided, such deceased member has paid or caused to be paid all assessments due, and such membership is not in any way impaired, and has not been forfeited, and, provided further, that such deceased member leaves no outstanding or unsettled contracts or claims, fixed or contingent, held by or owing to, the Exchange or any member or members thereof. If there be any such claim or claims, the amount thereof may be withheld until same are fully adjusted, liquidated and satisfied, and in case such claims equal or exceed the amount of One Hundred and Fifty ($150.00) the entire amount, due such membership, may be applied in satisfaction of such claim or claims. The Board of Directors is empowered at its option to determine, redeem, cancel and retire the memberships of active or living members, subject to notice being duly posted and the compliance with other provisions heretofore outlined in this rule as in the case of a deceased member, at a fixed sum of One Hundred and Fifty Dollars ($150.00).

It is further provided that upon the adoption of this rule February 6th, 1942, the Board of Directors shall transfer the sum of One Thousand ($1,000.00) of its Capital account to the credit of a new account to be known as "Membership Redemption Account," and shall transfer from current revenue on December 31, 1942, a further sum of Two Hundred and Fifty Dollars ($250.00) to the credit of the said Membership Redemption Account, and a like sum each and every year thereafter.

ARTICLE XI

Bonds and Licenses

Before commencing business as a commission merchant, co-operative association or dealer, it shall be necessary to comply with the requirements of the Live Stock and Live Stock Products Act 1939, and the Regulations thereunder, as set forth in Article Twenty (20), Part One (1) of the Act and Sections Thirteen, (13), Fourteen, (14), and Fifteen (15) of the Regulations thereunder.

ARTICLE XII

Shippers' Trust Account

Every commission merchant and co-operative association shall keep in respect of commission business, a separate account in a chartered bank to be known as a "Shippers' Trust Account" as set forth in Article 26 of the Live Stock and Live Stock Products Act 1939, and in the Regulations under the Live Stock and Live Stock Products Act 1939, Section Seventeen (17) of the Regulations.

ARTICLE XIII

Salesmen - Buyers

Section 1. All commission merchants, co-operative associations, and dealers and/or certified salesmen of any of them shall, subject to provisions of Article X, and Article XIV, be members in good standing of the Exchange.

Section 2. All members shall file with the Secretary of the Exchange, within five (5) days after the adoption of this Rule, or within five (5) days after date of his employment, the name of each person who is authorized to buy or sell live stock on his account at the market.

ARTICLE XIV

Rights of Shippers

Section 1. Any farmer, drover, or consignor, who ships live stock to the market, and who has a grievance based on reasonable grounds, may, in writing, directed to the Secretary, submit the same for consideration by the Board of Directors.

Section 2. Nothing in the Rules, Regulations and By-Laws shall be construed as in any manner prohibiting any farmer, drover, or consignor from selling his own live stock on the market, or any member of the Exchange from purchasing such live stock from any farmer, drover, or consignor, or in any manner prohibiting any person from buying any stock on the market, but the privilege of both buying and selling live stock shall be open only to members of the Exchange.

ARTICLE XV

Rates of Commission

Section 1. Rates of Commission shall be charged for the sale or purchase, or clearing, pro-rating, or rendering of special services in the handling of live stock at the market, by members of the Exchange, as set forth in the published tariff of The Proprietor of *The Alberta Stock Yards Company Limited,* by authority of the Regulations under the Live Stock and Live Stock Products Act 1939.

Selling Stock for Members of the Exchange

Section 2. Selling live stock for a member in good standing of the Exchange trading on the market, said live stock having been purchased on and not removed from the market, the rate of charges shall be one-half (1/2) of the regular selling rates as set forth in the published tariff of the Proprietor of *The Alberta Stock Yards Company Limited.*

Section 3. Members may sell live stock, if mutually agreed to between the principals in the transaction, at one-half (1/2) the regular commission for another commission merchant who is a member in good standing of the Exchange, if said live stock has been consigned to said commission merchant, for sale, provided the full rates of commission prescribed for selling such live stock are charged to the owner by the member for whose account such live stock is sold.

Through Shipments

Section 4. If "through shipments" of live stock are offered for sale, and not sold, a charge of one half (1/2) the rate per car of selling commission provided for such car shall be charged. This includes live stock consigned to this market and offered for sale and not sold, but forwarded to another point.

If "through shipments" are not offered for sale but are taken care of, fed, watered, billing and customs papers made, etc., a charge of Five Dollars ($5.00) per car for one (1) or two (2) cars inclusive, balance of shipment Two Dollars ($2.00) per car, shall be charged on each separate consignment. This includes live stock consigned to this market and not offered for sale, but forwarded to another point.

Prohibiting Commissions and Rebates

Section 5. No remuneration of any kind shall be given by any member to any person to introduce a customer or influence sales of live stock at the market, other than regular commissions under the rules.

No member shall pay a commission or allow any rebate whatsoever to any person acting as agent, or representing himself as such, of any buyer of live stock at the market, and any representation that such person acted as agent of the seller rather than the buyer shall be considered a violation of this section and shall be

379

punishable by penalties prescribed by the Board of Directors.

No member; or firm of which he may be a partner; or company or corporation which he may represent; shall directly or indirectly, charge or receive, by any device or indirect method whatsoever, less than the rates fixed and prescribed in sections of this rule, nor by any device or indirect method whatsoever, allow or pay any rebate or make any deduction from the rates of commission herein established; nor buy live stock from or sell live stock to any person, firm, company, or corporation engaged in the commission business at the market and charging less than the commission fixed herein, or granting any rebate or by any device or indirect method whatsoever reducing to shippers of live stock the rates herein provided; nor buy from or sell to or for, or have any business dealings in the Yards with any dealer or Yard trader handling live stock purchased from or through such commission men.

Contingent Salaries

Section 6. Persons, firms, companies, or corporations represented in the Exchange, may after charging commission as herein provided, pay a regular cattle, hog, or sheep salesman at the market a sum of money for his services contingent on the number of cattle, hogs, or sheep sold; said salesman may be in the employ of other members.

ARTICLE XVI

Hours of Business and Holidays

Section 1. The hours of buying and selling live stock at the market shall be determined by the Board of Directors, and notice thereof posted on the Bulletin Board, and same shall be subject to change from time to time as conditions may warrant.

Section 2. No business, such as the buying or selling of live stock, shall be transacted at the market, in any way, on the Sabbath Day, Dominion Day, Christmas Day, and New Year's Day.

Section 3. The Board of Directors in conjunction with the Stock Yards Proprietor shall have the power to declare holidays from time to time at their discretion.

Section 4. The Stock Yards Company shall be requested to raise and lower a flag provided by the Exchange on the Exchange Building at the opening and closing of the market each day.

ARTICLE XVII

Rules for Trading

Section 1. All trading operations in live stock at the market shall be governed and conducted under the Rules, Regulations and By-Laws of the Calgary Live Stock

Exchange. In case of any violation, or evasion of any of the said Rules, Regulations or By-Laws, it should be reported immediately to the Secretary, who shall place the same before the Board of Directors for their consideration and action.

Section 2. In order to maintain the trading at the market on a fair and equitable basis, it shall be deemed unbusinesslike and not in accordance with the spirit of the Exchange for a seller to offer or promise any buyer the first chance to buy the live stock offered for sale. All purchasers shall have equal opportunity to purchase by being present at the seller's recognized place of business when the market opens, and all trading operations shall be governed by The Trading Rules and Regulations Governing Operations at the Alberta Stock Yards, Calgary, Alta., as adopted at the Annual General Meeting of the Exchange on February sixth, 1942, and any amendments thereto, and which are hereby made Rules, Regulations and By-Laws of this Exchange.

ARTICLE XVIII

Open Order Privileges

Section 1. The "open order privileges" is an arrangement whereby any person, firm, company, or corporation, who has purchased live stock, or has caused the same to be purchased from any member, or from the said member's authorized employees and agents, shall be allowed to take delivery, and bill out, all such purchases without presenting a "title order," from the member from whom the live stock was purchased, to the Stock Yards Company.

In this Rule, the word "member," includes any partnership, firm, company, or corporation licensed to operate as commission merchant or merchants at the market.

Section 2. The Board of Directors shall decide who is eligible to the open order privileges"; and any person, firm, company, or corporation desiring to be placed on the "open order privileges" may make application to the said Board for same.

Section 3. No person, firm, company, or corporation shall be placed on or struck off the "open order privileges" of the Exchange, except by order of the Board of Directors, through the Secretary, and notice to that effect, in writing, shall be given immediately by the Secretary to the Stock Yards Company. Any member in good standing may obtain on request to the Secretary, a certified copy of the names of those who are on the "open order privileges" list of the Exchange.

Section 4. Any person, firm, company, or corporation, who shall be placed on the "open order privileges," shall file with the Stock Yards Company, a list of all persons who are authorized to take delivery, and bill out, live stock purchased by said person, firm, company or corporation, or on his or its account.

Section 5. Any person, firm, company, or corporation, his or its authorized employees and agents, placed on the "open order privileges," shall continue to enjoy such privileges and rights only as long as he or it shall comply with the Rules, Regulations, and By-Laws, and other conditions prescribed by the Board of Directors.

Section 6. No member shall establish an individual "open order privileges," that is, authorize by standing order the Stock Yards Company to deliver, without a "title order," any live stock weighed by said member to any person, firm, company, or corporation, who has not been granted the "open order privileges" of the Exchange; nor shall any member issue a "title order" for any live stock not sold or not legally in the possession of himself, or of the firm, company, or corporation he represents; but if any member issues a "title order" for live stock to any person, firm, or company, or corporation, not on the "open order privileges," the said member does so at his own risk and responsibility.

Section 7. A "title order" is a signed order issued by an authorized party, authorizing the Stock Yards Company to deliver certain live stock, yarded in specified pens on the property of the said Company, to the party, or his authorized employees; or, his agent, and his authorized employees as stated in the said order.
'Authorized party" means a consignor or owner of live stock and his authorized employees; or, an agent and his authorized employees.

ARTICLE XIX

Payment for Live Stock

All live stock sold by any member of the Exchange at the market shall be paid for by the buyers, who are on the "open order privileges," unless otherwise mutually agreed upon between buyer and seller, not later than one p.m. (1:00 p.m.) on the second Exchange business day following the day of sale, except on Saturday when payment shall be made by eleven a.m. (11:00 a.m.); provided the member, firm, company, or corporation making such sale shall promptly present an account of purchase at the office of the purchaser or of the firm, company, or corporation who guarantees the payment thereof. Nothing in this rule shall be construed as in any manner infringing on the strictly cash principle of trading.

ARTICLE XX

Guaranteed Payments

Section 1. All members who propose, or have agreed to pay for live stock purchased by, or on the account of any person, firm, company, or corporation at the market, from any member, shall file with the Secretary a list of the names of all persons, firms, companies, and corporations, for whom they propose, or have agreed to make such payments, and such list shall also embrace a declaration on the part of the member or members filing same, in such manner and form as the Board of Directors may prescribe, to the effect that they will pay for all purchases of live stock made from any member, by, or on the account of the party or parties therein named and after any member shall have filed such list of names, as above provided, he shall be held responsible for any sum of money which any person, firm, company, or corporation, whose name appears in such list, and his or its authorized employees and agents may have agreed to pay to any member for live stock, until the same shall have paid in full, or otherwise lawfully settled; provided, the member making such sale shall present an account of purchase of the same at the office of the member who has so guaranteed the payment thereof.

Section 2. When any member shall desire to cancel any agreement he may have made to pay for the purchase of live stock made by, or on account of any person, firm, company, or corporation at the market, from any member, he shall give the Secretary notice in writing to that effect; and the liability of the guarantor in such case shall cease, when, and only when, all purchase of live stock made by, or on the account of such person, firm, company, or corporation from any member upon the day of notification and prior thereto, shall have been paid for in full, or otherwise lawfully settled.

Section 3. Any member selling live stock at the market, on the account of any person, firm, company, or corporation, the payment of whose purchases of live stock and of his or its authorized employees and agents at said market has been guaranteed by any member, shall return the proceeds of such sale to said member guaranteeing said payment.

Section 4. The Secretary shall, on receipt of the list of names and also of the notice of cancellation, as provided for in Sections One (1) and Two (2) respectively, of this rule, notify all commission firms and traders in writing, who are members doing business at the market to that effect; and also, in case of a notice of cancellation, he shall promptly post notice of same on the Bulletin Board, same to be posted for a period of ten (10) days. Any member in good standing may obtain, on request to the Secretary, a certified copy of the list of names on file as provided for in Section One (1) of this rule, for his own use and for no other purpose.

Section 5. Each member shall be held responsible for the payment of the purchase price of live stock purchased by any person, firm, company, or corporation for whom he is clearing, if said live stock is weighed in care of said member.

ARTICLE XXI

Accounts of Purchases of Sales of Live Stock

General trading requirements set forth in the Regulations under the Live Stock and Live Stock Products Act 1939, with respect to Accounts of Purchases of Sales, Selling procedure, Pooling, etc.

Section 1. The Regulations under the Live Stock and Live Stock Products Act 1939 are set up and printed by the Dominion Government, and are available to all commission merchants, co-operative associations and dealers.

These Regulations are requirements that each and every commission merchant, co-operative association and dealer, together with their employees, are required to fulfil and they are hereby made Rules, Regulations and By-Laws of the Exchange, and any enforcement of the same will be under the jurisdiction of the Board of Directors and such penalties, as may be ordered by the Board of Directors for the violation of each and any of such regulations, may be imposed.

See Sections Eighteen (18) to Twenty-seven (27) inclusive of the Regulations under the Live Stock and Live Stock Products Act 1939.

Section 2. In case of variation between the chute count of the Stock Yard Company, and the receiving or scale count of the commission firm, the said commission firm shall report, within a reasonable time, any such difference, to the said Stock Yard Company. In case of overs, the amount realized for the sale of same shall be placed with the Stock Yard Company to the credit of the rightful owners.

Section 3. Each member doing business at the market and every employee of same, shall report all excess, or found live stock, to the Stock Yard Company as soon as possible; and in no case more than twenty-four (24) hours after excess is discovered, or live stock is found. Shortages and losses of live stock shall likewise be reported.

Governing Re-weighing of Live Stock

Section 4. Buyers or sellers may re-weigh any live stock they have bought or sold whenever in their opinion an error has been made in the weight. If there has been no error, the original ticket shall stand. In case of any dispute as to how much the live stock has shrunk, or been damaged in re-weighing, the Committee of Arbitration shall decide the matter.

Governing Condition of Live Stock

Section 5. The responsibility of the seller, as regards the condition of live stock shall cease on all live stock sold at the market, as soon as said live stock shall have been driven off the scales, and no live stock shall be fed after the sale has been made except as agreed upon between buyer and seller; provided that, on account of inability to get said live stock weighed on the same day of sale, the salesman shall have the privilege of feeding and watering such live stock a reasonable amount, until same is weighed.

Dealing With Suspended or Expelled Members or Non-Members

Section 6. Unless sanctioned by the Board of Directors, no member shall have any business dealings or relations with a person who is under suspension from membership, or who has been expelled therefrom, because of a violation, or evasion of any of the provisions of the Rules, Regulations or By-Laws, after notice of such suspension or expulsion shall have been issued by order of the Board of Directors through the Secretary. A member who undertakes to resign his membership, or transfers the same, after having committed any of the offences herein enumerated; or while being or having been tried therefor, or who shall have surrendered or resigned his membership by force of any of the provisions of said Rules, Regulations or By-Laws, shall be deemed a suspended or expelled member, as the said Board may determine within the meaning thereof.

ARTICLE XXII

Uncommercial Conduct

Section 1. No member of the Exchange shall be guilty of uncommercial conduct or unfair dealings with his fellow members, or with his customers. The term "uncommercial conduct" shall include the following:

The circulating of false reports concerning members on any subject for the purpose of injuring the business or credit of such member;

The soliciting of shipments of live stock which are either in transit or have arrived at the market. This shall also include shipments which have actually arrived at or on the property of the Stock Yards Company;

The organizing of, or proposing to organize a boycott against the business of any member;

The interfering between a buyer and seller to prevent the consummation of a bargain during its progress;

The influencing of a seller against a prospective buyer;

The failing to observe rules of business integrity and fair dealing in transactions conducted with customers or other members;

The using of foul or abusive language toward another member;

The committing of acts contrary to sound business ethics, whether specifically forbidden by law or by the Rules, Regulations and By-Laws of the Exchange.

Section 2. It shall be uncommercial conduct for a commission merchant or cooperative association to solicit business with the argument that his or its scale advantages, or the location and number of his or its pens are superior to those of competitors.

ARTICLE XXIII

Purchaser Must Report

Section 1. Every purchaser of stock cattle, or feeding cattle, at the market shall report as soon as possible at the office of the commission firm through which the purchase was made, any lumpy jaw cattle weighed to him, unless the same were purchased and specified as such; and in such case, unless prior to receiving such report the said commission firm has made settlement to the owner or shipper of said cattle, the said purchaser shall have the right to weigh said lumpy jaw cattle back to the account of said commission firm.

If the stock cattle, or feeding cattle, were purchased from a local dealer or trader, the purchaser shall have the right to weigh back to the account of the said local dealer or trader, within twenty-four (24) hours of the time of weighing, any lumpy jaw cattle, unless the same were purchased and specified as such.

Disagreements Arbitrated

Section 2. Should any disagreement arise as to whether any cattle weighed to a purchaser are lumpy jaw cattle, the question shall be referred for settlement to a committee of three (3) persons, two (2) of whom must be members in good standing. This committee shall be constituted as follows: one (1) member shall be named by the salesman who sold the cattle, and one (1) named by the purchaser, and these two (2) shall then choose the third member. Their majority decision shall be final and binding, and any award or finding of the committee, thus formed, shall be made under the same Rules, Regulations and By-Laws, and shall have the same effect as if made by any regularly constituted committee.

Reporting Communicable Diseases

Section 3. Any member of the Exchange having knowledge of the existence of communicable diseases such as Cattle Mange, Sheep Scab, Hog Cholera, etc., affecting the live stock at the Stockyards, and failing to report the same immediately to the resident officers of the Dominion Department of Agriculture, shall be fined or suspended at the discretion of the Board of Directors.

ARTICLE XXIV

Live Stock in Transit

Section 1. No member shall purchase live stock which has left the point of shipment and is in transit to the market; and no live stock shall be considered out of transit until it is delivered by the Stock Yard Company, and signed for by the party handling same.

ARTICLE XXV

Cruelty to Animals

Section 1. Any member having in his employ any person who may be found guilty of striking, pounding, or prodding any animal at the market, thereby crippling, bruising, or damaging such animal, shall be subject to a fine of Ten Dollars ($10.00) for each offence.

Section 2. It shall be the duty of any member to report to the Secretary, any and all cases of neglect or cruelty to live stock, whether at the hands of a member, an employee of a member, or other persons working at the market.

ARTICLE XXVI

Failure to Meet Obligations

Section 1. All members shall decline to transact business with any person, firm, company, or corporation, who neglects to meet his or its obligations to any of said members, so long as said obligations shall remain unsatisfied, when advised to that effect by order of the Board of Directors through the Secretary.

Section 2. When it shall come to the knowledge of any of the members that any shipper to the market owes unadjusted or unsatisfied accounts or sums of money to other members, arising out of transactions at the market, exclusive of loans on live stock, it shall be the duty of such member to assist the creditor member in the collection of said unsettled accounts.

Trading and Business Relations

Section 3. No member shall employ, or have any business relations whatsoever at the market, with any non-member who, after complaint shall have been filed with the Board of Directors against him, and after having been afforded the opportunity of a hearing, shall neglect to avail himself thereof, or who, after having had a hearing, shall have been held by the Board of Directors guilty of any dishonest conduct, or of violating or evading any Rule, Regulation or By-Law; and the said Board, in the best interests of the members and the community at large, is hereby authorized to pass upon and determine the question of guilt of any one thus accused, by a majority vote of its members duly assembled in regular or special session, and it may in a similar manner subsequently annul such disbarment.

Nothing in this rule shall be construed as prohibiting in any manner any member from selling live stock consigned to the market by any such person; or such person from selling his own live stock consigned to the market; or any member from buying such live stock from such consignor.

ARTICLE XXVII

Members Responsible for Acts of Partners and Employees

Each member shall be deemed and held to be responsible for the acts of his partners and employees for any violation or evasion of the Rules, Regulations or By-Laws.

ARTICLE XXVIII

Employment of Delinquent Debtors

No members shall employ or retain in his employ any person indebted to any other member, unless such person shall by word and act show intent to liquidate such indebtedness as soon as circumstances will permit. The Board of Directors shall decide in all such cases.

ARTICLE XXIX

Inspection of Records

Section 1. The books, papers and records of the Exchange shall be subject at all times to inspection by the Dominion Minister of Agriculture, or any duly appointed representative of the said Minister, and such information shall be given as the Minister, or his duly appointed representative, may request.

Section 2. All official records of the Exchange may be inspected by any member in good standing of the Exchange upon application to the Secretary.

Section 3. Any member, or buyer, who is not bonded may be required to produce a satisfactory certified financial statement for the Board of Directors whenever the said Board shall deem it necessary for the protection of other members or the general public.

ARTICLE XXX

Annual Assessment—Assessments

Section 1. An annual fee of Fifteen Dollars ($15.00) shall be assessed on each member, and the Board of Directors shall have power to levy an additional assessment or assessments, not exceeding Fifteen Dollars ($15.00), to meet all estimated expenses of the Exchange for the ensuing fiscal year, subject to the provisions of Article Six (6), Section Six (6).

Section 2. Any member who neglects for a period of thirty (30) days to pay any overdue assessments, or any instalment thereof, shall be suspended from the privileges of the Exchange, until such default is remedied. Should such default continue for a period of three (3) months, the membership of the member so in default, shall subject to the provisions of Article Eight (8), Section Six (6), be forfeited to the Exchange.

ARTICLE XXXI

Amendments to Rules, Regulations and By-Laws

Any Rule, Regulation or ByLaws of the Exchange may be rescinded, altered, or amended, or any new Rule, Regulation or By-Law may be adopted by a two-thirds vote in favor thereof of the members present at any annual, regular, or special meeting of the Exchange, provided that notice of the proposed change has been conspicuously posted on the Bulletin Board for at least ten (10) days immediately preceding any such meeting. The members present at any such meeting may, by a two-thirds vote, amend such proposed change in any respect germane to the original purpose or subject thereof.

ARTICLE XXXII

Seal

The Exchange shall have a corporate seal bearing its name and date of incorporation, an impression of which is stamped on the margin hereof.

General By-Laws and Rules of Order of
The Calgary Live Stock Exchange

ARTICLE I

Stated Meetings - Order of Procedure

At all general or stated meetings of the Exchange or Board of Directors the following shall be the order of business:

Call to order.
Reading Minutes of previous meetings—which may be dispensed with.
Correspondence.
Hearing reports.
Unfinished business.
General business.
Adjournment.

ARTICLE II

Business of Special Meetings

At all Special Meetings of the Exchange or Board of Directors, only such special business shall be considered as was expressly embraced in the call for such meeting.

ARTICLE III

On Debates

When required by any member, the mover of a resolution shall put same in writing. No debate shall be permitted except on a motion regularly made and seconded. A member, however, shall not be prevented from prefacing with explanatory remarks any resolution he may be about to make.

ARTICLE IV

Limitation On Debate

Every member who is about to speak shall rise and address the Chairman, and no person shall speak more than twice on the same subject, except by way of explanation, if objection is made thereto, unless a majority of those present vote in favor of giving him permission to speak again.

ARTICLE V

Question of Order - Appeals

The Presiding Officer shall be the judge of all questions on order and procedure, and, when the rules of the Exchange or of parliamentary procedure are infringed, he may call any member to order. A member may appeal to the Exchange on any question of parliamentary procedure not provided for by the Rules, Regulations, or By-Laws of the Exchange, or by a special order, and, if seconded on such an appeal, a majority of the members present shall decide the question at issue.

ARTICLE VI

Interruptions and Privileged Questions

No business, before any meeting of the Exchange, shall be interrupted, except by motion for the previous question to lay upon the table, to postpone, or to adjourn, and such motion shall preclude amendment or decision of the original subject until such motion shall be disposed of.

ARTICLE VII

Division of the Question - What Motions Not Debatable - Reconsideration - When In Order

A member may call for a division of a question when the sense will admit it. A motion to lay upon the table or to postpone indefinitely shall not be debatable, and a resolution once acted upon shall not be revised at the same meeting, except by a vote to reconsider. A motion to reconsider shall not be entertained except at the same or the next meeting after the former action, and then only when made by a member voting with the majority, or a member who was absent when the resolution in question was voted upon.

ARTICLE VIII

Application of Rules of Order - All Members

All questions of order or procedure provided for by these Rules, Regulations, and By-Laws shall be held to govern both the Exchange and the Board of Directors, so far as they may be applicable. In the absence of any provision in these Rules, Regulations, and By-Laws to the contrary, Roberts' Rules of Order, which are hereby made the standard parliamentary authority of the Exchange, shall govern in the determination of any question before any committee or other tribunal of the Exchange.

APPENDIX D

CLASSES OF STOCKYARDS

I am not exactly sure why, but for some reason there was a lot of honesty and integrity at the Stockyards. I think some of the credit for this high standard of conduct and professionalism goes to the men who sat down in 1914 and drew up the rules and regulations that were fair to everyone and did not show favouritism. Another factor is that the cattle business has always been done with a handshake, and it is still done this way to a large degree today.

Over the last twenty years, I have fed thousands of cattle in the US, many of which, I never even laid eyes on. I wasn't there when they were bought. I did not see them during the feeding period, and I was not there when they were sold. Yet, to my knowledge, the feedlots never short-changed me. If they did—I have to apply the old adage: "What you don't know won't hurt you." (Sometimes, it does.)

The old saying "a man's word is his bond" really applied at the Stockyards. In the forty years I was at Burns and the Stockyards, I only ran across about half-a-dozen people whom I did not trust. In a few cases, my judgement about them might have been wrong.

In spite of the basic honesty employed by the operators on the market, it was still a good idea to have stringent rules as were set forth by the Calgary Livestock Exchange. In the eighty-six years the market operated in Calgary, I am not aware of a single producer who did not get paid for his livestock—maybe not as much as he thought he should have gotten, but that is the way a market works. Markets can fluctuate; that's supply and demand.

I doubt if very many people know there used to be five different classes of Stockyards rated by the Alberta Government. The Calgary Stockyards were rated Class A.

A retype of the Order in Council is as follows:

REGULATIONS GOVERNING CLASSES OF STOCKYARDS

Regulations pursuant to The Alberta Live Stock and Live Stock Products Act, R.S.A. 1947, Chapter 88 and Chapter 56, 1954, Section 3A, Subsections (1) and (2).

CLASSES OF STOCKYARDS - ORDER IN COUNCIL NO. 581-55

1. In these regulations, unless the context otherwise requires:

(a) "Live Stock" means cattle, calves, sheep and swine.

(b) "Packer" means any person, partnership, corporation or co-operative association, engaged in the business of slaughtering or processing livestock to the number of one thousand in any three consecutive months or three thousand in any calendar year.

2. Class A Stockyard means any area of land together with the buildings, pens, fences, gates, chutes, weigh scales and other equipment situated thereon and used in connection therewith which is in operation as a public market for the purchase and sale of live stock and meets the requirements as set out under Part I of the Live Stock and Live Stock Products Act of Canada and has been declared by the Minister of Agriculture for Canada to be a stockyard.

3. Class B Stockyard means any area of land controlled or operated by any packer or his agent together with buildings and equipment used in connection with receiving, purchasing, holding or weighing live stock for slaughter or for marketing or for shipment to slaughter and which is situated adjacent to a packing plant and which is commonly known as a packer's yard.

4. Class C Stockyard means any area of land together with buildings and equipment owned by any person, partnership, corporation, co-operative association or packer and used on a continuous daily basis for receiving and purchasing live stock for slaughter or direct reshipment for slaughter, and is located in such a manner that it is not adjacent to any Class B Stockyard, and is commonly known as a live stock buying station.

5. Class D Stockyard means any area of land, together with buildings and equipment owned and operated by any person, partnership, corporation or co-operative association, where live stock is received from producers or dealers at regular times throughout the year and sold by auction for a commission or set fee per head; and is commonly known as an auction market or auction mart.

6. Class E Stockyard means any area of land together with buildings and equipment which is owned or operated by any co-operative association for the purpose of receiving live stock from its members or non-members, for sale by auction, charging a commission or set fee per head; such sales being held at irregular intervals throughout the year spaced to coincide with the marketing season for the product of the members, and commonly known as community auction sales.